Dokshitz-Parafianov Memorial (Yizkor) Book (Dokshytsy, Belarus)

Translation of *Sefer Dokshitz-Parafianov*

Original Hebrew and Yiddish Yizkor Book
Editor: David Stockfish
Published in Tel Aviv, 1970

Translation Editors: Joel Alpert and Aaron Ginsburg

Published by JewishGen

**An Affiliate of the Museum of Jewish Heritage
A Living Memorial to the Holocaust
New York**

Dokshitz-Parafianov, Belarus Memorial Book
Translation of *Sefer Dokshitz-Parafianov*

Copyright © 2017 by JewishGen, Inc.
All rights reserved.
First Printing: October 2017, Tishrei 5778
Second Printing: March 2019, Adar II 5779

Translation Editors: Joel Alpert and Aaron Ginsburg
Translation Coordinator: Joel Alpert
Layout: Joel Alpert
Image Editors: Aaron Ginsburg and Joel Alpert
Appendices: Aaron Ginsburg
Cover Design: Rachel Kolokoff Hopper
Publicity: Dorothy Lipsky and Myrna Siegel
Indexing: Joanna Shear

This book may not be reproduced, in whole or in part, including illustrations in any form (beyond that copying permitted by Sections 107 and 108 of the U.S. Copyright Law and except by reviewers for public press), without written permission from the publisher.

Published by JewishGen, Inc.
An Affiliate of the Museum of Jewish Heritage
A Living Memorial to the Holocaust
36 Battery Place, New York, NY 10280

"JewishGen, Inc. is not responsible for inaccuracies or omissions in the original work and makes no representations regarding the accuracy of this translation. Digital images of the original book's contents can be seen online at the New York Public Library Web site."

The mission of the JewishGen organization is to produce a translation of the original work and we cannot verify the accuracy of statements or alter facts cited.

Printed in the United States of America by Lightning Source, Inc.

Library of Congress Control Number (LCCN): 2017952900
ISBN: 978-1-939561-10-7 (hard cover: 456 pages, alk. paper)

Front cover insert from the cover of the original Yizkor Book
Other front cover images and back cover image from the interior of the book and the Appendix

Cover Credits

Cover Created by Rachel Kolokoff Hopper

Four men on the cover are from page 2 of the appendix: *Photographs of Martyrs of Dokshitz.* "First from the left: Zalman Gejdenson, murdered in 1943, age 20 by German Nazi bandits. All of his other friends pictured here were murdered in 1942."

Woman on upper left of front cover from page 3 of the appendix: *Photographs of Martyrs of Dokshitz*. "*Esther Gejdenson - murdered in May 1942 with her husband Rabbi Samuel Gejdenson and their daughter Sonia Gejdenson in Parafianov, near Dokshitz. They were the parents of Shlomo Gejdenson.*"

Man in the upper right on the front cover from page 5 of the appendix: *Photographs of Martyrs of Dokshitz*. "*Shlomo Gejdenson's Grandfather*"

Background cover photo by Rachel Kolokoff Hopper:
Old destroyed Jewish Cemetery in Lithuania.

JewishGen and the Yizkor Books in Print Project

This book has been published by the **Yizkor Books in Print Project,** as part of the **Yizkor Book Project** of **JewishGen, Inc.**

JewishGen, Inc. is a non-profit organization founded in 1987 as a resource for Jewish genealogy. Its website [www.jewishgen.org] serves as an international clearinghouse and resource center to assist individuals who are researching the history of their Jewish families and the places where they lived. JewishGen provides databases, facilitates discussion groups, and coordinates projects relating to Jewish genealogy and the history of the Jewish people. In 2003, JewishGen became an affiliate of the **Museum of Jewish Heritage - A Living Memorial to the Holocaust** in New York.

The **JewishGen Yizkor Book Project** was organized to make more widely known the existence of Yizkor (Memorial) Books written by survivors and former residents of various Jewish communities throughout the world. Later, volunteers connected to the different destroyed communities began cooperating to have these books translated from the original language—usually Hebrew or Yiddish—into English, thus enabling a wider audience to have access to the valuable information contained within them. As each chapter of these books was translated, it was posted on the JewishGen website and made available to the general public.

The **Yizkor Books in Print Project** began in 2011 as an initiative to print and publish Yizkor Books that had been fully translated, so that hard copies would be available for purchase by the descendants of these communities and also by scholars, universities, synagogues, libraries, and museums.

These Yizkor books have been produced almost entirely through the volunteer effort of researchers from around the world, assisted by donations from private individuals. The books are printed and sold at near cost, so as to make them as affordable as possible. Our goal is to make this important genre of Jewish literature and history available in English in book form, so that people can have the personal histories of their ancestral towns on their bookshelves for themselves and for their children and grandchildren.

A list of all published translated Yizkor Books in the project with prices and ordering information can be found at:
http://www.jewishgen.org/Yizkor/ybip.html

Lance Ackerfeld, Yizkor Book Project Manager

Joel Alpert, Yizkor Book in Print Project Coordinator

This book is presented by the
Yizkor Books in Print Project
Project Coordinator: Joel Alpert

Part of the
Yizkor Books Project of JewishGen, Inc.
Project Manager: Lance Ackerfeld

These books have been produced solely through volunteer effort of individuals from around the world. The books are printed and sold at near cost, so as to make them as affordable as possible.

Our goal is to make this history and important genre of Jewish literature available in English in book form so that people can have the near-personal histories of their ancestral towns on their bookshelves for themselves and for their children and grandchildren.

Any donations to the Yizkor Books Project are appreciated.

Please send donations to:
Yizkor Book Project
JewishGen
36 Battery Place
New York, NY 10280

JewishGen, Inc. is an affiliate of the
Museum of Jewish Heritage
A Living Memorial to the Holocaust

Yiddish and Hebrew Title Page of Original Yizkor Book

ספר־יזכור

דוקשיץ־פאראפיאנוב

אנדרטה לזכר שתי קהילות יהודיות

●

יזכור־בוך

דאָקשיץ - פּאַראָפּיאַנאָװ

מאַנומענט צום אַנדענק פֿון צוויי יידישע קהילות

●

העורך • רעדאַקטאָר :

דוד שטוקפיש

●

אירגון יוצאי דוקשיץ־פאראפיאנוב בישראל ובתפוצות

Translation of the Title Page of the Original Yizkor Book

Yizkor - Book
Dokshitz - Parafianov

For the Memory of Two Jewish Communities

Editor: David Stockfish

Organization of Former Residents of Dokshitz-Parafianov in Israel and Abroad

Foreword for the Translation

The effort to translate this Yizkor book started back in the early 1990s when I found this book in the Harvard Library. I wanted to find out about the town of my paternal grandfather John Alpert (a.k.a. Itzhak Alperovitz) so as to understand my own personal family history back to the "Old Country." I understood that I might not find any mention of my family, but it would at least tell me about the environment and history of their town. I withdrew the book and discovered that I was only the second person to withdraw the book since its publication in 1970. The other person took out the book in 1972.

I was aware of the Yizkor Book Project on JewishGen, which works to translate and post on its web site the translation of these Yiddish and Hebrew history of our ancestral towns. I decided to volunteer to be the translation project coordinator. This entailed raising money, finding a translator and then acting as the intermediary between them and Joyce Field, who headed the Yizkor Book Project at that time. It started with posting the necrology of Shoah victims that I had found already translated. We were most fortunate that early on Ralph Ginzburg found the solicitation for funds for the translation and donated nearly all the funds required to translate the book. I was fortunate to find Daniella HarPaz Mechnikov to translate the Yiddish in the book.

May this book serve as a memorial to the Jewish Community of Dokshitz, Belarus.

Joel Alpert

February 10, 2017

Dedication of the Translation

This book is dedicated to the memory of all the Dokshitz and Parfianov martyrs who suffered and were murdered in the Shoah. It is in their memory that this book is dedicated.

Acknowledgements for the Translation

Special thanks to Yechezkeel Levitan, *z"l* of the <u>Association of Former Residents of Dokshitz and Parafianov Belorussia</u> for permission to publish this translation of their original *Yizkor Book Sefer Dokshitz-Parafianov*. Thanks to Aaron Ginsburg for preparing the Appendix, to Professor Dan Bar-On for his article "Legacy of Silence."

Special thanks to Ralph Ginzburg, *z"l,* whose generous contribution paid for nearly all of the translation of the Dokshitz Yizkor Book into English in honor of his parents, Rafael Ginzburg and Rachel Guta Lipkin who were from the Dokshitz area.

Map of Belarus with Dokshitz Indicated

Parfianov is located 6 miles to the west of Dokshitz

Geopolitical Information

Dokshitz, Belarus is located at 54°54' North Latitude and 27°45' East Longitude and is 69 miles North of Minsk.

Parfianov is located 6 miles to the west of Dokshitz.

Alternate names: Dokshytsy [Belarus], Dokshitsy [Russian], Dokshits [Yiddish], Dokszyce [Polish], Dokšycy, Dokshitse, Dokshitsya, Dokschyzy, Dokshitz, Dugscitz

Period	Town	District	Province	Country
Before WWI (c. 1900):	Dokshitsy	Borisov	Minsk	Russian Empire
Between the wars (c. 1930):	Dokszyce	Dzisna	Wilno	Poland
After WWII (c. 1950):	Dokshitsy			Soviet Union
Today (c. 2000):	Dokshytsy			Belarus

Nearby Jewish Communities:
Parafyanovo 6 miles W

Yasevichi 13 miles NNE

Budslav 14 miles SW

Hlybokaye 16 miles N

Begoml 17 miles SE

Golubichi 17 miles NNE

Daŭhinava 20 miles SSW

Krivichi 22 miles SW

Plissa 23 miles NNE

Dunilovichi 23 miles WNW

Kozlovshchina 25 miles NW

Kraysk 28 miles SSW

Mstizh 28 miles SE

Kublichi 30 miles NE

Introduction to the Publication of the Translation

In 1995 Dokshitz descendant Joel Alpert created a web page on jewishgen.org about Dokshitz. The page enabled people to learn about Dokshitz, and with Joel's help gradually led to the creation of a community. Most chapters in the Dokshitz-Parfianov Yizkor book were written in both Yiddish and Hebrew, which implied that they may have been in Yiddish first. A few chapters by Zvi Markman were only in Yiddish.

Permission to complete the translation and place it online was obtained from the publisher of the Yizkor book, "The Dokshitz Partisans and Survivors Association in Israel," thanks to Yechezkel Levitan. The Association had published a partial English translation in 1990. Joel did some fundraising to hire a translator to complete the translation. A major contributor was my father's first cousin, Ralph Ginzburg, z.l. whose parents Rafael Ginzburg and Rachel Guta Lipkin were from the Dokshitz area. Many Ginzburg family members were murdered in Parfianov, and several Lipkin family members were also killed, including Rachel's brother Chaim Lipkind his wife, Perla Friedman Lipkind and their children, Rivka and Shalom. Joel placed the English translation of the book online in the Yizkor Books Project at www.jewishgen.org/yizkor/dokshitsy/Dokshitz.html. The original is on-line at the Yizkor book collection of the New York City Public Library Yizkor Book Collection.

Once the Yizkor book translation was complete, Joel and I started to work on printing the English translation. It has taken quite a lot of time to secure permission, and to edit and prepare an appendix with additional material. During that time, Joel went on to create and coordinate the Yizkor-Books-In-Print Project as part of the Yizkor Books translation project of Jewishgen.org. Several additions in the partial 1990 English translation were not in the original book. These are included in the printed appendix.

Kol Hakoved to Joel Alpert for making the Dokshitz-Parfianow Yizkor book available to the many descendants throughout world who don't know Hebrew or Yiddish.

This will be the first time the Dokshitz-Parfianov Yizkor book has been printed in its entirety in one language. Now *Tze ulemad uvahchu* "Go and learn and weep!"

Aaron Ginsburg

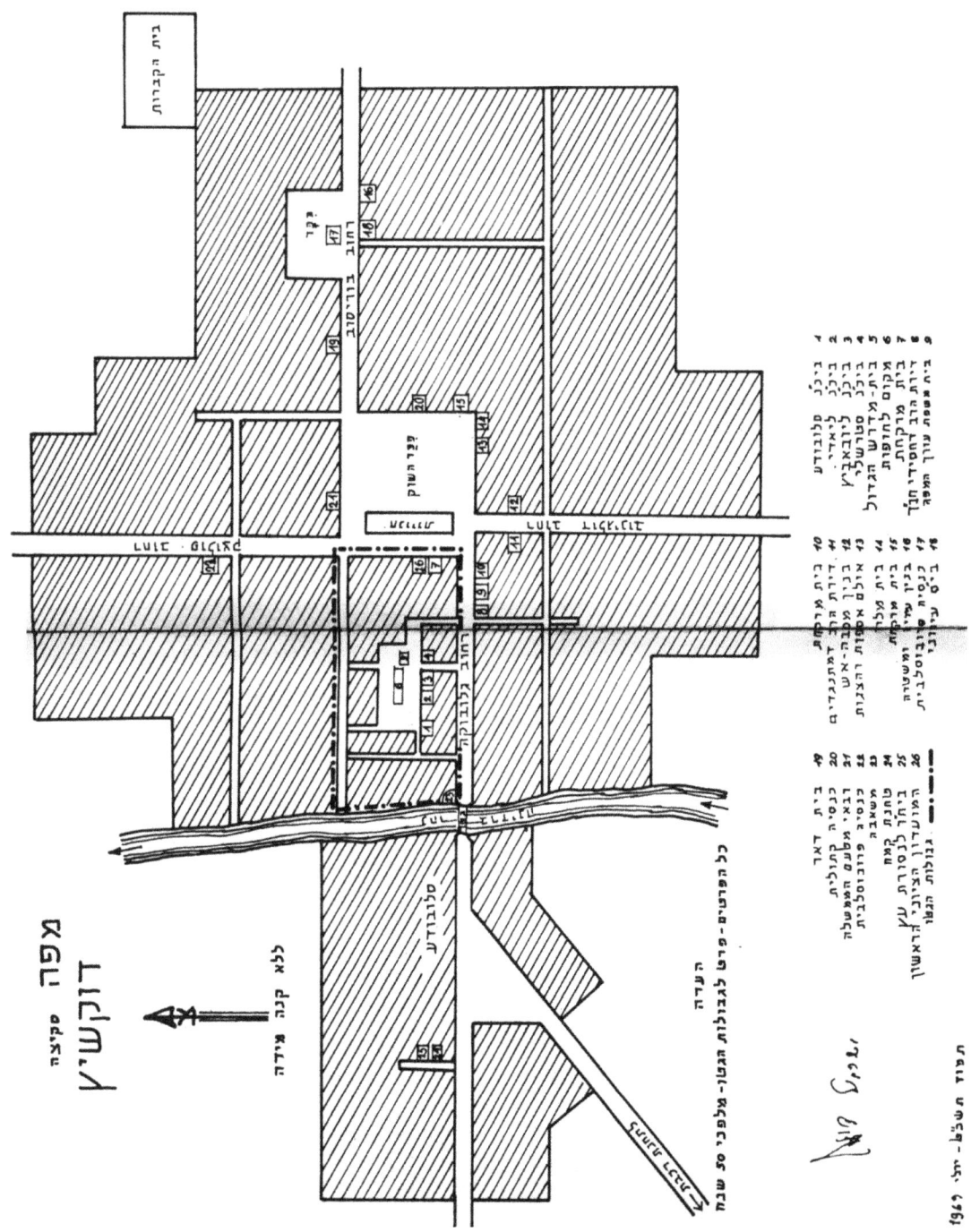

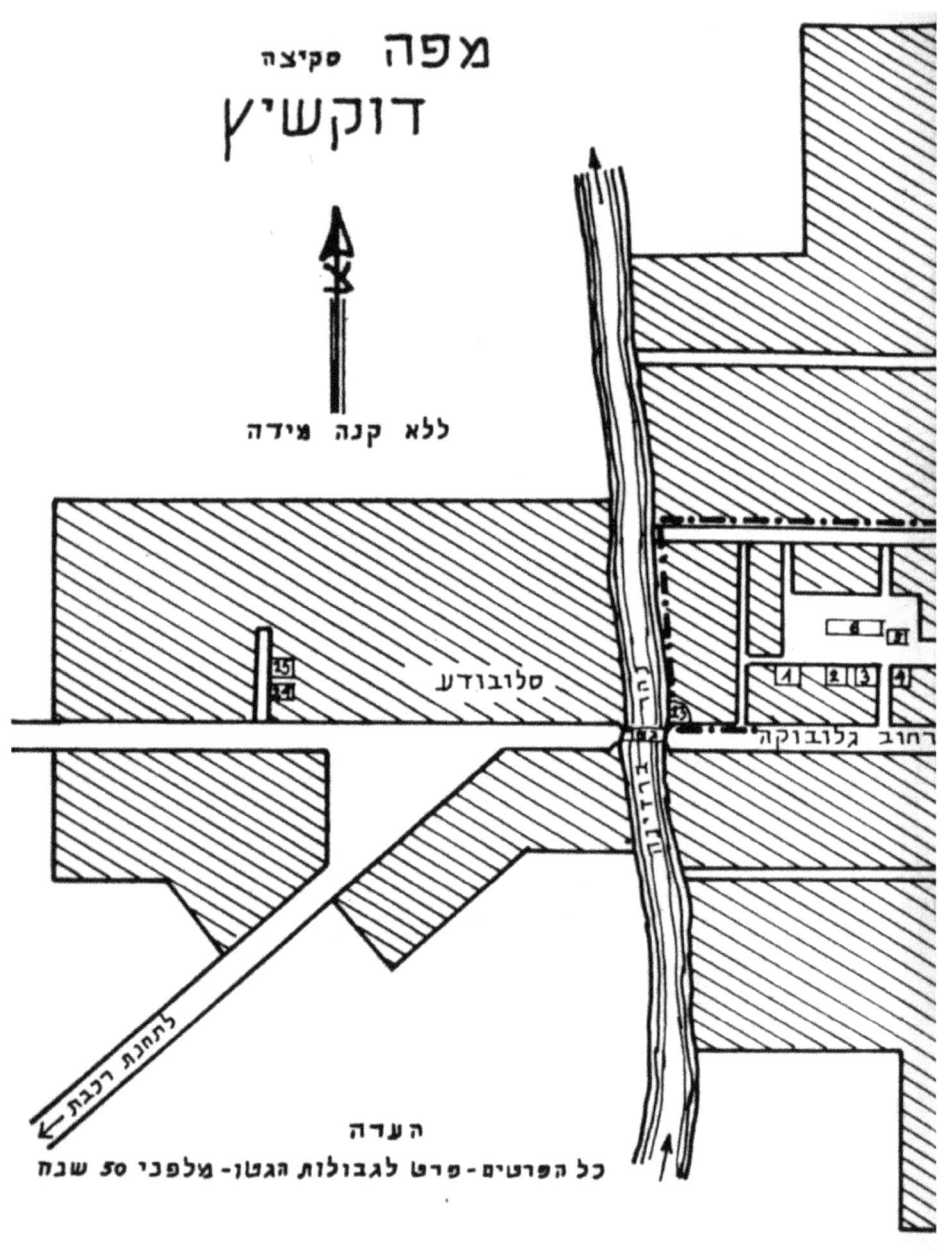

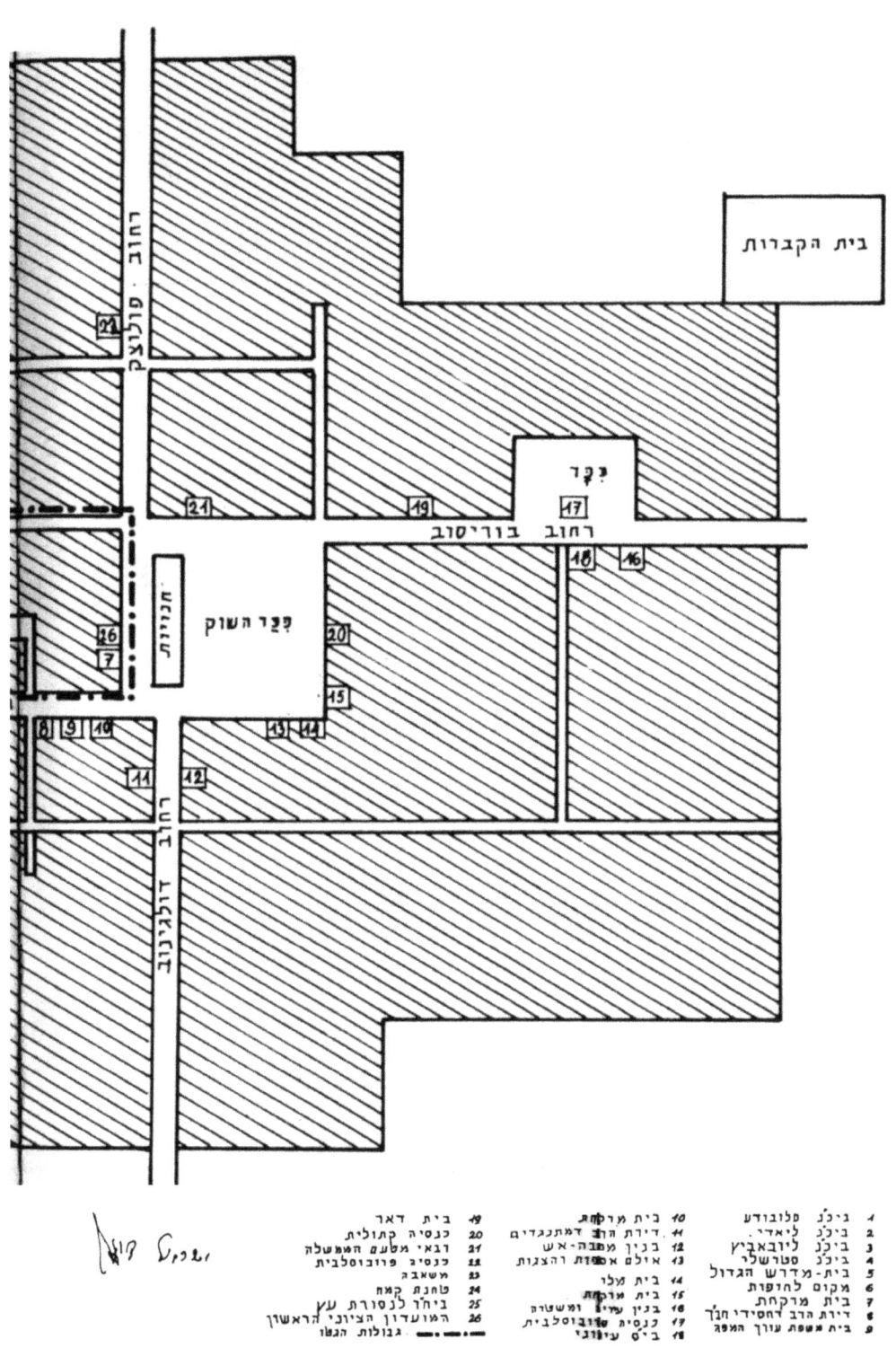

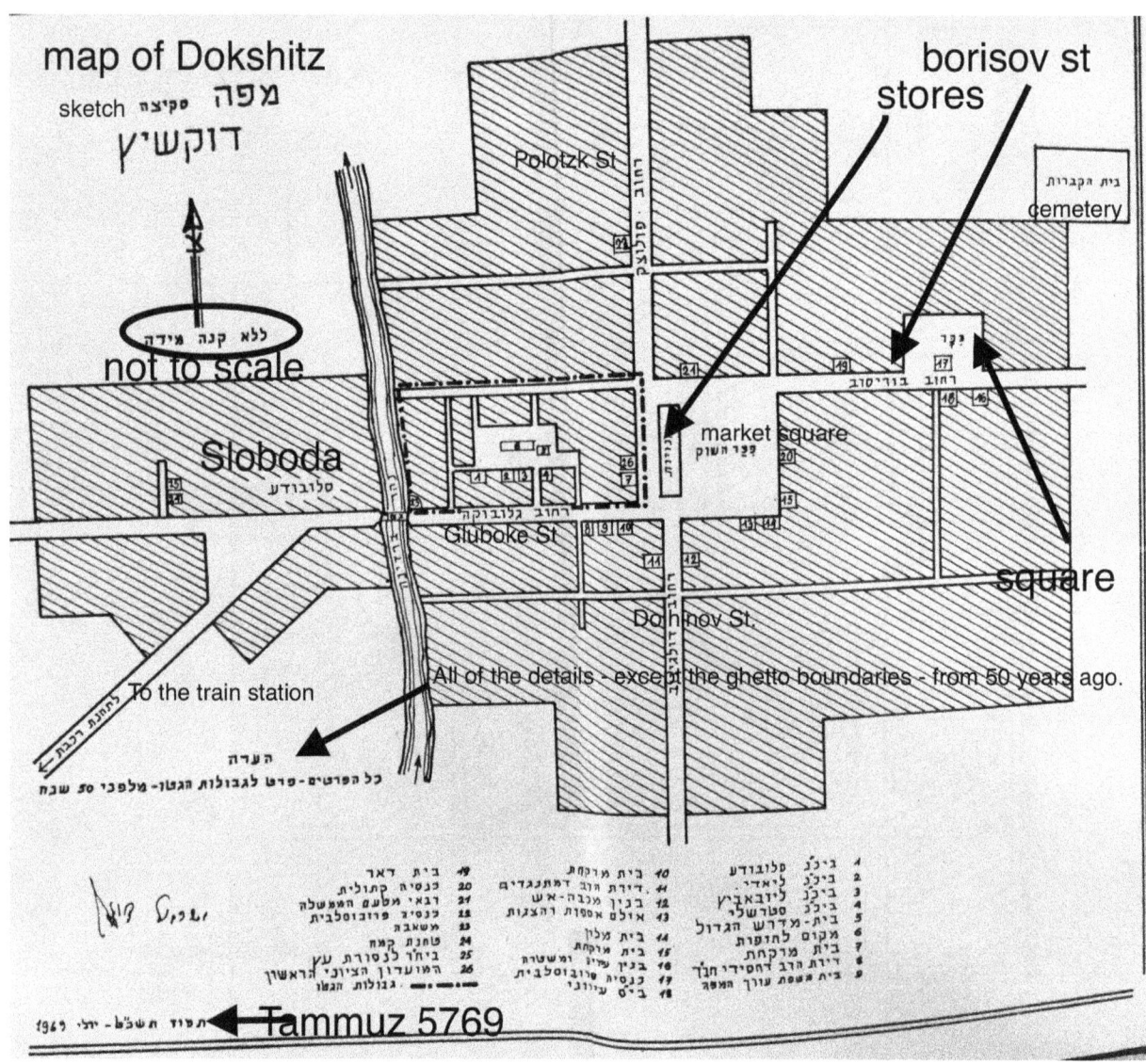

Key to the Map

Transated by Aviva Neeman

1. Sloboda Synagogue
2. Liadi Synagogue
3. Lubavitz Synagogue
4. Strashli Synagogue
5. Large Beit Midrash
6. Place for Chuppahs
7. Pharmacy
8. Residence of the Rabbi of the Chabad Chassidim
9. Residence of the map illustrator
10. Pharmacy
11. Residence of the Rabbi of the Mitnagdim
12. Fire Station
13. Auditorium
14. Hotel
15. Pharmacy
16. Municipality and Police Building
17. Pravoslav Church
18. Municipal school
19. Post office
20. Catholic church
21. Government Appointed Rabbi
22. Pravoslav Church
23. Water Pumping Station
24. Flour Mill
25. Saw Mill
26. First Zionist Cub
    - - - Ghetto Boundaries

Notes to the Reader

Within the text the reader will note "{34}" standing ahead of a paragraph. This indicates that the material translated below was on page 34 of the original book. However, when a paragraph was split between two pages in the original book, the marker is placed in this book after the end of the paragraph for ease of reading.

Also please note that all references within the text of the book to page numbers, refer to the page numbers of the original Yizkor Book.

The original book can be seen online at the Yiddish Book Center web site either with a reader or downloaded as a pdf:

https://www.yiddishbookcenter.org/collections/yizkor-books/yzk-nybc313745/sztokfisz-david-sefer-yizkor-dokshits-parafyanov-yizker-bukh

In order to obtain a list of all Shoah victims from Dokshitz and Parfianov, the reader should access the Yad Vashem web site listed below; one can also search for specific family names using family name option. These lists are continually updated by Yad Vashem, so it is worthwhile to periodically search these lists.

There is much valuable information available on this web site, including the Pages of Testimony, etc.

http://yvng.yadvashem.org

A list of this book and all books available in the Yizkor-Book-In-Print Project along with prices is available at:

http://www.jewishgen.org/Yizkor/ybip.html

Outside Cover of the Original Hebrew Book

Table of Contents

Contents of the original Yiddish and Hebrew version reorganized by chapter and including the images from the Yizkor Book. Captions translated by Daniella HarPaz Mechnikov.

Page   Contents of the Book

1   Foreward - David Stockfish

Chapter 1. This is Our Shtetl

3   Dokshitz - according to historical sources (Hebrew and Yiddish)

7   Only Memories Remained / Kalman Shultz (Hebrew and Yiddish

21   My Shtetl Dokshitz / Zvi Markman (Yiddish)

44   Memories and Impressions / Zelig Ben Moshe (Hebrew)

51   Religious and National Life / Zvi Bar Massada (Hebrew and Yiddish)

55   Professions of Jews / Zvi Rafaeli Gilenson (Hebrew and Yiddish)

57   Memories from My Shtetl / Shoshan Tchuchman-Drezin (Hebrew)

62   My Childhood Memories / Shechna Kanterowitz (Yiddish)

64   Jewish Youth in Our Shtetl / David Kopelowitz (Hebrew)

69   Memories from My Mother's Stories / Devora Matkman (Hebrew)

71   Memories from the Far-Far Past / Shaul Markman (Hebrew and Yiddish)

74   Dokshitz – Its Jews, Traditions, Holidays / Sara Rozov (Yiddish)

Chapter 2. Personalities From Our Town

87   Chaim Zamiri / by Nessia, Shmuel Zamir, Beila, J. Levitan, Sarah Rozov (Hebrew)

97   Aryeh Fogelman / by Offira (Hebrew and Yiddish)

101 "I, Chaya Bloch..." / Zvi Markman (Hebrew)

104 "Chaya Bloch - The Death of a Martyr" / Zvi Markman (Yiddish)

111 Sheynka Markman/ Zvi Markman (Yiddish)

113 The 16 Year Old Partisan Izia Katzovitch / Dov Katzovitz - (Yiddish)

120	Loyal To The End / Dov Katzovitz - (Yiddish)
122	My Family / Nessia Zamiri Kopelowitz (Hebrew and Yiddish)
125	Our Brother Yeshayahu / Dobbeh and Esther Sosman (Yiddish)
128	In Memory of Moshele Kuzinitz / Shoshana Meltzer-Weinbaum (Hebrew and Yiddish)
129	In Memory of My Brother Zosia / Malka Abel (Hebrew and Yiddish)
131	About a Dokshitzer Family / Sonia Komankowitz (Hebrew)
133	In Their Memory (Hebrew) - Photos

Chapter 3. Parafiaov

140	The Shtetl Parafianov / Chaya Foss (Markman), Moshe Mor (Markman) (Hebrew and Yiddish)
144	My Shtetl Parafianov / Shmuel (Ben Raphael) Markman (Yiddish)

Chapter 4. Holocaust and Heroism

149	In Ghetto Dokshitz / Yoseph Shapiro - (Yiddish)
156	The Holocaust in the Shtetl / (Mordechai Warfman) (Hebrew)
157	A Partisan's Story / (Boris Kozinitz) (Hebrew and Yiddish)
181	Memoirs of a Partisan / (Y. Sigaltchik) (Hebrew and Yiddish)
183	The Partisans Attacked Dokshitz / (Lydia Brown) (Hebrew)
183	In the Partisan Detachment / Shmuel Margolin (Yiddish)
184	With the Partisans and in the Red-Army / (Dov Katzowitch) (Hebrew)
204	Testimony of Batia Pren / (Batya Friedman) (Yiddish)
211	The Jewish Resistance in Dokshitz and the Surrounding Area / Shabtai Ruderman, Canada (Yiddish)
214	The Mass Grave of the Dokshitz Martyrs / Ephraim Lipshitz (Yiddish)
216	The Partisans (Yiddish) - Photos
217	At the Pit / Tzvi Markman – Peom (Yiddish)

Chapter 5. The Dokshitzers in Israel and the Diaspora

220	The Activities of the Dokshitz Veteran Organization (Dov Katzowitch) (Hebrew and Yiddish)
222	Dokshitzers in America / Nechama'leh Zalkind-Greber (Yiddish)

Chapter 6. Our Martyrs

225	List of Dokshitz Martyrs (By Streets) (Hebrew)
237	List of Martyrs Given by their relatives
240	List of Parafianov's Martyrs (Hebrew)
244	List of the Anti-Nazi Fighters of Dokshitz and Parafianow (Hebrew)
245	Those Who Survived
247	List of People of Dokshitz Killed in Gleboki

Appendix of Material not included in the original Yizkor Book

249	Introduction to the Appendix by Aaron Ginsburg
254	Material added in the 1990 English Translation: Another German Failure
256	Material added in the 1990 English Translation: People of Dokshitz Killed in Gleboki
257	The Friends of Jewish Dokshitsy by Aaron Ginsburg
262	Why Remember Dokshitsy? by Eva Fogelman
272	Despite Everything by Michael Etkin
322	From Dokshitz to Israel by Arie Henkin
344	Siberian Exile, Aliyah and War of Independence by Arie Henkin
353	My Story Three Years on the Run by Rachel Mutterperl Goldfarb
389	Small Hills Covered with trees by Dan Bar-On
412	Testimony from Trial by the Russian Government
418	Photographs of Martyrs
423	Indices of the Translation and the Appendix

Family Notes

Forward

For those who were born and grew up there, Dokshitz and Parafianov are more than mere geographic points on the map on the eve the flood of Nazism. Physically it is actually a world that is extinct, that has sunken. Yet, in the hearts of those few who survived it is a full world. Spiritually these two places are a world of childish joy and tears, youthful dreams and remembrances of a sparkling life, full of struggle, accomplishment, confidence and belief. Therefore, is the sorrow and rage over the barbaric murder of the hundreds and hundreds of Jewish families, women and children, young and old--the sacrifices of the Nazi executioners and their accomplices unforgettable.

After annihilating these two Jewish communities, what else remains to do for the few survivors but write a memory-book that shall both unite those nearest and dearest and stand as a monument to their unknown graves.

It took ten years of ant-work collecting materials, photographs and documents from the compatriots in Israel and abroad. Very few from Dokshitz survived, and from Parafianov they can be counted on a hand. These tiny numbers took upon themselves the holy responsibility of putting together this memory-book and of raising the necessary funds to publish it. There were immense difficulties, but the will to pass on to generations to come the stories of pre-World War II life and its tragic end at the hands of the Nazis encouraged the survivors through the painful effort to bring this book-monument to publication.

*

Here the book is in your hands. Not a large volume, only some 350 pages, but full of content, heart and soul, as expressed in the written works of thirty six writers--a loyal reflection, in Yiddish and Hebrew, of the rise and the destruction of two neighboring Jewish shtetles in Poland near the Soviet Border.

The Dokshitz-Parafianov Book is not just a Holocaust book, rather first and foremost--a book of the struggle in three stages of Jewish life there and here: the struggle for the establishment and glory of Jewish life in Dokshitz and Parafianov until September 1, 1939; the armed battle and active resistance of Jewish youth in the ghettos and forests against the greatest hater of our people--Nazi Germany; the admirable participation of our pioneers and fighters in the building and defense of the Jewish land until the establishment of the Jewish State and until today. All of this is presented in this book.

*

With the feeling of the completion of a work of great value, that will undoubtedly be a contribution to the literature of the Holocaust and heroism; with the knowledge of fulfilling a national and historical challenge of uniting two destroyed Jewish communities; with gratitude to the former residents of these towns in Israel and the Diaspora who aided in this holy work, we present this Dokshitz-Parafianov Book for reading, study and judgment.

David Sztokfisz
Book Editor

Tel Aviv, May 1970

[Page 11]

Chapter 1
This Is Our Shtetl

Dokshitz
(According to historical sources)

A Street in Dokshitz

In the "General Illustrated Encyclopedia" ("Vielka Powshechna Illustrovna Enciklopedia") published in 1895, volume 15, page 730, we find the following details about the town:

Dokshitz - A town in Minsk region, subdistrict of Borisov, bordering the Vilna district, not far from the source of the Berezina river; A population of 5759 (in 1892), after Borisov, the most important settlement in the province, trades in lumber and flax, has farming and craftsmen. It has two cerkovs (Gregorian churches), a Catholic monastery and a synagogue. The monastery was built in 1608 by the bishop Stan. Kishka; one of the two cerkovs was built in 1863 and the other was restored over the former Unitarian cerkov. Exact data is lacking as to the specific date in which the town was founded; it is known that there was a town in the place in the sixteenth century. During the Swedish war in 1708 the town suffered burning and pillaging. After the second division of Poland, Dokshitz was included in the Russian Empire and in 1795 became a district town in the Minsk region. In 1802, however, the town was annexed to the Borisov district.

In the Orgelbrand encyclopedia (Warsaw, 1899, volume 4), it is said that the population of Dokshitz in 1897 reached 3647.

The Yard of the Lubavich Synagogue

The complete, general, illustrated Gothenburg encyclopedia establishes that Dokshitz is included in the Disna subdistrict, in the Vilna district, and its population is 3004. It has a lumber and meat industries, breweries, a leather factory, an oil factory, a sawmill, and a windmill. A town from the sixteenth century. In the general encyclopedia "Ultima Tabula", published in 1930 in Warsaw (volume 3, page 88), it is presented that Dokshitz is found in the Vilna district, in the Disna subdistrict, 10 kilometers from the Parafianow train station, which is on the Molodetchna - Zahatcha railway. A lumber industry, leathers, oil factories, saw mills and 4081 residents in 1927. In August 1919, the Poles, after a bloody battle, surrounded the Bolsheviks, seized 7 canons, 7 locomotives, a large amount of ammunition and about a thousand prisoners. Dokshitz was destroyed in the end of May 1920. In a counter attack on June 5th 1920, it was taken again by the Poles, but on July 5th was conquered by the Bolsheviks. Dokshitz returned to Polish rule after a peace treaty with Russia.

In the "Powshechni Slovenik Geographitchni", published in Warsaw in 1925 under the editing of A. Malishevski and B. Ulshvitz, in volume c, page 291, the following facts and numbers about Dokshitz are given: A town, subdistrict of Donilovitch, Vilna district, not far from the source of the Berezina, 3004 residents. More details about the town are found in the "Geographic Dictionary of the Kingdom of Poland and Other Slavic Countries" ("Slovnik Geographitchni Krolevstwa Polskigo i Inenich Kraiov Slovianiskich"), published in 1881 in Warsaw (volume b, page 93): Dokshitz, a town in the subdistrict of Borisov, on the border of the Vilna district, not far from the source of the Berezina, in the third Polish area, the fourth Judiciary area and fourth military area, 205 wiorsetts from Vilna, 105 wiorsetts from Borisov, 162 from Minsk and 882 from Petersburg. There is no qualified information about the founding of Dokshitz, but a town existed in the area as early as the fifteenth century; after the second division of Poland, Dokshitz became a district town in the Minsk region and in 1802 it was joined with the Borisov subdistrict. The town includes a Catholic monastery built in 1608 by the bishop Stanislav Kishka who for this purpose ordered the "Turki" manor house to finance a school and a qualified teacher. King Zigmond the third authorized this will by privilege from January 18th 1609. The town was completely burnt during the Swedish war in 1708 and was built anew in 1745. There are two Prowslavian cerkovs, one, of the Unites, but it is not known who paid for its construction. In a certificate from 1514 is it written that it was built using funds of Prince Constantine Ostrogski; the second cerkov was built in 1864. The administrative district of Dokshitz includes 102 tiny villages, and the number of men in it is 1629. The council resides in Dokshitz itself. A population of 5600, mostly Jews. Structures of stone - two; wooden structures - 400. Trading mainly in lumber, grain and salt. The local population owns about 1300 morgs of land. Fairs are held on Tuesdays.

In the sources quoted there is hardly any mention of Jews, except for their number within the populace. The materials were given to us by the National Polish Library in Warsaw in 1964. It seems that there is no other documentation about the town in this establishment.

The Market on Tuesday

The Flood of 1931 Reached the House of Lazar Aharon

[Pages 18]

Only Memories Are Left

by Kalman Shultz

Dokshitz, my little town, so remote, so unpretentious - Much is the joy, the happiness, the love of life you have given us! Pressed between cities and forests, living your calm and tranquil life. The Jews, honest, hard-working people, feeling the ground tremble under their feet, they look up towards the heavens. Sprinkled with beech trees, the road traverses the forests and the villages from the Gleboki direction. The road is wide and silent, the noise of cars and trucks is unheard. Only the cart of a farmer hitched to a horse appears in the horizon, with a swish of a whip in the background. Around are grazing-grounds for the cows. Every Jew, of course, has his own cow. However, the herdsman and the pasture belong to the landowner. There is silence and only the herdsman's flute dares interrupt the bliss. But lo and behold! Not only the flute shatters the tranquility - A great sound suddenly is heard: " Ku ku-ku ku-ku ku-ku ku". There she is. Among the tree tops - the mockingbird... A spring sun. Its rays are caught in the pure white clouds. They play with them like a hand, gently caressing a young girl's hair. Again, a flock of storks visits the fields. The sweet chirp of a young fledgling waking to life. The croak of the frogs in the swamps spread wide. The buzz of bees.

A flock of snow-white doves flying among the trees. An eye-full of blossom and new life! A new spring has conquered the land. Summer. Fields of wild flowers like waves of a calm sea... The star-thistle flowers as exquisite bluish star-fish. Cherries, plumbs, pears and apples. At dawn, the farmers' wives make their way to town with baskets full of blueberries, raspberries, mushrooms and aromatic dried wild flowers for medicines in their hands. Autumn - sheafs of standing corn - like wigwams. The smell of dry hay... Seeds of wild flowers, scattering white strings, blowing in the wind, caught in everything as if in a spider web. Many flocks of birds migrating south. And the sun, setting like a great, red ball of fire. The morning frost... dripping... mud. A strong, continuous pouring of sleet. In the market appear seeds of the harvest and flax. The upkeep of most of the town Jews. And in winter - Whiteness and frost. Trees tops and house roofs covered with snow. Winter wagons. Skis. Long files of wagons taking wood out of the forest. The ice reaches the mouths of the wells.

And at home - plated windows. A blazing stoked fire-place, and the windows full of blossomed frost lilies. Large snowflakes fall continuously. The street is desolate. Only homeless dogs roam the town alleys. Flocks of geese enjoy a stroll in the streets and their white feathers are lost in the white background. Only the water drawer, in his frozen wet clothes passes from street to street, from house to house, the yoke on his shoulders. The housewives shall not remain without water in this cold... The first house. A bit secluded with gardens of lilacs and Tofuls surrounding it. The Faibush family lives there. They are well to do. He is the "go between" the landlord and the Jews. He has a business house for grains and linen as well. But... is that a trick played upon the ear? The sounds of metal glin-glin glin-glin glin... Is it possible? Is there a smith in town as well?

The Hebrew "Tarbut" ("Culture") School in the Shtetl

That is so. It is Erke, the blacksmith. He hammers out a plow. For only half a sack of potatoes he will fix a farmer's plow. Many mouths to feed at home, and the girls are growing up. There is no money and the only hope is the bellows, the anvil, the hammer and the hands... More trees and flowers. On the left a large house built of red bricks. It is a Jew with talent, drive and initiative raised it - and did not live to enjoy it... The house still stands, but the extensive family is every which way. Only the widow is left - with her blond charming daughter.

Songs, songs... "Maybe" - "The motherland" - "My soul desired" - "The dream" - Feelings and bliss. A place for the heart to overflow, between activity in the youth movement, a trip, a camp, pioneer training, the army and the anticipation of the "Aliya". Books - Bialik, Peretz, Mendalei, Marx, Mopassant, Rolan, "Flames", Everlasting Love", and Tolstoy. And there...? In Poland -

Hatred and malicious plotting of the gentiles... No! We shall not overlook the little house of Agatha. She and her daughter are the "Sabath-goy" - and the water drawers. The symbol of poverty, distress and the moral deterioration of the country. For only a few pennies she milks the cows, extinguishes the candles on the Sabath, washes the floors, washes the laundry, brings water and much more... Did she remain a friend in times of holocaust and distress?

On the opposite side, what do we have? The house of Disha and her sons - gone to America.

The Shomar HaTzair "Nest" in 1933

The Bridge on the River Berezina. Here the "Hora" was danced to escort the pioneers making Aliyah (Immigration) to Israel

The Group from the so-called "The Golden Youth" in Dokshitz

Disha is going to America, the street is full of chatter... the neighbors are whispering. Is it so? Yes. Her husband has sent her the papers... At first she objects, refuses. No! She will not desert her sister Malka and her children. Leave the house, the quiet religious town and go off to the end of the world... Where they scorn "Yidishekeit". There is chaos and noise, automobiles and skyscrapers... However, she finally decides. The preparations lasted two years, for many are the papers and arrangements. She has to go to the American consul in Warsaw and fill out questionnaires. Warsaw is a city of con men - when they saw the small-town girl standing in front of them, they traded empty pieces of paper for her dollars, and sold her a brass ring instead of a gold one. That is not all. Down blankets and pillows have to be made. For this, Geese have to be raised, fattened; with the first snow, as the feathers whiten, they are slaughtered. All the neighbors help plucking. The women work 'till the early hours of the morning. Plucking, yakking, giggling and gossiping. True, the work was plenty, but in the end Disha can be proud of the size and weight of her bed clothes. Also, dry cheese has to be prepared, *Gomulkes* (a pastry) and hard cotton towels, since the townspeople do not use the city-folk soft towels. Much is the work. Two days before she leaves, Disha takes leave of the synagogue. Then she visits the graves of her relatives. She is all tears; and here comes the final moment. All who were there will remember it forever. All the relatives and neighbors gathered round the house and filled the street. Chaim Wallwel, the coachman, loads the huge packs on to the cart hitched to two horses. Disha kisses and caresses the walls of the house and parts with her friends and neighbors tearfully. The coachman hurries: The train will be missed! The paring is difficult. She kisses the ground, but at last she's put in the wagon and she's off.

*

"Happy are they that dwell in thy house..." (Psalms 84, 5) With dawn a voice rises from this house day after day. Father, may he rest in peace, Lazer-Hiles. "Psalms", D'...

His lips mutter the prayer while his eyes look out the window searching for a farmer in a wagon coming to sell linen or rye. Often one hears: "A psalm of David..." together with "Patchion Lyon..." For father was a harvest and linen tradesman. Hard working, agile and honest. Loved and accepted by all- including the neighboring peasants. And mother - always busy. Milking the cows, baking bread, cooking, cleaning, doing the washing, knitting and sewing. Sabbath nights and holidays...

*

Youth. When everything is light and the blackest - is white. When the snow covers the windows, flowers of grace, a sun-ray of gilt. Everything full of light and warmth even the snow - even the frost. Arms folded, father walks back and forth telling an ancient legend from a time long past. A Hanukkah lamp glitters on the table - Holy! The candles flicker. Silence. Once there were a mother and her seven daughters. They stood erect, they would not surrender to evil! They were slaughtered before her. Mathityahu and his five sons, heroes, "The Maccabees", led the rebellion! A lesson for generations to come. Facing the many - the strong, stood the few, fighting, avenging winning. He tells of a small oil vase among the ruins of the house of God. Of Judas Maccabaeus, hero, bringing freedom and liberty to a tortured people. Imaginings and secrets. To a child's eye it is a short distance from reality to legend.

*

What is the value of regular days when compared to the holidays? Only yesterday we celebrated Purim, the happy festivities, with its gift sending, "Mahn-ears" and noisemakers - and already we get ready for Passover. So much to do. First, the kirch has to be checked, homemade. "Naliwax" kosher, made to perfection. We Steep wooden barrels in the river to make them kosher to hold water during Passover. A sack of "guarded" wheat is brought to the mill, and is ground into "matzah" flower under strict observation. The neighbors open a matzah bakery together - (Padrad). They bring new boards and planks; after being cleaned the new tables are ready for the kneading of the dough. Everyone helps: Fathers, sons, daughters, all in white volunteer for work. The women roll the dough until it's thin and fine, the youngsters make the holes with metal wheels, and the children pour the flower and the water.... The strongest of the men make and knead the dough and the most responsible put it in the oven. Like a commander in the front lines stands the baker near the oven. His face glistening in the heat shining with joy and perspiration. *He* and no one else, handles the work. *He* is in charge.

The first "matzahs" are taken out of the oven and are put in a basket on a white cloth. The matzahs - thin, round, fragile and fragrant - pass from hand to hand. First to taste are the children, for they can wait no longer, and then the rest. They taste and enjoy. They praise, they complement, they extol... So thin, so white, reviving! Taste of heaven! Here and there one hears blessings! "Blessed be he who gives us life...."

At home a "Kosher for Passover" corner is readied for the matzahs. The crate is covered with snowy cloths all around. The suspense rises... Everyone expects the porter impatiently. From afar one can hear the joking of Asar Zecharovitch about the towns rich, about their pretty daughters, fragile, spoiled...

Make way! Here he comes- and the basket of matzahs is already at home. An aromatic fragrance spreads across the room. Feelings of suspense, joy and holiness. In my memory of then... these moments...are like "the revelation on mount Sinai".

Done with the matzahs, we begin the work at the house. First, the brasswear is whitened and made Kosher: kettles, pots, pans, samovars and other utensils. After this the walls are whitewashed and then the cleaning, the scrubbing, the washing and the "mess"... At this time the tailor and shoemaker arrive to make new clothes and shoes for Passover.

The snow has already begun to melt and warm winds blow from the south. Dogs, cats and other animals loudly announce their presence and begin looking for a mate. Here and there a cow gives birth to a calf and the goat spawns kids... Outside, the rivers are overflowing. Many people gather on the Berezina bridge to watch the water spewing and angrily sweeping logs, branches, roots and planks. The people stand there with fear in their hearts, arguing: will the bridge hold? The older ones tell stories: Once, a bridge was destroyed by the flow, with a mill and many houses. Some say it was before the great fire; others say after...

Already the holiday is near. Everything spotless, clean and shiny. The Passover dishes are taken down from the attic. Everything gives off the aroma of the holiday. As the evening dawns, a last check is made: Father passes from room to room with a feather and a candle picking the crumbs of bread put there before. The next day the "hametz" is sold to a gentile and everything is Kosher for Passover.

How I long to relive these precious hours before the "Seder", to feel the Solemnity in every corner, the holiness and light.

To be again in the shiny house, near mother, radiant in her snowy shawl...Mother...!

*

The table is set- matzahs, wine, fish. Everyone sitting ready for the "Seder". Father, like a king- on a high chair among pillows. The children, in their new clothes- Does a deeper joy exist? The Passover holidays which are also the end of the days in the "Heder".

"What is different"? Here he is! I see him in my mind... Elijah, the prophet, walking across the room, sipping from a cup.

Oh story? Diminishing memories! Forced by them, was I! Flaming poetry coerced from my loins...all to no ado. Passover at home- that is childhood, the age of youth... Days of gold and glory.

Here is the echo of the Haggada stories: About the billy goat, a stick, wildcat and water.

I will run towards my sweet kids, press them to my heart... and the echo... continuous... the next year in Jerusalem!

Youth. The heart warm and wide. The blood racing through the veins.

Spring. "He and she" whispers of love, a first kiss. The shudder of bodies. Shameful pleasure. The hand on the hair.

Everything is a fire! Everything is a storm! Quickly! Rebellion! Charge every obstacle!

With dawn, belief and knowledge. Conversation. Song and dance for supper.

*

The winter and autumn. Schwistapfoli's forest permeates strongly. The lilacs in the alleys intoxicates in the evenings. The smell of roses and Tofuls diffuses through the air. The wooden bench at the corner near the brick house- "The Princes' Palace"- what vigor, how good the people are. In the streets, in the houses. What attraction to the youth movement meeting place, the regiment, the group. How sweet and beloved are the friends.

Is it possible? Are the winds warm in autumn as well? The falling rain mixed with the autumn snow, leaving thick mud on the roads, looks more clear... More beautiful. All this gathers the thoughts, collects the dreams... In winter, how white the snow is - how crisp the air! The ice - a crystal mirror. How good to skate. Oh life, how I love thee!

In the barn the gang sits on the hay, singing. The feelings flow, nostalgia, warmth and love all around. She sits near him - so close... here she is, whole, the sight of her, her voice, the light of her eyes, her body - her soul. Deep in the heart, the singing goes on. The Jorden river flows, it's pure waters whispering secrets. Oh, is our secret revealed as well? Do they know about the hidden yearning , the chaste, modest, relentless feeling?

"You are my Kinnereth". The Jordan river, the Kinnereth... love... the song goes on "Listen, how sings the spring! The song of rebels, the song of freedom". May it go on forever, boundless. Many days and nights, to the end of all generations - forever and ever. Slowly, the singing dies out and a conversation about wealth and happiness develops. "Life, it's sorrows and worth" "The sons' rebellion" "Youth and old age"

*

I shall never forget you, the "Rabbi" and the "Heder" (religious elementary school). I was but a child, but the "heder" memories are deeply imbedded in me. I was five-years-old when the teacher and his son came to father to speak about my eldest brother learning in his "heder". My brother would not go without me so I joined him. The master took me on his back and brought me to the "heder" When he got back to the "heder" he put me down. I stood at the doorstep, embarrassed and shy. I took in the "heder" with my eyes. Long, wide tables, and to them, sat little children on wooden benches. At the corner of one of the tables, sat the master with one of the boys near an open book, pointing with his finger and a belt nearby. "Say 'Kammatz' A, 'Kammatz' B, well? - Go on!" The boy is having difficulties. It seems he's crying. Is this it? I cannot remember how long I stood there with my finger in my mouth... A kid winked at me from one of the tables. I came closer slowly, but the rabbi scolded him. Under the table I saw some kids playing with buttons, I joined in. Finally, it was my turn. The rabbi sat me on his knees, near the open book, and began showing me the first letters. It seemed I was sitting on a hot pan.. I tried not to cry - it would not look proper for a five-year-old to cry. I was released with an affectionate pinch. From then on, every day I had my turn with the rabbi. I received many affectionate pinches, but once in a while my ear would be pulled... a sign to be careful, so that I should know I was mistaken with a phrase or a tune. The rabbi's barometer. Nevertheless, I loved the Alphabeth. Later, the Torah stories, sung... The walking home with a lantern in hand... The fence was broken in the days of youth and triviality. Suddenly, at dawn, for the first time in the "heder". Hebrew and Torah - Adam and Eve, the creation of the world, the shrewness of the snake... Cain and Able, Sodom and Gommorra. Is it all true? Maybe a lie and a falsehood? Oh, if I could only shed my burdens - as a child of then, straighten my back, take off my shoes, without any obligations, worries or promises. I'd run back to the rabbi, to the "heder". Most probably, scorn the modern lecture halls, the lavish schools - Nifty teachers smile to themselves, luxurious colleges... but I shall not be convinced! Happy is the man who acquired knowledge and wisdom in that tiny, poverty-stricken "heder".

A small and modest house. A large family resides here. It is a wise family having an understanding of contemporary times, and this is why it is the meeting point of the "Shomer-Hatzair" Many of the young come here to be educated, to live together. The house is busy with youngsters at all hours of the day: Girls thrown out of the Polish school for belonging to the "Shomer Hatzair" will find condolences here; when the time for "Pioneer training" comes, here is where the strategy for convincing the parents is formed. John Doe has to make Aliyah but has no money - here is where one looks for solutions. A trade must be learned. How? Which? Where? Here one talks about it. Someone has to buy material for clothing, shoes, a sweater, a dress; to crochet a shirt - here is where they'll come for a final decision. You've read a book and you would like to talk about it - here is where you'll find a listening ear. If the kids are not at home, you can talk with "mother" until they arrive. A good and kind woman. The boys - all witty, with acute minds and tongues... and the girls - all graceful and charming... You would like to know the news of the town - here is where to come. Just gossip...? Everything is talked about here. What happened yesterday at the youth movement meeting? Who's in love with whom? Who went to vilna and brought "Saccharin" Who was met last night? What happened in the Polish school? Who's to be married? What did Asar Zacharovitch say? Again about the argument of the two rabbis. A new teacher has come to the "Tarbut" school . Some new books at the public library. Something is wrong at the bank. Last night, the fire- fighters' band crossed the border into Russia. Who are the couples that will empty the Jewish National Fund donation boxes tomorrow? Again about the traditional fire-fighters' parade every Sunday in their shiny brass hats, the trumpets and the band. There is a movie showing at the "Dam-Ludowi". Have you heard? There is a radio with earphones already in Dokshitz - It's at the nearby café, they're actually talking... More youngsters crossed the border. Yesterday, we drank "Quas" at Mulai-Kugel, good "Quas". There was a fight with the communists. ÅRabbi Glinkin spoke at the synagogue against the youth movement members for desecrating Passover..."Firalaier Lat'kes"... Soon there'll be a "tea party". The ones training at night to ready themselves for the army transferred wood from the lord's house to the pauper's home. Drunken gentiles broke the windows of Jewish houses but received a beating. Shlomo and Israel received *certificates* to make Aliyah to Israel, the parting at the bridge. That loony happy guy said... The Jewish National Fund council in Dokshitz is raising a show. A few Jews were arrested for commerce on the border. The communists spread more propaganda. She's beautiful...

*

Many shall remember the small warm house, a heater, a couch, a table, an oil lamp, warmth, simplicity and modesty. Opposed to substance - the glory of the spirit... the life and the soul of every flesh and blood. Here, the heart shall open, a story is told by every man - young or old.

*

Miserable, bitter, unlucky in love, failing at exams, a sadness of the heart? Distress at home, unemployment, destitute or simply...in love... All in need. Sharing - some in joy, some in failure and misery. Here is that small house! Morning, noon, evening, a joy in the heart... A light shining in the window.

*

Can the pain be encompassed? Will the world ever understand the immenseness of the holocaust, the profoundness of the sorrow?

*

In the town: streets, alleys, squares, markets, synagogues and schools. Children, boys, women, grown-ups, elderly - everything is gone to dust.

Only stories are left, memories, nostalgia and a heart torn in infinite grief.

[Page 30]

Party in Honor of Mendel's Alyiah (Emigration to Palestine) and Henekh's trip for pioneer training. (On the picture is written: "Henekh to pioneer training and Mendel to Aliyah")

[Page 34]

The sawmill where the pioneers trained for making Aliyah

[Page 37]

**The "Hatzofeh" (Scout) Group on the way from Pireley Boats
(written on the photo: "on the way from Pireley"
and "'Hatzofeh' group - Hol Hamoed Pesach 1935")**

[Page 40]

**The "Hatzofeh" (Scout) Troup of Hashomar Hatzair (the Young Watchmen)
On Photo held by boy: The "Hatzofeh" (Scout) Troup**

[Page 42]

Wind Band that crossed the border to the Soviet Union

[Page 44]

The Great Fire in Dokshitz

[Page 46]

Committee of Keren Kayemet Bazaar
Written on the top: The Committee for the fourth Bazaar
of Keren Kayemet of Israel in Dokshitz - Purim")

[Page 48]

My Shtetl Dokshitz

(Memories, Manners, Images)
Tzvi Markman/Kibbutz Hatzor
Translated by Ira Lulinski and Aaron Ginsburg

Oh, Dokshitz, my shtetl, I come to remember you...
A life that sprang from pure sources,
I will never forget you
And I cannot believe that all is lost

Forests surrounded you,
Trees full of summer greenery,
A small river snaked its way
Under the dawn's rays.

As they used to say sometime ago,
Borders over the horizons..
Frequent wars and pogroms
And battles on all the frontiers.

Balakhovitzers, highwaymen,
Used to amuse themselves by
Cutting beards, breaking windows
Accompanied by a wild-devilish laugh.

Those days are forever gone,
A new generation arose
And people immediately began
To live in fear and apprehension.

Three churches and a mosque,
Mills and a brewery,
A market square in the middle of the shtetl,
Shops, warehouses-without end.

During the week they displayed
Their various types of merchandise,
Trustworthy Jewish merchants-
Poultry, grain, flax and hay.

Old houses, spacious apartments
Of timber, and also from brick,
Small houses they were not perfect.
They looked like fallen wings.

The businessmen, the storekeepers, the tailors, blacksmiths,
Coachmen, carriers, shoemakers,
And also just plain Jews-
Of virtually every type.

Bearded Jews, clean-shaven ones,
Also happy ones, sad ones
Those with clean clothes and those with dirty clothes,
Modern ones and frum ones.

Laborers, Klei Kodesh,
Everyone came to hear the maggid.
The shul and beis midrash were filled,
They also ran eagerly to hear a chazan.

People split hairs about a mishnayos,
Over a pshat, a halacha,
Politics, related a piece of news-
And occasionally; a schnapps, a bracha…

Thus did we live in peace.
Occasionally things upset
The routine of Jewish life-
Because of a rabbi or a shochet.

Little children grew up
And were always being educated.
Either in the Polish public school,
iIn the Tarbut, or in the cheder.

They played, well dressed and well fed,
with black or blue eyes,
There were also hungry ones in rags.
They were looked at with pride…and humility

The youth used to parade,
Dreaming, looking at the stars,
Singing songs, they used to carry on romances
Laughing so hard that tears came.

Engagements, weddings, circumcisions
And under the chupah of the chosson and kallah,
At nicely bedecked tables-
In-laws, friends and everyone.

Good citizens, paid taxes.
Even if a little bit was added on.
The mayor says "Dobry dzień":
For the city treasurer was his crony.

That's how, in great harmony,
We almost forgot that we were in the galus.
Amidst our neighbors,
We accepted the fantasy.

Often ideas arose-
A struggle for tomorrow and freedom;
In organizations and parties,
Comrades with enthusiasm and dedication.

At bonfires an oath was sworn:
Halutzim, Shomrim, and Zionists
Often a red flag
Was hung by Communists.

Discussions, lectures, debates
And farewell banquets,
Performances, speeches,
Bazaars and raffles.

The entire community used to turn out
And dance a fervent hora
To accompany a neighbor who
Was setting out for Israel.

Until Hitler's wild beasts,
Threw themselves into war;
With a bloody noise
A storm blew over the world.

The Red Army
Without a shot being fired
Opened wide horizons-
That became very costly.

They offered a better life
Work and education, happiness and peace,
Slogans, posters, banners…
Was it only a dream?

But the fascist powers
Broke through to the east,
Murdering and splitting brains,
Letting flow rivers of blood.

They drove the Jews-alive-
Into the pits
And with the blood and murder of children-
Thus in the history it is recorded…

It's hard to find a pen
That can express
What everyone feels in their hearts,
When the tears choke, choke…

In deep sorrow, heads bowed,
We now stand as the last witnesses,
To the killing of our parents, grandparents,
Sisters and brothers, children, relatives.

Forever gone, the sources overgrown,
Your shame and pain cannot be forgotten,
It's unbelievable that all was lost..
Oh Dokshitz my shtetl, I come to remember you.

[Page 51]

From Kheyder--to the Cemetery...

Dokshitz, my shtetl--you stand now before my eyes. From the earliest childhood years, with the kheyders where mischievous youngsters learned, with the school where teachers implanted Jewish and general studies in us.

I am reminded of a parade on *Lag Ba'Omer*, with the national flags and slogans, "Long Live our National Language!" Then comes a *Keren Kayemet* Bazaar with the lovely exhibits and drawings, which emboldened the youth to transform during a folk-demonstration from love and sincerity to a Zionist mindset. And the lively ebullient youth-organizations: *HaShomer HaTzair, HeChalutz, HeChalutz HaTzair, Beitar, Com-yung*. Everywhere a flurry of activity, discussions full of zeal and passion. Evening group meetings with heated arguments that sometimes ended in blows. And overall--there was joy! A comrade travels to the Land of Israel. The entire shtetl sends him off with song and dance, on the bridge they dance a "hora," and then the traveler commences on his long journey.

The noise of the matza hearth ovens announces the approaching Passover. *Milkhiks* [dairy foods], *Tisha B'Av*--with *shtekhekhtz* [little thorns thrown in beard in an Eastern European custom for the holiday *Tisha B'Av*]. Dressed up and festive girls, strolling to the synagogue on Rosh Hashana to hear the shofar blow. By the river a multitude of Jews stands shaking out their pockets, they free themselves of all of their sins from the previous year. Later, the pre-Yom Kippur atonement ceremony of *shlogn kapores* begins. On the eve of Yom Kippur, Jews wrapped in *talisim* [prayer shawls] and *kittles* [white robes] fast and pray more than a day and a night in the full synagogues, where the lights burn non-stop. *Kol Nidrey*-it is a tremendous experience for all the Jews in the shtetl.

Here runs the *shames* [sexton] with an *esrog* [citron] and *lulov* [palm fronds] to the women, so they don't miss this *mitzvah* [commandment]. And the streets become filled with joy as do all six *basey midrashim* [houses of study and prayer]-*Simchas Toyrah* is upon you, Jews. In a state of light drunkenness the congregation begins *hokofes* [circuitous procession around the synagogue the Torah scroll]. Blessings with "*Shehaklen*" [benedictions over drink] over full cups, entire families wishing a "*l'chayim*" [toast to life]!

Again, the gray weekdays return, with the old worries and troubles. Quietly a funeral procession goes to the cemetery and the pine-trees rock themselves to the cadence, and shade the fresh grave. And comrades enlist jokes and pranks from one another to bring out laughter, and also anger.

**At the Cemetery in Dokshitz
Gravestones of Yehudit (1917) and Isaac Markman (1926)**

Up the Mountain - and Downfall.....

Who among us does not recall a summer Sabbath day in the Swistopole forest, when a well-known rabbi decided to find his Hassidim in Dokshitz? After dividing the songs, listening to different melodies, a little dance, tickets were handed out. In the "folk-house" a play is performed well. The striving to perform in and to see theater becomes greater and greater: Particularly when the profits are designated for such life-important causes as caring for the ill, culture, *Keren Kayemet*, the Jewish school, *Keren Aliya*, Women's committee. This does not include only philanthropic aid, rather also moral and communal support, with exception of help to the ill.

1939. The Red Army marches into Dokshitz on those famous September days. All social worries fall on the state. But of the one-time Jewish institutions not a memory remains. Only the dramatic circle expands its activity and the chorus sings new songs about victory and happiness. But this does not cont6inue for long. . The accursed swastika with its four venomous snakeheads spread out its reign over Europe and also reached Dokshitz. A dark cloud set itself upon the Jewish heads in the shtetl. Yet even in those difficult days of the ghetto our brothers, the children of Israel did not lose the image of God. The strong assist the weak in deeds and help. And when the last hope was put out, they showed their valor, approaching death with calm, dignity and resistance. Is there any greater heroism than that of the Jewish mother in Dokshitz, who injected her own child with morphine, to ease his passage into death? Or the young man already shot through, with the bullet in his back, who jumped out of the mass grave and attacked the murderer? Or the captive young man, the soldier who took him to be shot, suddenly grabbed the gun out of his hand and ran with it into the forest to the partisans? Or the heroism of the Dokshitz mother who took her three daughters and with heads held high walked towards her murderers?

Now all has ended. There are no more Jews in the shtetl. Just a cemetery that once was, with the holy grave from whence come the last moan and silenced cry of old people, women, children: "Do not ever forget what happened to us! Always carry our memory inside yourself!"

Jewish Livelihood

Our shtetl, Dokshitz, did not differentiate itself from the tens of other and similar communities in the area. The center of the shtetl-the market-was the core source of livelihood. The church stood in the square with its low clock tower, which gave an uneasy, even a fearful, feeling as it chimed..... Opposite the church-the rows of shops, one across from the other, some eighty in total. The owners of these shops were considered middle class and they were more or less secure financially.

The four most important streets, which intersected in the market from four different directions were called: Polotzker, Borissover, Dolhinover, Gluboker. Many little streets branched out from these streets and most of them made their way to the synagogue courtyard-there was also another quadrangular place between the *beys-hamidrash* and the *shtibelekh* [little synagogues]: Starosheler, Libavitzer, Liyader and Slaboder. Opposite all of these houses of prayer were the workshops of the Dokshitz Jewish tailors, cobblers, gaiter/boot-makers, tinsmiths. The small muddy streets were inhabited by the wagon drivers and butchers. Here were the *kheyders* [small religious schools], where teachers ruled by whips, or the more liberal who punished a student with copying or learning chapters of the Psalms by heart, or blessing the new moon, or the "*Y'hi Ratzon*" prayer of the *Rosh Khodesh* [new month] service. Of course, the greater the "transgression"-the greater the "punishment." It was, however, a fact, that the students of the encouraging teachers learned much better than those who were whipped.

Several of the Youth of Dokshitz before their Induction (Draft) into the Polish Army

The part of the shtetl, inhabited by *Amkho* [your people], simple Jews, also made its living from the beer brewery, two mills, a sawmill and the special bakeries and ovens for baking matzah for every Passover eve. The machine for rolling matzah was new and was operated by a hand crank. Since there was no industry in the shtetl, there was not sufficient work for the five thousand residents nor sufficient livelihood. The so called lower class elements, the workless and moneyless, sought a bit of earnings in petty trade at the market, or in surrounding villages, not numbering many, because not far from us- some 7-8 kilometers, was the Soviet border. People only let themselves go in the direction of Gluboki and Dolhinov in search of work, the most important of them going to haggle first and sell the ripe fruit to the wholesalers or store it for winter. There was exchange with the village, buying and selling of wheat, flax, eggs, chickens and geese, which were bought in autumn, kept and tended in the garret, stable, cell or even in the anteroom until Chanukah in order to derive *shmaltz* [fat] for Passover and to use it for the delicious *latkes* [potato pancakes]. Feathers from the slaughtered geese were plucked for featherbeds, cushions and pillows. The work was done for *grozshn* ["pennies," lit. smallest amount of Polish money/coin], in the long winter nights.

The full picture of business for Jews in Dokshitz is not yet complete. We also had matchmakers, brokers, sextons, cantors, *ba'aley tfiles* [leaders of prayer services], psalm sayers [for the dead-it is the tradition that psalms must be read aloud for the dead from the time of death until the time of burial], shroud embroiderers, those who practiced cupping [for the purpose of bloodletting as a remedy for ailments], ritual attendants at the bathhouse and *mikveh* [ritual bath], cooks for weddings and suppers, waiters, guardians, porters-and not just a few charity collectors. And over all of them-the arrogance of certain wealthy people, even very affluent, in the shtetl: wood merchants, merchants of flax and seeds, millers, partners in pitch burning, cooperatives, hotel owners, restaurateurs, some land owners, those employed by lords, owners of the beer brewery and several big merchants who also received support from their relatives in America.

Regarding the support from overseas, it was known that almost a half of the Jews in the shtetl benefited from it. Nevertheless most people were over their heads with worries about income and the general economic position of the population was not very high. Therefore, the Jews created many institutions and organizations, which had as their mission to mitigate the necessities of the needy and also to morally, encourage and support them.

Education, Upbringing, Culture

Jewish children, who studies for some time in various *kheyders* were, both because of the obligatory school law and because of the impossibility of their parents paying for their education -- enrolled, from age seven on, in the Polish State Folk-School [*Poveshechne*]. The curriculum there, and the anti-Semitic spirit that reigned moved many parents not to send their children there. The community began thinking seriously about its own Jewish school for Jewish children. After much outreach to America and receipt of some help from there, it was decided to found a *Tarbut* [culture] school. This occurred in the year 1924-25. The school developed slowly. Notwithstanding the limited financial opportunities, six classes were started in which 150 students studied. Since there were representatives of all strata of the Jewish community on the school-committee, the curriculum in the *Tarbut* school was multi-dimensional and incorporated subjects like Polish, religion and others. A cadre of young "doers" and activists for the Zionist parties and organizations in the shtetl came from that school.

The Bundist and Yiddishist elements founded a Jewish folk-school with great effort where the teachers, working there for a "hunger-wage" [i.e., very little], displayed a lot of idealism and devotion. Both directions-The Zionist-Hebraist and the Bundist-Yiddishist, also influenced the students in the Polish school who were not estranged from the Jewish area and gave their contribution to the lively societal activities.

In order to insure the existence of the schools, which consistently found themselves in a difficult material position, dramatic circles were created, which in addition to giving, the satisfaction of good performances, also enriched the tills of the schools.

The library was an important stimulus for the cultural development of the city.

Members of "Achdut VeTkhiya" (Unity and Revival) - 1917

The Spiritual and Community Center

"Keep the book clean, do not tear it-because it is a communal possession!" Every book in the Dokshitz library had this stamped on its cover. The youth, after finishing one of the folk schools, still yearned for knowledge and wanted to study further, the folk library was their only "high school." Only a very few boys from privileged homes had the opportunity to continue in *gymnasium* [high school] in Vilna, three or four even traveled to France to study, while most young people used the library which possessed a rich collection of the better books of Jewish and general literature. The popular editions from the "*Grozshn* Library" [Penny Library] also gave the youth the impulse to contemplate, discuss and debate the works of the classics and the poli-societal problems.

And the librarians, as the schoolteachers, were committed to their work with heart and soul. In the cold winter nights they would hand out the books in the unheated library, directing the beginning readers and helping anyone to choose a specific book. The library also struggled for its material existence, because the membership fee did not cover all of its necessities. The used to hold presentations, productions and performances. The same idealists were very busy, over their heads, producing all of these productions.

The influence of the library upon the growing youth did not take long. The different party ideologies and movements which came from outside, with the help of the folk-library and its books, allowed for the fact that in Dokshitz all of the organizations that were active in Poland were represented. Our youth participated in *HaShomer HaTza'ir, HeChalutz, Po'alei Tzion, HeChalutz HaTza'ir,* Communists, later-Revisionists and *Beitar.*

The club evenings, lectures and discussions in the street and at home showed the political growth and Jewish involvement of the youth. There were membership drives for Zionist causes, separate from the *Keren Kayemet, Keren Aliya* and bazaars. Literary evenings and presentations have already been mentioned.

The first pioneers leave for *Hachshara* [training and immigration to Israel in a rural development movement]. At different times uniformed youth of *HaShomer HaTza'ir, Beitar* and *HeChalutz* would often march across the Dokshitz streets. The illegal communist youth pushes its conspiratory platform. The conflicts and meetings of the Zionist and anti-Zionist youth become more frequent. When one group has gathered for *Keren Kayemet,* the second delivers a contribution for *Mopar* (aid for the political prisoners). Illegal literature surfaces in the shtetl and from time to time a red flag is hung on the telephone poles. People also begin stealing across the border in to Russia, which was also full of much danger. But there were also some who were privileged to make *Aliyah* to Israel, or seldomly go to *Hachsharah* training.

Clearly, the Jewish struggle was also a result of the difficult economic situation in which the Jewish population found itself, especially the youth. The unemployment was high; there was not always enough food to satisfy.

Illness was also a frequent visitor in Jewish homes. In order to alleviate the need, the philanthropic institution *Mishmeres Khoylim* [lit. protector/guard of the ill] was founded.

Aid for the Sick and Needy

Mishmeres Khoylim was the only institution around which the greatest political adversaries gathered, tens of young people volunteered to help it. The newly created institution first aided the poor and in the case of a sick child or an old father, the medical help from the *Mishmeres Khoylim* was a great comfort, giving courage and real support to the family which lived in want and need. Calling a doctor or buying an expensive prescription was simply an impossible thing for such people. Therefore, *Mishmeres Khoylim* took this burden on, pro bono.

Besides this, the institution looked after the sick with a nurse team of two people, usually a young man and a young woman, whose job it was to follow and execute the doctor's orders. They sat with the patient at home, encouraging him/her and looking after all that was needed.

The managing committee also looked after the patients with a pot of compote, preserves and various jams which were prepared in the summer from berries, fruits and raspberries. In addition, the *Mishmeres Khoylim* leant various sorts of instruments to the patient, a thermometer, cups [for bloodletting], and the like. This aid is what determined the budget. Therefore, frequent campaigns, events and functions were organized. The Jewish community very positively supported the mission of the institution and supported it with all its strength. The most important income came from presentations with the participation of local very talented efforts, both in the dramatic arena as well as singers, musicians, etc. The presentations were always greatly enjoyed and on top of the aid to the *Mishmeres Khoylim*, they also brought a lot of liveliness and cultural activities into the shtetl, simultaneously developing stage talent in the young.

I remember an instance when because of a most serious illness the patient was not allowed to be transported to the hospital in Gluboki. Some 15-20 Jews volunteered to carry the patient on a bed, a distance of 30 kilometers. *Mishmeres Khoylim* also oversaw that dangerously ill patients could get to a government hospital in Gluboki.

Separately from the *Mishmeres Khoylim* the Women's-Committee was active -- a competent group of doers which achieved a lot for the institution.

One could also count the *Khevre Gemiles Khasidim* among the philanthropic organizations in the shtetl, as they granted interest free loans to the needy merchants, small-time peddlers and craftsmen. Furthermore, the *Kevre Kadish* took care of deceased Dokshitz Jews, taking care that they were buried according to the Jewish law and brought to the Jewish cemetery.

The Management Committee of the Bank

Pozsharne [Fire Brigade] and Self Protection

One of the oldest and most important institutions was the fire department, known by its popular name "the *Pozsharne*" which was kept busy putting out fires. In a shtetl like Dokshitz one heard the alarm sound often-bells and the scr4eams of frightened people "Fire! Fire!" Most of the houses and buildings were built of wood and furthermore-crammed together in narrow small little streets. The gates and entrances to the town were also made of wood.

At both people raised geese and in order to "lengthen" the day for them so they would eat more, people burned gaslights or lanterns there, which started fires more than once. The winter apples were kept in cellars packed in straw-truly a fire hazard. The heated ovens, the poor kitchens, were common causes of fire outbreaks, which ravaged many homes. A spark from a chimney was enough to cause an entire street to go up in flames and smoke.

The older generation used to tell often of the big fires in the shtetl and even the history of Dokshitz is organized according to the first, second and third fires.

The Dokshitz "*Pozsharne*" was supported by the community and government, but most of the firefighters were *Akhinu-B'nei-Yisro'el* [lit. "our brethren, the sons of Israel," members of our race/religion]. First of all, this was because many of the younger Jews had nothing to do and they were able to give a lot of time to drills. Furthermore, most of the fires broke out in

Jewish homes and, as already mentioned, destroyed many neighboring buildings because of the crowdedness. In the Polish neighborhood in the shtetl, one house was separate from another and the fire could become localized.

Fire Brigade in Dokshitz

Some 100 young people belonged to the "*Pozsharne*"-and outside of their own task, they were also in charge of Jewish celebrations and undertakings. Thus, the Jewish community was proud of and confident in its firefighters on account of their conversion into a self defense organization, when rowdy soldiers, or just anti-Semitic pogromists, wanted to make merry with the Jewish community. Or simply if the Jews smelled the danger of anti-Jewish excursions, they would ring the fire alarm and our boys, armed with axes, dressed in their brass helmets and *Pozsharne* uniforms, well drilled and disciplined, taught the ruffians, quickly they would mete it out, and before they could cause harm to the Jews.

Apropose the above-a few words about the Jewish-Christian relations in the shtetl. In the so-called normal times, both peoples lived in good-neighborly relations and seldom did conflicts arise. IN contrast, during times of crisis, the Poles and White Russians were the cause of clashes with Jews more than once. But our self-defense group did not allow the anti-Semites to carouse too much.....

Rest, Enjoyment and Recreation

The picture of Jewish Dokshitz would not be complete, without a description of the places of rest, enjoyment and recreation.

Several kilometers east of the shtetl, was the Swistopole forest that stretched to the Soviet border. Every Sabbath and holiday, that place was transformed into a mass meeting. Young and old came here to relax and enjoy their free time. The air there was delightfully fresh and a cool breeze blew steadily on hot summer days. Whilst the young danced, played, sang in special places or clearings-the older people lay in the shade of the trees, reading a book, a newspaper or having a chat. One could hear the playing of a mandolin or guitar from various directions.

There was also no scarcity of soccer games. The youth, who belonged to different organizations, held their get-togethers, circles/clubs and meetings in the Swistopole forest. The communist disposed youth relegated themselves to a hidden corner and ran their meeting there. In quiet corners young people would often lose their way, or young couples in love.....

People would put up a hammock between two close trees and rock until dozing off. Mothers would take their youngsters there for a walk-and thus, on such an afternoon, the forest was full of joy and fun.

In the shtetl proper, there were several fruit orchards, the property of the local priest, who leased them to Jews. On a Shabbes [Sabbath] after tsholent [a baked dish of meat, potatoes and beans often served on the Sabbath-a slow cooked dish, kept warm from the day before so as to avoid cooking on the Sabbath, which is prohibited] people used to go to these orchards and relax there from a whole week's work and from chasing their subsistence earnings. Also, the good owner, Mikulsky, rented his orchards to Jewish people who would tend the orchards. In addition to that rest, people went there to buy cherries, apples, pears. Lying on the grass people discussed politics, shtetl news, people also carried on romances, decided upon wedding dates and occupied themselves with...... gossip.

Smaller groups of young people also used to go for walks among the flowers, which were on both sides of the Glubok and Dolhinov roads. That area was especially good for young couples in love to walk in, and the trees on the road would have much to tell.....

The Laputa River, the Podamch swing, like the boulevard around the Russian Orthodox church, the little streets, were also never empty of young people strolling.

Until the angel of death came in the likeness of Hitler's murderers and their helpers-and all was annihilated.....

Members of the Fire Brigade in the Shtetl

Reincarnations of a Samovar

Clearly, I do not want to tell the whole story of our samovar here. For that end I would have to start with *Bereyshis* [lit. "In the beginning." The name of the first book of the bible, The Book of Genesis], when the earth came into existence and mountains and oceans were created, with volcanoes, earthquakes, explosions, dismemberment, gases, fusions, strata of different metal-ores, copper mines, melting ovens and foundries, factories and finally - - - the samovar body plant, which belonged to the immense Czarist empire of Nicholas the Second.

It would be enough, believe me, if I were to begin with my *zeyde's* [grandfather's] wedding. Why my *zeyde's*? Because every sensible person understands that wherever was a *zeyde*-there was certainly a *bubbe* [grandmother] as well.

I recall my *zeyde*, may he rest in peace, because he was truly a learned Jew, with a beard and *peyes* [traditional hair sidelocks] and with a *tallis-katon* [ritual four corner fringed undergarment] that reached to just above his knees; Additionally, a *shoykhet* [ritual slaughterer], a *ba'al tfilah* [person who leads prayer services], a *moyel* [person who performs the ritual circumcisions]. His name was Reb Tzvi-Hirsh, and I myself bear his holy name.

As you now know who my grandfather was, you might imagine what sort of a wedding they had put on for them.

In those olden days such a wedding was held in the big synagogue - calmly, leisurely, with respect, with klezmer musicians, with a *rebbi* [rabbi] and with a *badkhn* [traditional entertainer at a Jewish wedding who delivered humorous and sentimental rehearsed and impromptu rhymes and poems], a sexton, a waiter and a cook. And everything was filled out with all of the trimmings: a *kinyen* [traditional act required to validate the marriage contract, required before the witnesses sign the *ketubah*] with a welcoming reception, a *badekn* [veiling of the bride prior to the wedding ceremony], the traditional seating of the bride on a chair, congratulations, with a *chuppah* [wedding canopy], lifting the married couple in chairs, with *havdoleh* [traditional ceremony performed at the close of the Sabbath to distinguish between the holy Sabbath and the profane weekdays] and candles, with someone to arrange the wedding nuptials and the *sheyva broches* [7 traditional blessings with meals after the wedding], with *"harey-as"* [lit. "you are," the beginning words spoken by the groom in the wedding ceremony] just where it is supposed to be, a wedding meal with the *khosn's kitke* ["the groom's" twisted bread loaf] and delicious fish and meat, with rice, kasha and soup, with *kimelekh* [caraway seeded rolls] and compote and in addition, a nice *l'chayim* [toast "to life!" with drink] with a *kiddush* [blessing over wine] and *brachos* [blessings - i.e., over food and after meals], with good wishes and most importantly - wedding presents!....

The *badkhn* stood, immediately wiped his lips, curled his mustache, combed his yellow sparse little beard with his fingers, unbuttoned his long coat, glanced over his belly with pleasure and with a cantor-like voice began to read a sizeable list of important relatives from the groom's side and just regular relatives from both sides. And everything presented so ingeniously - according to one's origins, one's importance, with all of the titles and furthermore, in rhymes, which was commensurate with the level of a truly talented *badkhn*, who was actually also the *shadkhn* [matchmaker]: the scholar, the *shoykhet* [ritual slaughterer], the wealthy *Reb Lipeh* with his dear wife *Khyeneh-Soreh-Tzipeh*; the wealthy *gabai* [trustee or manager of an institution] of the *khevre kadisha* [the burial society] with his *eyshes khayil* [lit. woman of valor - his wife] *Brokheh Stishe*; *Reb Sholem*, the scholar and *dayen* [assistant to Rabbi, responsible for questions of ritual cleanliness and settling minor disputes] with his partner *Shosyeh-Khayeh*; the wealthy *Berkeh*, the spice merchant with his canary *Grunyeh- Merkeh* from the groom's side; the well versed in Torah [bible], the scholar *Reb Dovid Zisheh* and his second wife *Dobeh- Musyeh*; the wealthy, pre-eminent and philanthropic *Reb Yakov-Yosheh* with his blessed young efficient housewife *Yenteh- Dvosheh* - from the young couple *Heshl* and *Sorel* of the bride's side. And from all of the remaining relatives *Zalman* and *Khasiyeh*, *Nokhem* and *Basheh*, *Shmerl* and *Keyle*, *Yitzkhok* and *Beyleh* - and so it went without end: *Khayim* and *Boyrekh*, and *Zeyrekh*, and *Moyshe*, and *Khasheh* and *Basheh*, and *Bereleh* and *Pereleh*, and the aunt *Gnesyeh* and the widow *Feygeh-Pesyeh*, and *Zeyrekh- Kalmen* the *almen* [widower], have all publicly contributed, sparring no expense, because of life - one lives only one life on this world.....

And with many blessings, that the couple may live in wealth and honor to the age of 120 years, shall know no sorrows, poverty of danger, all jointly present as a gift a brand new copper samovar!!! And the *oylem* [crowd/audience] is asked not to sit like a *goylem* [dummy], lift their noses, fill their glasses, and let there be joy among the Jews, make a *l'chayim*, have a bite and be merry!.... [Translation note: Above passages by *badkhn* all in rhyme in the original Yiddish].

As is the case with Jews, not all well wishes are fulfilled, not all blessings become actualized, because the "creator-or-the- world" doles out his "merchandise" without guarantees. The young couple, that is my grandfather, *Reb Tzvi-Hersh*, and my *Bube* [grandmother], *Soreh-Rivkeh*, despite all of the spirited wishes, actually did not begin a very happy rich life. All five of my grandfather's vocations barely brought in even the dearth of earnings they did bring.

Why? First of all, a scholar: Well, when one studies Torah, does one get paid for it? It actually goes right in the bank of the court in the heavens in an account for the world to come. Secondly, a religious teacher. Well? One must have students. And if one does have several, do their parents pay enough fees to sufficiently support a family?

And now, a *moyel* [ritual performer of circumcisions]. What does one do if, just to be aggravating, only girls are born?....

So, a leader of the prayer services is actually just a thing of evil inclination or desire, a kind of "hobby." One's heart wants to pour itself out before the pulpit, yet that is also far from income.

What remains is a ritual slaughterer. This is actually a good profession among Jews, which gives honor and glory - but no money. Because not only the slaughterer lives off the neck of the animal, but also the rabbi and the *gabbai*, and the *dayen* and the *shames*, and the kosher-meat-tax-collector and simply good and pious Jews, and something is taken off the top for a *mikveh*, and for a bath and for an almshouse or hospital and for a chamber of ablution [for washing dead bodies before burial], etc.

In the event that it is the neck of something random, just any old ox - fine: perhaps he can make do. But in the event that it is a calf, a skinny sheep, or a truly old he-goat, than clearly - no "goatly" enthusiasm. Nevertheless, there is also no sin. A world of Jews live like this. So, it has been said of my grandparents too.

The samovar, with its bulging wealthy man's look, with its big beautiful carved spout, actually began to fulfill its duty quite intensively. What a samovar is to a Jewish home, I need not say, because without tea in the morning and evenings, furthermore after holidays and the Sabbath (if one has a non-Jewish maid she can set it up for a piece of Challah). Shortly after the wedding it must be set up with hot water for washing diapers and swaddling cloths, bathing children, filling flasks and compresses, clean away bedbugs, blanching poppy seeds, washing laundry and for warm water for baking bread. And many other things related to childbirth, women in childbirth, bathtubs, hygiene, purity of the family and purity of the dead, heaven preserve us, and so forth, and so forth....

Thus, they tended dearly to their samovar for many years, in bad and good times, with joy and sorrow, with happy occasions, with sad occasions, with births and raising children, they even made a wedding. And because one of them was my mother, who was the youngest daughter in the house, set aside for my father in the dowry along with five hundred golden rubles and wedding clothes, the samovar. And if the above- described history came to me as they say, by oral law - the further happenings with the samovar were closely connected to me. My father, born a village-Jew, knowing the "psychology" of animals well ("if one punches in the teeth, one gets it in the bones"), invested his dowry in a woollery, that is to say, putting oxen on "*brahe*" [malt grains]. When they get fat, they are driven to *Dvinsk* and one can earn a couple of nice rubles.

God is also a father, the fifth year came quickly. Then came 1914, and then the seventeenth year - and *Fonya's* [nickname for a Russian] "nap" was over.... For the oxen one received a few sacks of *dumskeh* and Kerensky's banknotes, which one could use instead of white paper. Therefore, one began dealing with lead and fire, a spattering of coal - one hardly returned with his soul from *Mordkhe Velvl* the furrier's basement, where everyone kept their goods and found the room empty and desolate. The "heroic" Polish legionnaires quickly got it into their heads to rob a Jewish home, rather than steal a piece of coal from a Red-Army soldier.

And since, in the time of war, such a samovar is a hindrance - it was actually thrown away. Later, it was found on a side street, a little dented. What is one to do at such a time? There is not meat, there is no dairy to be obtained, the result is - a pareve glass of tea....oh, for tea, doesn't one need sugar? Who says so, is saccharin so bad? So, that very tea with saccharin was my first nourishment. And from then on, I remained bound to the samovar in heart and soul. Who could write all of what we went through together? I will only recall a few curiosities:

When everyone in the house was taken ill with typhus, we needed rubber flasks for laying ice on the forehead. The flasks could be borrowed against collateral at the *linat-hatzedek* [hospice for the poor]. If one could have just seen me walking over there with the samovar. A second time, when my brother was laid up ill, I brought the samovar for collateral again. Seeing that I was sweaty and tired out, the administrator of the organization, *Reb Yoel*, the short one, called out to me:

"Do you know what, Sonny, why do you carry the samovar each time? Just bring the spout as collateral. Without the spout, one cannot pour in any water. You will certainly remember anyway and return the instruments you have borrowed."

Truly a wise man.

From then on, the samovar stood in the house for months without the spout, because we always needed medical instruments. If not a flask, then an enema, ten or so bloodletting cups, an enema syringe or other necessities, because no illness, may the Lord be blessed, ever went missing in a Jewish home. As one got better from the pox - a second fell ill with the measles, a third with scarlet fever, angina or the grippe. And almost everyone was used to pneumonia or rheumatism.

When my little sister became ill with diphtheria, *Monya*, the barber-surgeon didn't leave the house. He ordered that we make steam. The samovar lived again - although my sister was not saved by it, it nonetheless became important, dear. It was like a symbol that reminded one of past good days, when it cooked and satisfied, shpritzed and sparkled, grandfathers and uncles sat around with big black, yellow and gray beards, argued with enthusiasm about "the bull that gored the cow," or "two grasping one prayer shawl," etc. Sweating over the boiling hot glasses of tea, throwing off their hats, they would sit in *yarmulkes* with a *tallis koton*, placing their hands behind their necks, squinting, combing their beards, a little dance to a Hassidic melody - or even a Purim feast, or a Simchas Torah dinner. One didn't need a radio in those days, or a television, or a piano. Jews had other music. The poverty whistled, the stomach played, one's head drummed - where will I be for *Shabbes*?! Once *Shabbes* was already made, after a good tsholent with a kugel, after a bit of *zmiros* [singing] - the samovar would crawl out onto the table again, around which sat relatives, neighbors, close family. What could be nicer than reviving such guests with a glass of tea, and then with jam (during the week, jam wasn't used, except when a groom would come with his bride, or a man would return from America with a nice couple of dollars in his pocket, or a son would be released from conscripted army service because of an eye, a wounded ear and so on, or a Jew survived a robbery, larceny, avoiding some kind of unhappy occurrence, saying *goymel* [the blessing said by Jews after escaping great danger])?

But also in the long evenings of the cold winter nights when it was snowy outside, the blizzard clapping on the shutters, howling in the chimneys, the ice cracks, the windows are frosted - the house is heated, it is warm and the samovar boils on the table. Wives, women neighbors, who used to like to listen with pleasure as my older sister, Sarah, of blessed memory, read aloud parts of a book. She used to read chapters of Russian or Yiddish classics. And imagine, how the women just sat, drinking a glass of tea, listening to a story like "*Tuvye der Milkhiker*," ["Tevye the Dairyman"] when he turns to come back from his happy trip, after he drove that lost girl from the bounds of "*Yehupetz*" back to the country house in "*Boiberik*": how people filled his wagon full of good things; how he awakened his wife and seven daughters with it, who ran sleepily with a hearty appetite, to the roasted geese, the little turkeys and ducks, and desserts of cookies and tortes and preserves and all good things. And you could see the women were truly delighted, licking their lips, swallowing their saliva, they could feel the taste flowing through all of their limbs. Their faces shone, their eyes glowed - and at that moment, bursting through the door, was one of the women's husbands, on the threshold, *Velvl Kanareyke*. Carrying a big tray of dairy bourekas with half a loaf of black bread, he calls out to his missus:

"Here, sweetheart, eat a little something, because sitting for so long, you must certainly be near faint...."

This and similar curiosities aroused hearty laughter - and gray life got a little bit of charm.

There was always water in the well, one only had to take the pails and drop them about 700-800 meters. In order for it to fill to the top, an old hatchet or pick axe or any old iron shovel or weight was attached to the bucket and then you would let down and then steadily lift the bucket so the water wouldn't spill out. When this was done, both buckets were lifted onto a board, hung over the right shoulder and - *hayda!*

Well, setting up the samovar was not any great trouble: you take off the lid, pour in the water, cover it and begin looking for coals. Coals, what about them? A big deal! All week, one heats a bath, almost every year there was a fire in the shtetl, the whole month of *Nissan* [month in the Jewish calendar] matzah was baked in the hearth. When the wood was dry, there was clearly no question that there was coal left. And in the event that the wood is wet and it becomes ash before it burns fully? Also not a danger! One takes the axe, one chops small wood chips, which can successfully supplant the coal. Oh, it smokes a little, one must stand by a bit, regularly blowing and stirring underneath. So what? How long does it take? An hour and a half. However, when it hissed and white streams of fresh steam began to wind - it was actually a pleasure.

The pleasure was passed to me just after I became bar mitzvah age, because my older sister was already a bride-girl and my elder brother, *Velvl*, of blessed memory, was already a deserter of the Polish army (he escaped to Russia). The second sister, *Sheynke*, of blessed memory, was satisfied with scrubbing, cleaning and koshering, although I would help her carry to the bath. But to go in, where the big walled-in pot boiled, I didn't like to go because of a small thing, because there also stood all of the paraphernalia of the *Khevre-Kedisha* [burial society]: the stretcher, the tubs and ablution board, with the black cover and the white inscription: "Justice goes before Him as He sets out on His way." I don't entirely know why, but I didn't like it there....In short, when I used to hear someone at home mention that maybe it would be a good idea to set up the samovar - I quickly understood that this meant me. Because no one younger than I was at home, I actually felt dedicated to my duty with greatest craftsmanship; dedicating myself entirely. But the truth be told, I ate it like a bitter onion.

I was quickly aided. Grabsky became the finance minister in the Polish government. You may ask: what connection does Grabsky have to our samovar? You will soon hear that he does, and how, because if until him Jews paid "taxes" (duties) for businesses, trade, stores, undertakings, and so forth, Grabsky got to business, as if to say from the "socio-psychological" perspective: it isn't right, that only Jews of means should support Poland's governmental budget, rather the taxes should be divided so that all Jews, without exception, should feel that they have worth. Because, if not, they might, heaven forbid, be insulted, gather themselves and move to Israel. Such a tragedy for Poland must be avoided at any cost. Because imagine, how would Poland look without Jews? What would the protesters do? Where would they put picketers if there were no Jewish stores? Who could the students assault? Whom would Madame Pristorova be able to publicly denounce? What would the lords do without their advisors?

Thanks to Grabsky there were streams of endless different taxes, with reminders, punishments, interest and all the trimmings. Clearly, no revenue came to Jews from all of this, and without income in the first place, begging your pardon, people had nothing to pay with. When people didn't pay, the government authority appeared frequently, and after his demands, dunning, coercion and abuse -- they would produce a fresh note for a couple of *zlotes* [Polish money] for the "polite" visit.

That is how, unfortunately, it grew, without dew and without rain. When it became clear that he would not ever get such a sum, he would arrive with two ruffian helpers, write down everything that had any bit of value and he would utilize his assistants, who would, with more than a little pleasure, carry the things to the city council, and from there to auction.

Thanks to such a "campaign," we were finally free of the samovar.

At first I was actually happy internally, because I would be spared the chores of the samovar. I can also not say that we suffered from its absence. Its functions were immediately filled by a simple clay pot that my mother would shove deep into the oven without tire. The tea actually tasted a bit like clay. But, nonetheless, who are we really, Rothschild's nephews or Brodsky's grandchildren?

It was hard to look at my father. It really made him sick. He would glance over at the place where the samovar used to stand and let out a heavy sigh. He almost stopped drinking tea entirely. Why did the samovar have to leave him in this way? I won't posit a psychological analysis post facto. He lost much more in his life and, blessed by God, survived.

Once, when I left work, after receiving my wages at the sawmill, while walking through the market I wanted to buy a little something for Passover. I looked in all corners. Suddenly I saw a circle of people standing around a wagon belonging to the Polish cooperative ("Rolnick"). I drew nearer and saw, among a whole pack of Jewish trinkets, like brass pestles, candlesticks, copper pans, ladles and more -- sitting, like a king at an auction, our samovar. Poor thing, greened, dejected, lonely. To my amazement, its price was so low it was laughable. Clearly, it hadn't traveled an easy road. One could see this from the dented sides and its dirtiness. It was sadly missing a foot, had broken a wooden arm. Nevertheless -- such a samovar, which was once listed for some tremendous sum, like 3 - or 20 *zlotes* -- was now selling for only 4 *zlotes* ...

What is the wonder? Jews, after all, never bought at auction. It was a kind of habit of theirs. Well, and the gentiles? Would they trade their potato blinis with hot lard for a glass of tea? If they're drinking, they can have *samohonke*! And for that one does not need a samovar.

In short, I paid the four Polish *zlotes* with trembling hands and went home happy.

It would be unnecessary to describe the warm reception we got at home. In a couple of hours or so, it was already cleaned up, koshered, shining -- once again, taking its seat of honor. Once again, it was satisfied and humming, my father once again, poured glass after glass from the samovar for his close circle of good friends as a symbol of freedom and salvation.

Once more we took to our zigzagging, virtuous and difficult life. This is where I'll end my story. Not because everything ended, there is no more to tell about the samovar. With every year that it aged, came important events. But every history must have an end. And the end is, unfortunately, as difficult and tragic one.

When I returned to my shtetl after the Nazi hell, I stood in shock on a mountain of earth, which had once been my home, I heard a voice from our Christian neighbor across the street. He invited me to come into his house.

Just as I crossed the threshold my eyes are blinded -- from under the picture of the holy Madonna -- -- our samovar, the copper samovar. The Christian, seeing that I was stunned-still, began to stammer as if to answer:

"That is your samovar you see? When your sister was in the ghetto with her two little children, after the Germans shot her husband, I took some milk to her a couple of times. She then gave me the samovar, and said, 'Take it as a memento. We will never need it again.'" And he added, "If you want it, take it!"

"No, dear neighbor," I thanked him politely. "The samovar has already played its role for us. May it have better luck with you ..."

* * *

Memories and Impressions
Selig Ben-Moshe/Kibbutz Ein Shemer
Memorial candle to my parents, brother and sisters

A

Dokshitz dates from the eighteenth century, it is situated 60 kms. from Polotzek in Belorussia and about 200 kms. from Vilna. In 1920 the little town was captured by Poland and from then on belonged to the Vilna district. It had 4,500 inhabitants (before the war), 3,000 of them Jews and the remainder White Russians and a Polish minority (a few Tatar families as well). The railway that passed along the little town of Parpinov at a distance of 10 kms. was the only link with Vilna - ; the commercial and cultural center. This was almost the only link to the outside world. Many young people acquired an education in Vilna, some at high school and others at the teacher's seminary or the yeshiva. Vilna was also the basis and center of cultural institutions and political organizations, including "Hechalutz" and "Shomer Hatzair".

The "HeChalutz" (The Pioneers) in Dokshitz

After the German invasion of Poland in September 1939, the town was annexed by Russia and restrictions were imposed. These decrees (ban on Zionist activity) were a cause of great concern, but the fact that they were saved from the Germans inspired confidence and instilled hope for better days to come. The Jewish organizations were dismantled. "Hashomer Hatzair" went into hiding. This situation continued until the Nazis entered Russia (June 1941), when Dokshitz too fell under their rule. Only a handful of Jews were saved, they managed to flee or were exiled eastwards into Russia. Some of them were fortunate enough to emigrate to Israel at the end of the war and built their home there.

Dokshitz and its closest neighbors: Globoki (the largest), Dolhinov, Kornitz, Donilovitz and others all resembled each other. The Jewish inhabitants were concentrated on the main streets and the others, mainly Provoslav Christians, lived in the alleys at the outskirts of town. At the center of the little town was the market place which on the day of the market, once a week, was full of people and animals. The church, water containers to extinguish fire (most of the houses were built of wood and there were frequent fires), the police station, pharmacies and shops. At the square called "Shulhoif", in the name of the synagogues located there, was the center of "Tora ve Melacha" (learning and labor), most of the workmen and the poor lived here and most of the "heders" were at this square. This was obvious, for the municipal bathhouse was to be found here and the "Mikve" (ritual bath) which stood on the banks of the Barzina river which divided the town.

B

Dokshitz was a provincial little town, without any regular transportation and without proper roads, and nearly until the thirties even without electricity. (In most homes they continued to use oil lamps). There was a flourmill, sawing mill and beer brewery. Those were the only industrial enterprises. The majority of the Jews made their living from petty trade and the market day (once a week) when the farmers of the surrounding area would bring their produce for sale and in return would buy food and clothing for their families at the stores of the Jews. A large number of Jews were craftsmen: tailors, shoemakers, carpenters, milliners. Some Jews were also engaged in farming and they were poorly off. They carried a heavy burden of taxes. In the last years before the war they also felt the results of the competition by the non-Jewish population, in trade and crafts. It is therefore not surprising that many youngsters left school at the age of bar-mitzvah (sometimes even earlier) in order to help support the family or due to the fact that they were unable to afford tuition fees. They started to follow in the footsteps of their parents (even at this early age): trade, crafts (and sometimes idleness and degeneration).

Nevertheless, Dokshitz was a town with a very rich cultural life. The "heders", the schools, cultural institutions, municipal as well as Jewish, gave it (rightfully) its good reputation. In the days of Russian rule Dokshitz had a municipal high school and later on there were 3 elementary schools in the little town: Polish, Hebrew, (Tarbut) and Yiddish and about 10 "heders", a large public library (most of the books were in Yiddish and a few in Polish, Hebrew, Russian and German). The establishment of the "Tarbut" school was an important event and a turning point in the life of the young. Many children left the "heders" and the Polish school and moved to the Hebrew school. This was the foundation of the Hebrew enterprise which in due time formed the basis for Zionist activity and the pioneer movements.

Indeed, the Zionist pioneer movement reached our distant corner a few years before the establishment of the "Tarbut" school. The blue box of "Keren Hakayemet" arrived at a number of homes and from time to time someone would go on aliyah to Israel (those aliyot were shrouded in mystery and secrecy and aroused much admiration among the young), however near the thirties when the "Hehalutz" movement developed and the broad range of training kibbutzim were set up in Poland and the stream of pioneering aliyah to Israel increased, in Dokshitz too a branch of Hehalutz and Hashomer Hatzair was founded. It soon developed wide-ranging educational activity, organized many young people who in due time found their home at the cell.

The social and communal activity was not sufficiently developed and was very modest. Nevertheless, there were a number of institutions worth mentioning: the communal committee, the national bank (Yiddisher Folks Bank), the workers charity union, an institution of craftsmen for assistance and granting loans, a charity association, "linat tzedek"- for assistance at times of illness etc. The establishment of Shomer Hatzair. The Zionist movement was set up at the initiative of a few individuals. One summer day in 1927 a couple of youngsters, about to graduate from the Tarbut school (aged 13-14) met and after a lively debate about the situation of the Jewish people and Return to Zion, it was decided to establish an organization called "The Association of those who love the Fatherland". On the spot they drew up a set of rules for the association and it was decided to pay a fee to cover expenses. They would meet from time to time, read an article or two from "Haolam" (the World Zionist monthly) or from other Zionist literature, go on outings into the fields and forest and discuss the future. In due course the need for central power was felt, a "madrich" (youth leader) who would help to implement the plans. We came to the conclusion that a proper youth movement should be found, based on the Zionist idea and ready to further the workers' interests. That is how we arrived at "Hashomer Hatzair". Before that we heard positive rumors about the "Hashomer Hatzair" cell in Vilna and after some consideration, we decided that this was the right path for Jewish youth and that we should join this movement. We soon started to receive training manuals and literature and eventually we even received a visitor from the top leadership in Warsaw.

We had success. We received a serious addition of manpower when a number of older and more experienced members joined us. They had organizational talent: the late Haim Zamiri (Solovei); the late Kamankovitz and Shmuel Zamir (Solovei), thus the Dokshitz cell was founded. Why Hashomer Hatzair? The truth is that we did not know much about the Hashomer Hatzair ideology. We did not read Marks or Borochov and did not take an interest in the ideas of Hashomer Hatzair until the decision was taken, but we felt the abnormalcy of Jewish life in the Diaspora, the poverty and the hopelessness of the situation. We realized that the solution was to be found in Eretz Jisrael. We saw that the Hashomer Hatzair movement was above all another kind of youth movement, bent on implementing these principles, and we relied on it. Indeed, we were not disappointed.

However, so as not to create the impression that everything passed smoothly and that there were no problems, I shall name a number of elements that made our life difficult, however we were not at all surprised and accepted them.

In a little town such as ours life took its regular course for hundreds of years, according to the "Shulhan Aruch". Relations between children and parents and between the two sexes were based on a lack of equality and the ancient patriarch custom. Religious tradition ruled all parts of our private and public lives. It is therefore quite obvious that we faced serious problems when we set out to set up a free, pioneering youth movement . . . .

We should also mention the resistance and battle waged against us (usually secretly and under cover) by the communist and Yiddishist circles. They, of course, considered us another kind of danger, and against them too we had to conduct our educational activity among the youngsters and recruit them to our movement. However, the youngsters did not listen to them and joined the Zionist movement and its youth movement. In a relatively short period Hashomer Hatzair managed to recruit a large number of youngsters who were thereby saved from a life of boredom and degeneration, that was the share of many of their friends who had to leave school and find ways to make a living. Boys and girls aged 12 and over were received at the cell in a friendly and educational atmosphere and found their social environment and their future way in life here.

The Jewish Folk School in Dokshitz (1928)

The members of the cell were active in every Zionist and pioneering field of activity, spearheaded the collection of donations for the Zionist funds, spent time learning Hebrew, and its sounds could be heard all over town, scouts activities and outings drew the attention of children and youngsters and had a refreshing effect. The cell also focused on the glorification of physical labor (not greatly appreciated). We accepted and carried out work at sawing mills and covered part of the cell's expenses with the wages we received.

When the older members of the cell went on "hachshara" (training), towards their aliya to Israel, a certain crisis occurred in the cell's regular activity, however, we soon recovered thanks to a new generation of "madrihim" (youth leaders) that sprang from the members of the cell and continued the activity. The first to go on aliya from the cell arrived in Israel in 1933, and this went on until the war broke out.

In conclusion, we would like to mention our friend, the late Yosef Kaminkovitz, who was among the first to fall, hit by the bullets of the German murderers. One of the founders of the Hashomer Hatzair cell, who was among its devoted members, carrying the flag of Hebrew culture, he was not fortunate enough to arrive together with us at the kibbutz and realize his dream. We would like to commemorate all the Hashomer Hatzair members and the pioneers from Dokshitz, and all the dear Jews of Dokshitz who perished in the

Holocaust and did not reach the safe haven of Zion and witness the creation of our land Israel. We shall remember them in deep anguish and pain. We shall remember them forever - blessed be their memory.

The "Bnei Ha'emek" (Children of the Valley) group of Hashomer Hatzair (1933)

The Rabbi Reb Aharon Zelmanovitz (The Blind Rabbi)

Same article appears in Hebrew on pages 78 through 80.

Religious and National Life
Tzvi Bar-Massada (Tshukhman)/Kfar Hassidim

Our shtetl, Dokshitz, was no different than the other shtetls in the czarist occupied territory or in the rest of Poland.

Dokshitz was attractive, despite its wooden houses and the four broad long streets. In the center - the market with its shops.

The spiritual center of the shtetl was mostly at the synagogue-courtyard - five houses of worship in a row. Near them - the bath and the *mikveh* [ritual bathhouse] by the river.

All religious teachers and their schools could be found by the synagogue-courtyard. The ritual slaughterer, *Reb Yoykhenen Gordon* - a dear man, and the scribe also lived there.

I remember everything, all that went on in the *Beys-Hamidresh* [religious house of study] and in the four *shtibelekh* [small houses of worship or prayer rooms] of the Chabbad-Lubavitsh Hassidim. Some four-five *minyans* [prayer groups] prayed there regularly during the week, from the very crack of dawn on.

I remember the Sabbaths and the holidays, the nights of *slikhos* [the days preceding the Jewish High Holidays] and the eve of *Yom Kippur*.

I remember the large place encircled by a high fence. There used to be a synagogue there that burned down in one of the fires.

Bride and groom under the wedding canopy and Klezmer musicians, even from distant places, were brought there. The whole shtetl, invited and not invited, took part in accompanying the couple to this holy place.

I remember how Jewish children in the shtetl would leave the schoolrooms on winter nights with little lanterns in hand. And on *slikhos* nights people streamed in to the synagogue courtyard from all directions.

The *Hoshana-Raboh* [the last of the intermediate days of the festival of *Sukkes*/Tabernacles] night in synagogue is deeply engrained in my memory: or walking with *kapores* [traditional object for symbolically ridding self of sins, often a chicken/fowl] in hand on the eve of *Yom Kippur*; carrying all of the utensils every Passover eve to fire them and make them kosher for Passover in the big pot near the bath.

Tisha B'av [the ninth day of the Jewish month of Av, a day of fasting, commemorating the destruction of the first and second temples] left the strongest impression on me. The group of people walking to the cemetery after saying *Kinos* [lamentation poems] in synagogue - men, children and women.

I remember you, my shtetl, at the end of the First World War, when soldiers of newly freed Poland suddenly appeared on horseback - with their conceit and impudence, looting, violence - that infamous Sabbath when all synagogues were closed. The preying upon Jews with beards, the sadistic derision of those who were caught and the mutilation of the beards and *peyes* [earlocks worn by Jewish men] of believing Jews.

For a long time I could not forget that image. My father was thus caught and I followed as they took him. I swore to myself that I would defend my father if they dared to lay their hands on him - and it would be what it would be.

The Poles were the ones who gave me the idea to leave th4e accursed Diaspora and take part in the building of The Land [of Israel].

Until the final years of the First World War, people in Dokshitz didn't know of the existence of a national Jewish movement, about Zionism. Of the first who began to do something was *Lipeh* Levitan, blessed be his memory, a child from a wealthy family, he was an intelligent, nice and healthy young man. He succeeded in organizing several boys and girls and founding a Zionist organization called "*Akhdus Vetkhiyeh*" [Unity and Revival]. They rented and fixed up a nice meeting hall, a library, and they began to promote the Zionist *Shekel* [currency], selling stamps of *Keren Kayemet* and other activities. This group dreamed only of making aliyah to Israel. *Lipeh* was the first and only one in the shtetl who, in 1922, made aliya to the Land of Israel.

Committee of HeChalutz (The Pioneers)

The Hassidim in Dokshitz related negatively to Zionism, as did all orthodox Jews. When people heard about the Balfour Declaration they did not want to rejoice at all and they referred to it as the Balfour *Tsoreh* [plight/sorrow/woe]. When the British Mandate over Palestine was approved, some Zionist inclined people wanted to recite Psalms and a prayer of rejoicing - there was a strong opposition.

Lipeh worked on me as well. I was jealous of him. I was too young though and had to withstand regular interference from my father.

At that time the first Hebrew teacher came to Dokshitz - *Presman*. A dear person, the son-in-law of *Reb Binyomin-Meyer Tomarkin*, blessed be his memory, a good Jew who had influence in the shtetl. He opened the first Hebrew school in Dokshitz, despite the tremendous opposition from the extreme Hassidim. That school brought out a Zionist-Nationalist breath in the shtetl. The youth began to sing Hebrew songs. From time to time there were also Hebrew presentations - but with the Ashkenazic pronunciation.

That school also gave us good students, from whom there later became organizers and members of Hekhalutz and *Hashomer Hatza'ir*, who went for *Hakhshara* and later made aliyah.

After *Presman* came, his brother-in-law, *Tomarkin*, who did much in the field of Hebrew education, not the least of which was raising a generation in the national spirit. In those times long and interesting letters from *Lipeh* in the Land of Israel would arrive, in which, in a beautiful spirited style, he described the new colonization in the Jezreel Valley and in the Galilee. With talent, he described his visits to places mentioned in the bible, about which we studied in *kheyder*. Those descriptions delighted the hearts of young and old. *Lipeh's* letters were passed from hand to hand and blew life into dry bones....

After *Lipeh*, I became the second to organize the "*Hekhalutz*." I was not as successful as he. Individuals followed his example and after me, only two came to this country. After my aliyah, in 1924, the students in the Hebrew school became active, particularly *Khayem Solovey* and *Shmuel-Leyb Kaplan*, blessed be his memory.

Shmuel-Leyb was loyal and devoted to the Zionist ideal. For all the years until his death, he was the representative of the Palestine-office in Dokshits. He helped every person making aliyah, every *khalutz* [pioneer] from his first step to actually making aliyah. Various obstacles and reasons did not allow for his making aliyah himself. He was like the dear loyal ship captain who helped save lives until the final day, when World War II broke out. His place is with all of the holy and pure of Dokshitz's Jewry.

Since my leaving the shtetl in 1924, I have aspired to see it again - but have not had the honor.

Professions and Good Deeds of Dokshitz Jews
Tzvi Rafaeli Gilenson/Chafatzey Bak

From what did our Dokshitz Jews actually live and earn a living? One need not do any tremendous research to find the answer. This is simply because in those times in Jewish shtetls in Poland all of our Jewish brethren lived thusly.

Mainly Jews were in trade, some on a greater and some on a lesser scale. Whatsoever was purchasable was bought from peasants in the area: dry mushrooms, hides for fur coats, pig hair, wheat, flax. People also leased plots of forest from neighboring gentiles for copping wood and leased mills to mill the wheat. There were also fishermen, butchers, who traveled throughout the villages all week buying living cows, slaughtering them in the slaughterhouse and providing the shtetl with meat. There were also Jews who worked their own fields.

Most Jews were tradesmen, toiling people, who labored hard and bitterly to earn their piece of bread. Behind the city good blacksmiths served the area, shoeing horsed, fixing wagons. They stood all day by the anvil and bellows. Carpenters built beautiful works with simple tools, even luxury furniture, doors and windows. There were also glaziers, tinsmiths, locksmiths, tailors and milliners. The latter sold their own work in shops or booths in the market.

Tuesday was the weekly market - the day when all looked to make a week's earnings. There were bookbinders who had to read through each book first. People worked hard, the women also helped in the trade. It is a fact that there was no eight-hour workday - people worked late into the night.

There were photographers, thanks to whom photos of the shtetl remain.

Tailors were in different categories: simple, who sewed for the peasants [in the shtetl] and also the peasants in the village; tailors who sewed better clothes for Jews or military people and officers. (Among the so-called village-tailors was my grandfather, *Moyshe-Yerakhmiel Gilenson*. A simple Jew, not a great scholar, didn't even understand his prayers, but incredibly hardworking, virtuous, a good grandfather and father.)

Quite early on a Sunday, he could be seen on his way with his *tallis* [prayer shall] and *tefillin* [phylacteries] and a few sundry items in a little sack hanging on a stick. A cigarette stuck to his bottom lip. Thus he would be off for a whole week - to sew a fur for someone by hand, or clothing form crude fabric, which the peasants made themselves.

Friday afternoon my grandmother and the grandchildren would meet him as he returned home. There was tremendous joy. He had a gift for everyone. He would return by horse and wagon from the peasants where he worked and he would be loaded with all good things: rye for flour, potatoes. A live chicken and fruits - that's the kind of man my grandfather was.

Jews worked hard all week. But on *Shabbes* [Sabbath] they all used to go out in the street for a stroll. People talked about everyone and everything.

The tradesmen later organized themselves in an artisans union. The originators were: *Max Golts* - the photographer, *Shmuel Kugel* - the bootmaker, *Khayem-Rafoel Gilenson, Yitzkhok- Yaakov Biyelinki, Mendl Kozshiniyetz, Zalmen Freiman* - tailors, *Moyshe Friedman* - the bookbinder. The goal of the union was to defend the interests of their members from high taxes levied by the government upon the toiling craftsmen; to help in getting an artisan's card, without which one had no right to work; to administer the master craftsman and journeyman exams required by the government.

Committee of "Linat HaTzedek" Hospice (Hostel) for the Poor

There was a second organization - a specific Dokshitz accomplishment called "*Poaley Tzedek*" [Workers of Righteousness]. The mission was to help the needy, particularly during the time of illness. The medical help was at a lower level at that time. They purchased glass cups [for bloodletting], thermometers, hot water bladders, ice-bladders. In the summer they prepared ice in Gordon's beer brewery, the so-called "*Liyednik*" [summer visitor].

Reb Yoel, Der Kurtzer [the short one] and his wife did all of this work. People called him "the short one" because of his short height, although he had a great soul. More than once he was awakened in the middle of the night. He was always ready to help the sick.

**The Bazaar Committee benefitting the Keren Keyemet Le'Yisrael in Dokshitz
11th day of Adar Bet, 1935**

Memories of the Town Where I was Born

Shoshana Tschuhman - Draizin

The town of Dokshitz where I was born and spent the best years of my life, my childhood and youth, is deeply engraved on my memory. I remember its streets, alleys, houses, institutions, mountains, rivers and above all the people, who were so nice and kind. I loved to climb the hill near our home, where the Russian church was situated, and to look at all the surrounding area from there. I loved to wander along the boulevard lined with birch trees, named after Catherine the Great, and to stop near an old birch tree trunk underneath which there was a spring. This spring was the source of the Berezina river. The waters flowing through the narrow, long passage were beautiful to behold. The further away I got from the spring - ; the broader and deeper became the river. In summer, when it was hot, we loved to go down to the river to bathe and refresh in its water.

Dokshitz, which was under Russian rule until World War I, was considered a district town with a large and developed Jewish population. We made our living, as in the other towns in the Diaspora countries in that period, from trade, industry, crafts, and a few families from agriculture. There were no welfare institutions then with social-governmental assistance, as are to be found today in every cultural country. On the other hand, there were all sorts of associations among the Jews for mutual assistance to the needy. Among these we must mention the assistance to the sick, aiming at helping poor families if one of those supporting them fell ill.

As the population was mixed, there was quite some anti-semitism, particularly when the gentile youngsters in the area would come for a medical check-up towards their army recruitment. Those who were accepted as recruits thought it necessary to poke fun at the Jews, and if they would run into a Jew in a narrow alley, they would beat him up and tear his beard.

At the end of World War I Poland once again became an independent state. It was the town's destiny to fall under Polish rule, and it became a border town with Russia. As a result, it lost many sources of income, and this had an adverse effect on the economic situation of the Jews. On one hand, trade deteriorated, on the other hand the Polish government imposed a heavy burden of new taxes. This resulted in a movement to leave the town.

The first to leave town were the well- to- do tradesmen. They did not want to wait until they would be totally ruined and left Dokshitz immediately for Vilna, to find their luck there. Other groups, especially the young, also looked for a way to emigrate to another country, some to north or south America, and a few who were lucky enough to obtain a certificate, went to Israel.

A branch of the "Histadrut Hatzionit" (Zionist Federation) had existed in Dokshitz for a long time, but was not active. At that time the branch became active and started to play an important role in town. A branch of "Hehalutz" was also opened in Dokshitz, it became active mainly after the Balfour Declaration, when the United Nations decided in Geneva to set up a Jewish homeland in Eretz Jisrael. The decision to grant Great Britain the mandate over the country gave rise to false hope that the gates of the land would be open to all Jews. Unfortunately, reality proved to be different. The British closed the gates of the land and granted but a few certificates.

Our family was among the few Jewish families in Dokshitz to make a living from farming. We lived on a little side- street behind the town called "Podgorna" in the period of Polish rule, i.e. "under the mountain". This name referred to the fact that it was at the foot of the hill on which the Russian church was situated.

The first to settle here was my grandfather on mother's side, the late Joshua Selig Kabakov, soon joined by his son Shmuel Kabakov and his son in law, Menahem Mendel Shalom Chuchman, our father. All the members of the family mainly made a living from growing vegetables.

Grandfather was a staunch lover of Zion. He wanted to organize a group to go on aliya on foot to Eretz Jisrael and settle there, but this did not materialize. They did not own the land they tilled, for in the period of the Russian-Czarist rule, there was a law forbidding Jews from owning land. For hundreds of years the land had been concentrated in the hands of a few called "Pritzim". A "Paritz" called Proshinski owned huge areas of land around Dokshitz. He himself would lease them and my relatives were among those who leased his land.

Once a year the Paritz would appear in a splendid carriage drawn by mighty horses. He would arrive at the leaser's home and without descending from the carriage would call the Jew (Jid), who would come outside and pay his dues. When the Jew appeared, the Paritz would order him to take off his hat as a sign of honor.

Committee of Keren Kayemet LeYisrael in Dokshitz
11th day of Adar Bet, 1935

Our father built a factory for hides processing (borsika), in addition to the area of land we tilled. This factory was a cause of anger to the local Russian priest, who protested against the smells emanating from the borsika. He turned to court so as to remove my father's enterprise, but my father won the case. The priest was furious at this and took out his anger at the children who played on the hill near the Russian church.

Not far from our home stood a beer brewery belonging to the Gordon brothers. We children often used this proximity to visit the brewery to taste the fresh beer.

When the Bolshevik revolution in Russia broke out the Czarist rule came to an end, and the "Pritzim", Proshinski among them, understood that they would not be able to concentrate huge areas of land under the new regime, so they started to sell their lands. Ownership was mainly transferred to Jews. The Gordon brothers were the first to grasp this, and they immediately approached Proshinski and asked him to sell them the land we tilled. My father soon learned of this and he managed to prevent their scheme.

When my father appeared before the Paritz to reach an agreement regarding the sale of the land, the Paritz treated my father courteously. He proposed my father buy the land he leased and even the adjacent areas. My father told the Paritz he was unable to buy the adjacent plots, and then the Paritz suggested my father chose his own neighbors. My father started to promote the purchase of land from the Paritz.

That is how a Jewish agricultural neighborhood was established on both sides of the main road to Plotzak. The neighborhood was pretty and its inhabitants took care of it as best they could. We did not manage to hold on to our status of farmers for a long time because of the problems caused to the Jews by the Polish government. A lively movement of emigration started, and we too became part of it.

Our grandfather, the late Rabbi Joshua Selig Kabakov, did not have the good fortune to realize his dream of going on aliya to Eretz Jisrael, but his grandsons and his son Shmuel did. The first to go was our brother Zvi and then our brother Mordechai. Once these two had settled in Eretz Jisrael they brought over their sisters Hadassa, Ada and I. Two years later they also brought over our father, his sister Malka and our mother.

In Israel we made a living from farming. Our brother Zvi is at Kfar Hassidim. The family of my sister Hadassa and my own family are at Sde Yacov. Thus we realized the dream of our grandfather not only to go to Eretz Jisrael but also to be farmers there.

In conclusion, I would like to dwell on the day when we left Dokshitz, and our emotions when we took leave of our many friends and acquaintances. Although everything had been packed and was ready for departure, I could not believe that we were actually leaving Dokshitz forever. Only the sound of the carriage of coach-man Joseph-Itzhak made it clear to me that the miraculous moment for which we had waited for so many years had come.

Our best friends gathered then to accompany us on our way. I shall never forget the hundreds of eyes looking at us with both affection and envy. When we reached the bridge, the group burst into song and started to dance the "Hora". With calls of "See you in Eretz Jisrael" we took leave of our townspeople. Who would have thought that this was farewell forever and that we would never see those wonderful Jews again. I am overwhelmed by anguish when I remember that our little town was erased and that those lovely people now lie somewhere in a mass grave. Blessed be their memory!

Memories of My Childhood
Shekhna Kantorovitsh/New York

When my family left Dokshitz in 1921 to travel to America I was barely 12 years old. We endured all seven fires of hell brought with World War I. It is, however, in the nature of man to remember the good in life and forget the bad that one has endured. Those times of war when the various armies chased one another out of the shtetl, were very bitter times. But looking back with childlike eyes, I see only the good and happy times.

The memories that remain of Dokshitz bring me spiritual refreshment, a longing, which even 45 years have not succeeded in erasing. Something always bloomed in the shtetl, especially on Slovoder Street. Behind every house was a garden, full of cucumbers, onions, beans, grains and other vegetables. How nice the gardens looked when they started to bloom. Behind the gardens was a green field with thick grass. When the field began to green it was covered in a sort of golden blanket. Oh, how we children used to love to roll in the soft grass, or lie on our backs among the little yellow flowers and watch the blue sky. How beautiful God's world looked from that spot!

I remember the cry of the sexton, "Jews to the bath-house," or Friday evening, "Jews, close your stores, it is almost candle-lighting time!" In the week before Rosh Hashanah, the sexton would rap on the shutters in early morning and call out: "Slichos, slichos." He also announced all other community news.

But more than anything, certain curiosities that could take place only in such a nice Jewish shtetl as Dokshitz, are impressed upon my memory.

When I began going to kheyder, my mother used to give me a piece of dark bread for lunch, sometimes with cheese, sometimes without. Many a time this was the last piece of bread in the house. The other boys used to bring a roll or white bread. I used to wonder how it was that they got a roll and I got black bread. It didn't take long to discover the answer. Not far from our kheyder lived Sholem the bagel-baker. A little further, by the bridge, Libeh-Frumeh had a store where she sold cakes. Midday, the boys from my kheyder used to go to Sholem's or Libeh-Frumeh's. I also went along. They went to make purchases, and I did as well. But I was different in one way. I didn't understand that one had to pay. And so it went a long while until my mother heard about it. The baker and the shopkeeper never once asked me for money or refused me. Such dear people, they didn't want to embarrass a small child...

Other things that I remember: I must have been eight years old when this happened on a Saturday in the Slovoder synagogue. Although I was not yet bar mitzvah age, I was given the honor of maftir [the last person who is called to say the blessing over the Torah reading who then may proceed to chant the Haftorah] quite often. I would prepare to say maftir before Shabbes. It happened that Itshe, a son of the bath-keeper (I believe his name was Yoshe) wrote Tnoyim [the official Jewish engagement document] that week, so people wanted to give him the honor of maftir. In grief about the fact that I was not going to be called, I went off into a corner and had a sobbing fit. Yoshe noticed this and came over to me, gave me a hug and said: "Shekhnele, don't cry, I will let you say maftir." And so it was. He made the blessings. I chanted the Haftorah.

In the front of our house, we had a dirt patio with a bench. Across from our house lived Khaya-Tsishe. She dealt in all types of wares. She was a widow for many years. Later on she married a nice man, a scholar. His name was Shimon-Arye. He used to sit at home and study and Khaya-Tsishe continued with her sales and supported him. His Gemorah-nign [Gemorah - Talmud, nign - melody, melody to which he would study Gemorah], which was a pleasure to listen to, would travel to our patio. Women from neighboring homes would come sit on our patio to listen to Shimon-Arye studying. The women would talk and say that Khaya-Tsishe got a well-deserved reward in getting such a good man.

For today's generation, these vignettes will perhaps be no more than little shtetl stories. But I believe that they reflect the character of the general person from Dokshitz that I remember. The nice qualities that they had - not wanting to pain anyone or shame them.

May this all be recorded in the memory book of Dokshitz. May the children and grandchildren of the one-time Dokshitz Jews know from what kind of shtetl they come. When the historians of the future one day research the history of our time, they should know that there was once a shtetl like Dokshitz, where Jewish life bloomed, until the murderer, Hitler, came and annihilated everything. However, in the hearts of those who knew the shtetl, it will live eternally.

* * *

The Jewish Youth In Our Town
David Kopelewitz/Kibbutz Ruhama

Dokshitz, a typical little town in the Diaspora. The majority of its inhabitants were Jewish and their lives were guided by Jewish tradition. The Jews were religious, but not fanatical. They were divided into two rival camps: the Lubavitz Hasidim and the Mitnagdim (opponents). A young generation of proud, active and lively Jewish youth grew up this way.

Many years passed since I last saw my little town. I left it about a year before the outbreak of the War and the Holocaust. When I try to remember life in town, I see Dokshitz as a quiet and peaceful little town, far from the busy main road, hidden in a quiet corner. The faces of the people who lived there carried an expression of peace and quiet. In spite of the many problems of making a living and the hostile environment, the constant awareness of the surrounding hatred and anti-Semitism, everyone tried to create the illusion of security in his own peaceful home.

That is how our parents lived, as did the generations before them. I did not witness the Holocaust which also arrived at Dokshitz, and that is why the town remains in my memory just as it was in previous years and I can't visualize it any other way.

I remember its main streets, densely populated by Jews, each house close to the next, each yard close to the next. The gentile population was pushed towards the distant corners at the outskirts of town. I remember Market Street with its many Jewish shops "full of goodies". On weekdays not many came to buy there, but on Tuesday, market day, the place was full of people. From the early hours of the morning rows of carriages drawn by horses would ride towards town from all the villages in the area. The quiet atmosphere turned into commotion, turmoil and cries filled the main streets - ; the local anti-Semitic youngsters contributing their share.

As in the other towns of Poland at the time of the Pilsodski government and the "Andatzia", in Dokshitz too there was fierce incitement against Jews, and only because they formed the majority in Dokshitz, the gentiles were prevented from carrying out progroms. On market days the gentiles grew bolder and they tried to provoke a fight, sparing no means. Fistfights often broke out, but the Jewish youth, together with the "common people" retaliated. In most cases the Jews had the upper hand and the hooligans were chased away, however fears of tomorrow always persisted.

In this period, a few years before the outbreak of the War, incitement against Jews increased in all the large cities and many agitators were sent to the small border towns. As a result, anti-Semitism in Dokshitz increased, and the Jews slowly started to be pushed out of their well-established economic situation. The situation deteriorated. The future became clouded and all hearts were filled with apprehension. At the same time the general lack of security grew.

Such was the situation of the Jewish population in Dokshitz on the eve of the World War. I would like to go on and dwell on the essence of the Jewish youth, its activities and situation in those days.

The Jewish youngsters in Dokshitz started to get organized in the twenties at a time of relative quiet. The monotonous life did not satisfy the ambitions and aspirations of the local youth. They started to rise up against accepted norms, against their parents, against the existing order.

There was no significant class distinction in town, although there were both rich and poor among us. There were but a few industrial enterprises, and Jews did not work there as laborers, merely as clerks - ; therefore there was no background for the creation of different classes. The situation was not the same among the young. Here clear distinctions were developing, mainly for Helachic reasons.

New ideas and conceptions started to infiltrate the town. The majority of the well-to-do youth left for the large cities, once they had graduated from the "Tarbut" elementary school, in order to obtain a high school education. These youngsters, who spent the year in surroundings that were different from what they were accustomed to, started to absorb new ideas and made a clear class distinction. They formed the first nucleus for a change of atmosphere among the Jewish youth in Dokshitz, and when they returned to town they brought along new ideas and different outlooks. They inspired their friends with these new ideas and this caused a great deal of agitation. The quest for knowledge and general education grew. The municipal library turned into a regular meeting place for the many youngsters of Dokshitz. Naturally, they all started to read the books closest to their heart and status.

The agitation among the youngsters finally led to a clear development of youth movements and parties. The young people in town lived within narrow boundaries and wanted to develop into new and different directions, from the extreme left to the extreme right.

The largest and most important part started to organize into the Zionist frameworks. Youngsters of all ages and levels gathered at the local cell of "Hashomer Hatzair". Although the movement was semi-legal and its activities had to be hidden from the eyes of the authorities, this did not prevent the youngsters from joining the ranks of the movement and participate in all its activities. The youngsters went on outings in the framework of "Hashomer Hatzair", to summer and work camps. Robert Baden Powell's scout's movement on the one hand, and the positive activity on behalf of Jewish funds such as "Keren Hakayemet", "Keren Hayesod" on the other hand, were at the center of the daily life of "Hashomer Hatzair" in those days.

The main nucleus of the founders of this movement and most of its members came from among the educated young. It was considered a free, non-political movement.

Together with "Hashomer Hatzair" the "Hehalutz" movement was founded, which mainly included older, working youngsters, who decided to go on alyah to Eretz Jisrael. Here too there was a lot of propaganda activity. Work for the national funds, preparations for going to the movement's training kibbutzim and - ;finally- alyah to Eretz Jisrael. The older members of "Hashomer Hatzair" also joined "Hehalutz" as an independent body, mainly for training which was organized by "Hehalutz". The "League for Labor Israel" was formed in those days and this incorporated all the Zionist-socialist parties and movements.

A Group of Jewish Youth in the City

In the framework of the "League" there were many joint activities, such as the distribution of "Sheqalim" for the Zionist Congress, wide-ranging propaganda towards the elections and various collections for working Eretz Jisrael.

A cell of the "Beitar" movement was also formed, however its impact was not felt on the Jewish street. Another influential part of the youngsters turned the wheel into an anti-Zionist direction. This was the Yiddishist youth which was in favor of integration in the life of the Diaspora and adhering to the values acquired by the Jews in their places of living, encouraging the Yiddish language as our mother tongue and fighting an all out war against the Zionist idea. Some of the youngsters were attracted by this idea. This ideology did not in fact require great sacrifice or any revolutionary changes in the way of life. It was enough to join these ranks as a member, pay the dues and agree with the existing situation. Their program was cultural activity - ; literary "tea evenings" with lectures abounding with rhetoric, and above all reading Yiddish literature.

The Yiddishist youth partly came from a working background and partly from the intelligentsia. Some of them were inclined towards the leftist movements, the communist party, and slowly abandoned the Jewish nationalist identity. Many communists decided to implement the doctrine and moved to the Soviet Union.

Meeting of the Group of Hechalutz and Shomer Hatzair

The border with the Soviet Union was merely a few kms. away from Dokshitz and these youngsters were attracted to it. There was a time when they would stealthily cross the border each night. An example of this was the crossing of the Russian border by the orchestra which remained there. Although not everyone managed to cross the border and some were even caught, the very act indicates the atmosphere that existed in those days.

We also had youngsters called "Golden Youth" - ; mainly educated youngsters who decided not to join any of the existing parties. Their only ideology was a lack of ideology, they wanted to be part of the existing order of life and have proper relations with the Jewish public and to a certain extent also with the Polish population. These youngsters also adhered to certain values. They conducted cultural activities, but their general activity was without any ideological trend.

This picture of Dokshitz and its youth is engraved on my mind and I keep the memory to this very day. It is very hard to imagine that all this was destroyed in one stroke and no longer exists, as if it was an idle dream. May this article serve as a commemoration and eternal candle to the population of annihilated Dokshitz, to our parents who perished and to all the young people who lived there and are no more.

Memories From My Mother's Stories

Deborah Markman

The thirteen-year-old boy refused to go and herd his father's horses at night. After much convincing he did go out and was rewarded. When he reached the field, a few kms. from town, he saw a beautiful girl in the moonlight who was also herding her father's horses. The girl was as beautiful as the field, as a star in the sky above.

From that meeting on it was no longer necessary to urge him, for he was happy to go and herd the horses. He would await the appointed time anxiously and with a beating heart he would take the animals out to the field. When he returned home, lay down to sleep and got up in the morning, at the "heder" and at home he would dream about the girl he saw at night. He would roam among the market stalls, in spite of the Rabbi's ban, for he knew that he would see her there.

The love story between the boy and girl went on for seven long years, until the day they had longed for arrived - ; their wedding day. They were very happy and after the "honeymoon", on weekdays, the daily struggle to make a living did not daunt their love for each other. Their home was always open to guests and full of light.

From time to time an "Offitzier" would stay at their home or a "Pan". A Russian or Polish official, for Dokshitz was situated on the Polish and Russian border and its rulers would often be replaced. However, grandmother was very clever and knew how to get along with everybody, therefore all those who came to her home respected her.

When their first son was born, they were very happy and hoped to establish a large family. However, this did not happen. Some of the children died when they were still young, grandmother was very sad and found no rest. She asked the Rabbi for advice. The Rabbi listened to her lament and advised her to return to her husband and when the new baby was born he should have two names - ; thus advised the Rabbi - ; which should not be revealed until the day of his wedding. The newborn baby should be dressed in white linen, until the age of three, and this should be done with all the children to whom she would give birth. Grandmother listened to the Rabbi and acted accordingly. She dressed her children in white clothes, gave them various names, brought them up with a great deal of love and even had time for "Tzene veRe'na" (religious book of guidance for women)

However, although she was very busy, grandmother did not forget the poor of the town who were unable to lay the Sabbath table and she would send them whatever she was able to obtain.

Grandfather was busy at the butcher shop, many came to consult him about all kinds of animals, big and small, for he was a great expert.

The Sabbath eve was a particularly beautiful time. Grandfather would return from the synagogue, splendidly dressed and immersed in a different world. Daily matters were forgotten, worries blown away, and the Sabbath candles on the table created an atmosphere which only a Jew at ease with himself and his God could know.

The sons would sit around the table, sing Sabbath songs or listen to their father read the weekly Bible portion. A "Sabbath guest" - ; a "Talmid Haham" (religious scholar), a Yeshiva boy would sit at the table and tell the children stories from the Bible.

On religious holidays all the grandchildren would come to Grandfather, proud of their new and festive attire. One would say : "look, Grandfather, I have new shoes", and the other would say: "look Grandfather, how beautiful my dress is", and little Shaulik would ask: "Grandfather, did you see my new patch?"

Such was the life of the Jews in the little town of Dokshitz: holidays and weekdays, love and struggle, new clothes and new patches.

May these few lines serve as a candle commemorating my forefathers who I unfortunately never got to know.

Memories from the Far-Far Past

Shaul Markam (Markman)/Kibbutz Ayn-Shomer

I don't know why I remember these very things. But so it is. I have already been in this country over 30 years. Eating oranges - without stop. And yet, every time I peel an orange I recall the first orange I ever enjoyed. It happened so:

I was already a student in the Tarbut-school [culture school] in Dokshitz. Niyumke Glekhengoz, a son of wealthy parents, always wanted to sit by me. I don't know what was in his head, but he did not listen to the bright students. Every time the teacher asked him something he remained immobile and delayed and didn't know what to answer, until I quietly whispered the answer to him.

Once he brought an orange to school and began to peel it slowly in the middle of class under his bench and gave me a piece. The first time I saw an orange and the first I ever tasted. And every time I eat an orange here I remember that specific fruit, when I tasted it for the first time. I believe that I will always remember that first orange from Dokshitz.

You will probably say that it's not nice, but I know, just as I remember Dokshitz, this is how it was with scratching. From childhood on I used to run after my brother Nakhman-Reuven, 3 years older than I - I came, for the first time, to Rabbi Velvl "the louse's" kheyder. Why did he have such a nickname? Because he used to do the following: He used to stick his hand under his arm, take a louse out of there and say this verse with a melody, "If one finds a thief in the act and kills him," squeeze the louse between both knuckles of his thick fingers, with a sharp crack, then wipe the blood from his knuckles and end the verse, "you are not culpable for his blood."

...So, I look for the first time at Velvl the teacher's kheyder. The floor - of lime. A dark room. In one corner - a long table with benches on both sides. Small children sit there sprawled. Up front is the rabbi with his long beard. A stick in his hand. And all repeat after the rabbi, word by word, in a loud voice, the morning prayer from the prayer book. In a second corner is a big brick oven with a glowing fire, by which the Rebbetzin [Rabbi's wife] kept busy. She cursed the rabbi, the students, and the whole world with weighty curses. In the middle, a white goat walked around and little black fleas fell off him all the time onto the floor. Near him, a hen wandered about, squawking in a loud voice.

I stood still by the bench, confused by the uproar. Unable to contain myself - and wet my pants and cried hard. My brother got angry with me. He took me outside immediately. He tried to calm me down and dealt with my pants. He said that he would not allow me to run after him anymore. He would not take me to kheyder anymore. I could not calm myself - and I remember it until today.

Members of Hashomer Hatzair with their parents, the Markman family

The bathhouse also got me all mixed up. When our mother noticed us scratching ourselves, she would take out a few groshen [Polish currency], with a groan, and send us to the bath. We took a bucket, a towel, soap, a rag, and we went. My father held my hand so I wouldn't get lost. I looked at everything with curiosity. We came to the river's edge. A big black building - here is the bath. On the lean of the roof stood a gentile who poured water from the well and without stop emptied the buckets in the eaves.

Inside - a tremendous tumult. My father urged me on - not looking around, just undressing. One must manage undressing well, sleeve to sleeve - the shirt, the pants, and especially the tallis katon [the traditional fringed undergarment worn by Jewish males]. Lice stayed especially in the tsitsis [fringes]. After one bundled it all up, one went into the big room, where the clothing was hung quite high on special poles in order to exterminate the lice with the help of a heavy steam - and then one began to wash oneself.

I looked around: a tumult, noise, one almost couldn't see because of the thick steam. Slowly I could distinguish people on the upper benches. Everyone held a little broom made of white birch branches which he beat on himself over his shoulders and belly. There were also cases when one would lie stretched out on a high bench and another would beat him and rub him with the broom. Both would groan with great pleasure. Someone kept going over to the big oven with the red-glowing stones and poured a few buckets of water — then the steam would really increase and it was actually difficult to breathe.

My father would see how I was looking about. He would take my little hand, soap up the rag and rub my head, my back, my whole body. When I would start to scream that the soap was burning my eyes he would pour a few buckets of water over my head — and that was the end of washing. We barely could find our clothing, we'd leave the rucfuss, go over to the other room, get dressed and — back home.

When my father had tried to put me down on one of the benches, I went only to the second and quickly ran back because I couldn't catch my breath. The disinfection of the clothing didn't help much and the biting began again. Then I came upon an invention. In the winter nights, when the oven was heated up and the bricks glowed, I would pull my shirt up over my head and stand with my bare back towards the fire and scratch myself from top to bottom and bottom to top, actually until it hurt, but did not allow myself to sop. I remember it until today.

Dokshitz - Its Jews, Traditions, Holidays

Sarah Rozov/Kibbutz Ayn-Shemer

Reb Yoyel the Shoemaker and his wife *Khasiye*

Rebe Yoyel and *Khasiye* were very treasured and loved in the shtetl. Both were really an institution for social and — in the fullest sense of the word.

They lived by the synagogue courtyard in a little ben house, which glowed of cleanliness.

Reb Yoyel did a little work with shoes, from which he barely meted out some earnings. Although they were only two people (with no children), they lived in poverty. In order to perform a *mitzvah* [according to Jewish tradition, a commandment prescribed by God], they rented out their house for *Reb Berkey Yoshe's kheyder*. The most horned spot in the house, however, was occupied by a small cabinet with glass windowed doors on top. There were various medical instruments in the cabinet; two thermometers, some tens of glass and rubber cups for bloodletting, one hot water bottle, one ice bag and of course, one enema syringe.

This was a tremendous property which the shtetl entrusted to their hands.

When someone used to (heaven preserve us) become ill with a cold, *Moniya* the barber-surgeon would pronounce the diagnosis — "bedridden." He would prescribe castor oil and, whether it was necessary or not — cupping and an enema.

One would come to *Khasiye* with colladeral, sometimes a silver spoon, a cup or anything that had greater value than the cups. And both of them, by day or night, when anybody needed the first bit of help, they uplifted their "patients" with a warm word, a blessing, "to health." Being poor themselves, they felt the need and didn't shame people with their help.

There was a hospital. *Reb Mendl Kapelovitsh* was the head of the institution (who does not remember *Moshke Mendl's* store in the market?).

Reb Mendl Kapelovitsh used to give *Yoyel's Khasiye* [meaning Yoyel's wife Khasiye] sugar, she would rustle up a few *groshn* [Polish coins], buy raspberries and cherries, and from them she would make preserves (jam) and give it out to those who were ill, who had no opportunity to enjoy luxury - - and so, it was said about supporting the souls of the infirm (so it was said in the shtetl): a bit of raspberries for one's fever, or - - a bit of tea to make the tea sweeter.

Reb Yoyel used to concern himself with making sure that the infirm did not spend the nights alone, in case help was needed, or if the person did not feel well, or if one needed to perform cupping (*Khasiye* did this as well).

The Rozov Family

Reb Yoyel used to make sure that the *Mishmeres-Khoylim* [lit. protector/guard of the ill] would send a guard, a young girl or boy (this was also decided thoughtfully...). More than once *Reb Yoyel* would act as the controller making certain that the guard had come. Woe unto him who did not fulfill his duty. But usually the young came, not in order to "earn" a *mitzvah* [following the Jewish tradition that one should "earn" credits of prescribed *mitzvahs*], but sometimes a romance would grow out of such situations, or even a heated love might blaze up.

Khasiye, when she was younger and stronger, used to bake for weddings and other occasions and thus, add to their earnings. If it was a poor bride and groom, she used to bake as a *mitzvah*, to help the young couple.

They made do with their little bit, were happy with their piece. And so, they were able to save *groshn* by *groshn* and present a gift of a *seyfer-toyre* [Torah scroll] to the Lubavitsh synagogue.

Reb Yoyel used to always pray with the first *minyen* [prescribed group of ten men required by Jewish law to gather for prayer several times per day]. After prayers he would grab and usher out his only goat to pasture first. Clowns in the shtetl used to say: "A little man driving a big goat." When the goat was full then *Reb Yoyel* would go eat breakfast. Somebody always came before him. Even the goat. That was his defining characteristic.

This is how I recall *Reb Yoyel* and *Khasiye*, the older people of Dokshitz I encountered. We, who were children then, are now already grandfathers and grandmothers in Israel.

Where were they from? Where did they spend their childhood years, their youth? No one I asked knew the answer. They were materially poor, yet spiritually rich, full of purport, love and joy. This is remembered by all and they recall it with great respect. May their memories be blessed.

Reb Mendl the *Shoykhet* [ritual slaughterer]

I remember *Reb Mendl* the *shoykhet* - - a tall man with a full beard, playful intelligent eyes, and... always a pinch on the cheek of every child he encountered. He was a friend of children.

On the eve of *Yom Kippur* he used to slaughter the geese for *kapores* [tradition of swinging a fowl around, overhead to rid oneself of one's sins before atoning in the [tradition of swinging a fowl around, overhead to rid oneself of one's sins before atoning in the *Yom Kippur* service] so that, heaven forbid, no goose fat would be missing come Chanukah. When a boy was born in the shtetl *Reb Mendl* was the *moyel* [performer of ritual circumcisions]. On the day of a *bris* [ritutual circumcision] we children would wait for him as if for the Messiah.

During a celebration in the shtetl *Reb Mendl* would always remember us, the children, fully stuffing his pockets with *lekekh* [gingerbread/cake or candies], *teyglekh* [round dough-pellets with sweet coating], and tarts (it wasn't the cleanest practice but it certainly tasted like the Garden of Eden). He used to come to school, to class. It was all joy and happiness. What teachers? What lessons? We encircled him, each one stretching out their little hand. And he - - in the middle, amongst all of the lively group, a tall smiling guy. It wasn't so simple though to receive a snack: The boys had to show that they were wearing their *arba-knafos* [ritual four cornered garment] and the girls had to show that they knew how to recite the blessing over the Sabbath candles.

There was more than one instance when a young boy had forgotten to put on his *arba-knafos* on that very day and he would run home like a wounded rabbit and then return breathless to receive his share.

I remember: One time, in the middle of our teacher, *Yekhezkel Tomarkin's*, class, while I was reciting the poem, "*Hakoysel-Hama'aravi*" [The Western Wall], the door opened suddenly and *Reb Mendl* entered with full pockets. The teacher retreated to a corner, he had no control over us at this point.

Reb Mendl was a good religious man. Poor people used to come to the shtetl from various places. They had a place to stay the night at *Reb Mendl's*. It happened occasionally that in the morning after their departure something would be missing from his home. But this did not deter him from giving a place to sleep a second, third or tenth time. He did not take such instances to heart. The key for him was to fulfill the *mitzveh* of *hakhnoses-orkhim* [the commandment of receiving guests].

Teachers and *Kheyders*

One of our older people who remembers his *kheyder* years from tens of years ago told me about our teachers and *kheyders*. He asked me not to mention his name. It didn't seem appropriate. Today he is a respected man, a grandfather, it isn't appropriate that his grandchildren should know that he was such a prankster that the teachers were glad when he was taken from them.

He tells:

My first teacher was *Reb Velvl*. I studied with him for some time. In *Velvl's kheyder* there were some 20 students of various ages to whom he taught Bible and over whom he maintained discipline. A teacher would think that I wasn't with him for very long. But for a rowdy kid like me it was a long time.

I was taken from *Velvl* to my next teacher, *Reb Berke Yoshe*. That teacher had his own unique pedagogical method of teaching. Every Tuesday was the most difficult day - - exams. Everything that had been learned in the entire week, one had to know by heart on Tuesday. Whoever forgot a passage had his memory aided by the whip. More than one black-and-blue mark remained from one Tuesday to the next. *Berke Yoshe* did not get much pleasure from me. And me from him - - also not.

They tried a third teacher, perhaps it would be a lucky match. My third teacher was *Reb Binyomin Meyer Tomarkin*. There were other teachers with whom I studied: *Reb Shloyme Motles, Reb Yisroel, Berl Mordkhe, Berl Kurokin*.

At Berl Kurokin's children from wealthy and nobly pedigreed [pedigree is literal translation of *yikhes*. The implication is that the family is one with learned members.] families studied. At his *kheyder* though, the whip was even nobler... When we couldn't take the lashings anymore and the rear of getting a beating was great, we would stay for long hours in the toilet. We were certain that there we could wait out the wrath.

The nicest and best day of *kheyder* was the first day. Candies would fall on our childish heads. The older children would say that angels from heaven were throwing sweet things upon us.

But life in the *kheyder* was not really so sweet. Sitting from early until late in the evening on a hard bench, while the sun shined so nicely outside, repeating together aloud after the Rebbi read passages which we could barely understand. More than once is happened that I could not repeat with everyone because my mind was elsewhere. A pinch from the Rebbi would help bring me back to reality.

In the winter evenings we would run home quickly. A lantern in hand lighted the way. We would arrive to our good mothers half frozen.

That is how once upon a time we studied *Toyre* [Torah/Bible], which is, as is known, the best *skhoyre* [merchandise. From a well known expression that rhymes in Yiddish.]...

Holidays in the Shtetl

Every *yontef* [holiday] has its religious content, symbols and specific foods.

For *Rosh Hashanah* [the Jewish New Year], *Yom Kippur* and *Succos* they used to prepare round *farfelekh* [a kind of pasta] made of eggs and flour to symbolize the cyclical nature of the year.

Rosh Hashanah we used to eat more sweets. Apples dipped in honey, for a sweet year.

Shehekhiyanu [the prayer said for something new thanking God for "sustaining" one to realize the moment/event] was said over a piece of sweet watermelon. It wasn't very cheap, but whoever's pocket was a little deeper would buy a bit of grapes or dates, the fruits of the Land of Israel.

Baked goods for *Rosh Hashanah* were not just the usual. Different *challas* were baked for the Sabbath, like a ladder, so that all of the prayers would be able to climb up to the heavens...

For us children *Rosh Hashanah* left beautiful memories. First of all - - the new clothes and shoes. Dressed up in the new outfits we used to go to hear the *shoyfer* [the traditional ram's horn blown on the Jewish high holidays] blown. In the synagogue courtyard groups of young boys stood who used to "throw eyes" at us [slang, i.e., "check us out"], and we, the young girls would blush and, with hearts racing, duck into the women's gallery of the synagogue.

Before the *shoyfer* blowing "*lamenatzeyakh*" was said seven times. Whoever came early to say the "*lamenatzeyakh*" came out quite victoriously. We used to really pay attention to one another for fear that someone might omit a word or sentence. A holiday in which such a girl was caught in such a transgression was a marred holiday.

In the Lubavitsch synagogue *Reb Shmuel Moyshe Yishayes* blew the *shoyfer*. I remember it as if it were today, waiting with a lack of patience for that oment when he used to blow the *shoyfer*. I can still hear his *t'kiya g'doyla* [one of the requisite soundings of the shofar on the high holidays, a very long steady note] today. He used to get such clear pure notes out of that *shoyfer*, it would catch one's heart in synagogue and it was so quiet. Therefore I used to say the *lamenatzeyakh* to the very end, or sometimes not even be able to finish.

The second day of holiday, after supper and the sweet midday nap, we used to go for a visit. The aunts and uncles would meet the children for a simple strong glass of tea with sweet flat cakes and preserves. In the evening, the shtetl would go out for a walk on the Glubock, Barisof and Poletsk streets. When one would tire, one would sit to rest on a little bench, observing and chatting with those who were strolling.

The shtetl was so *yontefdik* [lit. holiday-like, full of the holiday spirit], so *yiddishlekh* [full of Jewish spirit]!

Yom Kippur

With the nearing of *Yom Kippur* the spirit would become gloomy, fearful. The Days of Awe. On the eve of *Yom Kippur* the very religious would go to the cold *Chabbad* [a "sect" of Hassidic Jews] synagogue where, for a few groshn the sexton would give a couple of lashes with the belt of his robe so people could atone for their sins.

My grandfather, *Reb Yisro'el Tzoduk* had many grandchildren. It was our family custom on the eve. of Yom Kippur for the grandchildren to go to our grandfather to be blessed. This was the nicest moment for me. I loved my grandfather very much. When he placed his hands on my little child head I wanted to stay like that forever with my grandfather. He would say the blessing in a crying voice, which I didn't understand and later understood: "May you hear your father and mother."

When I was in *Hachshara* [training and immigration to Israel in a rural development movement] preparing to immigrate to Israel, I was the only grown grandchild who used to go to my grandfather and ask: Grandfather, would you bless me? Then I cried together with him. Writing these words I see him and hear many of his warm blessings.

The fear of the Day of Judgment extended itself to some tens of Christians as well. They used to tell that they had seen a *"khapon"* (ghost) [see author's explanation further] with their own eyes, which drowned a Jew in the well. And every year the same Jew was drowned. Why a *"khapon"*? On the eve of Yom Kippur a Jewish woman told her son to go grab [khap] the white hen to use for shlogn *kappores* [pre-Yom Kippur atonement ceremony], (*"khap im on!"* ["grab hold of it!"]). A non-Jew must have heard this as if she were shouting *"khapn."* And so, he thought that *"khapon"* meant ghost. And Dokshitz Christians believed that on the eve of Yom Kippur Dokshitz is visited by the *"khaponÉ"*

It was nice when after *ne'ilah* [the last prayer recited on Yom Kippur] one would walk home with a kindled lamp in hand, so as to assure a bright year.

After the Yom Kippur fast the most religious Jews would pound the first stick of the *sukkeh* [tabernacle erected in celebration of the holiday Sukkoth, the Jewish Festival of Tabernacles, in which meals are eaten during the holiday] into the ground.

Sukkos and Simkhas Toyre

Sukkos was a joyous holiday. Especially the eve. of *Sukkos* when people would bring the *skhakh* [branches used for covering the roof of a *sukkeh*]. People used to build *sukkehs* attached to a wall so that a window of the house looked into the *sukkeh*, so stuff could be passed through the window into the *sukkeh*. Neighbors in one courtyard built a shared *sukkeh*. The wealthy built their sukkeh on the veranda, but they had to lift the roof and cover it with *skhakh*. But I think that the joy in building the *sukkeh* was much greater for the children whose parents did not have verandas.

The most joyous was *Simkhas Toyre* [Jewish festival celebrating the completion of the yearly cycle of reading of the Torah in synagogue]. The children received flags with various pictures on them, such as: Moses, or the Holy Ark with the doors opening. (That was a very precious flag.) On the tip of the flag we would put a potato or an apple and in that - - a candle. For *Simkhas Toyra* all went to the *hakofes* [perambulations with the Torah scroll] in the synagogue. Little children were carried. The bigger children pushed to get a chance to kiss the decorative mantle of the Torah scroll.

But the adults, especially the Hassidim, were completely out of their minds at *Simkhas Toyre* performing tricks. There were Jewish revelers in Dokshitz who, on that day, forgot all the years' concerns about finances. All of the knots left their faces, their eyes were bright, and there was joy and merriment. Hassidic melodies, dances, a good glass of spirits - - were not lacking on that day. Even people who were respected middle class citizens during the year allowed themselves certain wiles on that day.

The Hassidim used to go from one to the other. Taking a drink in one place, a bite to eat in another, moving to a third place and partaking in festival feasts.

Reb Meyir Mendl's goblets of liquor resulted in a joyous Hassidic melody warming the blood and people taken up with dancing on the tables until the windows rattled. At the end they would put *Reb Meyir Mendl* out on the floor and measure him with an arshin to see if he shrunk at all that year.

Every year they would measure him. He was the tallest and the skinniest guy in Dokshitz, full of confidence, also money (a soap maker?) - - it was remarkable. His son, *Shmuel-Leyb*, was the same way and was one of the most devoted *Halutzim* [member of the Zionist pioneer movement], who never got the opportunity to make *aliyah*.

Reb Yoykhenen Gordon, the slaughterer, who was a short serious man with a broad yellow beard year round, was not to be recognized on *Simkhas Toyre*. He put on a new skin. He had a very nice voice. So, what does a Jew do on such a happy holiday, when one is allowed anything? He knew many happy Russian melodies with Hassidic words. When he became ecstatic he went from window to window of the Hassidic houses and crowed like a rooster, and the shtetl gasped with laughter and happiness. These kinds of people brought joy to the holidays, they made all of the worries of the poor small shtetl be forgotten.

My Home

It is hard to believe that it was and is no more. I close my eyes and see the streets, alleys and market where my parents' house stood. I still see my father *(Shmuel Ahren)* sitting bent over the sewing machine, sewing hats and singing to himself, "Oh, how you ring, church bells." I see my mother, as she prepared for the Sabbath. And my brother, *Gershon*, as he pushed himself away from the sewing machine, grabbed his violin in hand, played a couple of minutes and sat by the sewing machine again. A winter Friday. People prepare for the Sabbath. The shtetl breathes with the smells of the Sabbath foods together with the cold air.

My father goes to *Fishkeh* the barber for a haircut. Or he went to *Yankev-Moyshe* where one could hear gossip of the shtetl, and talk about politics. All of the tradesmen in the craftsmen-union [lit. handworkers-union] went to Fishkeh the barber. There was a sort of shtetl "parliament" there. My father used to sit there for quite a long time and then run to the bathhouse. When he came home the house was already set up, the sewing machines shoved in their "Sabbath corner." My mother used to serve a hot glass of tea with a fresh pletzl [cake or flatbread], after that my father put on his Sabbath clothing and went to synagogue. Throughout the shtetl one could hear *Avrom-Moyshe* the sexton's voice ring out: "Candle lighting! Candle lighting!" When he was on *Gluboker* Street he could still be heard on *Polotzker* Street.

My mother lit the four Sabbath candles in two brass and two silver candlesticks, covered her face with both hands, said the blessing over the candles and after that added: "Just as the candles are lighted, so shall the souls of my children light." Until my father returned from synagogue my mother sorted the newspapers of the entire week, taking out the articles that they hadn't had an opportunity to read - - and after eating, reading these was one of the most important Sabbath pleasures for my parents.

When my mother married my father she brought him a very large dowry: two baskets. One was small and one large. Her library was packed in the large one, the Russian classics and even a small brochure by Karl Marx (which I found many years later in the attic.) She donated the books for the founding of a library. The second basked was for my mother's clothing, white "historic" handkerchiefs (that I played with later.) The first supper my mother cooked was a potato soup with herring. And my grandmother just had to see that my mother peeled the potatoes in white handkerchiefs. I can imagine what kind of uproar there was among all of the aunts and uncles! A bride without a dowry and furthermore she peels potatoes in handkerchiefs.

My mother loved the Russian language, which she had mastered, very much. Yiddish as well. My parents loved to read in general. They were active members of the "Bund." My father was active with the socialists ("sisilistn" as some Jews used to say/pronounce) when he was a young man.

As members of the *"Bund,"* they and other members (*Avrom* and *Libeh Khoydesh, Muleh Gleykhenhoz*) organized a reading parlor, helping to found the Yiddish library, one of the most important institutions for spreading the Yiddish language among the children who studied in the Polish school. That is to say - - teaching the children to read and write Yiddish, they become aquatinted with the literature. They organized Yiddish evening courses. The teacher was *Shimon Madeyski.*

We have him to thank for much joy and nice experiences.

Our first children's-performance, *"Der Friling Kumt"* [Spring is Coming] is unforgettable. I am certain that these were the first child artists in Dokshitz. The amount of pleasure we received from it is evident in the fact that until today I recall full sentences and scenes from the performance: *Reuveleh Kozak* was the bad winter, *Kreyneleh* - - the beautiful rose, I - - the queen, spring, who awakened the flowers from wintry sleep.

We Jewish children, who never saw a flower at home, wandered around in the cold winter evenings amidst fragrant flowers, thanks to the teacher Madeyski. If he remained living somewhere, or anyone from his family, may these few words of mine be brought to him as thanks.

Since there were no financial plans for holding the evening courses, to pay the teacher, the courses were terminated - - to the great regret and loss of the children.

My parents subscribed to the *"Folks-Tsaytung"* [People's/Folk-Newspaper]. For me and Gershon - - *"Di Grininke Beymelekh"* [The Green Saplings]. That was a wonderful children's journal. Later the *"Folks-Tsaytung"* also put out a weekly children's paper: *"Di Kleyne Folks Tzaytung"* [The Little People's Newspaper]. This was when the *"Bund"* was strong. Later on the Bundist organizations had less influence over the Jewish community and its place was filled by the Zionist youth organizations - - the *Hekhalutz, Hashomer Hatza'ir, Beitar.* A change to this position took place in our family as well.

Ideologically my parents were Bundists. However, at home the future and practical decisions for the children became the topic of conversation. Sending me to study in high school was a dream. Teaching me a trade so that I could remain in Dokshitz was also not a future. Boys and girls floundered about idly without a purpose. The only way out was joining one of the Zionist pioneer organizations, or the Communist party, which was illegal.

As *"Bund"* members it was difficult for my parents to be role models for their daughter to join *HaShomer HaTza'ir*. The education they gave us was something completely different. If the Communist party hadn't been illegal, my parents would even have been agreeable to my going that way.

Committee of Tradesmen (1930)

The youth that did not join any organization was faced with great hardships. Everyone thought to himself: "The *HeChalutz* and *HaShomer HaTza'ir* with its happy horah dance and excursions, the Beitar - - with the brown uniforms in various delineations. And the Communist group had its magic too.

With the help of my cousin *Mendl Markman* (today - - *Mendl Ashal*), I joined *HaShomer HaTza'ir*. For my parents it was a question of finding good company for their daughter. For me it was a life question. A question of building a world view.

Little by little my parents got used to the situation. The newspaper, *"Der Haynt"* started to come to the house, for which they subscribed with a neighbor (The *"Haynt"* was a more liberal paper). They took the *"Moment"* paper from *Reb Zalmen Taytz*. Despite the fact that income was low, my parents went without other things and subscribed to the *"Folks-Gezunt."* As a member of *"HaShomer HaTza'ir"* I had to read the newspaper, *"Dos Vort."*

In the long winter evenings, when the sewing machines would quiet down a bit, my mother would read aloud articles to her partners *(Khaykel der Kirzshner* [the cap-maker], *Berl Freys)* especially the novels, *"Urke Nakhalnik"* and *"Yosheh Kalb."* There was a pervasive atmosphere of study and work in our home.

My father was an active member of the craftsmen-union [lit. handworkers-union]. All management meetings and all gatherings took place in our house. Even if there weren't any meetings, father's friends from the organization came to visit for a chat: *Muleh Kugel, Moyshe* the bookbinder, Max Goltz, *Khayem Refo'el Gilenson* and others I don't remember. These people were connected to my father because of joint community work. They had a need to meet, discuss, politicize. Because how else would they there their happiness about *"Itshele's briv* [letter from Itshele]", or *Moyshe Kleynboym's* (today Moshe Sanah) sharp pen, and where should one have discussed what *Yitzkhok Grinboym* said in parliament?

The *Khabbad* and *Starosheler* synagogue was an important place for discussion. My grandfather used to come and tell my mother that my father was standing and discussing politics in groups more than praying. At the same time he would ask: "What's in the paper today?"

My grandfather, *Reb Yisro'el Tzaduk* was a tall, nice and intelligent man, pious but not fanatical. The big world interested him no less than his son, my father.

My grandfather used to say, "To live to see the end of the Poles!" He despised them. When my grandfather would come over and put on the headphones of the small radio we had, to listen to songs from "the olden days", that is to say Russian songs (*Dunayevski's* beautiful songs were in fashion at the time), his face would shine as that of a young man.

The *Khabbad* and *Starosheler* synagogue was an important place for discussion. My grandfather used to come and tell my mother that my father was standing and discussing politics in groups more than praying. At the same time he would ask: "What's in the paper today?"

Committee of Jewish Folk Bank (1929)

My grandfather, *Reb Yisro'el Tzaduk* was a tall, nice and intelligent man, pious but not fanatical. The big world interested him no less than his son, my father.

My grandfather used to say, "To live to see the end of the Poles!" He despised them. When my grandfather would come over and put on the headphones of the small radio we had, to listen to songs from "the olden days", that is to say Russian songs (*Dunayevski's* beautiful songs were in fashion at the time), his face would shine as that of a young man.

On Sabbath my mother would hand me and *Gershon* over to my father and she would say: "Don't forget to wish your grandfather a *gut-shabbes* [good Sabbath]."

How tragic it is that a generation has grown up without memories of grandfather and grandmother.

As I said, finances were difficult. Mother used to stay in the store and sell hats. As she treated the peasants very well, they paid her with the same coin. The peasant women would entrust her with their most intimate and asked her advice more than once.

My mother was also skillful at different community functions, organizing a tea-evening, a charity function and the like.

It was a real happening when a theater group would come to the shtetl, whether it was real art or lower level performance. It was a real holiday for the shtetl. It is worthwhile to remind the reader that there was a dramatic circle in Dokshitz as well, and that *Sheynke* was the star performer. I remember her in the role of Leah in *"Dibbuk."* I was still a little girl then. My parents wanted me to see theater and to become interested in the Yiddish classics. I went with a friend to see *"Dibbuk."* I was so taken in by her performance that when the dibbuk went into Leah I was terrified and I screamed along with her.

My parents' intention was good, but the play was too strong an experience for me.

My parents stood before a tremendous problem when it came time for me to go to *Hachshara*. They understood that it was a necessity. But we would have to separate. Meanwhile, Gershon also joined *Hashomer Hatza'ir*. It was difficult. We avoided talking about it.

It was my good fortune that *Yoysef Kaplan,* of blessed memory, visited my *ken* [lit. Hebrew, nest - - the word used for groups of Zionist organizations and youth groups]. The gang put forth that I should invite him to our home. They told him the reason, my parents agreed and my mother prepared a lovely dinner.

Yoysef Kaplan told my parents the entire truth about the difficult life of *Hachshara*. He gave my parents a lot of confidence, which brought results. We exhaled. My parents knew what a difficult way lay before me. Politically they were opposed, but they knew that there was no alternative - - and my onetime Bundists sent me to *Hachshara* with a heavy heart.

When I came home to prepare for *aliyah* I found my father to be even more active. His big dream was that the members of the craftsmen-union would have their corner, their own place where they could meet and gather. Thanks to his initiative a room was rented and that is where the club of the craftsmen-union met.

There were already rumors floating around about a war before I made *aliyah*. Antisemitism reached us as well. The situation was tense. People started to gather salt, soap.

The last day before my *aliyah* was the most difficult. My *aliyah* was an illegal one. It had to be a secret. I can still see today all of the people who stood in their doorways and escorted me with their sad eyes, giving me their blessing.

That is how I separated from my shtetl and from my family.

* * *

Chapter 2
Personalities from Our Town

Chaim Zamiri

Nessia, Shmuel Zamir, Beila, J. Levitan, Sarah Rozov
(Excerpts from the story of his life)

Chaim was born in the little town of Dokshitz in the province of Vilna, in 1908. His parents, Tzipi and Arie Solovey, dealt in trade and were well off. They were very popular among the townspeople and the farmers in the region because of their honesty and reliability.

He received his first education at the "heder", with a "mitkadem" (progressive) melamed (scholar). Chaim was very fond of the Rabbi and he always spoke well of him. At the same time, he also went to a Russian and Polish school. This was the period when the regime changed in the area. Chaim did not like the secular schools and when the "Tarbut" school was established, he moved there.

This was the time when "Hehalutz Hatzair" was founded in Dokshitz. Chaim and his friends were among the first to join the movement, he immediately stood out because of his qualities: reliability, honesty, enthusiasm, power to convince and above all his ambition to realize his plans. These qualities made him into the leader of the group and many youngsters, both younger and older than he, were attracted to him and influenced by him.

At the age of 17 he went on pioneer training and prepared himself to go on aliyah. However, it was impossible to implement this for there was a shortage of certificates. Chaim returns home and establishes the "Hashomer Hatzair" branch in the town and its vicinity. However, he does not leave Hehalutz", continues his activity there and is one of its leaders as a graduate of "Hashomer Hatzair".

Chaim undertakes many tasks, among them looking after the "Tarbut" school which lacks funds; activity at the Zionist and Eretz Jisraeli funds and above all attracting youngsters and children to the youth movements. Chaim was at the center of all these activities. "Bleemel Tag" (flower day) activities were organized for obtaining money, parties, amateur drama performances ("The sale of Joseph", "Tuvia the Milkman". The "Dibbuk" and others) and Chaim played the main role in them. They also undertook seasonal work with the estate owners in the area, delving pits mewing the meadows etc. This served for the maintenance of the "Tarbut" school; the money in the funds was regularly sent to Israel. "Davar" - the newspaper of the workers in Eretz Jisrael was regularly received at the branch.

"Hehalutz" had to compete with the other movements in town, which was close to the Russian border where the communist influence was deeply felt; the Revisionists also attracted the youngsters of the wealthier classes. A battle was fought for each soul and the rivals soon found out that it was impossible to resist Chaim and his friends.

Chaim himself was not fully satisfied with his activities - he wanted to go to Eretz Jisrael. In 1931 he went on permanent training and took the firm decision not to return to his little town until he would be able to go on aliyah to Israel. He joined the "Mesilah" organization, presently kibbutz "Mesilot." Chaim was active here for six months and moved on to "Hehalutz" training - ; kibbutz Tel Hai which set up a branch at Bialistock. This branch was in its early stages and had but a few members. There was not enough work, hunger and a deteriorating social situation. Chaim started to organize the place. He runs around for days and knocks on the doors of the factory owners in Bialistock and with his power of conviction he manages to explain to them that the pioneers are good workers. In order to prove this he appears at each difficult place of work; with his willpower and good sense he overcomes the physical problems and the employers invite a few other pioneers on condition that they work like him.

Chaim does not neglect social life either. He sticks to his principles, tries to keep the group together. He manages to establish ties with broad Zionist circles in Bialistock and thereby removes the branch from its social and economic isolation.

It was the aim of the "Hehalutz" center to expand pioneer training and infiltrate the large cities. Chaim was sent to Grodna and established a new training place there. Conditions in Grodna were similar to those in Bialistock and after many difficulties a branch was established and pioneers from all over Poland started to come here to be trained for aliyah to Eretz Jisrael.

Due to "Hehalutz" center considerations the Grodna training was transferred to "Hashomer Hatzair", and therefore the members of the branch belonging to Tel Hai were forced to disperse to other training points. Chaim accepted this and went to Lida to continue his training.

When the gates of Eretz Jisrael were opened and the first certificates were received, Chaim and I received permission to go on aliyah in February 1933, and after brief preparations at home - ; we left.

We arrived in Israel and were immediately sent to Ein Harod. In the first year Chaim, restless and full of energy, did not find a suitable field of activity at the established kibbutz. He was offered various opportunities for activity at the Noar Haoved (working youth) movement, but did not find this attractive. He was attracted to the mountains and the valley with which he fell in love the moment he set foot on the land.

In 1934 our daughter Nurith was born. Chaim was very happy and devoted all his free moments to her. He looked for a new venture and wanted to set up a sheep section at the kibbutz. The kibbutz management did not like this idea so much for everyone remembered the initial failure of the sheep growing section at Ein Harod. However, with his willpower and with the assistance of a small number of friends, the late Itzhak Rafaeli and Motke among them, they convinced those who were against the idea. Chaim left for a brief training period at Ayelet Hashachar, and in 1936 the sheep were acquired, and working with sheep became his chief interest in life. He found a source of joy in each professional achievement - ; increase in the output of milk, the birth of each little lamb; he was particularly happy when he started to work with the late Dr. Pintzi. He discovered a whole new world, spent every free minute perusing professional literature and studied genetics.

He would sit with the late Dr. Pintzi and with Motke till the wee hours of night in order to establish a logbook of the herd. Yet, however busy he was, he never forgot his family, for he loved us very much and shared all his achievements and failures with us - ; we were indispensable to him. All the sheep business was conducted in our modest little room.

In 1944 our daughter Aviva was born and two years later - ; Tzipi.

A year before the War of Liberation Chaim was called upon to be in charge of purchasing at the kibbutz, and when he finished this task the sheep breeder's organization asked him to provide training. Chaim hesitated for he did not want to leave his job with the sheep, however, his health had deteriorated and after a while he accepted the organization's request.

He would go to work in the morning and return late at night, and would devote all his free time to the herd, he had very close ties with the shepherds. He continued to conduct the logbook of sheep and would work on this on Saturdays and in his free time.

When the State was established Chaim was sent to other countries in the Middle East by the Ministry of Agriculture in order to buy sheep.

In 1951, when there was a division at Ein Harod, our daughter Zohar was born. Chaim passed through a difficult crisis with the division. As he was not a political person he was unable to accept the idea that the kibbutz and society could be destroyed because of political strife.

From the start of the division he took the stand that a peaceful and friendly agreement should be reached. He adhered to this stand, in spite of all the tragic events at the kibbutz. The majority of the members of the two groups did not agree with him and Chaim abandoned his activity and devoted himself to the problems of sheep. At that time he went to Turkey to buy sheep and bring them to Israel, however, his heart was with what went on at the kibbutz. His letters are full of sorrow and pain. He was not in good health at the time and while he was still in Turkey it appeared that he had a heart problem.

When the rift at Ein Harod deepened, many members of the kibbutz realized there was no solution or compromise. Chaim, together with a few friends who shared his views, set out to rehabilitate Ein Harod by dividing the productive branches and rehabilitating them. His time is spent trying to find the means to do so and this is the peak of his activity and tension.

In 1956, during the Sinai Campaign, Chaim is recruited with a kibbutz vehicle and gets as far as Ismalia. He was proud of this campaign and happy to be able to take part in it.

Once the kibbutz is rehabilitated on the hill, Chaim leaves his position and returns to his sheep activity. A while later he is appointed trainer at the sheep section management.

When the rest of my family arrives in Israel, my sister and her son from Russia and the 2 children of my sister from South Africa, Chaim sets out to help them get settled, takes care of all their problems and is a pillar of support to them.

In February 1962 when he returns from a visit to the Negev, he suffers a massive heart attack. His life is at risk. When he recovers, the doctors ask him to take care because his life is in danger. But, all the rules of being careful that apply in such cases were not made for Chaim. He continues his travels, even adds tasks and occupations. The period and his work oblige him to advance and he studies and teaches others. Deep in his heart he is aware of his situation, he withdraws and only those closest to him know what goes on, and suffer together with him.

We lived with the bitter verdict for three years. Every time he went on his way we worried, and when he came back late we were out of our minds. His love knew no bounds and he would give us all his attention. His death was not sudden but reality is far different from what is expected. He left us broken hearted.

By Nessia

*

Chapters of Life

We were cousins, Chaim and I . . .

Our grandmother was a central figure in our family, she was full of energy. When she became a widow she had to take care of a large family (twelve sons). She was a very diligent woman and conducted wide-ranging business affairs. She would tell us, her grandchildren, that she even had good connections with the Czarist regime and managed to obtain rights from them which other Jews were unable to get (there were regions at the time which Jews were not allowed to enter, trade restrictions etc.). She was proud of the fact that she conducted her business by memory, for she was analphabetic.

There is no doubt that Chaim inherited her energy as well as her organizational talent.

His father Laibe (Arie) and his mother Tzipa (Tzipora) came from Dokshitz, they conducted a large trading house for building materials, paint, various farming equipment, lighting, foodstuffs etc. They set it up by themselves, were extremely successful and were considered the richest grocers in town. Customers were the farmers of the vicinity who trusted the Solovey house and were sure of its honesty.

There were three children in the family: Chaim, Shmuel and their sister Lea. The father passed away and the mother and her two sons, who had married in the meantime and begotten children, remained in the Diaspora. All of them perished in the Holocaust and except for the late Chaim and myself noone is left of the Solovey family.

Lea, Chaim's sister, studied at the gymnasium outside Dokshitz and Shmuel at the local gymnasium. It must be mentioned that Dokshitz was a town abounding with Jewish and general culture, and the Jews were enthusiastic Habad Hassidim.

When Chaim's older brother and sister finished their studies, they joined their parents' business. Chaim himself moved from one school to another in town - ; at first he studied at the "heder" and at the age of 10 he moved to the Russian gymnasium. When the town was conquered by the Poles in 1920, a Polish gymnasium was also established and Chaim moved there.

There was an awakening of Zionist activity in town and a "Tarbut" school was established. Chaim left the secular gymnasium and started to study at the "Tarbut" school. This is quite astonishing, for his parents were not Zionist and only his brother Shmuel absorbed the spirits roaming through the Jewish world and was active on behalf of Keren Hakayemet leJisrael. Chaim drew his love for Zion from him. The majority of the youngsters in Dokshitz went to the "Tarbut" school. One of the teachers called Tamarkin, a fervent Zionist, inspired his students with a national spirit.

While he was still at school Chaim already organized youth meetings in town, invited lecturers to speak about Eretz Jisrael and Zionism. The teachers were usually Zionists, but there were others who were inclined towards the labor movement. Chaim looked for a way to the labor movement of Eretz Jisrael through one of the teachers. He despised business and saw his way of life among the working people. That is how he arrived at "Hashomer Hatzair", and he invited Shimon Polotnikov (presently member of Gan Shmuel) to our town in order to tell us about this movement.

I remember there was a great deal of commotion towards the visit and most of the youngsters participated in the meeting. Chaim announced the establishment of a "Hashomer Hatzair" cell and he headed it. He brought all the educational systems of "Hashomer Hatzair" to our little town - ; scouts, organization into divisions etc. He determined who would be at the head of the divisions and he even attracted those youngsters who were far from Zionism in general and working Eretz Jisrael in particular. Even idle youngsters off the street were drawn to this movement.

The Hehalutz Histadrut (union) in our town included all the movements of working youth of Eretz Jisrael (except for Hashomer Hatzair there was also "Gordonia" and "Hehalutz"). At these youth meetings Chaim met his future girlfriend, Nessia, who was a member of "Hashomer Hatzair". Many of the members in those days are presently in Israel, dispersed over various kibbutzim. Some at Ein Shemer, Manit, Hatzor, Dan and Beth Zera.

Chaim was the center of attention when he appeared at "Hehalutz", he was an excellent speaker with great power of conviction.

His students at the kibbutzim remember him fondly for he influenced them to leave their town and find their roots in the fatherland.

In 1930 Chaim arrived at the training camp, together with the "Mesila" group - ; presently kibbutz Mesilot. He left this training camp for social reasons, and perhaps also political doubts. He joined the Tel Hai training camp of "Hehalutz" where he found his friends from the Dokshitz "Hehalutz".

In mid 1933 Chaim went to Israel in spite of his parents' opposition, they wanted him to stay with them and help them in the business.

When Chaim came to Israel he not only realized his personal and pioneering dream, but he also served as an example to all the youngsters who hesitated to leave the Diaspora. He did so although he recognized that his presence abroad as leader of "Hehalutz" was essential.

I went on aliyah to Israel about a year after Chaim and he was my only relative there. My first Sabbath I spent with Chaim at Ein Harod. He wanted to make my visit pleasant and took me on a horse-drawn tour of the area, he never ceased praising the beauty of nature and explained to me how to settle down in Israel. When I was at Ein Shemer, my meetings with Chaim were rare - ; each of us was busy with his own affairs, but our children made us visit each other. We felt that Chaim was very fond of our children, noone could imagine that this bond would suddenly be severed.

In our family Chaim was the older, more experienced brother, often a substitute for my parents. My sons were very attached to Chaim, loved and respected him. We all loved him. That is why we are so deeply saddened at his early death.

By Shmuel Zamir (Ein Shemer)

*

To His Memory

Chaim is no longer. Hard to believe! - ; The heart refuses to accept this bitter reality. Shall we never see him again?

With a heart full of sorrow I shall try to write a fraction of what one could write about my dear friend Chaim who was so loved and devoted. It is hard to write about him for it seems as if he is still among us.

Chaim was very close to me, like a brother. With his honest wish to become involved in the problem bothering you he rekindled your belief in good. I had deep feelings of respect for him and was extremely fond of him. Although we grew up in the same little town I did not know him, until we met at "Hehalutz". We came from a different educational background - ; I studied at the Russian school and he received a Hebrew education and was fluent in the language from an early age. When we met at "Hehalutz" this was already his home. He had no problem in throwing away all the customs of the young of that period, and devoted himself entirely to the new way which was so positive and contrary to the lack of purpose of the other youngsters in town.

He inspired everyone with his simplicity, his boundless devotion. He set up a branch of "Hashomer Hatzair", where he concentrated the crème de la crème of the young. He devoted day and night to propaganda, education, activities. He managed to kindle a beam of hope in all of us - ; we felt we had something to fight for, for Jewish youngsters would no longer sit with their parents in a dark corner in the Diaspora and spend their time at a shop or buying produce from the gentiles at the market - ; there was a loftier purpose to life.

Chaim was the first to go on "hahshara" (training) at Tel Hai and many others, in spite of the parents' opposition, followed him.

I went to Israel before him and did not follow up his activity in the Diaspora, but the fact that so many of his students are dispersed over all the kibbutzim and the various movements shows how blessed his activity was.

I welcomed Chaim when he arrived in Israel, at the Jaffo port in 1933. At that time my links with Chaim were not only social, but we were relatives as well, and I was very happy that my sister Nessia linked her life to his. I was a little concerned at their joining Ein Harod - ; would the energetic Chaim find his place and be content at Ein Harod, which was already very established at a time when there were many groups all over the country battling to find work in the orchards and all other fields of labor?

However, I soon re-discovered Chaim. Even at Ein Harod he was not satisfied with the existing situation; here too he found a challenge - ; he chose a new branch at the kibbutz. No need to describe his activity at the sheep section, for this is well known, and for generations to come the story will be told.

We shared part of our life with Chaim, and not every period was glamorous, but he almost always had the upper hand and found a solution for the problems that arose. He had a rich and energetic personality.

Chaim devoted much time to rehabilitating Ein Harod Ihud, he accompanied each plan with pride and devotion, each house and each building at the kibbutz. During the days of strife he knew to distinguish between what was important and what wasn't, and to him the most important thing was to build the new kibbutz.

The gracious and good heart has fallen silent. I am shocked and pained. How can I write about my dear brother Chaim, while I am still unable to accept the fact that he is no longer. He was taken away suddenly while he was still at the center of activity, taking care of his family and of all of us, and ready to contribute to finding a solution to the problems of our life.

His personality will serve as a candle to us and will brighten our path. Blessed be his memory!

By Bila (Yifat)

*

Fellow townsmen and students commemorate Chaim

A small town on the Russian border. Little streets, densely populated alleys; a market at the center of town and little shops, which barely provide a living for the families. This is where Chaim was born. The young who organized into pioneer movements were the only bright star in the somber daily life. Chaim was among them and grew together with the movement. It was to him we, the young and others as well, turned. I remember him: broad shouldered, dressed in a short leather coat, a cigarette dangling from his mouth, broad forehead and kind but stern eyes. He was alert, active and capable of making others act. He was extremely upright and steadfast. Not ashamed to say what he had on his mind if he thought this was the right thing to do. These qualities did not make life easy for Chaim, but they gained him respect with his opponents (indeed he had some) and admiration from his many friends.

Indeed, his life was not easy, but that is what he wanted. He was so dynamic that it sometimes seemed as if he was looking for trouble. We would tell him: "Chaim, turn down the volume" but he did not want to listen. He would fight, overcome, and be happy. He merely wanted to live a rich, full and intensive life. He was a simple man, with a good sense of humor, liked to listen, faithful to his job, movement and a friend to everyone.

Sara Rozov (Ein Shemer)

*

The late Chaim's activity in Dokshitz

Everything that happened in Dokshitz in those days should be seen in the background of the economic situation that followed the Polish occupation in 1920. The Russian border was at a short distance from Dokshitz. The majority of its inhabitants were craftsmen or grocers and made a living off the farmers in the vicinity. The change of regime brought an end to the sources of living for many people. Daily life deteriorated from day to day and poverty was rampant in town. Many of us were hungry and torn. The young were in distress and looked for ways to extricate themselves from the dire situation. Many youngsters joined the communists (who operated underground) and some joined the "Bund". We saw the Yiddishists as one body, it was impossible to distinguish between them and they had their own solutions for the troubles of the Jews.

Against this bloc the pioneer youth stood up, they wanted to go to Zion. New voices were heard in our little town. When a cell of "Hashomer Hatzair" was set up Chaim was among the leaders of this movement. Thanks to his activity our branch did credit to the movement, as proven by the fact that so many of the members of Hashomer Hatzair in Dokshitz are in Israel at the kibbutzim. The Hashomer Hatzair cell brought new life to our town. The sounds of the Hebrew language were heard on its streets. Hebrew songs, enthusiastic dances, lively conversations, culture evenings - ; many youngsters were drawn to this.

At that time the "Tarbut" school existed in our town, but it did not have a solid foundation. Because of the poverty many students did not pay tuition. In order to solve the problem of the school the "Hehalutz" people in town, together with "Hashomer "Hatzair" undertook many different campaigns, such as cutting trees in the forests in order to sell the wood, baking matzos on Pessach eve for a small fee and street collections etc.

Among the most lucrative activities were the performances for the general public. I particularly remember one performance - ; the Lanski "Dibbuk". Chaim played the role of the Rabbi with great success, he would usually play the main part in most plays.

In addition to all the activities we organized on behalf of the "Tarbut" school we would go to the rich homeowners in our town and ask them to donate money for this institution, and we would approach the parents not to send their children to the Polish schools and transfer them to "Tarbut".

We did not only care for the "Tarbut" school which would close down when there was no money for its maintenance, but also for the children - ; many of them were hungry and did not have proper clothing, shoes etc. We tried to take care of all their needs as far as this was possible. A free hot meal was organized at school. We even managed to obtain sums for this from the authorities, and this was very difficult.

We tried to bring teachers from Vilna ("Tarbut" center). They had a pioneer spirit and we educated the youth in our town in this spirit.

The "Bund" and the communists gathered around the Yiddishist school. There was fierce competition between them and the Eretz Jisrael Haovedet movement centered at Tarbut".

The late Chaim came from a well to do home, yet he mingled with common people and was among the most active to help the needy. In this respect he served as an example to all his friends in the little town. There was much work and many efforts had to be made - ; one had to go from one to the other and convince them. Chaim was very good at this. As the poorest part was concentrated at "Hehalutz" everyone needed personal attention, it was necessary to obtain money for going on hahshara (training), finance aliyah to Israel and even buy the stamp for sending a letter to the "Hehalutz" center.

Chaim stood out with his energy, was a good and devoted friend, demanded much but also served as an example to others, he did himself what he asked of others.

I was not as close to Chaim in Israel as I was in our little town, for we went our separate ways. Each of us settled at another kibbutz, but even from a distance he was like a brother to me.

Israel Levitan (Yagur)

Outline in Memory of Arie Fogelman R.I.P.
Who gave his life in the War of Independence
Born: Jan. 12, 1923. Died: May 31, 1948 Near Latrun.

Arie Fogelman

Beginning to tell about our Arie, I halt and wonder: Which is the Arie that should be told about? Arie the weak kid in the Diaspora? Arie the growing teenager in the homeland? Arie the realizer of Zionism? Maybe Arie which is gone? Alas, many a face did our Arie posses - faces never fully matured.

In childhood he was a weak and sickly child. He became orphaned from father at a young age and never heard neither kind and encouraging words nor moral teachings. He was a "son of old age", "a child of entertainment " for his mother, sisters and brothers. Despite the lacking materialistic conditions he was bestowed love from his entire family.

His childhood year passed similarly to other kids in the Diaspora, studying in the "Tarbut" school, and in hostile surroundings and atmosphere which gave birth to a longing of days to come. The compensation for the Diaspora life and the rest of the burdens of the soul was to be found in the "Hashomer Hatzair" youth movement, which he joined at an early age. He found there a kind and loving instructor, Zvi Markman, who was a friend and father to him. Arie was loyal to the movement and attached to it wholly. From it he gained the strength to strive towards the future and the Aliya to Israel.

At home a turning point is reached, an agitation is felt. The eldest sister has begun training towards Aliya. The mood has changed in the house and all conversations are about Israel, making Aliya and around these subjects. A regeneration has taken place in the homely atmosphere and it cut through the Jewish Diaspora atmosphere.

A long time passed since the sister made Aliya until they began to believe her letters and until it was decided to agree to wishes of joining her and her family in Israel. When the fateful decision was made, the preparations began, all accompanied by a tens feeling about the future.

The Aliya to Israel was marred by the separation from Simcha, the older brother, who was then in the Polish army. A year after his service, when he planned to make Aliya, the second world war broke out and he found himself fighting in Polish uniform. With the entrance of Germany into Russian-occupied territory, he joined the partisans and went through many a dire time until he came to Israel after the war of independence.

With the Aliya of the family (mother, sisters and Arie) to Israel a startling change took over Arie. No more was he Leibale of the Diaspora. He became an Israeli, a growing boy, turning into a young man, studying in an Israeli school -"Pika" school in Petach-Tikva and living in the homeland.

His stature was erect, his face shone with pride and heroism. A all-Israeli kid, returning to the homeland and grasping it with all his binding love.

Immediately coming to Israel he joined the "Shomer Hatzair" where he found his happiness and integrity of his life. This is where he found his best friends with whom he went through life, and on his last road.

Here his personality blossomed; his love of Israel strengthened. Every inch of blue skies in the homeland, every chirp of a bird and the smell of earth made his heart flutter, overtook him, made him their private and personal possession.

The financial difficulties at home did not allow him to peacefully continue his studies. Despite his acknowledgement of the importance of education, he would not continue to sit and study, while his sisters support the family and take care of his every need.

With the decisiveness of an adult, in spite of his tender age, he deserted school and began to help the family financially. He started out at the packing house (of citrus fruit). First, as a fruit picker, and later, due to his success and accomplishment, attained the position of a packer and moved to work in the "Yachin" factory, thrilled at being able to help the family.

The youth movement took the place of school. He gave more and more of his time to the "Shomer Hatzair" both as a student and an instructor. The movement became his second home, and later - his first as well.

He inhaled into his soul the air of the homeland, its beauty and majesty. He was deeply affected by his surroundings and molded this love into his pupils who worshiped him and saw a perfect role model in him.

At this point in his life he began to conquer the land with his feet. There was not a trail nor road which he did not tread feeling the country's earth beneath his feet. It was a time when the people began forming methods for defence against the evils to come. Weapon training had begun. Comportment under fire, fighting strategies and all other practices needed by a people out to defend its land and freedom.

Arie was out of the house for many days due to these marches and training, and even when he arrived, he would not spend much time with his family. In those days the commune of "Hashomer Hatzair" was founded in town. He was of the first to join and it became his home.

However, his time with the commune did not last long. At the time a call came to join the watchmen. As always, he followed the call and served as a watchman in Vilhelma.

The youth became a man, leaving the familial framework and choosing his own way, linking his life with that of his country and his people. From there, not long was the way to the kibbutz and the realization.

As the movement turned to the settlement, he moved to kibbutz Sarid which became his one and only home. In the farmstead and in his life he found fulfillment and it seemed that he reached a state of rest and security.

He was a herdsman, and in the wide expanses of nature he saw his life realized. A devoted and loyal herdsman since devotion and loyalty were a part of his personality. He would worry about his mother which was left alone, about his sisters who should walk in his footsteps and give of themselves and of their strength to the workers movement and the building of the country, and about his brother who stayed still abroad. He planned in his mind to take a break from the farmstead when his brother makes Aliya, in order to work and gain money to help his brother get settled in Israel.

He used his time in the farmstead to study different subjects. He felt his lack of education and tried to compensate for it on his own. Among other things, he studied Arabic in the hope of forming a link and conversation with our neighbors in better times to come.

He fitted in well socially and his loyal friends carry his memory in their hearts forever, as he was kind, friendly and loved.

With the outbreak of the independence war, he was made military instructor on the farmstead. He was to train the people to protect the farmstead and their lives. However, he was not a long time in this duty. He requested vehemently to be sent with the warriors. After many a request, his wish was granted and he joined the fighters. He took part in the battle of "Mishmar Ha'emek" and his reactions were full of hope and glory. He believed that justice will prevail, he mourned the death of his friends and promised to avenge their deaths.

He was sent to an officer's course, after being found suited to lead due to his good traits. Alas, the course did not last long. The war became more difficult and a need arose in more warriors. The course was terminated, the people received new soldiers who had just made Aliya, and with them, they went out to battle. A battle which was to be his last - the battle of Latrun.

This battle also came only after his insistence, since he had just come back from an operation a few hours earlier and was ordered to rest. He refused, saying he could not peacefully rest knowing his men are out to battle and he is not at their side.

It was a rash and bitter battle. The soldiers were inexperienced, not knowing how to contain their fear, the language and weapons unfamiliar to them. The weather was stifling hot and the strong enemy covered the hill with heavy fire.

There, on his last road, he succeeded in showing once again, his heroism and love of man. He was wounded and kept going in order not to cause chaos in the lines. Just then, while trying to encourage two of the soldiers, who, for fear stayed in the front in spite of the order to retreat, came another wound.

With the last of his forces he convinced the two to retreat and stayed alone forever... No one ever saw him again. For a long time it was unsure if his bones would be buried in Israel - but he was granted at least this honour.

The blow was hard and perpetual. His image will forever be inscribe in the hearts of his family and friends, all weeping and mourning the sorrow of the loss.

Ofira (his niece)

"I am Chaya Bloch..."
by Zvi Markman, Kibbutz Hatzor

Chaya and Chana Bloch

Although twenty-five years have passed, still, I see her in her supreme heroism, her blue eyes looking with mocking scorn at the hangman. He is vested in a brown uniform, adorned with medals and decorations of valor with swastikas noting his being an S.S. officer. He sits comfortably in an upholstered armchair behind the green desk. With a leveled hand movement he waves at the blue smoke rising from his cigarette. The servant meekly takes the remnants of food from his desk and hastily leaves the room.

Hana Bloch - of a simple Jewish family, her father having made a living trading in horses. She was the youngest of the family, having an older brother and a married sister by the name of Haika. Haika, voted a member to the city council with the rise of the Soviets to power, whose doom was sealed by the S.S. entering the town.

For the last few days she's been wandering from village to village with her infant in her arms. No one notices, no one will help her, no one will give her shelter. Broken and exhausted she returns to the house of her parents. She can suffer no more and makes her mind up to present herself at the police station of her own free will. The young Hana is lost in deep reflections. Suddenly, she rises, takes her sister's identity card forcefully, kisses the baby and with quick steps walks to the police station. There, she hands over her sister's reporting order to the policeman on duty and says: "I am Haika Bloch..."

Now she stands in front of the S.S. officer. She does not feel the nearing end. Only one thought enters her mind: Succeeding in tricking this Uberstumpführer that she really was a member of the city council and that she should pay for this. The heart beats strongly, the eyes fixed on the interrogator, following his every movement. He is still quiet, polite. There is pleasure which can be read from his features. He beckons her to approach. She is slightly pale, her blond tress made golden by the rays of the sun falling through the window. Her knees slightly quivering, but her spirit strong. Trying to stay quiet, something not too difficult for her as it is her nature.

Only three years ago she terminated her studies at the public school. After the arrival of the Red-Army she finished an accountancy course, and lately worked in one of the city offices as an accountant. How happy she was being independent and making a living honorably. She is always smiling, always neat, nice and her voice sweetly sings poetry and the song of life. However, the end is here - and she has seen no more than eighteen springs.

The officer turns to her with a satanic smirk on his face: "A pretty girl like you surely wouldn't want to die, and so I advise you to tell me everything you know about the Soviet action men: Who are they? Where are they? What is their plan of action against us? You yourself must understand that there is no point in resisting. The communists will never return, and you have no need to risk your life. If you cooperate we'll find work for you, maybe even in my office". She stood still, not a word. Slowly, the smile left his face, he lowered his eyes to the desk. All of a sudden, his fist exploded on the desk. Fire and brimstone flowed from his mouth. He came to her, grabbed her tress and began pulling and yanking to and fro. A shiver went down her spine, she almost broke down weeping, but she got hold of herself and her tears dried and did not run. She decided to confront this "filthy beast" in shape of a human being. He landed a heavy blow upon her face, and she fell like log, unconscious. - Talk, you cursed Jew! She did not move nor answer. She continued being silent. He brought the burning cigarette to her pale cheeks, to her forehead, took his anger out on her. There is nothing left to do. He ordered her to be taken to the cellar until she regains consciousness.

*

She awoke with dawn. The sun snuck in through the bars of the small high window. Her entire body ached. Her cracked swollen lips hurt, blood covered her face. A deafening noise and a throbbing head ache almost blurred everything around her.

With great difficulty she managed to rise on her feet and approached the barred window. The streets were empty. Military vehicles passed constantly: Tanks, armored cars, armed soldiers with steel helmets on motorcycles - everything flowed eastwards... Fancy cars with sharply dressed officers, looking fresh, smiling, as if they were off to a party or on holiday, passed by. It's hard to get accustomed to the idea. Did they really win? Maybe it's all a temporary glimmer?

Quickly pass squadrons and squadrons of airplanes. The earth, as if shaking under the noise of the engines. No one stops them, no one resists. The road is open for the progress of the Nazi filth. Cities and villages swallowed whole, or burned in a title wave of fire and explosions. The Red-Army is organizing to repel this awesome force but it is helpless. Outside the sun is shining, a hot summer day in the midst of July, but the cellar is infested with a bone shuddering, humid cold, and a pain of gnawing hunger is unbearable. Her head is spinning and her world darkens. She falls helplessly to the floor. Suddenly, cold water is poured noisily upon her. She awakes frightfully. Oh, murderers, what have you done? Why didn't you let me sink into the unknown darkness, not to wake again?

*

Again, she is in the same spacious room with the same face opposite her. She repeats her thought: No, nothing will help you, bastard. You'll never get your information from me... No no no! More beating, more threats. Day and night, the tortures of the merciless Nazi machine repeat themselves. Hana opens her mouth and words escape her like a volcano erupting, facing the astonished officer. - "We are millions and your devil's power will not destroy us all. Our brothers will avenge our blood. If you succeed today - not forever will you do so. Bitter will be your fate. With your blood you shall pay for your cruel deeds. I spit in your face! I'd rather die than live among animals like you. You shall be dammed forever"

A bullet from the Nazi's pistol extinguished her voice, but her words are not forgotten with her death. From then, until now, they reverberate in the heavens...

*

In Dokshitz there is a school named after Hana Bloch, and at every assembly Hana's name is read first and a choir of students answers in one voice: "She died a martyrs death for her people and her country..."

Zvi Markman, Kibbutz Hatzor

The Death of a Martyr Chaya Bloch

A daughter of a simple Jew - ; a coachman who swung himself with horse and wagon across the dirt roads around Dokshitz, both summer and winter, in snow and rain, heat and cold. He drove from market to market, from shtetl to shtetl. On the way he would stop in villages to feed the horse [alt. to let the horse out to pasture] and in the meantime would have a chat with the peasants, asking who had a horse to sell or trade, perhaps someone might buy a colt from him?!

More than once, in a winter blizzard, he was stuck in a village overnight. He thus wove friendships with many peasants through the years and felt like a fish in water among them.

It also happened that while wrapping up the deal on a purchased or sold horse they would make a hearty toast, "l'khayim" [to life] and get a little tipsy, and then for a bed on a shabbes evening stretching out in the straw in the wagon, meanwhile humming a tune from Hillel, or a "y'hi ratzon" [Heb., words from a prayer, "let it be God's will"] from Rosh Khoydesh [the beginning of the Jewish month] prayers, sometimes even turning out a "kebikartel". The sun already having set low, people would run late to light the Sabbath candles, as they say - ; "mit di halobliyes in l'kho doydi" [lit. with the shaft of the cart in the "l'kho doydi" prayer (which is a prayer welcoming the Sabbath). An expression implying that the weeks work hangs over into the Sabbath.].

Sabbath at home, a strong smell of freshly cooked peppered fish, brass candlesticks with burning candles, the kidesh-khalleh [challah/egg bread that is blessed and eaten as part of the Sabbath ritual] covered with a white Sabbath cloth. The wife - ; dressed up, with her prayer book in hand, and the two daughters, like roses - ; all this filled his soul with quaint warmth, a true neshome yesire [lit. an additional soul, which a Jew is said to have (or supposed to have) on the Sabbath].

After prayers truly elevated song left his mouth, real conversation with the angels - ; angels of heaven, angels of peace, who hovered in the space of his home - ; guests, who came to pray with the holy Sabbath.

So it went for years and years. Who knows how much more pleasure from his children and grandchildren might have been his destiny, if not for the unforgiving, murderous hand that cut the life-thread of grandfather.

It has already been over two weeks that it has continued, with an incessant deafening noise, the loud creaking, the steel armored tanks, marked with black gloomy swastikas, holocaust and destruction peer out of the hollow long tubes.

Motorcycles with guns float by with diabolical speed. In them - ; brown figures in steel armored helmets - ; the culture-bearers of Nazi civilization which, like an angry river tore from its shores, pouring with lead and fire and overtaking ever greater areas. The ground shook under the weight of the heavy machines, the air became full of terrible roaring of their motors. Groups of rugged bomber airplanes sow destruction and fire. Without end, cars full of stuffed, self-satisfied soldiers and officers float by - ; armed to their teeth. They drove as if to some happy recreation, a ball, a holiday.

Everything draws to the east, almost without any resistance. No obstacles. The Red Army fled, helpless against the mighty machine, which suddenly, murderously unleashed itself upon with an assault.

Finally the storm is past. Gone onward, far away, leaving garrisons and the new macht [lit. power, i.e., German vermacht] organs here and there. Even Dokshitz had the good fortune to get an SS garrison.

Blunt and arrogant, because of their intoxicating victory, they begin to rule over the subjugate population. One of the methods, the "persuasion" - ; three people are shot openly, after they are forced to dig their own graves.

A hunt for communists commences immediately, Jews and Soviet activists. Khayke Blokh, the older sister of Khane, is called to report to the Gestapo. Her fate is sealed. She was deputized in the city council during the Soviet occupation. She is pregnant, due to give birth any time now.

Deathly fear consumes the house. Their father hitches the horse and wagon and in the dark of night tries to drive his daughter and grandchild to his peasant friends. Perhaps he might succeed in sustaining her, saving her from death.

But the effort is futile. They drive from village to village, from house to house - ; but everywhere the doors are closed. He sets forth money, he is prepared to give all that he has, even his horse and wagon - ; but he cannot find a single volunteer. People help with a groan, with a kind word, but nobody will take the risk.

Broken, they turn to go home.

Not seeing any other way, Khayke decides to present herself to the Gestapo. Khane senses what must happen. She looks at her unlucky sister, tears fill her eyes. How long has it been that Khayke has been so happy about becoming a mother? How much tenderness and love has been awakened in her towards her tiny bit of a child? As a bird spreads its wings - ; so did she sit, bent over the cradle, guarding her new joy, singing sweet lullabies. Now she must leave the child without a breast, without protection. No! This will not happen! I will not allow it! I will replace her - ; Khane told herself. She went to the cradle with determined steps, gently kissed the child and, with the paper in hand, set off in the direction of the Gestapo.

It was a summer day in July. The sun blinded one's eyes with its sharp rays. Khane walked without looking around, as if she was not afraid and did not regret her steps.

The street was empty of people. She walked to the bridge, which divided her birthplace, Slobode from the other part of the shtetl. The Berezine River flowed peacefully east. On both sides, going on foot from the shtetl, the land was covered with a green carpet of grass, softly bending and sprinkled with yellow fuzzy flowers, which opened thanks to the warm sun.

Khane stood still for a while, looking down. Various images from her youth and childhood swam in her thoughts.

There she was, running, a three year old girl, on the same grass with a jump-rope, getting all tangled up and wandering in the smelly tall grass. Now she sees herself bathing with her girlfriends, filling their mouths with water and squirting one another - ; drowning one another. Now she falls into the river with her clothes on, barely crawling out and running to her mother crying.

Wives and their husbands, Jews from the shtetl, stand before her eyes with siddurim [prayer books] in their hands, shaking and swaying their sins out of their pockets.

Yes, Simkhas-Toyre [lit. happiness of the Torah. Jewish holiday, the day closing the feast of Tabernacles, when the last section of the Torah is read in the synagogues]. With a colored flag standing on a desk in the men's synagogue. Her little hands outstretched reaching to give the Torah scroll a kiss.

All seems so distant to her now. Nervous, uncertain, her thin white fingers twisting her long blond braids. She tears herself from the place and goes onward. She knows what she's going to. Now she passes the building that used to house the local chapter of the club where she used to spend evenings and Sabbaths with friends, boys and girls. After studying in the Polish "Povshekhner" school she hankered after a Yiddish/Jewish word, a little Jewish history. Yes, she remembered, what was she called? If memory serves, it was Dina, Rabbi Eliezer's daughter, Bar-Kokhba's bride. When the Romans captured her she was forced to call her beloved from her captor's prison so that he would open the dams of water and thus buy her freedom. She used that fateful moment to strengthen Bar-Kokhba's fighters, calling them revenge, to victory over the enemy, giving her life for the honor of her people. Oh, how much heroism must she have had?

She, though, wanted to live. Life wills itself like that. How much time did she have left?. A white cloud partially covered the sun, a mild breeze stroked her face. She lifted her face, as if awakened from a dream. Opposite her the windows of the Gestapo were already blackened.

*

She turned to the left. A few minutes yet remained in which to enjoy the free air. She breathed deeply, with quick steps went to her onetime school, which was now transformed into a barracks.

There were tall maple trees with white flowers and buzzing bees flew from flower to flower. They were finding sources for their honey collection. She noticed them in particular now. Such small, nothing little beings, attracted her attention. Interesting, when she had learned about them, their love of work, their difficult burden as insects. People are different today. Nobody thinks about the other. She hadn't let anyone support her.. And the child, for what was he guilty?..

With her heart beating, quickly, so as not to be late - ; she opened the door of the division.

*

A tidily furnished room. Folded in a soft armchair near a green desk, in a shiny, pressed, brown uniform with black swastikas on the sleeves, playing with a cigar with pleasure - ; sat a tall, lanky blond SS officer. His shiny boots were stuck out of the other side of the desk. He tapped impatiently with one toe of a boot on the other. He kept picking up the phone receiver, grumbling something short and abrupt into it, accompanying each order with a humble glance at the hanging portrait of the mustached Führer.

-- Oh, such a pretty girl! [in German] - ; he said, with spirit, when Khane stood opposite him.

With a sharp look he measured her, and with false politeness to her he said:

-- I think, that such a young pretty girl, won't want to risk her life and had better give us accurate information. Who? How much? What are your Soviet activist colleagues' plans? You, as the city-deputy must certainly be well informed. Keeping the truth from us makes no sense. Your communists will never return. Our victorious army presses onward, in a short time all of Russia will lay at our feet.

Khane stood still. Her thoughts worked feverishly. This means that he thinks I am Khayke. Do I really have the opportunity to save her, making it possible for her to raise her child? Encouraged by the thought she totally lost her fear, she felt confident.

The officer stood with his feet apart, one hand in his pocket and in the other his cigar. He waited with tension for her to begin to speak.

-- I don't know - ; she answered, indifferently.

-- That is a lie. You know quite a bit and very well. Who are your people? Answer quickly! Well, you are not here on vacation. You are in the SS headquarters, we take advantage of all options to get you to talk. Where are all of your communists hiding?

-- I don't know! -- She repeated.

-- You do know! -- He screamed. His face got red, his cheeks nervously twitched. - ; You will not play games with an SS officer. You cursed Jewess!

His voice got louder and more menacing. The veins on his long throat stuck out, his eyes were slits. As a tiger springs upon its prey he grabbed her by the hair and began throwing her from side to side.

Proudly, with an attentive gaze, she looked at him, answering nothing. Her perseverance agitated him even further.

-- Who are your colleagues? - ; He roared hysterically, and slapped her face with the force of his whole body.

A red stream burst from her nose and got her whole face wet.

Seeing her own blood she got even more resolve - ; not to give herself up. With a mocking look she ordered her persecution and pain.

The telephone rang. An order was requested of him -- The result of the investigation. He ordered her to be thrown in the basement to have time to think.

Pain and misery, angst and anger marked her heart. Hungry and tired. Her feet couldn't stand any longer. Holding herself with both hands against the cold smooth wall, she slid down to the cement floor.

The sun sent its last setting rays through the little grated window, the warm summer day disappeared into a dark night. Dark clouds covered the horizon. No stars, no ray of hope.

Sitting like this her eyelids, as if filled with lead, got heavy and closed themselves.

In the dark unconscious the again saw herself standing in the blooming garden around her home. The flock returns from the fields, it smells of hay and freshly milked milk. A young goat, a white one, approaches the hedge to pluck off some grass, the goat glanced at her. She outstretched her hand - ; the goat ran away scared. Everything began to grow distant, the hedge, the house, father and mother. As if she was looking from far away, as if through a fog, the sunset became a fiery circle, and departed with blinding speed, leaving behind it a desert, veiled in black smoke. It took one's breath away. She turned, wanting to run away. But opposite her flowed a river, raging and frothing, it spurted and boiled, washing away everything in its way. There they push against one another, the fireball and the water. The earth around is seething. It is burned. And here - ; a gush. She was awakened from the world of dreams with cold water, back to bitter reality.

And above in the research room, the forty year old son of a Prussian baron was pacing, the SS officer, who was bestowed with many awards for his longtime Nazi activity - ; would he not be able to break the stubborn will of such a "nothing" Jewish girl? His anxious glances stop at the Führer. It seems that he looks at him with angry suspicion. His eyes get sharper, his brow furrows, and his black mustache thicker and pricklier. The Führer gnashes his teeth, curses and menaces. On this we are stuck? So long in officers training, fed with race theory? Press forward by any means necessary and with any amount of work, forge yourself an iron head and a tiger's heart . You are becoming upset and powerless against a Jewish girl?

Ashamed and guilt ridden he stands opposite the portrait. His entire career is in the balance. He would like to be a conqueror, ruling over broad areas around the Volga, Dnieper, to live in a marble palace. Tens of servants serving him, kneeling and bowing.

His daughter would play piano in a white ball gown. All will marvel at her talent. He would show the aptitudes of the superior race. But in order to achieve this he must earn it!. And here, for several days already, he has been unable to make progress. He cannot allow this. He must get his, he will make all efforts.

-- Quickly! Bring in the Jewess!

*

Therefore Khane was awakened with cold water.

Her knees quivered, her head burned, her mouth chattered and twitched. She was hurt nonstop with all of the hellish methods of the modern Nazi-techniques: with tongs and fire, with lead and barbed wire, her fingers twisted and broken - ; but her spirit was strong and unbroken. She was silent and unrelenting.

When she felt that her hour was near, she began talking. And words crept out of her mouth like snakes, cutting, piercing as if with spears. Fiery sparks flew from her eyes.

-- My colleagues are all those who fight against you. You will not always drink our blood. You will be eternally cursed, you murderer! The revenge against you will be big and terrible. There will be another world - ; and it will bring your punishment, you will be tied to the post, you and your name will be erased from the all names. Your brutal tortures will not scare me, I spit on.

A shot cut off her words.

*

Now, 25 years since then, in the shtetl of Dokshitz - ; a school has been erected in her name. Every morning at roll call, the name Khane Blokh is the first one called. And a chorus of children answers in unison: --

"She fell heroically defending her people and land."

*

Your name, Khane Blokh, will be forever in gold,
Fashioned of sun's rays, in all great days.
You wanted to save a sister and her child:
With your young life and boundless love.
We weep for your youth, when at times
Pain and regret press our hearts
And from the tears, flowers bloom in the valley,
Where birds sing out their song.
With the glow of hatred in the deep blue of your eyes.
The executioner was madly reflected with his sword.
Your eighteen years stood unbending
As black oaks, rooted in the earth.
The enemy did not kill you.
You were not slain, it's a lie!
Your spirit lives and blossoms in full bloom
And escorts and helps us to be victorious.
Your pride sprouts out of every tree
And wafts out of every flower!.
And lights the stars in space,
Shining light upon people everywhere.
Your flesh has certainly long turned to dust
And harsh winds have blown it far away.
Yet all that loves and believes, sings out its pride in you,
Time will never erase the symbol of your courage!

Tzvi Markman (Khatzor)

**Sheynka Markman (Skibin) and Leyb Pollack
in the production of the play "Chasia the Orphan"**

Sheynka Markman

Translated by Ira Lulinski and Aaron Ginsburg

Who in the shtetl did not know Sheynka, the daughter of Mendel & Bayla? She was always full of love for life, energetic, hopeful, and proud even though her luck did not go well.

Her older sister, and her spiritual mentor, Sarah, died at the young age of 28 years. For six weeks, Sheynka, with great trepidation and pain, was constantly with her in the Pinsk Hospital.

Shortly after that she learned of the death of her much beloved brother Velvel, who had, because of his Jewish ideals, deserted the Polish army. He went across the border to the Soviet Union and tragically perished.

The parents were broken; ill and despairing over the heavy blows that befell them, one after the other. Also, they were very poor and in great need. They became entirely forlorn. She, however, did not dwell on the awful things that befell her. In time she found an interest in helping other sufferers and unfortunates. Sometimes she sat for hours and wrote touching letters to relatives in America asking them to come to help their needy ones in difficult times. At night she would often sit by stranger's beds, comforting the sick and easing their pain with a compress on those that were ill and she applied medicated plasters to a burning forehead and administered drops at the prescribed time. And thus gave the family a little relief.

For Passover, she went to work baking matzahs for the poor. Everything fell into place-people would work half the night kneading, rolling, perforating and baking. For a wedding of a poor couple she helped with cooking, baking, arranging flowers and havdalahs, singing, dancing, so that the simcha would be greater. Often she would go around with a basket and gather things for a poor family for Shabbos.

Her greatest joy was to act in the theater. Her earnings went for different purposes: caring for the sick, the Yiddish school, the Tarbut school, Karen Kayemas, Hachnassas Kallah. She did not spare any effort and she learned all the roles every month. If it was a new play she would take on the most difficult roles. The more tragic the role-the better the outcome. I remember when she played the role of "Khasia the Orphan", the teacher from the Tarbut School, Mr. Nielevitsky, asked her, "Where does your dramatic talent come from?" She smilingly replied, "In life I act, on the stage I live."

Not infrequently it would happen that a wandering troupe would come into the shtetl and need her help. Would she take a role? She would fulfill their request. In many instances she was offered a material reward. But she would not accept it. She only agreed to take a few tickets for her friends, those who couldn't go the theater because of a lack of means.

Thus she lived, with the people and for the people.

When the horrible catastrophe came, her pain was more difficult than others. As a political opponent, her husband, Itzhak Skibin, was among the first of the people who were shot in the Holocaust. She was left in great distress with two small children.

When, with all the Jews from the shtetl, she walked on her final road. she went down with her niece from Budeslav in her arms, and sang this old song:

> Oh world, oh world, don't worry,.
> Your day will come,
> Not forever will be your sorrow,
> Not forever will be your affliction!

These sentences should act as a monument for her life, her deeds and death.

Zvi Markman/Hatzor

The Heroic Sixteen Year Old Partisan, Iziye Katzovitsh

I never imagined that I would have to write the life history of my brother and pass on the story of his heroic death, in his best thriving years, to future generations. His glorious battle and his death in a link in the chain of suffering and valor of the *Dokshitz* Jews.

In the year 1927, the dentist, *Manya* and her husband *Shmuel Katzovitsh* had cause to celebrate: They gave birth to their second son - - *Yitzkhok*, called *Iziye* by his parents and friends.

A few winters and summers flew by. *Iziye* is already attending synagogue with his father. In *Dokshitz* it was called the "*Starosiyeler Shul* [synagogue]," in which *Reb Leyb*, may his memory be a blessing, prayed - - *Der Dokshitzer Rebbi* [The Great *Dokshitz* Rabbi]. He, like all who prayed, prayed with great enthusiasm and purpose - - they didn't even know that they had already fulfilled their obligation.

Many years have passed - - and until now the melody still rings in my ears. Somehow I remember the terror and tragedy of "*Yizkor*" [memorial prayer remembering family members who are deceased]. Young fathers and sons leave the synagogue. Their close relatives are still living, their time has not yet come.

The 16 Year Old Partisan Iziye Katzovitsh

Iziye is growing bigger and bigger. This is how it was with the gang: The first sign, if you can climb 2-3 steps on the ladder to the attic of the synagogue. The sexton, *Reb Alter* kept a few brooms, *skhakh* for *sukkes*, and several broken benches and lecterns up there, which have been meant to be fixed for years already.

Understand that a father did not allow one to crawl up there, but a few of the gang already climbed up and a few Bar-Mitzvah youth stand below encouraging.

You have really made it, you become a guy [colloquial, you are "cool"], if your father lets you carry the *tallis* [prayer shawl] bag home from *shul* [synagogue]. The *tallis* bag is gentle-soft, a gold Star-of-David embroidered on it. It has a familiar smell, comfortable - - as you carry it home, held with both hands...

The second stage is winter. That is when one displays expertise in sledding. There are two slippery spots: 1) On *Dzike* Street, a long sloping path, which winds from *Yehuda-Peysakh's* store past *Mendl Zalke's* house. 2) From the *beys-hamidrash*, near the *Starosiyeli* and *Ladi* synagogues. *Peyse* the shoemaker who lives there, is always angry that it is so icy, and that he might, heavens forbid, fall, while fetching water. Therefore, he often spreads ash on the area — small medicine against the plague.

When winter departs, icicles hang from the roofs, long, like *tsitsis, lehavdil* [Heb. Lit. to differentiate. Used when listing or comparing the profane and holy.], and when a deft youth hits them with a snowball they fall down with a melodic sound.

Later, water streams in all the streets, all in one direction, to the *Berezine* River, which empties into the *Dnieper*.

When the snow is gone, one can play in nut or buttons.

Nuts do not have any special history. They can be divided into Turkish, walnuts, common ones, twins and whistlers — those are the ones that have a little hole and you can whistle with them.

Buttons do have a history, because they were cut off of old winter clothes: the buttons are scratched and crunched. How often they were played with, in the cold in the wind, in the rain. But the children pay no mind. If at all — they are interested in metal or tin buttons. They are not so good to play with, but every child had several of these in his pocket in reserve. There are even some really old ones, rusty "*Nikolikes* [playful diminutive of the Czar Nicholas' name]," with two-headed eagles on them [the two headed eagle was a symbol of the Russian Empire and its Royal House]. You could also find a tin button with a star — a reminder of the first Bolsheviks. New Buttons with an Eagle wearing a crown — a brother who served in the Polish army, coming home on leave brought this. Buttons with a helmet and two hatchets — a symbol of the *Dokshitz* firefighters. The last phase presented buttons with lilies from *HaShomer HaTza'ir*, from *Beitar* (with menorah's). These were our buttons.

Every time had its own Zionist parties in *Dokshitz*. There were often disagreements, but there were no great rifts.

Iziye studies in the "*Tarbut*" school and later in the Polish "*Povshechne*" school. After classes he would go to *Yisroel-Aaron's kheyder*. He was also a member of *HaShomer HaTza'ir*. In *kheyder* he studied *Tanakh*, in "*Povshechne*" he often heard, "*Zjidi do Palestini*" and in the *HaShomer HaTza'ir* group — about Israel, kibbutz's, pioneers, Trumpledor. Who knows if the decision to fight for Jewish honor to the end didn't fall into his head even then... *Tov lamut b'ad ameynu, b'ad artzeynu* [Heb. It is good to die for our nation, for our land]... and also Samson's last cry: "*Tamut nafshi im Plishtim*" [Heb. Let me die with the Philistines]...

Later we will see what kind of strength and courage a little boy from the *shtetl Dokshitz* showed.

The wheels of history ran on their way. The German-Polish war broke out. The Poles were sweet to the Jews — real saccharine. In their stride — the Russians occupied *Dokshitz*. After two short years, the Germans came into the *shtetl*.

Shortly before the outbreak of the war my family moved to *Gluboke*, where our father was from. Both *shtetls* shared the same fate. In *Gluboke*, as in *Dokshitz*, the Jews were confined in a crowded ghetto. The mass murders of Jews began immediately. In order to achieve speed and efficiency the Germans assigned a *Judenrat* with Jewish police. In the end of it all, their fate was the same as everyone's, but in the beginning they thought that they were "one-of-us" in the eyes of the Germans. They solicited various things for the enemy: boots, leather, gold, and dollars. They also organized our going to compulsory work duty.

We spoke about the *Judenrat*, and I remember *Iziye's* timely judgment well: "The *Judenrat* are not friends of the Germans, except in that they fulfill the enemy's orders, they are suspect and we should beware of them."

A wave of pogroms swept over all the *shtetls*. My family managed to avoid the brunt of the first pogrom in *Gluboke*. In the second — it was ruined.

On the 20th of July 1942 the Germans demanded that all Jews stand in the *mark-platz* [marketplace]. I, along with a few other people, was held by the Germans outside of the ghetto, working in a printing shop.

At two o'clock *Iziye* came and told me that mother said: "Run, my child, try to save yourself." He didn't go to the "*platz*," but ran away from the ghetto into the field, lay in the rye and came to me at work via back roads.

In the evening we returned to our ghetto dwelling. It was empty. Mother and father were already gone.

The weather on the day of the slaughter was nice and sunny; therefore it was even more terrible to hear the sound of rifles and machine guns in the middle of the bright day. In contrast, the Christian side of the city was quiet. But they were also scared to leave their homes and see the terrible picture of murder...

At three o'clock in the afternoon we suddenly heard resounding footsteps. A police officer was going home. He didn't carry his rifle over his shoulder, rather in his hand, obviously just having finished his "work." His name was

Molinovsky, yemakh-shemoy vezikhroy [may his name and remembrance be erased].

At dusk we returned to the ghetto. I remember two Christian women walking. One of them had a son in the police. She asked the other woman: "Did you take anything?" Apparently she had been robbing the empty dwellings. They saw us at this point and got a little flustered. But one of them, with real impudence, asked: "Why weren't you there?" Upon seeing the wild hatred one could immediately feel their insecurity and it became easier. May they tremble from our revenge, may it not be borne by them easily.

Immediately after this we decided to run away from *Gluboke*.

But where does one get weapons?

We tried to speak with other guys, but it seems that the rumor spread to the Jewish police.

Once when *Iziye* fell asleep in a stall, exhausted from work, some police came in and searched around his bed and under his head. Understand that there was no weapon to find, but they took a little money. They were not happy. The police called us a "The *Dokshitzers*." They claimed that we would be the ruin of the ghetto.

Around then the refugees from *Dokshitz* arrived in the ghetto. *Tuviye-Shloyme Varfman* (currently in Acco) was among them. We were very happy to meet one of our own. He told us how he lived for ten days with his brother near *Kruleveshtshine*, on an island, in the middle of mud.

While on the island he met a young Pole, *Lukhovski*, who lived on a farm on the *Krulevishtshine-Dokshitz* road, and worked as a brigadier fixing the roads. He could acquire some weaponry for a small price. As it is known, the Germans were initially good to the Poles, later they changed their politics and oppressed and persecuted them. This Christian lived some 20-25 kilometers from *Gluboke*.

After the pogrom the Germans gave an order to enclose the ghetto in a boarded fence. During the day we searched for a spot where the boards were loosely nailed. We stood and talked until the moment of action when we pushed two boards until they gave way. We replaced the boards and left two stones as a landmark.

At night we escaped with *Tuviye-Shloyme* through the prepared opening and ran through the fields towards the *Kruleveshtshine* road. We had to cross the train tracks twice, which were guarded by the Germans and police. We lay in the dark by the tracks and at the moment when we saw that there were no guards there — we quickly ran across.

It took days for us to reach the familiar Christian. We went into the stable and waited for one of them to come. The peasant woman came right in, she was frightened, but *Tuviye* calmed her down, telling her that her son knows about us. She brought us coffee.

In the evening the son brought a rifle, bullets, and a revolver with nine bullets.

At night we returned with our weapons. It was easier travelling this time. Our luck was that it was a very dark night, but before *Gluboke* we stumbled upon a thorny hedge — a long and tall one, around the rye storehouse from the earlier "*Zagotzerno*" near the train station. Obviously, we avoided and walked around the obstacle more than a good kilometer.

This was my first night walk in a field. My friend used to travel a lot by night before the war, which helped us to orient ourselves on the roads. Also, I traveled to *Krulevshtshine* and *Dokshitz* twice during my studies in *Gluboke*. Then it was just a plain walk. Working in the printing shop I had the opportunity to look at a map of the *Gluboke* district and I studied it well. This was very useful to me later.

We brought the weapons into the ghetto and hid them. We decided to escape in the coming days. We worked for the Germans and searched out opportunities to steal a little ammunition.

In the end of the spring, 1942, two young men came to the *shtetl*: *Friedman* from *Dolhinev* and the second guy from *Postav*. They were already partisans. It was known in the ghetto that we had weapons and people told the two guests. They agreed to take us along, but had other demands. They did not want to take *Iziye* along because he was little. I told them that I would not go without him. That same night, a group of ten of us left the ghetto.

Little *Iziye* ended up being a real guy among guys. He was well liked by the other partisans for his boldness and fairness.

Winter, 1943. The partisan movement in White Russia had grown and strengthened. The detachment we were in was over in the *Minsk* area. We were put in a new "Bolshevik Detachment," near *Leavisk*. There were 6 Jews in the detachment. *Iziye* was already 16 years old and counted as an adult.

Near *Leavisk* was the German garrison, "*Kosina*." The leader of the "Bolshevik" decided to defeat the garrison. *Iziye* left with the detachment. A few went as an ambush and a few went to attack the garrison. *Iziye* was asked to go with the ambush, but he refused and went with the attackers. The partisans were successful in taking over the garrison. *Iziye* ended up as a heroic youth. During the march to and from "*Kosina*," it turned out that the partisans discovered, but were not going to carry the heavy machine gun, "*Pulimyot*." It's really a good name, "*Pulimyot*, [Russian lit. machine gun]" but nobody wanted to carry the 24 kilo weapon. *Iziye* took the gun by himself and carried it a big piece of the way. He told me later: "I decided to show them. They always laugh at the Jews. They are older than I and are really soldiers, but I have to show them what a Jew really is. Secondly, we really needed the *Pulimyot*.

That's how *Iziye* became a "*Pulimyotshik* [machine gunner]" in the detachment. The comrades began to treat him with respect. They called him "*Yuzik*," which was easier for them to say.

Little *Yuzik* participated in many operations on trains and bridges.

At the end of July 1944, when the Germans felt their end was near, they gathered all of their military from the villages circling the *Leavisk* forest and wanted to put an end to the partisans.

The partisans knew of this immediately and got a small group together in the forest to hit the bases and the main strength went to the *Berezine* marshes. The goal was: to tear out of the German ring at night.

Izik asked to come to me, but he wasn't allowed. They went some 15 kilometers in the forest — quietly and without notice. On the way from *Pleshtenitz* to *Leavisk* there was a group of Germans hiding that opened fire on the detachment. *Izik* was able to get close to the Germans and open fire on them harshly. The partisans were encouraged and crossed over the main road. Many ran away and were lost. The remaining way was even more difficult. They walked between German positions, without food, without water and without leadership.

That is how they arrived at the *Berezine* marshes near *Ziembin*.

In *Ziembin* there mer many Germans and police. They guarded the important bridge over the *Berezine*. Around *Ziembin* were large forests and marshes. This was the general headquarters of the partisan group in the *Barisov-Minsk* district. The Germans bombed the forests and took control over every bridge and road. The partisans lost one another. The commanders and those who had horses continued to tear through.

The fascists made the circle smaller. *Izik's* hut was soaked in mud and torn apart. He was left barefoot, torn and hungry. German groups searched and rampaged through the forest.

Suddenly, he saw a group of Germans. He hid behind a trunk of a chopped tree. The end was near. "*Tamut nafshi im Plishtim*" — he reminded himself [see top of page 162 for translation].

The Germans decided to take him alive, in order to torture him. They neared and he let them. He tore the ring out of the grenade I had given and put on him. When they came to put their dirty hands on him a terrible blast was heard. *Iziye's* grenade exploded, killing him dead and of the lowlife — the three Germans were killed. The others crawled away. They had never seen such a boy, they will remember him. The Germans retreated and did not want to move further forward.

A couple of hours later partisans passed by and saw the corpse of the heroic *Yuzik*. A dead German lay next to him...

He remained in the forest and it is not known where his bones are, he never came to be buried in Israel.

May his memory remain forever with the *Dokshitz landslayt* [citizens of Dokshitz].

Dov Katsovitsh / Petakh-Tikva

Loyal to the End...
(In Memory of *Izzi Plavnik*)
Dov Katsovitsh/Petakh-Tikva

Izzi's father, *Nokhum*, came to *Dokshitz* before the outbreak of the First World War. The Czarist government expelled him and his family from the village of *Kreytzi*, where they had lived for generations. *Reb Nokhum* married *Mashe Gulkovitsh* in *Dokshitz*. They had three children.

As a village-Jew and someone who knew the area and forests well, he did some work in the pitch business (extracting tar and turpentine from tree stumps). He was beloved by the peasants, and the *shtetl*-Jews [i.e., from bigger town, town-folk] treated him as one of their own, even though he was a village Jew. *Reb Nokhum* was a proud man, a businessman and beloved by all. One could hear stories without end, at night in his home about the once-upon-a-time village life of working the ground, about the fields, the forests and rivers...

This affected young *Izzi*'s spirit, which already understood that the road back to the Polish, the White Russian village — was closed. And he began on his path of envisioning a life in a Jewish village, in the Land of Israel. It is true that the country is still desolate and almost completely unsettled, but he can see how trees are being felled here, how forests are being cleared, new settlements are being created. So, why could it not be possible to achieve this in one's own land?

He studies in the *Tarbut* school, one year — in the "*Povshekhne*" school (folk-school). He would get a beating from Christian children, but he would return the hits — then they would stop bothering him.

He marches into *HaShomer HaTza'ir*, the strongest youth organization in the *shtetl*. He becomes one of the most loyal and committed members. Ignoring his mother's opposition, he travels to do *Hakhshara* in *Tshenstokhov*. He knows that the *Hakhshara* builds him a path to make *aliya* to Israel and realizes his dream.

The outbreak of the war in September 1939 greets him in *Tshenstokhov*. After much peril and difficult experiences he finally returned to *Dokshitz*. A week after his return home the Soviet army arrived in the *shtetl*. Jews breathed a little easier that the German terror had passed and that the antisemitic Poles would now not dare to raise their heads. The socialist groups were enthused and even grabbed along those youth who were Zionistically inclined. *Izzi*, however, correctly assessed the situation and knew the relationship of the new government to his movement and to the Zionist idea at all.

...September 1939. A heavy, cold autumn rain falls. From *Borisov* Street there are long winding rows of tired and wet Red Army soldiers. They are suddenly at the market and further, all the way to *Glubok* Street. It is 5 in the morning. Several older Jews, with their *tallis* bags under their arms, let themselves into the *beys-hamidrash*. They stand a while watching the marching soldiers. From time to time a Jew stands under a roof overhang to get out of the rain. There they are still marching on the "foot-bridge." People hurry to prayers.

Every once in a while they see a young boy cut across the road, in the free space between one military unit and the other. One can clearly sense that he is holding something hidden under his jacket. The Jews recognize him. That is *Izzi Plavnik*. Yesterday evening he was in the *HaShomer HaTza'ir* meeting place, he saw the library books scattered on the floor, the newspaper torn off the wall, the "local" looked like another pogrom had hit. Just the flag, the blue and white one with the symbol of *HaShomer HaTza'ir* on it, was tied with red ribbons to the pole. *Izzi* didn't think long. First of all — save the flag. He came to the meeting place at dawn, untied the cloth, lay it close to his heart so the flag would be warm, so it wouldn't feel alone in the demolished place. Now he runs with it, cutting across the path between two troops and knocks on the door of his friend *Henekh Frankfurt*, on *Poltotzk* Street. The *Frankfurts* are still sleeping. He knocks on the window. *Henekh* comes out and the two lay the fan in a tin container and bury it in the garden — until better times.

Until today the flag of *HaShomer HaTza'ir* lies buried in the *Dokshitz* ground, as a witness and symbol of young dreams and of *Izzi's* idealism, represented by the flag.

Loyalty to Jewish national values and to his people showed itself first after the German murderers entered *Dokshitz*. The living hell for the Jewish people began in the year 1941: ghetto, *Judenrat*, tributes, murders, mass-murders. *Izzi's* family was killed. He understands that he can no longer stay in the ghetto. He was able to escape into the forest — and there he led a life of a fighter in a partisan detachment. In a tragic fight with the Germans *Izzi* fell, weapons in hand.

His life and battle serve as a sign and wonder for future generations.

Dov Katsovitsh/Petakh-Tikva

The Frankfort Family

My Family

I left Dokshitz 34 years ago when I was 20 years old. I vividly recall how sad I was when I took leave of my family and my mother who was bedridden because of her illness.

The memories of what the town looked like and its personalities have become vague, but whenever I meet people from Dokshitz I remember the personalities because of their nicknames ("Tsunamen") which existed in almost every family. The events in my little town that occurred when I was young are deeply engraved on my memory. Most of the memories are enveloped in sorrow and but a few offer some consolation.

I would like to use this opportunity to write about my mother and my relatives who perished together with the other victims of the town. I don't remember my father, he passed away at the outbreak of World War I, when I was only two years old.

My mother was left with 7 children, two sons and five daughters. I can see her standing before me, burdened by the need to feed us and take care of all our needs. I don't understand how she managed to carry out her many tasks. My mother was a perfect housewife, managed a shop and even found time for charity. A "Yiddische Mame" - ; in the full sense of the word. Very orthodox and strict about the rules of kashrut. During religious holidays she looked glamorous when she blessed her seven children. We would sit around the long table, the candlesticks shining and a festive meal spread out in front of us. We sinned, according to mother's standards, but she pretended not to notice. She did not say a word, for during the religious holidays we would sit around the table with her and she considered this her achievement.

As the youngest daughter my mother showered me with love and affection. There was a very strong bond between us and I too loved her very much. When I joined "Hehalutz" differences of opinion arose for my mother, like many other parents, tried to prevent me from going to Eretz Jisrael. It was hard for my mother to accept the fact that I would not be at her side when she would be old. Nevertheless, she continued to treat me with devotion. In the end she even accepted my aliyah and helped to prepare it. My mother died from heart disease at the Dokshitz ghetto.

Chaim, my oldest brother, was the central figure among the children in the family. At an early age he undertook the burden of looking after the family. As he was a businessman and gifted accountant he was very popular in the business life of our town. He set up a cooperative together with five wealthy men - ; a trading house that supplied merchandise to the grocers in the town and its vicinity. He would bring his earnings home and his family was his first priority. He wanted to take care of us, his sisters. Although he was strict we showed him respect. Chaim married late and although he had to take care of his own household he continued to take care of us.

His wife Lisa from Gleboki was a kindhearted and sensitive woman. She had excellent relations with us. Chaim too tried to prevent our aliya to Israel, but in the end he understood that the future of our town did not look very bright and he saw the dark clouds casting their shadow over the Jews in Poland and agreed to let me go. Chaim even financed the cost of my trip to Eretz Jisrael.

During the Russian occupation, at the outbreak of the War, Chaim moved with his family to another town where he was employed as an accountant and here he, his wife and son and daughter came to their bitter end.

Moshe Aharon was 5 years younger than Chaim and had a different character. He did not have a talent for business like Chaim. On the other hand, he was kind and easygoing, liked by the whole family. He joined the cooperative and it was his task to find buyers outside. He was successful in this due to his pleasant nature. He was a Zionist and absorbed the "haskalah" spirit blowing through the Jewish world. His circle of friends was also Zionists and our home became a center for this circle. Although they did not plan to implement their ideas they contributed much to spread the love of Zion.

Moshe Aharon married Lea, the daughter of Ascher Shapira, and left home. When I came to Israel he had two sons. When the Russians entered Dokshitz my brother suffered tremendously. He found it difficult to get used to physical labor, but the Russians forced him to do so in order to earn a living. He fell ill with diabetics and died at the Dokshitz ghetto together with the members of his family.

The Kopelovitch Family

My sister Sara Esther was the tragic figure of our family. She did not find her place among the many children. She excelled at her studies and was among the few to graduate. As it was impossible to be accepted at the university in Poland, she tried to move to Russia, but failed. Life in the little town was too narrow-minded for her and this caused her permanent bitterness. She was a cause of concern to her mother. My good brothers made many efforts to find a suitable husband for her. She married and moved to Vilna, but did not find her luck there either. During the economic crisis in Poland in the thirties Esther-Sara lost her money and lived in poverty. She, her husband Yehuda and their two little sons died in the Vilna ghetto.

Four sisters remain of the Kopelowitz family. I built my home at Ein Harod with my childhood friend, one of Dokshitz's best young men, Chaim Solovey-Zamiri. In 1965 in the month of Nissan, Chaim passed away. My sister Bella found her home at kibbutz Yifat, together with her family, and she knew many ups and downs during her 37 years in Israel.

Rosa, our oldest sister, arrived in Israel 6 years ago with her son Shimon, the only one left of her family. She lost her husband, a son and a daughter in Karasna. The Nazis murdered them all. The 2 sons of my sister Ida, who is in

South Africa with her husband Miram Poliak, came to Israel with their families. We hope that their parents too will come to Israel together with their son Joseph, and that the remaining members of the Kopelowitz family will no longer have to bear the sufferings of the Diaspora.

Nessia Zamiri (Kopelowitz)/ Ein Harod (Ihud)

In Memory of My Brother Isha'ayahu
By Doba and Esther Sossman

Our parents, may they rest in peace, Baruch and Faighe Sossman were killed about two weeks before Passover, just then, when the slaughter did not as yet begin.

It was midnight. We were at grandfather's house, where we then resided. We heard knocks on the door. Five gentiles walked in, residents of our town, friends from school. They ordered us to stand facing the wall, and tied the hands of father and mother, my brother Isha'ayahu, Ziama Lifshitz and his wife Duba, Isha'ayahu's wife Shifra and the three-months-old twins. My father lost control but my mother began to beg and to try to convince them. They then released me and my sister-in-law with the babies. They took my brother, my husband and his parents, all still tied up, out of the house and dragged them to the pit. My brother and my husband, Ziama managed to escape, and my husband was killed later during the second slaughter.

I will now describe how we hid: In my grandfather's house, where we lived at the time of the second slaughter, we were nine persons: My sister Duba, my sister-in-law Riva, Isha'ayahu and his wife Shifra, Mula Kuggel, his wife and two sons and me. Isha'ayahu built three hiding places there. It was not possible to stand inside them, but only to sit.

At four o'clock in the morning Isha'ayahu stepped outside and saw that the ghetto was surrounded. Somehow, we managed to descend to the hideout but without the children. At that time the Germans were already inside the house. Through the slits in the floor beams we saw how the Germans tore the babies apart holding their legs. In the hideout we remained nine persons. We stayed there ten days without food nor drink. We smeared our lips with our own urine. We had only the air that came through the tiny slits of the hideout and we began to swell up. We then decided to leave the place for we knew we could take it no longer under any circumstances.

Yishayahu Sussman, May the Lord Revenge His Blood

Isha'ayahu took it upon himself to lead us, since he had been a soldier and also knew the area well. On his order we all crawled out in a straight line up to Gordon's pool. From there we walked to the house of a gentile of the Karpovka village (4 k"m from the town) who knew us. The gentile took us to his barn and brought us food but ordered us to leave the following day.

Swollen and barefoot we continued towards Gleboki, where we still had family and so did my brother's wife. The gentile promised us that Gleboki was still full of Jews and that word of slaughter had not yet reached the town. My brother led us to Gleboki through the Krolevshtchisna road, through the fields. On the way, we had to cross the railroad tracks where a gentile with his son noticed us and notified the Germans. Not far from there was a bushy grove and when we reached it, we were shot at. It was 22:00. We laid there until 02:00 and when the shooting ceased, we crawled 3kms further. I could see shepherds herding their flock to pasture. We had no other choice, we approached them and said nothing. They, also said nothing and among them we entered Gleboki.

The loss of parents, brothers and sister; the screaming of the babies, only three months into this world, never ceased to ring in our heads. My brother raves like a madman, never finding rest. The slaughter has begun again. They called the younger ones to come to work and then they shot everyone. Isha'ayahu screams: "I want revenge and I'll have it!"

Yes, thirty years have passed since my brother Isha'ayahu died a hero's death, in order to avenge. He was my younger brother, born in 1910, a handsome man and well developed in all areas. when the slaughter began in town, my brother's burning desire was to avenge the spilt blood of the Jews, the innocent blood of many children, his own, his parents, brothers and sister.

He fought like a lion in his cage to find a way for revenge. During the last slaughter in Dokshitz, we stayed alive thanks to Isha'ayahu who took us under German fire, in an abominable way, to the Gleboki ghetto. Isha'ayahu immediately set out to leave for the forests. He joined a group of young men and left us to wait until he could come and get us. His plans did not work. He returned barefoot and empty handed. The Russian partisans stole everything he had and sent him back. Alas, he did not give up. His will to avenge had not left him. He organized a group of 12 men and planned to take more Jews out of the ghetto. After wandering from place to place, Isha'ayahu met a group of partisans from the brigade named after Medvedev, near Miadel. There were gentile partisans from our area there and they had known Isha'ayahu before. They presented him to the commander of the brigade and recommended him.

The commander gave him a mission. If he succeeded, he and the women with him would join the partisans. He was told, as well, that a few comrades have already been sent on this same mission - none came back. Isha'ayahu is not frightened. There is nothing to lose, and he accepts the mission.

The plan is: To reach the train station of Molodetchna, find out from the train conductors which trains pass there and when. Not far from the station there was an ammunition dump with rifles and grenades. The order is to blow up the train and bring the weapons. The time: Ten days. Isha'ayahu sets out. Ten days pass and my brother does not return. We are forced to leave the place. The next day - the eleventh - my brother arrives. He has done it. Two trains with soldiers and guns, headed for the front, were blown. Isha'ayahu and his peers killed the guards and brought the weapons for the partisans. Thus, his will was done -blood for blood.

Isha'auahu became the commander of a special group. He was joined by another hero - Yodel Yassin, born in the village of Tamilovitch, near Dokshitz. These two never missed an attack against the Germans. Every night they would burn the German camp in the vicinity. The militias and the Germans in the area lived in fear. Komulka, the commander in Dokshitz, put a price on their heads, saying he wants Isha'ayahyu Sossman dead or alive - only then will he have quiet. After every operation Isha'ayahu would come back happy and singing. We asked him: "What is this happiness?" He then answered: "I'm avenging! My life is short". The night before he was killed his group had performed an important operation. In the morning, the commander wanted to know how the operation affected the populace and they left to check. Isha'ayahu wanted to join them and they wouldn't let him. "Rest", they said,

"More work in the evening". Isha'ayahu refused. He joined them on his mare. When they reached the village of Trestchanitza, he falls into a trap. A battle ensues and my brother Isha'ayahu gives his life as a hero.

He was buried with much magnificence. The partisans mentioned his courageous acts. He lays on a hill near the village of Trestchanitza, near Dokshitz. His friend Yodel Yassin fought to the very end and was killed.

Mula Kuggel never even left the hideout. His life ended there - waiting. His wife and children came out with us but went another way and did not come back.

Dobe and Esther Sossman
Written down by Yossef Shapiro, Ra'anana, Israel

In Memory of Moshele Kuzinitz, Son of Pivel and Dishka Kuzinitz

By Shoshana Melzer Vinboim, Beit Hannania

He was only 19 when he gave his life in a battle near Warsaw, and still so fond of life. Moshale was a studious fellow, serious and shy. Speaking with the girls in his class, he was embarrassed and would blush. We all loved him as a loyal peer and friend. He was a loved and loving son. He could not stay in the rear while bloody and bitter battles took place at the front lines. He wanted to take an active part in the front. Moshale studied in the "Tarbut" school and managed to study for two years in a "Yeshiva" in Vilna before the Red-Army arrived. With the founding of the Yiddish school he entered the ninth grade with the rest of his age group. Together, we finished the eleventh grade, already in the midst of Siberia, in a Kolchoz near Nuvosibirsk... The conditions were unbearable. We had no warm clothing and no warm footwear. We would take turns using a coat and a pair of boots. Often, we would be undernourished and life was harsh. Moshale, nevertheless, succeeded in finishing his studies with distinction.

Two years after public school, he constantly wrote to the military school, trying to be accepted, but being part of a persecuted people, he was turned down again and again. This saddened him tremendously. "How could I sit still without avenging my people's shame and suffering?" He would say. As he had no alternative, he accepted this fact that so grieved him. He applied to a higher academic school and was accepted, but this was not to be. The situation in the front lines worsened. The Red-Army began mobilizing westwards and it was then that Moshale received his much yearned for draft notice. After three months of basic training, he was sent to the front lines. He did not attain victory, his life was extinguished in battle. His parents and the holders of his memory mourned his death. Blessed be his memory!

Shoshana (Melzer) Vinboim/ Beit Hannania, Israel

In Memory Of My Brother Zosia

As a matter of fact I find it overwhelming to write about the great love I felt for my little town of Dokshitz. It is not a matter of longingly remembering its landscape and fields, for they are not ours - ; but it is a longing for the simple people of Israel amongst whom we lived. It was a town with a few hundred families, which without government help managed to set up a rich network of exemplary educational and welfare institutions. I think of my brother Zosia, devoted to his family, who from the age of fifteen had to make a living. He used to tell me: "what a pity that I remained at home while I was fed up with the little town." I, the youngest of the family, enjoyed too much freedom and I often realized how sorry my brother was not to be able to join the movement, and that his days were without meaning. Whenever I think of my brother I remember his kindness and simplicity. I remember something that happened after the war of 1917.

One day, my brother went to the market and came home carrying a handsome boy on his shoulders who had lost both his legs. My brother said he had found him begging at the market and struck up a conversation with him. He soon found out that the boy had been wounded in the war and lost both his legs. Zosia carried him to our home and lovingly took care of him for two weeks. My brother would work and save money in order to buy artificial limbs for the invalid. He then sent him by train to the nearest town with a letter of recommendation to the Rabbi. He considered this a natural thing to do.

Because of his kindness he refused to abandon our parents and go to Israel. He claimed this would be an escape and that we should help our parents overcome their difficulties. He often supported me when I went to the movement and my parents did not agree to this.

I remember your letters, always in the same style. You would ask me for help, for the ground was burning under your feet. And I wanted so much to help, but was unable to do so. You had a wife and children and according to your letters you were happy in the midst of your family. You refused to run away and be saved and you took the road, together with your family, from which there was no return. I see you in front of me, but your face is not clear, for my eyes are filled with tears.

Malka Abel/ Ein Shemer

In Memory of my Brother Zosia

About a Dokshitzer Family

Dokshitz, the town where I was born - ; I can see it now just as I left it 25 years ago, when I went on hachshara (training).

Dokshitz was a typical little Jewish town, surrounded by gentile villages which lent it its special character. The low houses were lined up along 4 main streets from which alleys emanated. The majority of the town's inhabitants were engaged in trade and crafts and barely made a living.

The social life of the older generation focused on four synagogues at a place called "Schulhoif". On the other hand, the majority of the young belonged to various youth movements such as: "Hashomer Hatza'ir", "Hehalutz", "Beitar" etc. There were two schools: "Tarbut" and the Polish elementary school. In order to continue studies one had to go to Vilna, Gleboki or other places. Our home, which I fondly remember, stood on Koschiosko street (Gleboki-Gasse) no. 6. Boys and girls used to spend the greater part of their free time at our home.

We were a family of 6: grandfather Abraham, grandmother Zlata, mother Hava-Rahel and the three children - ; Joseph, Moshike and Sonike.

All the inhabitants of the little town knew each other and it sufficed to say that I was "Avremel Shimon's ainekel" (the grandson of Avremel Shimon) for everyone to know immediately to whom I belonged. We did not know our father for he died when we were still very young. My grandfather supported the family and in due time my brother Mosheke helped him.

The life of the Jews in the little town was not easy. My mother also took an active part in supporting the family and assisted in trade - ; the main income was from the sale of linen and grain.

My mother, a very lively and smart woman, petite and full of energy, managed the household and educated her children. She had a very difficult life, but she knew how to overcome and always found moments of joy and mainly the joy of bringing us up and teaching us. Her joy was even greater when her children were cited as a good example to others. This is what gave her strength and satisfaction in her miserable life.

My brother Joseph was a gifted student, clever but physically weak. He very much wanted to continue his studies, but our limited possibilities forced him to quit. He taught himself, had a broad knowledge and was called "a walking encyclopedia". He studied accountancy and became an expert in his profession. It was his fervent wish to go to Israel and join kibbutz Ein Shemer. He spent two years on hachshara, but did not go on aliya for he did not manage to obtain a "Certifikat".

Once my second brother Moshe finished elementary school he became a great help to my grandfather. His sense of business and excellence were enough for him to start work. Moshe was a healthy boy, handsome and kindhearted. He belonged to the "Hashomer Hatzair" movement but the burden of making a living did not allow him to leave home. In due course he married Mattele Halbanowitz, and they built a home. They had a son, but I did not get to know him. I hoped all this time that he managed to escape the Nazi beast, but to date nothing has been heard of him.

I remember my mother's last words before I left for Israel: "Sonika, I always want to be near you and live together with you. Remember this - ; as the parents of Mendel Markman - ; to live at a kibbutz. . ." She was very much attracted by kibbutz life and was sure that in the future we would live and work together in Israel.

It is with deep sadness that I heard what happened to our little town and to my dear family in the war. I can imagine those terrible last days they passed, the suffering of the innocent victims. My relatives are deeply engraved on my memory as if they are still with me today. I must mention a number of families to whom our home was a second home: the Rozov family (Der Hittelmacher), Liba Rozov who I loved so much. The parents of Batia and Shaul Markman, the Solovey family, Kamankowitz who lived opposite us and the Kloner family and many others who are no longer with us today. Blessed be their memory.

Sonia Komankowitz/ kibbutz Beit Zera

The Tschuchman Family

In Their Memory

Left: Lipeh Levitan as a HaTzofim (Scouts) Commander in Israel
Right: Joseph Kamenkovitz, one of the first theorists and directors of HaShomer HaTsair, killed in the Ghetto

Left: David Kleiner, son of Tombstone Engraver. One of the first pioneers, fell defending Jerusalem in the unrest of 1936-1939
Right: Lipeh Levitan under arrest in the Acco (Acre) Prison

Left: Isaac Abelson, one of the first Marxists, tragically killed in the Soviet Union
Right: Monya Shapiro, the male nurse

Left: Alter Yofeh, artillery-man in Red Army during World War II
Right: Zalman Ori Tsiklin in the Polish Army

Left: Doctor Fanya Scheinman who injected her two children with morphine in order to prevent their murder at the hands of the Germans.
Right: Grandfather and Grandson, Israel ----, Died in the Ghetto

Left: Chaya Reyzl Ziskind, Died in the Ghetto
Right: Nachman Reuven Markman

Left: Zusia Musin and his Family, of Blessed Memory
Right: Shaul Ziskind (the Butcher) and his wife, both killed in the Ghetto

Simch Lenkin (center) in the Red Army

The Schultz Family

The Zalman-Natan Pollack Family

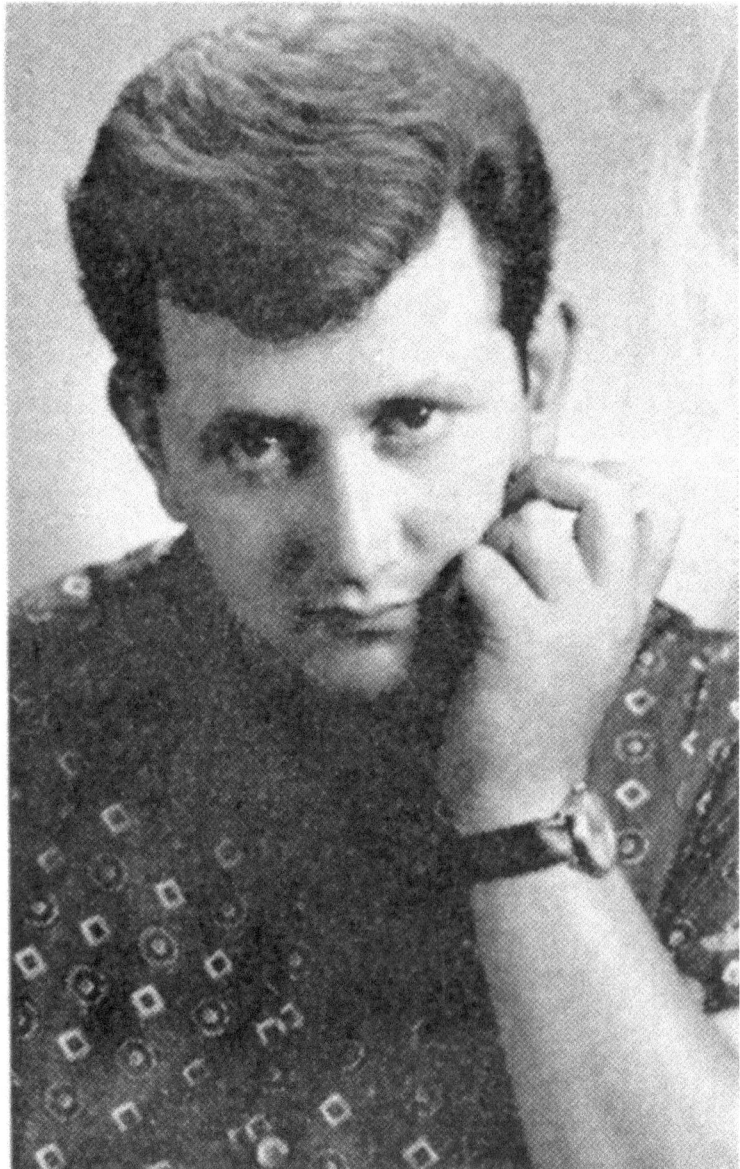

**Zeev Zeitlin, Son of Tzvi and Grandson of Velvel from Dokshitz,
whose name he bears (Velvel in Yiddish is Ze'ev in Hebrew)**

The young man grew up in Israel, Learned to be a pilot, yet worked in the ground troups of the Air Force. Musically talented he founded his own band. In the 6 Day War (1967) he served in the communications force as a communication commander. Months after his release from the Israeli Defense Forces, he met his end in a fatal traffic accident en route to Haifa. May His Memory be Blessed.

Yosef Shloma Levitan, of Blessed Memory.
A distinguished citizen of Dokshitz. Died at an old age in Petach-Tikva, Israel on the 27th day of Kislev, 1970. May His Memory be Blessed.

Chapter 3

Parafianov

The Town of Parafianov

By Haya Foss (Markman) and Moshe Mor (Markman)

Parafianow was a small town and it's train station serviced also the town of Dokschitz, 10 km away. It's houses were spread over a wide area, on both sides of the railway. One the one side were the residential houses, and on the other, the railroad buildings, the police and the clerks. The municipal authorities and the Catholic church were situated about 2 km from Parafianow, in the village of Parafianow. In the village itself, lived the manor lord, to whom belonged most of the lands around and also a liquor factory. There were about 130 families in the town, half of them Jewish. In the 1920s up to the depression in 1929, most Jews worked in the lumber trade and all adjacent jobs. Two big saw mills were built in town where the work was done at the maximum rate, in order to keep up with demand, and trains fully loaded with lumber would leave the town often. The Jews had a large number of stores and also a monopoly on the butcher shops. The authorities hurt the Jews by transferring the right to sell meat to the Poles. The rural population and the non-Jewish part of town was mostly Bialorussian (White Russians), the minority of which, were Catholic. They talked in their own language and were not fond of the Polish authorities, which tried to bring people from far away places in Poland to influence the population's attitude toward the regime and to promote antisemitism. Normally, the Jews and gentiles had a good relationship. The Christians would take part in the Jewish festivals and cultural events. The fire department building served as a theater and festivity hall for the entire populace. Jews and Christians work together under the same roof and in relative quiet. The town boasted one synagogue and its two main streets were populated mainly by Jews. Up to the year 1937, Elchanan ben David Markman performed as cantor (leader in prayer), circumciser, and officiant. He also served as slaughterer in the rural area and in the nearby town of Krolevshtchizna. In 1937 a young rabbi took his place. The town Jews held Zionist notions. Adults and young men busied themselves with the national funds, and not a house was to be found that did not give generously to this sublime cause. The youngsters studied in a public Polish school and in the afternoons went to the Hebrew school, under teachers brought to town especially for this purpose. The younger generation was active in the pioneer movements in town, and were raised on the values of "Hashomer Hazair". Comrads went to pioneer training organized by "Hachalutz" and "Hashomer

Hazair" movements. Thanks to this, some of the town people reached Israel before the war.

A Group of Keren Kayemet in Parafianov (dated June 21, 1939)
Bottom left in white pants: Szloma Gejdenson, father of the former United States Congressman Sam Gejdenson

This handful of boys organized plays in Hebrew and raised a library which included some of the best Hebrew and Yiddish literature. The library was in the slaughterer's house and was handled by his sons and daughters. These same youngsters organized a string ensemble, which played in the cultural activities of the youth and with the cooperation of the town's people. After the treaty signed by Russia and Germany in 1939, the Russians entered Parafianow. As a result of the change of regimes, a major change took place in the town and in the nearby area. Jews were given responsible duties. A Jew was put at the head of the municipal council - Aharon Levitan. The religious services were not abolished by the new authorities. The postal communication between the town's people and their relatives in Israel was maintained. Some of the youth returning to the town after it's high school studies, began studying in the municipal schools in the area, to obtain a general and professional education.

The "Tarbut" (Culture) School in Parafianov (1932)

With the coming of the Hitlarian army to the area in 1941, the town became a nightmare. The first thing the Germans did when they entered the town was hang Aharon Levitan, the local council chief. The Jews were, in fact, allowed to remain in their homes but the Germans took some of them to work and forced the Jews to pay them different sums of money every once in a while. In October the Germans concentrated all the Jews in a ghetto, which was a side street in town, and put seven, even ten families into a small house. The Jews worked communally and lived in atrocious conditions. They youth was drafted to do cleaning and field work. The Nazis began to persecute the children and demanded they be employed doing manual labour, knitting and doing needle work for the Germans. Thanks to this, the children stayed with their parents. The guarding of the ghetto was put in the hands of local youth. They organized a head count every day. Making false promises and lying, the Germans demanded more and more produce and monies, as a condition to the Jews' remaining in town.

On May 31, 1942, at 4 a.m.. the Germans, with the help of the local police and dogs, surrounded the ghetto. The Jews were ordered to dress in their finest clothes and to take all their money as they were being transferred to a nearby town for work. On the way they were taken to the fire department building, where they were undressed and beaten to shock them. In their underclothes they were led along the long main street, the gentiles looking from all sides. Thus they were taken close to a small village, where a big pit, destined to be their grave, was dug. They were lined up in a row and shot mercilessly. The pit was covered with earth and plaster and eyewitnesses told that for a long time the earth would rise from the river of blood flooding the surrounding area. A number of young men managed to escape in different ways from the murderers and ran to the nearby forest. Some joined the partisans, and some were handed to the police by the local farmers and were killed by the Nazis. The slaughterer's daughter, Haya Markman, visited the town coming back from Russia, and saw the unknown common grave. Only the fact that the place is higher than its surroundings led to the discovery of the grave in the wide field. The Jewish possessions were taken by the local populace. Some of the houses are in the hands of the Russian authorities. There once was a small town, Jews had inhabited it for generations, made a living, and led an extensively developed cultural life in it, until the Nazi murderers arrived. Now there is not one Jew left.

Trip of the students and graduates of the Hebrew School in Parafianov (1937)

My Shtetl Parafianov

Shmuel (Ben-Refoel) Markman
Until the Holocaust

Our *shtetl* had about 150 Jewish families. It was not a poor *shtetl*. Most of the Jews were traders of small goods, had businesses, where one could purchase anything. There were also tradesmen who worked the land and people with free professions.

There was a *beys-midrash* in the *shtetl*, a ritual slaughterer, *kheyders* [traditional Jewish one-room schools], where the children studied with learned and qualified teachers. Our youth was active in various organizations: the *hashomer hatza'ir*, *hekhalutz*, *mizrakhi*. There was a *g'milus khasidim* office [charitable organization] which supported those in need with an interest free loan.

The youth in *Parafianov* was connected with the neighborhood *shtetls* of *Dokhshitz* and *Gluboki*. We used to joint activities, parties and lectures.

We were a big family: my parents, six brothers and two sisters. The siblings had 16 of their own children. I also had uncles and aunts with their children, which numbered some 70 people — almost half a *shtetl*...

I want to write the names of my brothers and sisters and their families here, perhaps someone of them survived.

My eldest brother was called *Yoysef*, his wife — *Khane*. They had three children: *Berl*, *Khashke* and *Nekhomiye*.

A second brother: *Yekhezkel*, his wife *Nekhome* and their children *Roza*, *Sholem-Ber*, *Reuven* and *Mirl*.

Moyshe and *Rokhl Markman* and their three children: *Zelig*, *Avroml* and *Khaye*.

Yankev and *Zisele Markman*.

My sister *Sheyne*, her husband *Hirshl Rafalson* and her daughter *Khaye*.

Soreh and *Yoyne Kuladitzki* with their daughter *Rokhl*, *Khaye* and *Mirl*.

The "HeChalutz HaTzair"(The Young Pioneers) in Parafianov (1926)

League for a Working Israel (1932)

Activists from the Zionist Movement and the Keren Kayemet

The "Ra'ananut" (Vivacity) Group of HaShomar HaTzair (1930)
On the Banner: The "Ra'ananut" (Vivacity) Group of HaShomar HaTzair in Parafianov - Troup B

The Holocaust

In the second week of the German-Russian war, the Germans came into our *shtetl*. The first sacrifice was an uncle of mine, *Ahron Levitan*, whom they shot.

Later the ghetto was created, people rushed around for different jobs, always asking for contributions, money, gold, furs — until they took everything from us.

The first *aktziye* [German action] was on May 30, 1942. Early on Sabbath morning they gathered everyone in the ghetto, everyone in one place, by the firehouse. They tore everything off of everyone, beat everyone and marched them to a mass grave.

I took an opportunity and ran towards the forest. They wounded my hand, but I was able to escape to the forest. I met another three Jews there, also wounded, who were able to escape. They were my two cousins *Khonekh* and *Shloyme Levitan* and *Reuven*. A couple of weeks later the Germans caught *Shloyme* and *Reuven* and hanged them.

Khonekh and I later met up with others who were saved from Parafianov: the brothers, Yaakov and Yitzkhok Kastrol, Motl Bigun, Rokhl and Moyshe As.

We thought only of how to take revenge. The first case was when we met a group of Partisans in the forest and asked them to help us. They gave us three grenades. *Khonekh, Motl* and I went to *Parafianov* and threw two grenades into the house of the commander of the train station. He was the boss of the whole *shtetl*. He lived there together with his soldiers. However the luck of those nefarious people had it that they did not suffer greatly from this. But they lived in fear the whole time after.

Afterwards we joined the Partisans from the "*Zshelezniak*" area and from *Batkes*. We gave them various bits of information, carried out Partisan assignments, like destroying train tracks, bridges, setting mines on the highways, because we knew all the roads and areas well. We hid not far from *Parafianov* in the forest. Later on we were gathered into the Partisan lines and I fought with weapons in hand. But no matter how much we did, it was all too little...

Chapter 4
Holocaust and Heroism

In the Dokshitz Ghetto
By Yosef Shapiro / Ra'anana

Sand pit near the Jewish Cemetery, where the Jews of Dokshitz and the surrounding towns were shot and buried

Until September 1939, Dokshitz numbered some 9,000 citizens, of which there were approximately 4,000 Jews. The main businesses of our brethren sons of Israel were: merchants, retailers, a small number of manual laborers and farmers.

Jewish children in Dokshitz got their education in the Tarbut school and in kheyders. The youth and younger generation could thank the big folk-library (5,000 books) for their additional education.

The shtetl also established an independent free-loan treasury in each of its six beys-midrashes, in addition to other benevolent institutions that helped in times of need. In terms of parties and society, our youth participated with great satisfaction in all of the then existing Zionist youth organizations, as well as in the illegal Communist party. Officially, there was no existing "Bund" in Dokshitz.

The Soviets Occupy the Shtetl

Just after Rosh Hashonah, September 1939, on Sunday night just before Monday, when the Jews of Dokshitz lay in a deep sleep, a large number of Russian tanks, tore into the shtetl with tremendous noise and uproar. Not one shot was fired.

The Red Army's march through the shtetl lasted a whole week, day and night.

The Jews took the occupation by the Soviets indifferently. Only some people with certain fear. It wasn't with our will and agreement. However, it was better than the Germans. All of the Jews were in agreement about this. Although we were isolated from the rest of the world, news of what was happening to Jews in the Polish areas, what the Germans had undertaken, reached us. They suffered there from humiliation, hunger and deadly terror.

With the occupation of the Red Army, Dokshitz was sealed as a part of the Soviet White Russian Republic. All Zionist groups and parties had shut themselves down anyway. The philanthropic institutions also stopped their activities and the library closed. The beys-midrashes, in contrast, remained active.

The Russians sent ten Jewish families into deep Russia with the beginning of the repatriation of Gev. When Polish citizens from the Soviet Union returned in 1946, six Jewish families from Dokshitz returned. I do not know about the fate of the other four.

The German Bombardments

On the 22nd of June, 1941, on a nice sunny early morning, when the Dokshitz sky was a dazzling clear blue, the birds were singing happily and free, flying back and forth to their nests, singing praise to the creator of the world, the German silver "Meserschmidt"-bird suddenly appeared and began bombarding the shtetl in a barbaric way, sowing death and destruction. They especially destroyed Jewish streets and paths, Jewish houses with all their belongings.

There was great panic and confusion. The bombardment came unexpectedly. People started to run, but didn't know to where. Some ran with bags, some with children in their arms, some dragged the sick with them, blind, paralyzed. People ran from place to place, between burning houses, falling walls and ruins. Calls for help, screams, cries, moans and sighs of the wounded carried above the shtetl. The voices went up to the heart of the heavens and tore at one's heart.

A red flaming cover, full of smoke-clouds quickly consumed the first briefly blue sky. Our shtetl became tragic and unhappy all at once. Many were killed and many were left without a roof over their heads. Many families ran away to Russia.

In the beginning of July, in early morning hours, the German occupation of the city began. Well scrubbed and closely shaven, the Wermacht soldiers marched through Dolgenev and Gluboke streets.

Hopelessness and Fury

The German army entered Dokshitz on July 3, 1941. They immediately demolished the beys-misdrashes and burned the Torah scrolls and the holy books, destroyed the cemetery, chopped down the trees and broke the tombstones.

The first Jewish sacrifice during the German's occupation was Raphoel Markman (Otrubker). The murderers shot him. The second sacrifice was Dovid Mushin, from Keyder Street. There was a great fear of being shot or stabbed to death for nothing. People were afraid to go out into the streets. At night people didn't light any lights. Whoever had a little food at home for their family was happy. Most people just went hungry. There was nothing available.

During all of this, the Christian underworld grouped itself around the Germans. They immediately pointed out to the Germans which Jews had worked with the Russians. They were immediately shot, their homes destroyed in pogrom style and robbed. Itshe, the shoemaker from the synagogue courtyard was also shot in this way.

The Germans chose a Polish city-commander (Komulka), with very special broad proxy to torture Jews.

They instituted compulsory work only for Jews. People were murderously beaten at work. The most humiliating work was sought out for them, for example, cleaning the most horrible filth just with one's hands.

In the month of Elul [the 12th month in the Jewish calendar, usually in early autumn], on a Saturday morning, the German murderers gathered some

50 Jews from the shtetl and took them to a dug out pit, where a young boy, who had committed some small sin, was shot before their eyes in order to instill fear in everyone.

On a given Sunday they took some 30 men to work. I was also in that group. It was by the church on Borisov Street. We were forced to clean and scrape manure with our bare hands and we were beaten with rubber sticks until we bled. We returned home slaughtered and swollen.

While the men were away at work the German murderers plundered and robbed the homes. Destroying everything they could get their hands on. They took whatever they liked from the homes.

The Germans empowered the peasants with the right to point out to them whatever Jew had dealt with them dishonestly in trade, or issues of money. When a peasant pointed out such a Jew -- he was immediately shot.

On Rosh Hashone evening, 1941, the Germans took 8 Jews, pointed out by the peasants, to the Jewish cemetery where they were forced to dig graves with their hands. After this difficult forced labor, the Germans shot them. I saw the entire thing from a distance with my own eyes from the other side of the field, from Eliyahu Ritman's barn.

The girl, Leahke Blokh ["ke" on name is a diminutive of name Leah] was among those shot. She handled herself heroically. Before being shot she shouted at the Germans:

"Do not think, you murderers-gangsters, that in spilling my innocent blood and that of my brothers, that you will win the war. No! Our spilled blood will take revenge upon you!"

The Creation of the Judenrat

Daily Jewish life became more difficult and less bearable. A Jew's life was wantonly at the mercy of the Germans and Poles. They could do whatever they wanted with a Jew. There was no one to whom one could complain.

In time there was also a Judenrat established by the Germans, (Yakov Botvinik, Zelig Levitan, Dovid Varfman, Shloyme Pliskin, Moyshe-Yakov Feygin) to help them carry out their anti-Jewish policies. Thereafter a law was established that Jews must wear yellow patches. The punishment for not wearing this mark of shame was death.

On the first day of Rosh Hashone we, the young men, went to work, as on every day. The older Jews gathered in private homes to pray. The German and Polish police knew of this, came immediately, beat the worshipers, demolished the homes.

On the second day of Rosh Hashone the Germans did a search of the horses that were there. They took their handkerchief's and looked for dust on the horses. Bitterness and pain came to he whose horse had a bit of dust on it. Many lay ill for several days from those beatings.

On the morning after Rosh Hashone there was a decree that before two days are over everyone must bring all valuable items, such as: gold, silver, money, copper, brass, lead, jewelry, clothing, textiles and furs. Such decrees were not seldom. And all of this under the threat of the death penalty.

On a certain Friday gendarmes appeared in the shtetl. Not knowing the significance of this, people interpreted it differently. People waited fearfully for something to happen. Happily it was a false alarm.

Once, a German officer came through and gave some sort of an order. The work, however, did not turn out as he had wished and he called the head of the Judenrat and beat him hard until he bled.

In the Ghetto

In November, 1941, the order was given to create a ghetto. The plan for the ghetto was decided. All had to be done at a quick pace. It is a given that the ghetto was created quickly and diligently by Jewish workers.

The ghetto and its area encompassed the area from the bridge to Gluboke Street, to the side of the synagogue courtyard: Polotzk Street, from the side of the synagogue courtyard, until Gordon's beer-house and the Berezine River; the marketplace, from the side of the synagogue courtyard.

The ghetto area became enclosed by boards, fences and barbed wire. Only a small entrance was left through Bod Street [the bath street]. A border checkpoint was established across the width of the street, before the entrance. On one side of the street was a German guard post and on the other side -- a Jewish guard post to monitor that nobody took anything out of the ghetto, nor brought in any products. In the exit tower there was only a German watchguard.

One Sabbath morning, if I am not mistaken it was November 30, 1941, it was decreed that everyone should pack their things and gather in the marketplace. Only one half hour was given to do this.

Exactly on time, all of the Jews gathered in the marketplace. All of the Jewish possessions were immediately taken. The inventory was taken to Lapute Court, a little bit also to Bloy Court.

After that there was another decree that within three hours the Jews must go through the entire ghetto and literally straighten it. Obviously, no real order could be made in such a short time period. The ghetto was full of pits and mounds, crooked streets, clumsy doorways, dirty and muddy. One would need several thousand people for such a situation. The narrowness -- great and unbearable. This was on a cold winter day. The frost burned, snow poured down, terrible winds blew. Cold and hunger sat in one's bones.

All kinds of illnesses quickly began to spread through the ghetto, one just had to breathe -- and one lay dead. There was a great shortage of medical supplies, no medical aid.

This caused the Judenrat to appeal to the German authorities for some intervention. They told the authorities that it could not go on like this anymore. It is impossible to remain in such a small space. There is no food, no medical supplies. Filth everywhere which drives the spread of various illnesses. Furthermore, this is not ideal for the Germans because epidemics spread not only among Jews, but they can also spread to them.

The Germans agreed to enlarge the ghetto, adding Keydarum Street until the end of Dolganov Street.

It actually got a little roomier, but we paid with many sacrifices.

The ghetto exit was only for the workers, nobody else was allowed to leave. Because of this life in the ghetto became more difficult, everyone felt the tremendous shortage of foodstuff. It grew more expensive. The food rations for a person was 200 grams of bread. One received nothing besides the bread. One was shot for bringing in the smallest little item into the ghetto. The control at the ghetto tower was very tight.

Even if someone were to succeed in bringing something into the ghetto, it was very difficult to get. Everything was very expensive. No one received any money, but rather traded in clothing or other things. Not everyone had something to trade.

In addition to all of this, the Germans demanded something new each day.

One Tuesday evening, before Purim, the Germans surrounded the ghetto. It was a very dark night. It was very difficult to hide or run away. The Germans were able to grab some 65 Jews and send them away. At around 5 o'clock in the morning we heard a loud shooting from Piask pit, where we used to take sand (Borisov Street).

In an announcement by the Germans it was decreed: shooting of anyone associated with the partisans. There were no partisans then, no contacts -- certainly not. But the long announcement by the Germans reminded us youth, gave us the idea, that we must escape to the forests to fight the Germans from there, with all of our ability to take revenge for our killed brothers and sisters, close and related.

We Decide to Escape the Ghetto

The question of leaving the ghetto was not an easy one. First of all, where does one acquire weapons? Secondly, how does one get oneself out of the ghetto? We (Yoysef Kremer, Leybe Tiles, Libkin, Tsiklin and the writer of these lines) discussed these issues very seriously and decided to wait until there was some sort of upset, some happening, in the ghetto, in order to use the opportunity and to leave.

In the meanwhile, at night, our group got to work, we dug a deep and wide tunnel behind the beys midrash. We took axes, knives, iron bars, products and other things that one needs for the road.

With time we established contact with the surrounding peasants from whom we hoped we might get some help getting to the forests.

Life in the ghetto, in the meantime, went on as before: difficult work, hunger, cold and always the fear of death.

One Sunday, a day before Lag Ba'Omer 1942, it was announce that there would be a count and it is forbidden to leave the ghetto. According to the count there were 2516 Jews in the ghetto at that time. We understood that something would happen after the count.

At eight o'clock the following morning the ghetto was surrounded with a tight watch inside and outside. The Germans and their assistants entered the ghetto and started grabbing people -- whoever they could grab.

Taking advantage of the tumult that was created a few friends gathered in the tunnel that we had dug. Two friends (Aron Kagan and Khayim Lipshitz) were sent to the peasants with whom we had established contact. Alas, they were killed in executing this mission.

Looking out of the bunker we could see the Germans grabbing mostly children, little and big and throwing them on wagons, like dead one on top of the other. Many children suffocated right there.

The Germans took about 650 Jews. They were immediately transported to the Folks-Hoyz [lit. folk-house, public/community house] on Borisov Street. They freed approximately 200 Jews there and told them to go home. They had German work cards. 450 Jews were shot.

In a couple of hours a group of Jews came to us and called us to go help bury the dead. They told us that after the aktsiye [action/campaign] the ghetto would be made smaller because the peasants intervened claiming that they want their areas, which were taken when the ghetto was enlarged, returned to them.

Our plan to leave the ghetto was met with several difficulties from the side of the Jews in the ghetto proper. They didn't believe us --- and it ended up that we would wait for another opportunity.

Meanwhile, many Jews organized their own hiding places. In the course of the campaigns it became clear that whoever could hide himself has a chance of saving himself.

130 Were Saved

The first liquidation of a Jewish population in the ghettos in the Vilna area took place in Dokshitz.

From very accurate information from the Dokshitz Jewish community, 130 people remained living. 110 of them were able to evacuate when the Red Army left, when Germany attacked Russian on June 22, 1941. 20 people stayed alive in various partisan groups.

In the beginning of 1946 the refugees saw to it that the Jewish cemetery and the big mass grave near it, where some 10,000 sacrifices were buried, not only Jews but people from other communities as well, should be appropriately marked.

The Holocaust in Town
by Mordechai Warfman

June 1941. The Germans have arrived in our town. The ghetto was created and the Nazi conquerors appointed a "Judenrat" (a Jewish council) and a Jewish police whose job it was to implement the Nazi orders and to be responsible for the Jewish acts. They had to supply man power from among the Jews, according to a quota set beforehand. The overcrowding in the ghetto was unbearable. We lived three or four families in a small apartment. The first "Action" in our town took place in "Hol Hamoed" of Passover in 1942. Despite the fact that part of the ghetto residents were executed, life went on as usual, as if nothing had happened. Two of the townsmen, Arie Lifshitz and Pesach Velble, were found dead in the synagogue, as the Germans did not have time to take them. A day after Lag Baomer (33 of the Omer), the second "Action" took place. A considerable part of the town's Jews were exterminated in this "Action". The Germans demanded a hundred young healthy men for work from the Jewish police. I was among the hundred chosen. The Germans led us to the Polish school and ordered us to run and sing. The soldiers beat us with sticks until we bled. At noon we were sent back to work. The third "Action" occurred immediately after "Shavuot". This was the last "Action" which was supposed to completely exterminate the whole Jewish population of Dokschitz. Many Jews tried to escape this bitter end by hiding in sewers or bunkers. My uncle and I hid in a bunker during ten days. At night we would leave to search for food. A day before I escaped, I heard screaming from the house next door. It was the house of Nahman Zalkind and his daughter Masha Kosowsky. Nahman Zalkind, his daughter Masha Kosovsky and her children - the elder daughter, Riva Zlate and the son Jacob were taken brutaly by the Nazies. The son Leibel was in German captivity from 1939 and nothing is known of him to this day. The youngest daughter, Libe Lea survived and lives in Israel. That night, my uncle and I escaped and crossed, on our way, the Berezina river. Under German fire, we managed to escape and began looking for partisan units. We finally found a partisan unit and joined it, fighting between the years 1942 and 1944. I remember the attack we effectuated before the arrival of the Red-Army in June of 1944. The Germans ran for their lives. We set up an ambush their path and succeeded in killing 200 of them and also imprisoned many. When we were near Polotsk, Malnikov headed the partisan unit of which I was part. Later, Alchziov was appointed in his place.

On June 28, 1944 we succeeded in contacting the Red-Army. They let us join their ranks after letting us rest for a month. I was sent to the Minsk area where I was given an artillery course which lasted two months. After successfully passing the course, I was sent to the Visla area, about 30 km from Warsaw. Toward the middle of January 1945 we opened an all out attack. We advanced all the way to the Oder river and made camp in its vicinity for two weeks until the bridges were built. We crossed it under the cover of darkness and arrived all the way in Berlin where we fought bitter battles in the streets. After the war I remained in the regular army for another year and then returned to Russia, from which I moved to Poland, where I stayed a few months and came to Israel.

A Partisan's Story

By Boris Kozinitz, Dokshitz-Tel-Aviv

I was born in 1919 in Dokshitz, a small town near Vilna. In 1931 I finished my studies in the "Tarbut" school and in 1934 entered a Polish school. I was later an apprentice at a tailor shop. In 1941 I was drafted to the Red Army and was stationed in the town of Zelba, near Volkovisk, close to the German border.

With first light on June 22, 1941, the Germans crossed the border and invaded the Soviet Union. Our regiment retreated with fright towards Baranovitch, but retreating, we avoided the cities already taken by the German tanks. We turned to the Minsk road, between Mir and Stolpzi. Here, we were overtaken by the Germans. We - my friend Molly Wand, two soldiers from the Red Army and I, managed to escape from the road and slip to the forests.

After a half-day in the forest we found out that Minsk had fallen in the hands of the Germans. For two days we hid in the forest but our hunger had become oppressive, so I went by myself to look for food. I reached a Polish village where I was fed generously by a Polish farmer who even filled my bags with food for my friends in the forest. The farmers told us that the Germans announced to the villagers that from now on they could make use of all the property left by the Soviets at their withdrawal (meaning the lands of the Kolchozs, the Sovchozs and all the materials in them).

Back in the forest I told my friends that we were surrounded. They suggested giving ourselves up to the Germans of our own free will but I was adamantly opposed. I decided, on my own, to reach my hometown which was 400 km away. My decision influenced that of my friends, who did not want to join me but decided to stay in the forest. I parted from my friends heartily and made my way again to that village where generous farmers supplied me with civilian clothes and food.

As the Germans opened up the Soviet camps and jails, the roads were filled with political prisoners. This helped me present myself as a "released political prisoner" and using secondary roads I turned towards Molodetchna. The first town in my way was Ivinitz. The town resembled a ghost town. Its Jews locked themselves and dared not go outside. A Jew whom I stumbled upon explained that looking for relatives in this town was useless; it would be better to leave soon since danger was lurking ahead. Due to lack of choice, I left Ivinitz and on my way to Molodetchna I slept that night in a pigsty in a field. No farmer would let me enter his home. The Germans had warned in a special announcement that prisoners of war - Red Army soldiers or Jews, should not be housed.

Before arriving in Molodetchna it was hinted to me that my shaved head could arouse German suspicion, since every man whose head is shaved is sent to P.O.W. camp. With a farmer leading his cows, I managed to get to town. Another Jew told me that the Germans were treating the Jews brutally, forcing them to do hard work and with bare hands - without equipment - they are forced to fix the roads. I realized that this town would not be a good hiding place, not even for a short while, and turned toward the town Stary-Vileika, where my brother Jacob lived, but reaching his house was impossible. He lived close to the rail way station and at the time the non-Jewish residents of the town were busy pillaging train carts full of sugar and liquor which were left behind by the Russians. The streets were swarming with drunkards. In spite of everything I succeeded in reaching the place and found out that my brother and his wife, Hasia, escaped to Russia.

I kept wandering. I spent the night at the attic of a woman who worked as a cleaning lady with the N.K.V.D. There was no order in the town so I could still rest my head someplace. She led me up to the attic and I was fast asleep. In the middle of the night I heard some poles breaking into the woman's house to search it. They even reached the attic but luckily, I was not discovered as I hid under the hay.

In the morning, I was told by the woman that a Jew was just shot to death for refusing to give up his bicycle.

At nightfall I arrived in Dolginov, which I found in utter confusion. I spent the night with my relatives, the Mirkens, and at dawn continued to Dokshitz.

My Homecoming

I arrived in Dokshitz on the 29th or 30th of June in 1941. Notices were posted on the streets telling all former soldiers to present themselves at the German headquarters. Thanks to my ragged farmer's cloths, I was not recognized. I entered the house of my relatives who immediately sent word to my parents. My father, Mendel, promptly arrived and took me home where I hid for many days.

The Germans forced the Jews to do dirty hard labor. Later the Jews were sent to help the farmers at their tasks. Nothing was received in exchange for this labor.

The first two victims of the Germans were Musin, a deranged man, and Markman, who was shot to death in his home. In July, the decree to wear the yellow patch, was made public.

In those days I turned to the community to sign up for work. The workers were concentrated every morning and in small groups were sent to work or to temporary camps. The discipline in the camps was extremely strict. When Zalman Raskind was a few minutes late for work, he was ordered to crawl on all four and a German soldier flogged him twenty-five times. We watched, suffered and kept quiet as we saw the strong and healthy Zalman Raskind shiver with pain at every lashing. In our hearts we swore revenge and little did we imagine that in a short while most of the town Jews would not be among the living.

The Germans began choosing the craftsmen from the group of workers. I was sent to cloths workshop, and with its primitive equipment we worked for the army. On this work, was my fate dependent during the horrible times of the Nazi occupation. A local authority was appointed in Dokshitz. As head-council, the Germans appointed the so called "quiet" Pole, Kovalsky; As chief of police - Komolka, who was a master sergeant in the Polish army. He was born in Poznan but spoke German. He collected twenty-five policemen such as himself: The brothers Winitch, the brothers Litvin, Yochniewitch, Taragonsky etc. In their brutal and cruel treatment of the Jews they surpassed even their German masters. Komolka used to be a prisoner of the Soviets but in their haste they did not take him with them. The Germans released him and now he served them loyally. In 1951 Komolka was caught and hanged after a trial in Poznan.

As "mayor" was appointed Spitchonk, who hid the Jewish family, the Kramers (now in the U.S.A.). This man perished as a result of a partisan grenade.

From Germany arrived the "hangmen": Hartman, whom I worked for Until the "final liquidation", and his helpers: Ungerman, Dimenovsky, Strathoff and a few "unterams".

When the Gestapo arrived the first thing done by it was "taking care" of the Jews who were active under Russian rule: Gronam Kloft, Abraham Levitan, Zalman Tzicklin and others. After four days of torture they were taken outside of town where they were shot to death, their grave unknown until today.

The Germans allowed the second group of victims: Israel Freedman, Hana Bloch, Razel Freedman and others to be buried in a common grave. This happened in the month of August in 1941. It was then that we began to receive news of mass killings of Jews in neighboring towns like Berezino and Begomel. In these murders took part the aforementioned policemen who were so good at their job that some of them were promoted.

The terrible danger awaiting the Jewish population slowly seeped through into our consciousness. With Hartman's permission I began sewing at home. My payment was bread rolls, sometimes a loaf of bread, a steak or a bit of tobacco. Despite the rumors and news of mass killings of Jews, we still insisted on disillusioning ourselves that this was the fate only of the Jews living in the east, in the territory under Soviet rule.

Already was noticed a shortage of foodstuffs although a veritable hunger was yet to come. The Jewish children were unable to renew their studies in the schools for these were shut down at German orders. Also, praying in synagogues and houses of the Lord on new-year's-day was forbidden. Only in Yom Kippur, after chief Komulka was bribed with money and a new suit, were we allowed to pray in a remote house. however, already early in the morning, during the hour of "shaharit" policemen showed up, which he himself sent, and dispersed the faithful.

In the period between June and the holidays, we were made to pay every two weeks different payments- in Zloty, in Dollars, in gold or in shoes and furs .

The Ghetto in Dokshitz

In September 1941 the area commissioner made public an order to set up a ghetto in Dokshitz. The ghetto area began from the synagogue yard and included some adjacent alleys and part of the main street, Kostiushko.

On a Saturday all Jews were ordered to move into the ghetto within two hours and to take with them anything that can be loaded on a hand-wagon. Once again, the Jews needed to bribe the enforcers of the decree so as to lengthen the time allocated to the transfer to the ghetto. As our house was to be found inside the area allotted to the ghetto, we were spared the burden of transfer. However, in our house settled four other families. The Judenrat, set up immediately after the German conquest was moved to the ghetto as well. The Judenrat people did all in their power to help and make things easier. In fact, they did manage to reopen the synagogue and set up a clinic. At first, only one nurse was employed - Sonia Want. Later worked there also the doctor Shim'on Gleichenhous, a native of Dokshitz, having spent most of his years in soviet Russia and managing a field hospital in Vilna. Running from the Germans, the man hid with his relatives in Dokshitz.

All experts working for the Germans received permits (Sheinen) to perform their work. My father and I received schänen as well in order to sew their cloths.

Hunger creeped in on the 3000 souls residing in the ghetto. Not even the 300 gram bread - per - person was given out regularly and often was given very late. If not for the large number of craftsmen and men employed at the camps that were able to leave the ghetto on a daily basis and buy or exchange valuables for food, many a person would have died.

In Passover Taf shin beit (1942) rumors reached us saying that in all towns east of Dokshitz: Dolginov, Olchanovitch and Butzlav within Polish territory there were no Jews left. This was a project called "judenfrei" by the Nazis. Fear and horror took their hold on the Jews at the face of extermination, the fate of the Jews of the aforementioned towns.

The First Pogrom

The first pogrom took place in April, 1942. The local police, without help from the Germans, barged into the ghetto and began to rage and take vengence upon the Jews from the days of Polish or Soviet rule. Stumbling upon a Jew they would arrest him; others were simply taken from their homes. Among them were my uncle, Zalman Freiman, and his wife, Pesia, who ran away from their home seeking refuge in ours. The woman alone managed to escape while my uncle was caught.

Early the next morning a group of youngsters were ordered by policemen to deepen the hole from which mainly sand was taken out, and which was found in the vicinity of the Jewish cemetery. Now, the arrested Jews were led there and shot. The murder was witnessed by many Christian habitants who were there at the time. We, too, in the ghetto heard clearly echoes of many shots and the single shots finishing off the wounded. The group of youngsters which had dug the grave was sent back to the ghetto. With my uncle Zalman, caught and killed, were murdered our neighbors: Katzovitch, Friedman, Sossman, Bloch and others. It should be noted that some of the Judednrat did not take part in this murder, and did not help local police in the arrest of the Jews. After this pogrom many began building hideouts and the younger generation began considering joining the partisans who were at the time already working in the forests. However, a young man wanting to join, not in possession of a weapon, was not accepted. A weapon was impossible to obtain since neither Red nor Polish armies passed through the town. Many a Jew began residing with Polish neighbors.

I was obliged to remain in my home since the entire ghetto would suffer, had a Jewish craftsman joined the partisans. I continued my work but the rest of the household commenced digging bunkers. A hole was dug under the kitchen floor 2.70 meters deep. We covered it with thick beams over which we poured much sand. The opening to the bunker was a chimney. We dug a tunnel from the garden to the bunker which supplied us with air to breath but hid it with rocks. This is how we readied ourselves for the second pogrom.

The Second Pogrom

The second "Action" took place in the month of May, 1942. At daybreak the ghetto was surrounded by the Polish police and Germans who were later to be joined by Gestapo and Gendarmerie. The Jews, forewarned, took to the bunkers. It was the Judenrat's warning who after the first pogrom posted guards around the clock to watch police and German stations. The Judenrat even planned an organized escape; one of the bunkers, in the school was to be used as a gathering point. It was useless. This hideout could contain no more than fifty persons and escape without weapons was as good as giving ourselves up, since the partisans drove away anyone coming to them weaponless. In the entire ghetto there was not one pistol to be found. Another reason keeping the youngsters from leaving the ghetto was the disinclination to leave their family behind - parents, children, woman, brothers and sisters. Most decided to hide within the ghetto.

All of our family hid in the ghetto as well. With them hid a few neighbors, together about twenty persons. My father vehemently refused to hide in the bunker and remained in his house. From our hideout we clearly heard the policemen's footsteps and the screaming of our beaten father. The German for which we sewed clothing recognized him and ordered him to be left alone. In the afternoon my father knocked on the bunker's entrance telling us the pogrom was over.

Deeply shocked we looked at the toll taken by the pogrom: The bodies of the murdered lay in the streets and the roads and sidewalks were flooded with blood. In the houses, on the beds lay shot people as well - sick people who couldn't get up from bed. In the neighbor's house lay the elder Mordechai Ze'ev Schultz with his eye flowing out of its socket. This was my first sight of a Nazi victim.

On the bridge was Yehuda Pessach Kaplan picking up the brain of his little child, Hannan, who was clobbered by the Germans. The child's body was no more. All Jews caught in the bunkers or in their homes were concentrated in the place near the club, about 200 hundred meters from the big hole. There, the Germans checked which of them was in possession of a shein. The ones employed by the Germans were released and the rest were taken to the common grave and there shot to death. In this pogrom died 350 Jews, among which was found rabbi Sheinin. He did not hide. The murderers found him in his house praying, a Talit and Tfilin around him. When taken by the murderers to the murder place, the rabbi became happy, saying he was sanctifying the Holy Name. Was he insane?

After the "Action" no one left for work. In the afternoon the "Sonder-führer" and Komolka showed up at the Judenrat saying that since the ghetto population was down 12%-15%, the area of the ghetto will be made respectively smaller. The street Kostiushko and the adjacent alleys would be taken out. Relatives had no time to mourn their dead, having to move into a smaller and more populated ghetto immediately. The oppression was unbearable. Nevertheless, plagues did not burst out because the Judenrat was very careful about hygiene. The bathhouse worked daily.

The Last "Action" and the Final Extermination of the Ghetto (end of May, 1942)

It happened on a Saturday. At 4 o'clock in the morning we were wakened by our neighbor and relative, Zeinell Kazinitch, telling us the ghetto was surrounded. Enforced shifts were posted near the river, at the ghetto border. On the other side of the ghetto, bordering the main street, shifts were posted as well. The ghetto is surrounded from every which way, and there is no way to escape.

This time, as in precedent cases, the Jews imagined they could save themselves hiding in bunkers.

In our bunker, as well as our family, hid the neighbors; Lipkind, Markman, and Freiman; aunt Pesia (grandfather was killed in the second "action") and others. All in all 20 persons. Since the space was not sufficient for us all, some of them moved to another bunker which we dug under the floor.

When the Germans entered the ghetto they found no one except for Judenrat members, their families, and the chief of Jewish police - Warfman. This time they did not hide, as in the second action since the ghetto Jews denounced them for hiding in the past instead of trying to save Jewish lives by way of bribery. Now the Germans found them in the Judenrat building, used also as the apartment of the Judneltester, Ya'akov Butwinik. The Germans now took their anger out on these Jews beating them savagely. They were later taken to a side alley near our hiding place.

At eight o'clock in the morning the Germans found our trail and began taking apart the oven under which our bunker was built. With the first rays entering, the shouting began: "Juden, heraus"!

No one answered their calls and they threatened to throw in a hand - grenade if we didn't come out.

There was no reason left to remain in the bunker. I was the first to come out and was given a blow in the neck with a cudgel. I scurried out and was beaten savagely in the legs. I was surrounded by Gestapo armed with sub-machine guns and bats. I crossed quickly the corridor leading to the door, skipped over the balcony , and not sparing a look back, I was already on the other side of the street, leaving the Gestapo murderers behind.

The ones left behind were beaten mercilessly. My father was hit in the head and bled profusely.

All of a sudden I found myself near a group of Judenrat men: Warfman, his wife, and his daughters. Inside of an hour 70 Jews were taken to this place. we were all taken to the ghetto gates and there sat down under heavy guard.

Sonder-führer Hartman arrived and seeing my father's bleeding head, ordered one of the policemen to bring water and turning to my father said: "Haben sie keine angest, sie wärden leben belieben" ("don't worry, you'll stay alive"). Naturally, we did not believe this.

More and more Jews were brought. Some of them wept and some lay on the ground and did not get up. Next to me sat Gdallia Levin, the tubercular, and whispered in my ear: "Take a good look at the trees and the houses, you shall not see them again. These will stay after we are gone, nothing changed, but we will not. The world will keep on existing but many Jews will not be in it". I remember his words, until today. They are engraved in my memory forever.

In the afternoon the Judneltester, Butwinik, was led to the police station in Gleboki, so that he could not escape. On the way he saw a group of farmers waiting impatiently for the end of the ghetto extermination so that they could pillage the houses of the murdered. They told him that extermination had begun. remembering the discontentment after the last "action" he decided to turn on his tracks, but the two ghetto policemen with him decided to keep going toward the Gleboki ghetto hoping it was still there.

When Butwinik reached the ghetto gate he was arrested immediately and taken to the concentration area where I found him among the other arrested. A Gestapo officer came to him, and taking some bullets for a Russian rifle from his shirt pocket, said: "Look what the Judenrat men are busying themselves with". He slapped his face and ordered him to sit down under heavy guard.

At that moment, a man, David Glazer, asked the policeman for a match to light a cigarette. When he was offered the match, Glazer began running towards the ghetto. They shot at him but missed. We thought him insane since it was impossible to escape from the surrounded ghetto. Later, when we met in the Gleboki ghetto, he told me he had been hurt in his leg from the shots but managed to reach shelter. He dressed the bleeding wound by himself and arrived in the Gleboki ghetto after 4 days and nights.

When the Germans collected 350 Jews they ordered us on our feet. They put Butwinik at the head and told him to lead us. Surrounded by four rows of policeman, we were led through Pilsodsky street. The people standing on both sides of the sidewalk, looked at us indifferently. We thought we would be led to the "Club" where they would make a "selection" but no, we were led straight to the big hole. Passing the club without halting, I lost my last hope of survival.

††Near the hole we saw we were surrounded by many policeman and Germans. People trying to escape were shot at once, near me lay the first killed. The Judneltester jumped into the hole but a German pulled him back

saying "you, as a Judneltester, have to see all your community being killed and we will kill *you* last". At that moment Lipkind charged at Komolka, hit him in the face and jumped into the hole. The German asked the Pole if he should take him out and Komolka answered: "No, there's no need, he'll be shot soon anyway".

On any account I saw two who ran away and were already far from us. A sub-machine gun opened up on them, they fell down and when the shooting stopped, one got up and recommenced running and the other lay motionless. The police shot him a few times and he died.

At that time, I was approached by Sonder-Führer Hartman and was called aside. He called also my father, my stepmother Gutte and her daughter Haya. My brother, Haim, approached Sonder-Führer Ungerman presented his shein and added that he was employed by the Germans. As an answer he received a slap in the face. He began to run towards the Jewish cemetery and I clearly saw that he succeeded in reaching it. However, there are gentiles from the town present at the killings and they told me later that my brother was killed by Gend'arm Witwizky from Gleboki who ran after him with a submachine gun.

Next to me stood Sarah Markman, our neighbor. She told the Sonder-Führer she was my wife. He did not respond and she stayed in our group. Yasin, the shoemaker, and his wife were also added to our group, but their children were to be murdered. The Sonder-Führer took us back to town. Near the hole, the Jews were massacred and were ordered to undress beforehand.

About 200 hundred meters from the hole we were put in a garage and locked in. Only now did I notice that the brothers, Zelka and Samuel and my sister, Sarah, were not with us. In my great despair I hit the guiltless Sarah Markman.

Silently, we sat awaiting our slaughter. At twilight we heard shouting from the street. Through a narrow porthole we could see another group of Jews being led towards the hole under heavy guard. The screaming and howling did not subside and after a while even grew louder. We understood that they were now being killed.

At sundown the door opened and in came Sonder - Führer Ungerman, gend'arm and S.S. men. Some of them were leading Butwinik's daughter and her husband. They gathered all the women and asked me whom they should take and whom to leave. "According to the law" - they said - they could spare the life of only one man of every profession. Father immediately answered that he was ready to die as he was an old man and I was still young. I then said: "You should know that I can only sew and cannot cut, whereas my father can cut beautifully. The Germans took council together and decided to spare us both. They took all the women with them, locked the door and were off. In dead silence we stayed seated all that night. The next day Komulka arrived in the morning and told us that we would all stay alive. We would not have to wear the yellow patch, and we would be able to roam the town in liberty. Also, we would receive living quarters but we would have to work obediently and loyally. "You will receive a horse and a wagon to transport your belongings and equipment". - He added - and left.

We returned to the ghetto. The sights there were horrible. The doors and shades were shattered. German police looking for gold roamed the streets. The closets in our house were broken, nothing left in them. Everything broken and in chaos. I knew of a hideout where we hid some valuables but did not approach it to check.

Just when we were taking our sewing machine to take it to the new place Komulka showed up. He asked why weren't we taking our personal belongings with us as well? I took some bedclothes with me but I did not need much at that point in time.

All the craftsmen were concentrated in one house. Facing us, in the yard were all the Jews found in their hideouts. They were ordered to undress and were left only in their underclothes. Later, they were taken to a big warehouse. Through our window we saw how more groups of Jews were constantly led and how the pile of cloths gradually grew. They were photographed one by one and in groups, while being beaten savagely. Many were friends and acquaintances. Barefoot and naked some of them held money or valuables which the Germans took.

So passed the second day of the "Action", us not eating a thing in over 48 hours. However we did not feel hunger. On the third day of the "Action" we saw them being taken out of the warehouse and made to run to the hole in files, one man leading the way. Less than thirty minutes later we could hear the shots echoing. They were murdered. The extermination of the Dokshitz ghetto lasted 17 days since very many hid.

For nine days we stayed in this house witnessing all the horrors taking place in our town. During all that time no food entered our mouths and all I swallowed was a little medicinal alcohol which I had remembered to take with me when I left home. I gave ten liters of this alcohol to the policeman that took me home and thanks to this alcohol my spirit did not break.

Through the days the following people were brought in to join us: Gitlin, the blacksmith; Izsche Plavnik, the carpenter; the brothers Reitman, the locksmith; Freidman, the mechanic and Joseph Gurwitch, the tailor. So were gathered twelve "expert" craftsmen and we had a woman with us, Butwinik's sister to see to our needs.

On our fifth of sixth day in the house we saw Butwinik's brother-in-law led to the warehouse. He was a refugee from Warsaw named Schimek, but I cannot recall his family name. When Butwinik saw Schimek being undressed and made to run to the warehouse he broke down and cried and with him all of us. With the tears still in our eyes we could see the policeman put on Schimek's leather coat and boots.

At the same time a nurse injected herself and her children poison in the warehouse. Her eight-year-old daughter was taken out lifeless and her son dropped dead near the hole. She, herself, it was told, did not reach the hole.

On the eighth day of the "Action" everyone was taken out of the warehouse. I saw Judek Golkowitz - probably already insane - at the head of the row. He did not understand what went on around him and was beaten cruelly in his underclothes. Among the sentenced I saw the sisters Shleifer. They were dressed only in very short night-dresses. They pulled at their dresses constantly, embarrassed. Thus, naked and embarrassed, they were led to their death.

At the end of that day Dr. Gleichenhous was brought to the warehouse. He was undressed and beaten harshly. Every now and then he would fall down and almost lifeless he was dragged to the warehouse. When Komulka heard that Gleichenhous had been caught he ordered him brought to his house and from there he was taken out thrashed and bleeding beyond recognition.

There were not very many Jews left in the town and the killings took place every two to three days. On the last day of the extermination (the 17th) a last group of Jews was caught - 20 persons. After the destruction, we came to know that this group survived, escaped from the ghetto and hid in the ruins of a Jewish house on the way to Gleboki. A shepherd boy found them and turned them into the hands of the police. Among them were: The teacher Juttkovsky and his wife, Holtz, the Koplovitch family and others. I cannot describe what they looked like when caught, after having spent seventeen days without food and in horrible fear for their lives. Some farmers also said to us that one woman, Gutte Markman, succeeded in crawling from the big pile of the murdered and in reaching one of the villages about 4 km from Wieczery. A farmer sheltered her during four days and then threw her out. Looking for new shelter, she was caught by peasants who turned her to the police.

Thus in June 1942 came to its end the Jewish community in Dokshitz.

How strange and horrible was it that only we - a small group of Jews, were left alive continuing our work.

Organization of the Workshops

Two weeks later we were transferred to another house, in the market square, above the pub. It was a seven room apartment where workshops were organized for shoemaking, tailoring, carpentry, locksmithy, and blacksmithing. The mechanics worked in town. We ate what the Germans threw to us and the blacksmiths earned a little "on the side" working for the farmers in the vicinity. We shared our food like one big family.

After some time Sonder-Führer Strothoff came to visit us, wanting to know "how we were doing". He asked how it came to be that we were left without our families. During the extermination, he said wringing his hands, he was in

Germany. Was he a scoundrel or an honest man? I wouldn't know. He went on to say that everything was the fault of two people - Stalin and Hitler. "I have no need for this war" he said "I'm a judge. These two want this war but I have nothing to do with them".

After the extermination we began to think of escape. I proposed killing a visiting German, throw his body to the cellar and take his weapon. With a gun we could join the partisans. Unfortunately, I was always opposed by the mechanics. They said that since we were left alive we should not make other plans and just continue our work. Because of this opinion they were later killed.

One day a German truck stopped near the house and from it stepped out two Germans. One of them, a man by the name of Finster, came in to the workshop and ordered us to fix the truck. We were very frightened as we were never asked such a thing from an unknown German. This German, Finster, came from the Gleboki ghetto and took dairy products from the dairy in Dokshitz to Gleboki. He began questioning us about our relatives in Gleboki. We did not answer. So he put in the corner a few kilos of butter and cream and handed us a letter from Max Butwinik, the brother of the Judenrat's chairman. In his letter Butwinik made it clear to us that we should try to reach him in Gleboki. From there we could run away - we'll have the means. We understood the letter very well. As it turned out, Finster would sell weapons for gold to the Gleboki Jews.

When the German left we began discussing the idea. How would we get to Gleboki? Again we were not all of the same opinion and stayed divided for three months.

In the beginning of September 1942 a decree was made public by the commissioner of the Gleboki area that Jews could not reside outside the ghetto. The Sonder-Führer tried to object since he could not find other craftsmen but it was useless. When the second order arrived all thirteen of us were transferred to Gleboki. I was content with this fact as I believed I could get hold of a weapon there and join the partisans.

In the Gleboki ghetto

We were taken through the gate to the Judenrat. We were given a place to sleep and were left alone for a few days. Then we had to sign up for bread-cards and to go to work. From the moment I reached Gleboki I knew I was not staying and immediately began finding out how to escape.

It turned out that many young people had already escaped from this ghetto and joined the partisans in the woods. I indeed, I heard many had come back from the woods because of the weather conditions and the bands of criminals, but despite all this and despite the nagging doubts I did not give up on the idea of running from the ghetto. I began looking for contacts and ways to acquire a weapon. I managed to purchase a rifle with 14 bullets from world war I. I bought the gun from some farmers dealing in weapons in the ghetto. I prepared forged Arien documents printed in the press of the county commissioner by the Jews working there.

With the gun and documents in my hand -hidden in the cellar- I awaited the right moment. I did not tell my father about my acquisition but hinted that I would probably be leaving him soon as I did not want to end up another victim in the big beetroot hole-the killing place of the Jews and Russian P.O.W.'s.

At that time there were 8000 Jews in the Gleboki ghetto. Here were concentrated the remaining Jews from all the ghettos in the area. Despite the begging, the bribery, the flattery and the fact that the Jews filled all their requests, the everyday killings of Jews did not come to an end. The victims were taken outside the ghetto and murdered in Barok grove.

Knowing all this, I dared not come out. I came out only when it was absolutely necessary.

During the first week in this ghetto we organized the first group. From the Dokshitz community were Glazer, Plavnik and I; from Gleboki - Friedman and Swiedler. We wanted to enlarge and strengthen the group and in a short while we had 14 men. Some armed and some not (Kopelovich, Kantrovitch and Radoschkovitch). Many more asked to join us but we could not comply as they were weaponless.

Father found a bullet in my pocket. I was forced to tell him my secret and added that in the next few days I would be running from the ghetto. Father started to cry. It was impossible to take him with me because the wounds he had from the beatings in his head had not healed yet. I hoped that after I got settled in the forest and the wound healed, I'd take him to me.

Two partisans appeared in the ghetto - The brothers Friedman: one from Postov and the other from Dolginova. They gave us the address of the contact man, Yashka, who lived in the village Domislav, near the town Miadel. Moreover, they explained in which forests and where we could find the partisans from the "Avengers of the People" regiment. They, themselves, stayed in the forests in their base "The high Island" among the swamps.

Our group of warriors decided on one of the days in the end of September at 9 o'c as the running time. We would run from the ghetto, from one of the houses near the concertines.

when I commenced parting with my father he cried and begged of me not to leave him. "If we are together at least I'll know when we're killed" he said. This way, he'd live on the rumers reaching him. He knows that I'm going to my death and not to life. It's happened before that runaways did not succeed in passing the concertine and were shot then and there. If he hears that partisans were caught, he'll be sure that I'm among them.

He cried continuously, begged and did not leave me alone that whole night. That night I slept in the ghetto in my cloths with the gun in my hand so as to not be taken by surprise in case someone informed the Germans. I decided to look for another group of partisans since I was sure my friends had left. However, in the morning I found out that they didn't want to leave without me, saying I was the only one that knew how to manage in the rear as I had already been in this situation when the war began. We postponed the escape for two more days and left the ghetto at10 o'c. I promised my father I would come back for him in a month of two. Each one took a small bundle of linen, a sweater and the cloths on his back.

We cut the fence, and one by one, took to the open field. The Gleboki train station was a big railway intersection making it difficult to cross. However, we made it and turned towards Wolkolati.

The Road to the Partisans

After putting a few kilometers between us and the railway we decided to stock up on food supplies. We knocked on the window in one of the farmhouses, and addressed them in the German language. When they saw we were armed, they became scared and gave us all that we wanted. We left immediately and reached the forest at dawn.

We continued and after a long way knocked again on the doors of farmers. We got from them wagons and horses and that same night, reached one of the contact men, not far from Wolkolati. We hid in the barn all day long and continued at dark. The contact pointed out a forest where we could hide also during the day and even meat Partisans.

As a resting place we chose a location where we found traces of partisans - dead fires, remnants of food and clothes. In this forest we met two Jewish partisans from "The people's Avengers". Their names were: Sagalchik from Dolginova and "Zoska of Estonia" (a Jew from Estonia). They set out on orders from their regiment, which was staying on the other side of the Berezina, in the Plestchenitz area, near Minsk. They went on reconnaissance since the regiment was getting ready for fighting in the western area, and to get food. They took us with them then and we were introduced to their commander. They promised us that we would be accepted to their group as we were young, without families and armed.

On the way, we stumbled upon a group of Moscovite infiltrators made up of about 20 men. At first, we thought they were disguised policemen. Their commander was Dergatchow, an officer in the N.K.V.D. To prove they were Russian, they showed us a new submachine gun manufactured in 1942 With dawn, we all set out to the "High Island" where the whole platoon would meet.

Dergatchow presented us with a document of the "Great Earth" (Russia was so called) which showed that all armed forces operating in the Villeika area were to be under his command. Unfortunately, Dergatchow did not live up to our expectations. He turned out to be a drunkard and a bully with only pillaging on his mind.

Impatiently we awaited the arrival of the regiment. At first, only one company arrived, they were supposed to ready the camp.

When the platoon arrived we were presented to the commander, Sokolov. He liked us and was willing to let us join his men. Meanwhile, a conflict developed between him and Dergatchow. The latter refused to give us up and Sokolov threatened to take us by force. If Dergatchow did not submit, he would send his gunners and disarm his ten men. At this, Dergatchow gave up.

One by one we were taken to the headquarters and interrogated as to how we escaped.

In the regiment there were about fifty Jews, and a Jewish unit was organized with Sagalchik at its head.

The Miadel Operation and the Freeing of the Miadel Ghetto

The October festivities nearing, the regiment decided to celebrate this date with a few military skirmishes in the Miadel area. As the first operation was planned and assault on army barracks in Miadel.

In the beginning of 1942 the whole regiment gathered for a census. Sokolov, by now appointed commandeer, spoke. He explained to his subordinates how the operation would take place. We would start out at 9 p.m. and reach our destination at midnight. Each company knew it's job and the Kazachstany, Kaliosov, second in command, headed the whole operation.

I was very tense as this was for me the first battle.

The regiment set out and the headquarters was left in the cemetery under the protection of the Markov regiment.

Our Jewish unit had the following mission: We would ambush the Germans on the Narotch stream bank. We knew the Germans planned to come to the aid of the guard from the other side of the stream.

Our commander, Sagalchik, was also a guide, as he had lived in Miadel for many years and was familiar with the area.

When we arrived everything was quiet. Suddenly shots were heard. We laid down and awaited the Germans. When we received the sign to attack we ran to the houses where the Germans and Lithuanian sharpshooters were. The battle lasted a few hours and the Germans dispersed. Some of them enclosed in a monastery and from there shot at us and others charged us, but we held them off. At dawn we were called to help the group storming the monastery where our men already had positions. When we neared the monastery which was only 200 meters from the ghetto gate, we talked to Sagalchik about freeing the ghetto. According to the plan we were supposed to take from the ghetto only men vital to us: A doctor with his equipment; medicines; the dentist Simchelevitch and others, but with Sagalchik we talked about freeing the whole ghetto.

Meanwhile we received orders to set fire to the monastery. It caught and burned all through the night, the shots not ceasing. In the tumult of the battle we slipped away and with the buts of our guns broke down the gates and into the ghetto.

Despite the shots in the ghetto, there was no one in sight. The windows were all shaded. We walked up to the first house, knocked on the window, but no one answered. Only when we addressed them in Yiddish, did the windows open. We told them what was happening in the town and said that now is their chance to run away. We explained to them where to go, where the "High Island" was and about our Jewish unit. The news traveled very quickly and about 80 people began running away. Leaving the ghetto, only one woman was hurt (now she is living in Israel). On the way a 70-year-old woman died. All the rest arrived on our base safely. The wounded were sent for treatment together with the wounded in battle.

At dawn the battle was renewed. The Germans received aid from the surrounding barracks and we began to retreat. On our way back, we were shot at by the Germans hiding on rooftops, but we managed to retreat slowly. Meanwhile, Sagalchik left us to settle an account with a farmer's wife, who informed on the Jews. She was hurt by him.

I received an order from the unit commander to charge into a house from which Germans were shooting. Storming into the yard I saw, facing me, a German with a machine gun and policemen laying next to him. I succeeded in jumping away and immediately out machine guns shot at the yard killing all the murderers. Again, I went into the yard and pulled the boots off a dead German laying in a pool of blood. This was my first sight of German blood.

Outside of the town we stopped to gather our wounded from the town streets. Morning had broken and the Germans, noticing us, shot at us continuously. The commandeer's lieutenant, fatally wounded, sat next to me. He died on the way. The German losses reached 32. The Jews of Miadel and others, having reached us in many ways, were transferred by commissar Ivan Matvelvitch Timchuk to the rear. I would like to note the friendly and humane attitude shown towards the Jews by this man. Jews would join us, constantly. However, once, when a group of Jews, about 70 women, children and elderly folk, tried to reach us with a partisan as a guide, they were found by a shepherd. He immediately notified the Germans in Dolginov. The group and it's guide, save a few, were shot to death.

The Luban Operation

A few days later we received an order to blow up an alcohol factory and to confiscate all the farm animals and pigs in Luban, near Vileika. At night we began shooting at the factory. The Germans dispersed without resistance.

We then set fire to the hospital and the buildings near it. From there we turned to the sovchoz to get the livestock. Seeing the flames, the livestock refused to budge. In spite of this we succeeded in taking from the farm 300 cows and 300 pigs. In this operation we lost not one life.

In the Gleboki Ghetto

After these operations, and after we stocked on meat and cereals for the winter our regiment moved to the other side of the Berezina, to the islands among the swamps, in the vicinity of Plestchenitz. The camp and the H.Q. of the brigade were set up here.

Our task, all winter long, was to ambush the Germans.

All this time I thought of going to the Gleboki ghetto to release my father and bring him to me. This was not an easy task since it was forbidden to operate outside our military frame. Also, Gleboki was 200 km from us and we needed to cross two railways. Despite this I managed to convince our commandeer, and we set out accompanied by maybe five friends (Glazer, Friedman, Kopelovitch, Katzowich and two others whose names escape me). This was in February 1943.

without further obstacles we arrived in Wolkolati. From our contact men we found out that from the offices of the Wolkolati council it was possible to "acquire" a typing machine, money and other thing for our brigade. Also, there was a dairy supplying dairy products to the Germans. It should be noted that partisans never operated in this area. We set to work. With axes we broke the dairy equipment, set fire to all books and documents, and destroyed the installations. When we began breaking into the council hall through the windows we were shot at. This was unexpected and so we ran away and reorganized at dawn.

We reached the ghetto a bit late. I slipped my friends through the gate near our house where my father lived. We wore white robes and on one noticed us. When we knocked on the door we frightened the household. I fell in my father's arms and that night tried to convince him and the rest to join us.

In the morning the entire ghetto knew of our presence. In the evening arrive the Judenrat representatives and the Jewish police and asked us to promptly leave the ghetto. They were willing to give everything that they had for us to leave immediately.

Our order for letters for type-setting and a printing press was filled. That whole time I spoke to my father trying to convince him to leave the ghetto. The wound in his head had not healed and I promised that he would receive the necessary medical treatment with us. Alas, he did not possess the strength to set out on this long and dangerous road. We decided that I would come again in the spring to the ghetto and then he will join me.

We took with us 16 other men, all armed. These were: Yassin - a cousin of father's, Roderman the shoemaker, Pessia Zeplovitch and others. I alone, set out with the 16 men. The rest stayed behind to recruit more men.

On foot we reached the first huts, where we confiscated wagons and horses and we were quickly on the "High Island" awaiting the rest of the men from the Gleboki ghetto. A few days later five men arrived and we headed to the brigade.

Episodes

Here are some episodes that are engraved in my memory: Among the new men who joined us was a boy named Weinstien. When he just arrived he was told to guard a spy from Villeika, a Russian clerk. He was to stand guard from midnight to 2 a.m. I warned him not to fall asleep but despite my warning he slept like a log and the spy escaped. After and alarm, the spy was caught but Weinstien was sentenced to death. He was tried at absence. The verdict was carried out, but became common knowledge only afterwards.

On the way to the Zazorna village - as if he were taken to a trial - he was shot. He was a 17-year-old boy and had just arrived from the ghetto. This made a horrifying impression on all the Jews.

After Lederman's two sons, Motel and Yerucham, escaped from the ghetto, the Germans badgered him as Judneltester and accused him of having contact with partisans. They advised him to have his sons return or they will kill many Jews in the ghetto.

At that time some Jewish partisans - brothers Lederman, Friedman of Dolginova and Yerachmiel convinced Sagalchik to send people to the ghetto in order to enlist more Jews. They left from Yezurna, where the regiment was stationed. This was a month after Weinstien was killed. They were delayed at Yashka, the contact man's place, and as it turned out Gordon arrived there from ghetto Gleboki with a letter from Lederman to his two sons. Gordon gave the letter and went back to the ghetto. Partisans went to the ghetto two days later.

A week went by and the regiment received no news from them. The contact with them was broken. After a week the bodies of Yerachmiel and Friedman were found on the way to Gleboki and the Ledermans were in the ghetto. They were let into the ghetto after handing their weapons to the Germans. Despite this, the Germans arrested them after ten days. During the arrest shots were let off and Yerucham, the older, was killed. The younger managed to escape after killing a few Germans. He ran to join some partisans. Not to us of course, but to the Polotzk area. Judneltester Lederman was also arrested and led to Minsk where he was killed.

As our reconnaisance figured, Friedman and Yerachmiel were killed by the brothers Lederman on the way to the ghetto. It is a fact that their boots and leather jackets were still on them and there weren't mutilated as would have been German victims.

The Transfer to the Naliboki Forests

After these happening we returned in February to the other side of the Brezina. There we received an order to mobilize toward the Naliboki forests. The entire brigade set out right away in winter wagons and on horses to its destination. We traversed fifty kilometers every night. We crossed the railway, 5 kms long, in broad day light under the eye of the Germans who dared not attack us.

A few days later we reached the Naliboki forests. Here we met other Jewish partisans from Bailski's regiment. We also saw a family camp made up only of Jews. We were cheered up seeing another Jewish unit in the famous regiment in Bailorussia.

We made camp in the towns near the forests. I made the house of Graff Tishkevitch my base, while the camp was built in the forest. These were non-camouflaged clay huts. A big force of partisans was stationed in the forest, but before we could get settled, we received an order to return to Polik. We left the camp leaving some of our men to help construct a new brigade. Among those who stayed behind were Glazer, Ziskind and others.

As time went by they reached responsible and honored positions in the brigade. Glazer was made "Natchalnik" in the special division, but because of friction with the H.Q. he was killed under vague circumstances.

Back to the Old Base

On our way back we stumbled upon a group of Polish warriors from the A.K. (Armia Kraiova). Crossing a stream not far from Lida, our scouts were seen by an unknown group of partisans. The strangers immediately shot the horses of our scouts to prevent them from running away. However, we heard shooting and hurried to help them. A skirmish ensued where both side suffered losses. We then offered a cease-fire and each group went on its way. In spring 1943, the entire brigade moved to the Pleshtchenitz area. A hospital was set up without equipment, tools, medicines or bandages. The brigade's head doctor, Shtshaglov, was named general director of the hospital. He was a Jew who ran from the Minsk ghetto in 1942.

With him escaped the Jewish writer, Dubin (to him I told of my experiences in the Dokshitz ghetto and he put them on paper), Gurewitch, Tonik and others. The commander of our Jewish unit, Sagalchik, was named administrative director, and I was in charge of equipment. The cook was Susman, a woman from the Dokshitz ghetto.

The hospital was situated in the Pleshtchenitz area, between two villages: Hodaki and Lesniki.

At first there were not many wounded, but at summer, with more military operations, the number rose.

In May 1943 the Germans began combing the forest intensively. We had to retreat to the East, to Polic - an island in the midst of a 100 km of swamps and dense forests. The island could be reached by boat only, and this made transportation very difficult. Then we found out the Germans besieged us. 10000 partisans were under this siege. The brigade deserted the island hospital and decided to break through from its side. A special German force was concentrated east of Polik.

The Germans posted guards in all the villages in the Minsk area and from Miadel to Polozk. Retreating, the partisans found themselves under fire, many were wounded and the siege became tighter around us. All along the roads and railways there were Germans posted. Cut off from the world we continued working in the hospital giving aid to the injured who were brought to us in the boats.

Once, we received a man seriously wounded in the leg. He was †† a partisan and had stepped on a mine. His leg was bandaged in a sheet and during the three days that it took to bring him to us, no medical aid was given to him. When the wound was opened, we saw that he had blood poisoning.

Dr. Samuel Shtshegolov decided to amputate the leg, but had no equipment or anesthetic. I was sent to the hospital of the nearest brigade, not far from Polik, to obtain the necessary tools. The saw I brought was not good for the surgery. Nevertheless, time was running short. Sending the patient through the fire line to a hospital was not feasible due to the blockade. The Doctor decided to sterilize a regular saw in fire.

The patient was put on a table, two men held his hands and head; and his leg was held by me and another man. The doctor cut the skin off the leg and sawed it. This was the first time I attended such a barbaric amputation. The patient screamed and cried that he was being tortured. The operation lasted a half hour. afterwards he was put in a tent and he slept. He was soon well and survived.

Some days later, the partisans broke the siege and we were forced to leave Polik. The moderately wounded were sent back to the brigade, while six of the gravely injured (the amputee among them) were carried by us. The wounded groaned and were a burden. Transferring them, we lost two to three hours.

When the last of the injured, a partisan, and I left, we were 50 meters from Polik, and the Germans had just arrived there. We had to sleep in the swamps. I was so close to the Germans that I could overhear their conversations. An injured, with bullet holes in his lungs groaned all night. The next day we somehow transferred him to the hospital on the island.

A few days later the siege was finally broken and we remained on the island until the wounded were well again. The hospital was transferred to Zadorna village, in the Plestchenitz area, not far from the brigade's H.Q. It was given the name: "The people's avengers brigade in the name of Voronietzki"

Revenge of the Jewish Partisans

During an entire year - from the summer of 1943 to the summer of 1944 - we stayed in the village with the hospital. Once in a while, we would follow the brigade to battle, but our main duty until the arrival of the Red-Army soldiers, was to supply the hospital with foodstuffs and guard it from the enemy. However, we did not, for one minute forget our obligation to avenge the tortures and murders of our relatives.

In the fall of 1943, Sagalchik, Friedman, two Russians and I went out to obtain foods and decided to penetrate Protniki village, near Krivichi, where Germans were stationed. In this village resided a family by the name of Kamaiko. We had heard that the sons of this family would dig in the Jewish graves and take the gold teeth from the Jewish cadavers.

On the 11th we reached Protnik village. We left the wagons not far from the village and after finding out where Kamaiko's house was, we broke in. The house was full of Jewish furniture, crystal utensils, money and other articles from the houses of murdered Jews. First we gathered all that we needed. This was not difficult as everything was there for us to see. Never had partisans reached this village because of its proximity to the German barracks at Krivichi.

After taking the things and beating them, we broke their arms and teeth. We had no permission to shoot them without a verdict from the specialized department. We left feeling we had avenged our people a bit. Later we found out one of them died and the rest stayed in the hospital for a long time.

In the winter of 1944, this unit, made up of 12 men, set out again to obtain foodstuffs. This time we decided to avenge the Dolginov Jews. We decided to take a risk, enter the town, and reach the Jewish cemetery where a Christian family that helped exterminate the Dolginov ghetto, resided. The name of the gentile escapes me. One of the family worked for the "polizei". Sagalchik hit him in the head until blood spurted out. Meanwhile, the unit took the pigs and the cow. Then, we drove two men only in their underclothes out to the freezing cold. We ordered them to set out on the way we would take back. At that moment the Germans noticed us and opened fire from sub-machine guns. They probably thought we were a large force. Luckily, they chose a defensive strategy, remembering the times they were hit by the partisans.

We began running with our two prisoners. Five km from Dolginov we ordered them off the road. They understood that they were to be shot and tried to run away. Our bullets were quicker. Two days past before the Germans took them.

This action was, in fact, illegal, as the Dolginov area belonged to the special department of the Kutusov brigade. We were not permitted to operate there. There was a very strict rule saying one brigade could not operate in the area of another. Death was the punishment for breaking this rule. However, since a headquarters unit took part in this skirmish, we managed to conceal the matter.

The Second Siege

In spring 1944 the front lines reached Witbesk, 200 km from our base. The Germans knew they would have no choice but to retreat, and so wanted to "clean up" the rear and empty it of partisans. In order to do this they took 6 to 7 divisions out of the Witbesk lines. First they tried to besiege Navel Veliki-Luki, but were beaten. The Germans, running away, began putting pressure on us. From the other side, the western, from Molodechna, we were also charged. Now we were in "tweesers' from both sides.

Following the brigade, which went out to battle many times, we were forced to retreat from the Zadorani village. With the brigade we reached the Tzana village, near Bogomil. Here, the brigade took to the west, deserting the hospital. A few men, wounded and Typhoid-stricken, set out in 60 wagons in an unknown area, towards Polik, in the hope that they would survive the siege.

I walked at the side of the transport all night long, not keeping up with the team in the front, and caught up with them in the morning.

The Germans again posted guards in the nearby villages, setting fire to all communities suspected of sheltering partisans. This action was a heavy burden to us. The population ran to the forests a hunger spread in the area. Unable to feed the sick, we sent the healing back to the brigade.

The situation worsened in July when the siege tightened. Seventeen days went by without food or help for our wounded on the island near Polick, where the Germans were stationed. We could hear their voices.

In the night we heard the sounds of artillery, telling us the Red-Army began its attack. Bombs fell on Polick where there was a German camp. During the whole second siege we were ready for the Germans to find us. The wounded were hidden among the swamps. We kept them alive with the little food that we had. We had a ready - made plan in case the Germans found us.

Once, we heard explosions from the west. We sent scouts that came back to tell us the Russians were nearing. I then decided to go together with Sagalchik to Polick, where we hid some supplies. When we arrived, it seemed no one was there. We shot a few times and were duly answered... The Germans opened fire, but from the other side of the Berezina. We took the supplies from the hiding place and headed towards the island. A couple of days later the hospital was transferred to Polick.

Freedom

In July 1944 the Red-Army arrived. The wounded were transferred to the sanitary department, the partisans received orders to report in Minsk, for a partisan parade. There, we met our brigade. We took part in the parade where 25 brigades marched.

In Minsk our brigade was dismantled, and most were sent to the front. I was sent to Dokshitz, to the militia, to organize the local authorities. Dokshitz was burnt and destroyed. The center of the area authorities was moved to Parafianow, 10 km from Dokshitz. Two Jewish families returned to Dokshitz: Kramer and Shapira. Most of the time I stayed in Parafianow and did not visit Dokshitz, where my relatives died. My father was killed during the extermination of the Gleboki ghetto. Except for my brother Jacob, who ran to Russia, no one was left of my family.

After the war I moved to Vilna. I married Lucia Kaminkovitch from Dokshitz. Her mother, Zina and her sister Sarah were killed by the Nazis before my eyes.

In 1957 I returned to Poland, as I was told that Poland agreed to let it's Jews make "Aliya". I stayed in Poland a year and eight months and on November 4th 1958 I arrived in Israel.

All that was told here is but a small part of the experiences that I and the others went through in the Dokshitz ghetto and with the partisans. A more detailed description would call for an entire book and I am in no state to do this. Until this day these memories haunt me and cause me pain.

All I have put to paper is but a small monument in memory of the martyrs, together with the monument built in Dokshitz. Today the place is used to heard cattle, and no trace is left of the horrors that occurred...

**Ceremony at the unveiling of the memorial
for the Victims of the Nazis in Dokshitz**

Memoires of a Partisan
By Y. Sigaltchik

... I was told that units in the regiment was being organized for sabotage in the railways (the regiment received explosives from the regiment of "Batia"). I approached the commissar and asked him to supply me with explosives for sabotage operations. He received me politely (even with a smile on his face) and agreed that I find three more men for the job. We would be supplied with explosive materials and an exploding mechanism. Destination - The direction of Gleboki. That same night the four of us left: Michael Itzchak Friedman, Kolka Doroschenko, "The Estonian" and I. We had with us 2.5 Kilos of T.N.T. (an explosive), the exploding mechanism and 50 meters of fuse. The next day, towards evening, we arrived not far from the Parafianow-Krolevshtchizna railway line. At 10 p.m., when we reached the railway, we heard the rumbling of a receding train. With our hearts beating we placed the explosives under the right track, tied the fuse and retreated. Minutes later we heard again the wheels of an approaching train. In the distance we could make out the diffused light of the engine headlights. When the train reached the exact position, I pulled the fuse and all four of us began to run. An incredible sound of explosion was in the air. We reached a village five kilometers from the railway, stopped and ate. We could not sleep for all the excitement and joy. Early in the morning we sent the farmer, in whose house we took refuge, to the sabotage scene to check the results. Hours later the farmer returned saying the junction between the railroad and the main road to Porplishtcha is blocked and only military vehicles are allowed to pass. There is a great fright all along the tracks. Two specialized engines with lights arrived and the Germans ordered many local farmers to help clean the debris. The effect, it seems, was tremendous. In the afternoon hours, the railway was fixed and traffic was renewed. Traffic had stopped for fourteen hours and the sabotage caused great damage to equipment and loss of German life.

On that night, October twelfth 1942, we crossed the railway line again five kilometers away from the explosion. We heard the voices of the railway guards calling each other. We slipped between them and took to the road from Dokshitz to Gleboki; Not far from the farm was a solitary farm belonging to a Pole by the name of Patzvitch - a loyal and trusted friend of Michael Itzchak Friedman. When we knocked on the door and asked to come in the household was shocked. Never before had they seen armed Jews. We openly discussed the purpose for our visit with the farmer and asked that he go tomorrow, with dawn, to Gleboki and give a letter to the Zeevlotzki family (relatives of M.Y. Friedman). His two brothers, Eliahu and Moshe, were in the Gleboki ghetto as well. The farmer agreed to fulfill our wish and added that the Gleboki Jews are leading their life as usual, going to work without German hindrance. He said he visits Gleboki every now and again and even meets with the Solovitchik and Friedman families. The farmer fed us and took us to his son's house which was about two hundred meters away. The next morning Michael wrote a letter to his relatives: "Do not prolong your stay in Gleboki one more hour. Do you not sense the ground burn under your feet? The towns around you are empty of Jews. The Germans have supposable concentrated the experts in Gleboki. This is terrible deceit: your are doomed to death at any moment. Do not waste your time. Come to us, to the fighting partisans. We have weapons and many dead Germans to our credit. We are waiting for you"! At 3 p.m. Patzvitch returned with a letter from Eliahu Friedman and Molia Solovitchik written very briefly: We will arrive at midnight.

And so it was. At midnight exactly we heard their footsteps. Patzvitch let them in and we began a deep discussion. We told them of our sabotage operation at the railway. Rumors about a train derailed and about its passengers killed and wounded had already reached Gleboki. When we said it was our work, they did not believe us and were convinced only when we showed them the fuse and exploding mechanism. We suggested forming a group of 40 to 50 young men that would leave the ghetto and join us, and asked that they obtain weapons in any way possible. We promised to wait in a certain place from which we would lead them east. Among the present was Molia Solovitchik, an uncle of Michael Yitzchak. When he heard the details of our plan he recoiled: He is a husband and a father to two children and could not possibly take to the forest in the winter with them. The others agreed immediately to return to the ghetto and to organize the young people to leave.

They will leave the day after tomorrow and they ask that we wait somewhere near the town. During the conversation I found out that my cousin, Levi Yitzchak Koton, is in Gleboki. I demanded from the two that were returning that they join all people from Dolginov that are in Gleboki. They promised to do so. They left before dawn and the next day we started towards the arriving. We set the rendezvous about five kilometers away, in the Wolkolat-Danilvitz, Miadel junction. We met them at 10 p.m. - 14 men and 4 women. In the group, among others, were the brothers Lederman, Eliahu Friedman, Levi Yitzchak Koton, David Glazer, Menashe Kopilovitch, Beinish Kozinitch - all from Dokshitz. Michel Finkelman, Yerachmielke (I cannot remember his last name), Motke from Kazian, Milchman from Gleboki, Yochleman from Hidutzishuk, Pesach Isakson from Radoschkovitz and others. Among the girls I remember two by the name of Sarah - one from Gleboki and the other from Swintzian, Chernitchka from Danilovitch and Tzipka Solovitchik from Gleboki. They brought with them three rifles - one with no handle and another without a sight. They only had two or three bullets for every gun. Nevertheless, the guys were great - brave and daring.

The Partisans Attacked Dokshitz

By Lidia Brown

(Out of "The Ghetto War Book" edited by Itschak Zuckerman and Moshe Bassuk, Publisher: Hakibbutz Hameuchad, Ghetto Fighters Home. In the name of Itschak Katzenelson. Taf shin yod daleth, 1954)

In 1943 the Partisans attacked two towns in the area: Dokshitz and Krolevschcizna. Many Jews joined them. The Germans fearing the same thing would happen in Gleboki, ordered the lieutenant to the chief of the Judenrat, Judel Bland, to gather all the Jews as if to send them to Lublin (to Maidank, if seems). A deathly silence fell over the ghetto. Only solitary women were seen on the streets. The Germans opened fire - but, still, no sign of life: However, when they entered the ghetto, they were received with a raging fire. Grenades were thrown at them.

The Germans took over the houses one by one, throwing grenades into each window. The fight lasted a few hours, but when the Jews saw the Germans were winning, they took hold of their ready made bottles of Benzine and set fire to the houses. A cloud of smoke darkened the town, The Jews escaped every which way. *

* According to testimonies of partisans from the area there are some discrepancies in this story.

In the Partisan Detachment

by Shmuel Margolin

(From materials from the Jewish Historical Institute in Warsaw. Testimony of K. Mirska)

Dokshitz (according to my estimation) numbered 2,100 Jews.

On August 15, 1941, sixty-eight Jews were grabbed and shot in the market. On May 2, 1942, German field-gendarmes came and took 595 Jews, children, women, elderly people, and shot them immediately.

On May 28 the White Russian Police came with Germans and killed the remaining 1,500 Jews. They were held for eight days without bread or water, children were thrown into graves alive.

On February 13, 1942, I left with a group of Jews to the *Veliki Luki and Nevel* area. There were still 48 Jews in the group: After a long time of wandering in the forests we encountered the brigade that was Stalin's namesake. I was first put in the "*Komsomolski* detachment" and secondly

Pulemyotni group. There were White Russians, Tartars, Jews and others in the Partisan movement. The brigade numbered some 300 men.

Then we started to operate against the Germans. Our first operation was at the *Indral* station in *Lithuania*. We tore out the water pumps there and killed 15 Lithuanian police. On May the 8th, 1943, we went to the *Zshabki* station between *Molodetshne* and *Polotzk*. We took down a transport of 60 wagons with Germans and tanks. All of the Germans and the arms were destroyed. On May 19, 1943, we took down a transport between *Krivitsh* and *Vileyka*. One and a half kilometers from the *Kniyanigin* station we took out a second transport of 28 wagons with military and SS from the 122nd division "*Teutn-Kopf*". I got 15 Nazis on my own and shot them myself.

On September 8, 1943, we captured a German officer with two soldiers. We shot them.

The relations between the Jewish partisans and the White Russian partisans were very good, we were friendly. I was rewarded with the order of the "Red Fan" and the partisans order "*Suvorov*" [named after an 18th century Russian field marshal] medal of the second degree," a "*Za Boyeviye Zaslugi*" [Russian: lit. for military accomplishments. I received the "*Za Pobedu Nad Germaniyei*" [Russian: lit. for victory over Germany] -- medal in the army.

I was a sergeant. When I came to the partisans I was a simple soldier. After the fall of *Veliki Luki* and *Nevel*, our brigade joined the troops of the Red Army. As a member of the Red Army I was in Estonia, Latvia and Lithuania. We left *Memel* for *Elbing, Koeningsberg, Yustring* and *Berlin*. I was an artilleryman in the army, I commanded an artillery gun. Currently I am demobilized.

With the Partisans and In the Red-Army
By Dov Katzovitch, Petach Tikva

I was born in Gleboki and after a year moved to Dokschitz with my parents. I was raised and educated there, going to the "Tarbut" school. In 1939 I returned, with my family, to Gleboki. Gleboki's population was 12000, of which more than 7000 were Jewish. The Jews' main work was small time business. There were many craftsmen: shoemakers, tailors, blacksmiths, tinsmiths and liberal professions.

When the Poland-Germany war broke I was living in Dokschitz. On September 17, 1939 the place was conquered by the Russians, and in December 1939 my family moved to Gleboki.

From 1936 to 1939 I attended a Polish high school in Gleboki, which turned into a Russian high school when the place was taken in 1939 by the Soviets. There were 6 Jewish students in my class. Altogether there were 50 to 60 Jewish students in the school.

On June 22 1941 I received my diploma and that same day, coming back from school, I heard a radio transmission about the war breaking out between Germany and Russia.

On the second day of the war we could see convoys of military and civilian busses heading east from Lithuania and from the western Russian border. Among the fleeing were many Jews from Lithuania and from the western towns of White Russia. In Gleboki people began contemplating as well. Hesitations of this kind were to be found in my family also. In the family were another small brother and a small girl, and the house was very orderly - the decision was not easy.

The old Russian border was 40 to 50 kilometers from Gleboki. At the time of the Russian occupation one was not allowed to cross the old border. Many refugees, arriving at the town of Disna, on the old border, were sent back by the Soviet border guards. If their papers were from Western White Russia, they were not permitted to cross. Only those that arrived with the Russian forces were allowed to cross (Russian clerks, etc.). So there was also a doubt as to the worth of escaping, as it was seen that not everyone was capable of doing so. Some, though, did escape. The Germans began bombing Gleboki and Disna. Gleboki was bombed on the fourth day of the war on June 26, 1941. Civilian quarters, and not military, were bombed.

On June 28, 1941 the Germans entered Gleboki. The next day they set up their "Feld Comandantur" (local military headquarters) in our house, as it was big and in a central place. The family was not yet thrown out. The Germans took most of the house and the family stayed in a back room.

The next morning, on June 29, a German soldier came with a gentile neighbor, age 15, asked for my bicycle and took them. A few days later the "Feld Comandantur" was moved. A new unit - Geheime Feld Polizei - showed up in town. They were a secret military police. They arrested five Jews, among them a doctor named Gheler and an ex-businessman called Ghitleson. They vanished and nothing was heard of them since. No German authority answered as to where they were or what happened to them.

A rumor in town said they were executed outside the town. This caused shock in town, since these people were not communists and were badgered by the Bolshevicks as well. The Jews explained that they were arrested because they were Jewish. It was hard to believe that they were executed for no reason whatsoever.

The Germans put up signs from the "Feld comandantur" which says:

1. Wanted people for local police. It was noted that the candidates should be after military service and know how to handle firearms.

2. All Jews are to wear a white band on their left arm.

Many Jews had cows for domestic uses. German soldiers went to the grazing area, asked who the shepherd was, where were the cows that belonged to the Jews, and they were confiscated for army use.

Not all Jews wore the white bands immediately. The Germans had not yet learned to recognize the Jews by sight. Ten days later the Germans set up a *Judenrat* (a Jewish council) made of three people. Among them, the merchant, Lederman, and Rubashkin the shopkeeper. The next day it was said that all Jews age 14 to 50 are to gather and fix the road.

Forced Labor

The Jewish men were gathered in the central square. A Jewish interpreter stood near a German sub-officer. They demanded a military file. One of the Germans brought a machine gun, placed it facing the file, loaded the gun and began playing with it in front of the people. The people were divided into small groups and every group went off with an armed soldier. Some went to mend the road leading to the town, and others went 500 to 700 meters with the group. If a small defect was found in the road, the German would order a large part of the stones to be taken out and fixed with stones brought from afar. This was before noon. After a lunch break of half an hour, I was sent with a large group to mend the road leading to the town. On the road were German convoys. They understood that the workers were Jewish and shouted: "Juden, Du habst dem Krieg Gewollt" ("Jews, you wanted the war"!) - well, there you have it". This was shouted even by officers. Others laughed: "Das ist das derweilte volk" ("These are the chosen people")

Finding a small defect in the road, the Germans would order a quadrilateral hole dug, large rocks to be arranged on its bottom, medium sized rocks over them, and small ones on top of that. In another hole they would order an opposite order of work. Sometimes they would order a pile of rocks to be moved from one side of the street to the other and arranged in geometrical shapes, without any explanation. The work went on this way for quite some time.

One day I was sent to the high school, where two weeks before I had finished my studies, to do some cleaning work. The place was a communications center, and there were many cars with telephone switchboards. One of the German guards, a communications man, ordered me to straighten a hole in the ground. When I finished, he said the hole was not straight enough and I had to re-dig it. The German shouted that all Jews were pigs and that they should all be killed. He moved his hands as if loading his gun and ordered me to dig again saying it was to be my grave. Another officer needed some benches moved to an assembly room and saw me. He sent me to do this and so I was saved.

Rumors circulated in Gleboki that in nearby towns Jews were murdered by the Germans and the local police. Most local police were Polish. They suffered under the Russian occupation and accepted the Germans liberators. The orders, documents and bulletins of the local police were all in German and Polish.

Convoys of Russian prisoners began marching through the town, all in chains. There were tens of thousands. Their clothes were torn and many were wounded. The Germans escorting them had sticks with which they would beat them ceaselessly. Among the prisoners, according to their uniforms, were air force soldiers, artillery men, young people - nevertheless, they did not object, although the Germans were few. The first rows of prisoners would have the bicycles and equipment of the Germans, and even these were beaten for no apparent reason. Sometimes, the prisoners would be put into Jewish synagogues to sleep. Since their clothes were torn, they would wear a Talith and parchments of the Torah. There could be seen on the streets soldiers wearing pieces of the holy scriptures and Taliths on the streets. Apart from the prisoners going to the jails, there were groups of Russians with no German escort. These were former Russian prisoners that had escaped from jail.

Two days before Yom Kippur, the Germans decreed that they were creating a ghetto for the town Jews. Notices were posted saying there should be distinction between Jews and non-Jews so that the Jews could not influence the non-Jews. To this end were allotted a few streets at the end of town and gentiles living there were evacuated and installed in the empty Jewish houses.

It was announced that Jews were not allowed to buy groceries and to sell things. At that time a Jewish police was organized and the white band was exchanged for a yellow star of David, the diameter of which could not measure less than ten cm.

One star of David on the chest and another on the back. Jews were not allowed to walk on the sidewalks outside of the ghetto, nor walk in couples. Walking was permitted only single file near the tip of the sidewalk. Sometimes, the Germans leading the Jews to work would force them to sing Soviet or Jewish songs.

The local police and the German authorities demanded furs, diamonds, boots, fabrics, silver and gold from the Judenrat. They promised that in return for this bribery, the Jews would come to no harm. The Judenrat and the Jewish police knew where to find these things and demanded them. My family, having worked as dentists and denture makers, had gold as well. At first, they asked for 150 gold Rubles, and later for 300 gold Rubles. According to the Judenrat, the gold was given to the Germans and the local police.

The Jewish police did not wear the yellow patch. They had a white band on their arms, which showed: "Juden Polizei".

In the beginning, the Polish police would get friendly with the Jewish police. They would drink with them and blackmail them. Sometimes the Jewish police would be cruel to Jews for not being on time for work or not filling the bribe quota. The Germans, talking to the Judenrat, convinced them that the Jews will be given autonomy, and that this suffering is only because of the warlike acts. The Germans would often point to the map of Russia and said they would conquer Moscow quickly, two weeks at most. They understood it was difficult to take Russia in winter, and so everything had to be finished until winter. Looking at the map, they would always be amazed to see that after Moscow they would still have much more, and would ask if it is cold in Siberia.

Retreating, the Russians took with them thousands of prisoners. The people saw the huge quantities of men in the Russian jails. Some of these convoys, led by N.K.V.D. jailers, were bombed by the Germans on the way and would disperse. Some prisoners joined the German police. Near Gleboki, was an ex-monastery called Berezowich. Under the Russians it was a jail. The Germans made it a prisoner camp. The prisoners were held outside - in the cold and rain, with no food. At nights they would be shot with sub-machine guns and killed by the thousands.

A month after the beginning of the war I was sent to work in a printing press. A German brought in a text for green propaganda leaflets, saying all the Soviet marshals are imprisoned. At the end, in brackets, it said that whoever presents this leaflet is a "deserter" from the Russian army and as such, will be treated well by the German authorities.

A few days after the printing I saw a group of prisoners led by a German and some held the green leaflet. One of the Germans hit a prisoner although he had a green leaflet. There were no cases of escapees from the prisoner camp, although the prisoners were young and healthy. Some of the prisoners appeared in town. Most were Ukrainian. One of them, a Russian citizen, but of German nationality, was released. These were well dressed, ate well and walked unescorted.

Organization of the Gleboki Ghetto.

The Judenrat oversaw the accommodations of the Jews in the ghetto. Many families in each room, of course. The ghetto was made up of two parts, a large one and a smaller one, where it was more crowded, of course. Before, the poor Jews lived there and some gentiles. Now, the gentiles were moved to the Jewish houses that were emptied. Fencing the area allotted for the ghetto was commenced. A number of streets were blocked across by a high wooden fence. The two ghettos were connected by a narrow corridor. Not far from the German-Polish police station a gate was made in the fence. This was the only entrance or exit. On the inside stood a Jewish policeman and on the outside a German.

The Judenrat and the Jewish police were in one of the houses. In the cellar was a prison for Jews that had not gone out for work for some reason or Jews that did not pay the bribes.

In the house facing the Judenrat, the Germans allowed a 10-bed hospital to be set up... for a population of more than 7000. All Jews were given yellow identification cards, since the text was the same given to the general population. Under nationality there was a blank, under religion there was "Mosaisch" - The Moses religion, and in brackets was written "Jude" - Jew.

The Germans had no office inside the ghetto, nevertheless, they constantly walked around. If a Jew met a German, he would have to stop and take off his hat until the German passed.

In the fall of 1941, Gypsy wagons were brought into the Gendarmerie yard. The Gypsies were brought with their women and children. The Germans laughed at them and called them "wald juden" - the Jews of the woods. A rumor spread that they were to be put in the second ghetto with the Jews. To prevent this, the Judenrat asked for another bribe quota for the Germans. It turned out that the Gypsies were shot with their women and children before dawn. This event caused severe shock to the Jews as it was not clear why the Gypsies were shot. It only went to show how cruel the Germans were.

Every morning groups of Jews would set out to do forced labor. The winter began, it snowed and the Jews were forced to clean the snow from the roads as the German transportation could not pass.

Jewish refugees from all the small towns around Gleboki began arriving in the ghetto. They told of the horrible slaughter going on. In most cases the Jews would be told that they were being transferred to a bigger ghetto, and to pack their belongings. They were told of the concentration areas. The ghetto was surrounded by German and Polish police and from the concentration areas they would be led to pits dug ahead of time.

At the end of the fall, on October 1941, a German, civil authority arrived in Gleboki. Gleboki was decreed the center of the county - " Gebiet", and in Gleboki was the " Gebietskomisariat" - the civil authorities.

The administration men wore the uniform of the NAZI party, with a red band and a swastika on the arm on a white background. The Jews thought, that with the arrival of a civil government would stop the violent harassment. Actually, the Gebietskomisariat's men would take to the surrounding towns to organize the Jewish slaughter.

There was a "Religion, Nationality and Jews" department in the Gebietskomisariat. It's chief was a German called Havel. Often, Havel would invite the head of the Judenrat - Lederman, or the head of the Jewish police - Yehuda Blank, and demand a bribe. Sometimes, he would arrange matters in the work of the Jews.

Among the Gebietskomisariat's men was a German named Witwitzki. He was a circus performer and resided in Gleboki as a Pole. As it turned out, he was an under cover German. He knew, personally, many people from Gleboki, and was one of the organizers of the slaughter in Dokschitz.

In the beginning of the winter (the end of Dec.1941 - beginning of Jan.1942), there was a change in the Germans' attitude toward the Poles. The official language ceased being Polish and became Bialorussian. The police was also renamed The people's Bialorussian police. They received black uniforms with a gray collar and gray sleeves.

Arrests were begun among the Polish population. Former land owners were arrested and even priests. Between the ghetto and the Berezowich camp was a "Stalag" (Stabiler Lager - a permanent camp) and near it a grove called Borok. Deep pits were dug there, 3 to 4 meters deep and tens of meters long. The stalag prisoners killed or frozen to death during the night would be brought there. Also, in the morning, they would kill all the suspects arrested the day before, and they would bury them all in one pit. I was told this by the Jews working in covering the bodies of the murdered.

The First Slaughter in Gleboki

On the second day of Passover in 1942, I awoke in the morning and saw havoc in the ghetto streets. I lived on the outskirts of the ghetto. The family dressed in a hurry as heard they were arresting people in the ghetto. The arrested were taken from their beds early in the morning and led to the Borok grove. Two people, trying to escape were shot immediately. The local Bialorussian police would enter a house, take out a number of people, without any order. Germans stood in the streets, and as a large group gathered, they would count off a hundred, and take them to Borok, where they were shot. During the arrest, the local police was also violent to the arrested, they beat them with the buts of their guns. It should be noted, that policemen that had drunk with the Jewish police the night before, were also cruel to the Jews. Among the killed was a Jewish policeman. It seems there was a German decision to execute a hundred men exactly. On that day, some people did not go out to work. When the Judenrat complained to the Gebietskomisariat, they pretended that the whole thing was the local police's doing and promised it would never happen again. To prove this, they released the arrested men that had not yet been killed and before the evening, even some of the dead men's clothes were returned to the ghetto.

The next day, life went on at the ghetto as if nothing had happened. Only there were more widows, orphans and bereaved parents.

In the beginning of spring, end of April, beginning of May 1942 I saw many wounded men wearing rags around the ghetto. These were people from the town of Sharkowshtshisna. It seems, that during the slaughter in this town, some people, men, women and children managed to escape to the forests. Some were caught by local farmers and handed to the local police station where they were immediately shot. Others, with the help of Polish or Bialorussian farmers (the population was mixed), or without them, managed to hide. The Germans understood that they were unable to catch all of them and so announced that escaped Jews returning to the Gleboki ghetto would come to no harm. Jews began to leave the forests and to come to the ghetto. They looked injured, flee bitten, swollen. The Jews in the ghetto understood what would happen to someone trying to escape and hide in the forests. The Germans wanted to put all the escapees back into the ghetto and achieved another goal: They scared off potential runners. These, saw the ones returning, and were frightened.

The Work

Since the Germans wanted to organize a Bialorussian civil government, they needed many forms. They did not have paper, or did not want to give paper to the local government and began taking packs of Polish and Russian forms from the archives and sending them to the printing press. I was put in a group whose job it was to bring the packets and sort out the papers according to size. We would print on the back side. We would print receipts and forms for the local Bialorussian councils. Most of the men in the press were Jews, only one Christian worked there.

The press was situated a kilometer away from the ghetto and we would come there every morning. Then, the workers were allotted a house near the press and could not return to the ghetto as they began working in shifts. I could see my parents in the ghetto only once a week. The press workers were given a small salary to sustain themselves. They would buy groceries from the neighbors.

Since there was an austerity regime in the occupied area, they needed tens of thousands of food stamps. These, too, were printed in the press. Most of the work was forms for the local councils. I got the job because my grand-father had a printing press and it's workers helped me get in.

The forced labor the Jews had to do during the winter was mostly shoveling the snow off the roads and cleaning for the Germans, since German convoys would constantly pass through the town and sleep there. Also, they worked as porters at the train station and in the slaughterhouse.

In the press where I worked, we printed also identity cards for Jews and non-Jews. Many non-yellow forms were passed on to Jewish acquaintances in the ghetto, so that they would have "Aryan" papers in case they escaped. Sorting out the papers, we found packets of Christian birth certificates and baptism certificates which were also passed on to Jews. One Jew succeeded, with one of these birth certificates, to escape from the ghetto, set himself up in Vilna, and wait out the war. Today, he is living in Israel.

When the Jews went to work they would take with them (Unseen, of course) clothes, rings, watches and other valuables. While working they came into contact with gentiles to whom they would sell these for money or food.

The Jews' contacts with the P.O.W.'s were limited to the mutual forced labor. The Germans tried to prevent mutual influence. The only place where Jews met with P.O.W.s was the Borok grove, where the wagons full of "Stalag" dead would be brought.

The majority of the population was hostile, but there were, nevertheless, cases in which the horrors of the Germans and the executions of non-Jews generated revulsion especially with orthodox gentiles, and there were cases of aid. Many Christians would say to the Jews: "Run from the ghetto, you'll be killed in the end." Though this was but advise, and not a willingness for real help. Only with the deterioration of the Polish-German relationship, specially after the founding of a Polish government in exile in London, did the Poles incline more to help the Jews. They, themselves, were persecuted by the Germans.

The Polish minority was small and the population was mainly Bialorussian.

There were no political parties, trends or youth movements. Neither did schools, "haders", yeshivas, studying or lecturing exist. However, there was a religious culture, religious manners. On Sabbaths, we would go to prayer before work, if it were possible and even in the most difficult of times, one prayed in one's house. Matzas were baked from leftover flour, in a symbolic way.

Self Sacrifice

In the town of Dokschitz was a family by the name of Bloch. They had three girls, of which Haya was older and Hana a younger. Before the outbreak of the war, Haya married and conceived a child. She was a member of the local council ("Deputat") during the Russian occupation. Two weeks after the place was taken by the Germans, the police, already organized by the German representatives in the area, decided to arrest all those active in the old regime and to execute them. The policemen came to the Bloch home and asked for Haya. The young Hana understood immediately what they were after and said that she was Haya. They caught her, tied her up, tore her clothes and took her naked through the town. After a long night of torture, she was executed. (Now the highschool in Dokschitz is named after her. In times of celebrations and festivities, she is remembered as one of the schools heroes, having given her life for the life of her sister and son. The story was told by survivors from Dokschitz).

There were a few contacts through local gentiles, in exchange for a lot of money, or through Judenrat representatives from other ghettos whom the Germans forced to come to the county center. There were no contacts with the outside world. All radios were confiscated. People did not receive news papers and knew nothing about what went on in the country and in the world.

The Children in the Ghetto

Little children were also force to wear the yellow patch. It was a gloomy sight, those five-year-olds with a patch. There were no kindergartens or schools. No medical aid was given save the small hospital which only operated for a short time. Only a small number of Jewish doctors took care of the ghetto children. The children were the ones who suffered most from the terrible conditions and the hunger. Children over the age of 12 were force to do hard labor and children under 12 suffered from the fact that their parents worked and could not care for them.

All kids looked old for their age because of the troubles they went through and the worries they had, specially the girls, wearing long, torn, black dresses and black head covers.

In the town lived two or three families that had converted to Christianity decades before the war. They lived like Christians, but were put into the ghetto nevertheless, in the end of 1942. However, with the help of Christian friends, they disappeared from the ghetto and remained alive.

Rebellion, Underground and Partisans

There were a few escapes to the forests from Sharkowshtshisna, and later some returned because of German promises to the Judenrat that the returning would come to no harm. People escaped from adjacent ghettos as well, but the Jews were forced to return because of threats and lack of help from the local population. Once, escapees from a ghetto met a group of Russian escaped prisoners. The Russians robbed the Jews. Also, the prisoners threatened the Jews that they would kill them if they tried to join them so they wouldn't lead the Germans to them.

At work, exchanging merchandise with the neighbors, a rumor circulated that groups of Red-Army soldiers appeared in the forests. They were reputed to be well dressed and well armed (meaning not prisoners, but real soldiers). The soldiers promised the population that the day was near when the Red-Army would be back. They even paid for the food they received from the people. The population's attitude towards them was reserved, but sympathetic. The reason for this was the evident continuation of the war and the cruel treatment of the Germans.

My friends at work and I received a verification of this rumor when the Germans posted announcements and pictures of "bandits" still at large, with a German threat of killing anyone helping them. The Germans published propaganda against the partisans. Articles about German victories against the partisan groups, etc. The result was quite contrary to German expectations: The population understood, and so did the Jews in the ghetto, that an armed underground movement was forming.

One day, late in May 1942, I was standing not far from the press and I noticed a fellow who, by his looks, was not Bialorussian. He asked me about my work, the situation in Gleboki, etc. I understood I was talking with someone in contact with the partisans, and although I suspected that he could be a German police spy, I took a chance and told him what went on. He asked me for a number of papers proving a place of residence, a sort of substitute for the German identity cards. I gave him what he wanted and he promised to return in a couple of days. He also hinted about groups of armed men lurking by. He said if I happened to run into them I should say I was a friend of Fiodor's. The man did not reappear but I decided to obtain a weapon and run away from the ghetto.

The Second Slaughter in Gleboki

In the beginning of June 1942 a group of Germans arrived in Gleboki. 10 to 12 men from the security services. Their uniforms were different that the ones of the army. They wore black ties and there was a sign of a skull on their hats. These were professional killers, executioners. It was noted that even the German soldiers and police treated them with fear. The policemen told the Jews that these new ones had limitless rights and could do whatever they liked. A rumor circulated that they came to exterminate the ghetto. They often visited the ghetto and the Judenrat. Once, when they left the ghetto in armored cars, the rumors were that they exterminated a ghetto in a small town. They drank large quantities of wine and gave the clothes of the murdered also to the police and to people who took part in their parties. A few days later, they left the town, not hurting the place. The locals breathed again, relieved, but not for long.

On June 16 they were back and on June 19 when the Jews were waking up for work, a group appeared in the ghetto and ordered the Judenrat to gather all the Jews in the market outside of the ghetto, near the Jewish cemetery for a count. The Jewish police announced this and hurried people out to the streets with their children and small bundles of valuables and food. In this time there were many who had built shelters and hiding places in the ghetto but the majority had no time to use them, and many did not know of their existence.

That day, June 19, 1942, at 10-11 a.m. the workers being near the press, I heard shots and bursts of machine guns and I understood what went on. The town was ghost like. No one dared go out.

At 4 p.m. my younger brother, Itzchak arrived at the press and said that the whole family had gone to the so called count. My mother told my brother to run away and come to me.

Towards the evening I returned to the ghetto by a side road through the fields to see if anyone was left of my family. On the way I met two women holding big bundles, speaking Polish with each other and telling each other about what had happened. I recognized one of them for I had gone to school with her son. This son was one of the policemen in the local police. It seems that the son knew beforehand what was to occur and advised the women to profit from the Jews' things. When she saw me she was shocked for a minute and then started to scream: "Why didn't you report with the rest of the Jews?" I did not answer and walked away.

When I arrived in my parents' house in the ghetto I found the door open. The apartment was empty. A neighbor came in and said she was also in the "count". There was a German sitting at a table. Everyone had to pass in front of him and he separated them right and left. The group on the right was told they'll be going to Borisov or Warsaw to work. From this big group small groups were taken by German and local police and by S.D. men to the Borok grove - and from there the shots were heard. More than three thousand people were executed on that day.

The next day the Jews were ordered to go to work and when back they told that the German employers pretended innocence saying: "What is going on with you, this police really isn't good"! But in most cases the Germans were crueler. They beat the workers saying they would soon be next. The bodies of the dead were left uncovered for two days and after covering them, a wagon was brought with clothes to the Judenrat. The clothes were distributed among the needy. Many recognized their relatives' clothing. Among the local police, one of the most inhuman was my neighbor, Taragonski.

How I Came to the Partisans

About a week after the second slaughter I met an acquaintance, my age, from the town of Dokschitz. His name was Shlomo-Tuvia Warfman (today residing in Israel, in Akko). He told me he escaped from Dokschitz after hiding in a cellar for a few days. Then, he reached a small grove among the swamps. Not far from it stood a lonely house and in it lived some well-to-do farmers which supported him. The son of the farmers, who knew my friend and me since before the war, worked as a foreman on the road in Gleboki. The Poles, at that time, also suffered cruel treatment from the Germans. They helped Warfman with food and clothing. I found out that I knew the family as their son, Stanislav Lochovski, went to secondary school with me. It so happened that a couple of days later I was walking from the ghetto to the press to work, I met Stanislav and greeted him. The pole was shocked, it seemed, but said to me: "Come to me, bring some money. I have arms for you". I told Warfman about this and we decided to go from the ghetto to Stanislav and ask him for weapons.

One rainy night, my friend and I took a board from the fence, left the ghetto, and put the board back so as to not be found out. We went out towards the swamps, to the secluded house which was 15 kilometers away. We went according to a map I had found in the press and had memorized before. We went through fields and crossed the railway. This was very dangerous as the railway was heavily guarded. After midnight we reached the house. The Poles opened the door and had us enter the attic of the stable. In the morning, they brought us coffee, milk and food (this was the first time in over a year that I ate a regular meal). During the whole day we remained in the stable. Before sundown the family brought a rifle with *one bullet* and a revolver with nine bullets. Stanislav said that the gun belonged to one of the "Blue Division" (volunteer Spaniards, helping the Germans). He found the gun on the road.

We had with us only a small sum, three hundred Ruble. However, we said it was all we had and the family gave us the weapons. We were left with no money.

We stayed at the farmer's house all day long and at night we returned to the ghetto. On the way back, near the ghetto, we were lost because of the dark and we stumbled upon the barbed-wire fence. The guard, it seems, noticed us and ran towards the noise, but we hid among some nearby bushes. When the guard returned we went on. We reached the ghetto gate and found the two stones we had left as a sign near the loose board. We returned to the ghetto the same way we had left it. In our house we had a cellar where we hid the weapons. The men of the house, seeing us return, were frightened to see the weapons. We warned them not to say a word to anyone. The absence from work and the overly populated neighborhood near our house caused the rumor to reach the Jewish police. I hid the weapons in a better place and moved back into the house near the press. My brother and I slept in the storage room near the house outside the ghetto. Although I had to go to work, I did not since I knew we would be running away in a few days. In the Jewish police it was decided to quietly confiscate the weapons and to, somehow, get rid of us, saying the Germans could destroy the whole ghetto because of us (although the Germans did this without reason anyway).

Once, while my brother was sleeping, two Jewish policemen came, took him to the Judenrat cellar, beat him and demanded he give the weapons. He said he knew nothing. He was released after 24 hours and I was called to present myself. I let it be known that I would not come and that if, indeed, they tried to arrest me, I have in my possession a hand grenade... The Judenrat men were scared the Germans would find out about the weapons and backed off. So, except for the Germans, the Judenrat and the Jewish police also became our enemies. They interfered and threatened at any attempt to revolt or escape from the ghetto.

In July 1942 two Jewish partisans arrived in the ghetto: Zalman Friedman from Dolginov and M. Friedman from Postawy, after having resided in Dolginov in the time of the Germans. Since it was known in the ghetto that Tuvia, my brother and I had weapons, these partisans were also told. They invited me to the ghetto and said they belong to a partisan group and were sent by their leader to obtain false papers, watches, money and leather for boots and shoes.

They also said they would be willing to take in some young Jews in case these had weapons, as this was a imperative condition with the partisans.

The commisar of the Soviet partisan regiment was a Russian named Ivan Mitveivitch Timtchuk, a friend to the Jews. The envoy, his helper, was a young Jew by the name of Abraham Friedman (now living in Hulon). The partisans agreed to take me and Tuvia, but would not take my brother who was only 15 years old. I talked it over with my brother and we decided that I would go alone and when I reach the platoon, I would ask the commander, in person, to let my brother join. The partisans agreed to take my friend, Milchman Zalman, although he did not have a weapon. We acquired some money and at night, left the ghetto - a group of about 10 men, most armed, and some being relatives of the Friedmans'. We reached a small village where a partisan contact man lived, hid there during the day, and during the night arrived at a swampy area near the Nevery Kriganovka village where we found about 25 Jewish partisans and about 600 Russian partisans with their leaders. Platoon equipped with arms, guards and a reconnaissance patrol. Sort of a small regiment of partisans, wearing rags but with a high moral and ready to fight. Some were commanders that had hidden in the forests or in the villages since the beginning of the Nazi occupation. Some escaped from jail. Some wore German uniforms and uniforms of the local police. The regiment doctor was a Jew from Minsk, Stcheglow, a major. There were nevertheless partisans who laughed at their Jewish peers, but the influence of the doctor and the commisar were a restraining factor.

Moreover, many Jews knew the area very well as well as some of the locals, and this was a valuable asset to the Russian partisans since they did not know the area nor the people although the attitude towards them was friendly. The partisans told of successful ambushes and raids from the past - winter and spring 1942. I remember a story about a successful ambush near the town of Ilia. A convoy of about 40 local police was destroyed there. Also, there would be groups of saboteurs leaving from this regiment to blow up German trains.

Companies from that same regiment would take off at night to a distance of 30 to 40 km and blow up bridges on roads and destroy small police stations. The regiment had many contacts in the villages. The food and horses were obtained in the villages. Sometimes the Germans would murder the whole family of a collaborator with the partisans. The raids were very quick. They were done after careful planning and far from the main base in order not to have the Germans suspect the place.

The regiment had a special unit of about four men, a sort of interior/exterior security service. In the beginning of the operations they would pass quietly through the villages, since there were many informants to the Germans. When the regiment grew and there was a need for more supplies and wider reconnaissance, it became impossible to hide the existence of the regiment (it's name was "The Avenger"). The informants in the towns post a serious threat to the existence of the unit, and after an informant informed, German formations would storm the villages. Of course, the searching was useless, since by the time an informant reached the police and by the time the German police was organized, the partisans were tens of kilometers away. Finally, the regiment commanders found an ingenious solution. They gave an order to pass through the villages at night, cause a ruckus, to "make an impression" and to show off to the natives as if there were many more partisans than there actually were. To show they were a force to contend with.

Many of the partisan contact men and agents were sent to local police stations with news of partisans. This attained two objectives:

A) The contact were trusted by the Germans.

B) Cases were invented, and five or six informants would come from different directions to confuse the Germans.

The Germans could do nothing and did not know which direction to take. The German leaders would become angry and started beating on the informants, some of them being real informants with genuine information. In a short while the Germans themselves stopped the flow of informants and prevented themselves from receiving any information about goings on. Indeed, the partisan regiment began moving around freely even in the day time. The partisans had exact information as to German police movement. The Germans were forced to move only in large group for lack of information and fear of ambushes.

I know of a partisan ruse using two Jews. Two Jews were sent in the morning to Swir village, 2 km from a strong police station. They pretended to be drunk, badgered the local and asked them for money and Vodka (there was a standing order in the regiment which forbade robbing and mistreating the local population). One of the villagers, a collaborator with the Germans, ran off to Swir to say that two Jews are terrorizing the village and it would be easy to capture them. The Germans, hearing this, were raging. They mounted their horses, some without saddles, and laughingly planned how they would torture the despicable Jews. At that time a partisan ambush of more than a 150 men with machine guns lay on both sides of the dirt road.

When the commander saw the informant run towards the town he was happy and said: "We did it!" Even the partisans were not aware of the plan and the patrol unit wanted to shoot or arrest the man running to inform. A half hour later the group of horsemen came to capture the Jewish "bait". Twenty of them were killed immediately by the cross fire from the ambush. The company commander was Markov, a local Russian married to a Jewish woman. The "bait" was his idea. The incident and it's enormous success, as well as a catch of weapons and equipment, and the bait idea made the Germans a laughing stock in the whole area. This happened in spring 1943.

The German cruelty towards the local population, like the execution of hundreds of villagers (there were no Jews left in the area), the burning of whole villages and houses with their residents (the Germans would force the locals into a house and set fire to it with them inside), caused the population to rebel against them. The partisan regiments changed from hundreds of men to brigades of thousands. There were areas of hundreds of square km where the local authorities were not German. The Russian army command sent hundreds of paratroopers with automatic rifles and radios to the German rear in order to strengthen the partisan movement and train it. It reached such proportions that there was a temporary air field in the German rear where even Russian planes would land. This occurred from the end of 1942 to the middle of 1944.

A special emphasis was put on local propaganda. Airplanes with military equipment also brought newspapers and bulletins. The partisan leaders would hold assemblies in the villages to explain themselves to the locals.

Near the swamp area was a small Jewish town near the Narotch lake. There was a Jewish ghetto in this town made up the town Jews and Jews from nearby towns until November 1942. There was also a gendarmerie station in the town and a platoon of fascist Lithuanians was stationed there. It was decided to attack the town and exterminate the gendarmerie and the fascists. The Jews in the partisan regiment were concentrated in one platoon, the third platoon. The commander of the platoon was a Jew by the name of Jacob Sigaltchik (today living in the Magshimim settlement in Israel). It was decided that during the attack on the town, the ghetto would be released. The attack took place on the night of November 9, 1942.

Not all the fascists were killed, but some were, their positions were burned and above all - the ghetto was released. Thanks to this, about fifty people were saved, most of which are living in Israel today.

After the releasing of the ghetto, the Jews were settled in the heart of the partisan area and remained there until the place was liberated. In December 1942 the partisan leadership decided to organize an underground press. I was sent, together with a group of partisans, to the Gleboki ghetto, to break in during the night and obtain the necessary materials for printing. I knew the place and also knew what to take. The operation was handled with a quiet entry to the town and the goal was reached.

In the beginning of 1943 hundreds of newspapers and leaflets appeared within a radius of hundreds of kilometers. It should be noted that in 1943 local policemen and Ukrainian fascist troops also began defecting from the German service. They went over to the partisans. The regiment succeeded in many ambushes, in putting mines on transportation routes and on railways, and in attack on German posts. In the summer of 1943 the Germans planned an all out attack between Kursk and Oriol. On orders from the general headquarters, all partisan regiments took to the railways and blew them up all during one night. The partisans called this "the rail war". In the midst of the German attack on the Russian army, their transportation was cut off from Brest (The Polish-Russian border) to Smolensk, a distance of about a thousand km. This caused the Germans a stoppage of supplies in the midst of the attack.

In the summer of 1943 I found out that there were still about 2000 Jews left in Gleboki. With the permission of my commander, a group of Jews, including my brother, was taken out of there. These, later fought with the partisans. My brother, despite his young age, was a brave warrior and was greatly appreciated by the partisan commanders. Many of the Gleboki ghetto people got hold of weapons. Some ran to the forests and when this was known to the Germans, they decided to exterminate the ghetto. They did not enter the ghetto for fear of resistance, as the residents had weapons, and so surrounded the ghetto and bombed it with fire bombs. The houses were built of wood and the ghetto went up in flames and with it went it's people.

The Germans understood that the partisan movement posed a strategic threat to them and so took out of the front lines a few divisions and besieged wide areas. They would burn the villages to impede the partisans from receiving food.

They bombed the forests with fire bombs, but thanks to the partisans' vigilance and knowledge of the area, they succeeded, in most cases, to break through the ring, before it was tightened. Small groups would be left in the forest in order to deceive the Germans. They would make much noise and convince the Germans that they had the main force.

In a German "purge" during May-June 1944 my regiment broke through a German ring. My brother was in the leading part, while I stayed with a small group, within, to create a deception. The regiment, indeed, broke through but suffered heavy losses and scattered (the order was to reassemble near Borisov, next to Zambino, on the banks of the Berezina, in case were dispersed). The single groups were caught over and over in German ambushes and reached a new gathering place without leadership, without food, with wounded and sometimes - without weapons.

I was told by one of the partisans with my brother, that the Germans surrounded them in the forest. My brother was already hungry and barefoot for a few days and when he understood the Germans might catch him he began shooting at them and, by doing this, of course, showed where he was located. When he ran out of ammunition, he laid down on a hand grenade and when they came to capture him alive, he himself up with them.

Inside the German siege, our group shot from many different places in order to lead the Germans into the forest. The group moved from location to location and stayed near the Germans at all times, however, the Germans could not capture us. They shot in the forest in complete chaos, for fear of the group, but doing this they showed us where they were.

Two days later they understood their mistake and the forest was in utter silence. The partisans from the deception group decided two days later what this silence meant. I was sent with another partisan on reconnaissance. We walked in the forest parallel to the road and checked 5 km. We found nothing suspicious. We tended to think that the Germans had left. When we returned we found fresh footprints of German spiked shoes. My friend left the road and entered the bushes while I began to check what was happening. When I turned around I saw three Germans sneaking behind me, one of them only three meters away with his hand extended to grab my gun. I jumped to the side and ran between the bushes. The Germans fired, entered the forest and kept running. Our group heard the shooting and thought my friend and I was shot. I lay in the mud, among the bushes, until evening, and at night joined my group.

A few days later the Germans discontinued the siege for the following reasons: The Russian attack on the German army was developing; There were rumors about a second front and about the ally invasion of Europe.

In July 1944 the German army began its retreat. Many of the German police and other Germans remained in the forests and were surrounded by the partisans. So the roles were reversed. The Germans went into Russian captivity by the hundreds. They feared partisan captivity which meant - death. I saw hundreds of Germans take to the streets with their hands raised, asking army units to imprison them. The Russians were so sure of their victory that they did not even bother capturing them, and only showed them the way east towards any town, where there was a garrison to handle them.

The Russian army was very humane to the German, despite the partisan anger and the population which demanded lynching.

The commander of the local gendarmerie and a local German, part of the German police, were caught near the town of Miadel. The Russian army command tried them publicly. Locals whose family was tortured and killed by these two testified against them. They were hanged after the verdict was announced. The locals came in masses and clapped when the verdict was read. A number of local Jews, back from the forests by now, did not attend. It is said that two Jews, there, were in tears seeing these murderers swinging from a rope.

1944. When the Russians liberated the area, many people joined the Russian army, but many partisans were offered posts with the local authorities. I had no family left and so joined the Russian army. After a short training, I was sent to the front lines and took part in the Visla river crossing and the battles for the release of Shlesien. Together with the regiment, I took part in the Oder-Nisse crossing and in battles in Poland and Czechoslovakia, near the city of Glatz, in the battles of the Sudeten land - and so I arrived in Dresden in Germany. Across the river we could see the ally armies. The war was over but despite the German surrender, there were Ukrainian and traitor Russian Platoons (from the Vlassov army) still fighting. My regiment took part in the extermination of these bands. I stayed in Germany for a short amount of time and then returned to Russia. At the time the Russo-Japanese war had begun, but my regiment stayed in the Kaukas.

I fought with the Russian army from 1944 until the beginning of 1946. I received medals and a high honors from the Russian army for my diligence in fighting the Nazis and for fulfilling my duty. On the way from Germany to Russia my regiment passed through Auschwitz and I then saw the piles of ashes and bones, the shoes, the glasses and ruins of the gas chambers and ovens. There were other Jews in my regiment, some of which had excelled in fighting the Germans. An artillery regiment was attached to my regiment under the command of a Jewish major by the name of Kaplan, holding the highest honor of the Russian army - a golden star and the title: hero of the Soviet Union.

Some Personal Reflections

In the times of the ghettos the best characteristics of the Jewish nation turned against it. Jews are very attached to their families and so many fathers and sons, having the chance to escape - did not. In many cases partisans came back to the ghetto to die together with their loved ones. The Jews, out of their revulsion of murder, did not believe in a massacre of one people by another. Arriving in Israel and to other countries after the war, the compensations began. The Germans had a condition - only those who did not actively fight them, would be compensated. Because of the financial distress and the need for these compensations, many Jews Hid the fact that they actively resisted the Germans. A national asset is so lost. The asset of the documentation of Jewish heroism and their fight against the German murderers.

I was released from the Russian army in 1946. I studied and worked until 1958. I married a Jewish girl who had, together with her brother, took part in partisan attacks. We gave birth to a son, named after my father. I finished my studies in Russia, and worked as a high school math and physics teacher.

In 1957 an agreement was signed by Poland and Russia allowing Poles and Jews, former Polish citizens to immigrate to Poland. I moved to Poland and immediately requested to immigrate to Israel. I arrived in Israel on January 31, 1960. Since 1961 I work in a high school in the name of Y.H. Brener in Petach-Tikva.

Announcement in the newspaper about the death sentence for the head of the police in Dokshits, Komolka, in the days of the German occupation.

Body of the paper clipping:
One time Ghetto - murderer sentenced to death in Poland.

  Vienna, Austria, June 17, (ITA). Stephan Komolka, the onetime commander of the Facist White Russian Police in the Polish city of Dokshitz was sentenced to death in a Polish court today. Komolka participated in the mass killings of Jews in the Dokshitz Ghetto.

Testimony of Mrs. Batia Pren about her Experience in the Dokshitz ghetto and with the Partisans of the Kotozov Brigade

by Batia Pren

I was born in year 1922 in the town of Dokshitz in the Vilna District. My parents were musicians. Our family included five children and our parents; all but one of which were slaughtered in the Holocaust. This one brother survived because he served in the army and afterwards stayed to live in the town of Tashkant. Later, he moved to Poland.

We studied in town. I finished seven years of learning in 1935. Later, it was difficult to continue studying and I stayed at home. When the Red-Army entered the town in 1939 I began to work at the local post office. My father, being a musician, could not find enough work, and so I helped with the household income. When the Germans entered the town in the summer of 1941 I quit the post-office job and tried to escape to Russia. During our escape we met officers of the Red-Army who ordered us to return immediately to the town and to our jobs - They did not believe us when we said that the Germans were close to our area.

So I worked at the post office until the last moment, and helped running the branch. I stayed and work that whole night and in the morning, the Germans entered the town.

In the Dokshitz Ghetto. Young Jewish women peeling potatoes.

The German Takeover of Dokshitz

The Germans started making trouble. immediately entering the town, with the help of the cooperating Poles, they began to steal property and put fear into the population.

I remember an evening when we sat so terrified as to not even take our clothes off. Suddenly - a knock on the door. We were forced to open the door, since the Germans would forcefully enter if their knocks went unheeded.

The door opened and a German soldier entered accompanied by a Polish cooperator. They demanded we give them boots, clothing and other things. We kept the good clothing hidden and gave them the rest. When they saw the boots on out feet, they ordered us to shed them and hand them over. That same night, they were back for a cock which they had seen in the yard. Then, the German aimed his pistol at my father, pushed him against the wall and said: "You are a Jew, and as you know, Jews do not live among us". We remained rooted at these words and we understood that our end was near. Meanwhile, they took the cock and left. For fear of death, we went to our relatives' house - we could not stay at home. The rumors about what the Germans were doing to the Jews caused us tremendous fear. This lasted about three months until Dokshitz was made into a ghetto.

The Murder of Jews in Dokshitz

During the evenings I had talked about before, when the Germans visited our house, they killed Scheinman the shoemaker. They then came to the house of Rabbi Laib Shainen (our neighbor), took him outside to the yard, put his head on a brick, and with another brick they hit his head until blood spurted out. By a miracle he stayed alive for a short time after that but in excruciating agony.

The Death of My Father

Some time after the incident with the cock the Germans took seven Jews, one of which was my father. They said they were looking for a communist, but actually it was not the name or occupation of the man that they were really interested in, but the number of persons. They had to show their officers that they had carried out their orders.

My father's name was Israel Friedman and in the town there was another man by the same name who was politically involved. They looked for this man and when they heard that my father had the same name, they took him with no further questions.

The S.S. soldiers took the seven Jews, held them for three days, shaved their heads, led them to an area where they were forced to dig their own graves , and shot them on September 16, 1941.

They also forced other people to do hard labor such as digging graves and trenches.

We suffered from a shortage of food stuffs. We had flimsy relations with the locals, and those who still had things to sell, sold to us what little they had.

We wore yellow patches on our clothes and we were forbidden to walk on the sidewalks. We also had to take our hats off for every German soldier.

The Ghetto in Dokshitz

In the winter, in the end of December the Dokshitz ghetto was formed.†† The Germans appointed a managing council to the ghetto -"Judenrant". The head of the Judenrat was Ya'acov Butwinik.

The Judenrat fulfilled the Germans' wishes without being abusive towards the Jews.

The ghetto was made up of a few streets. Life was difficult as each house was filled with fifteen to twenty people. The ghetto was guarded on the outside by Polish and Russian cooperators, but not from the inside. We'd go to work in groups and it was very difficult to bring food into the ghetto. I remember a cold winter, when we had nothing to warm the house with. We looked for a way to light the stove. My younger brother sneaked quietly into the market, to buy wood. He was very frightened and careful but was found by the guards. He made a deal with a Polish farmer to bring his wagon with the burning wood into the ghetto. A guard walked behind him, he was arrested and taken to the police station. They held him for over half a day and we were worried sick. We ran to the Judenrat and he was finally released after receiving 25 lashings with a rubber stick. He barely made it to the ghetto. His entire body was covered with blue marks. I shall never forget this. A group of people got organized to leave the ghetto and my elder brother was one of them., The escape was canceled when everyone was made to understand that the whole ghetto would be exterminated in case of escape.

The Germans continued in demanding all valuables from the Jews as well.

The Extermination of the Ghetto. The First Action.

On the eve of Passover, 1942 the Germans began the extermination of the ghetto. They killed fifty to sixty men in this first act.

They gave an order with specific names and murdered them in Dokshitz. The main grave was near the old Jewish cemetery. I did not know who the first killed were.

The Extermination of the Ghetto. The Second Action.

The second extermination act took place on "Lag Ba'omer" (the 33rd day of the Omer) when 50% of the ghetto residents were murdered. The Germans went from house to house and gathered the Jews from wherever they found them. Those who hid in the pits and the bunkers stayed alive for the time being. The ones gathered were taken to a German officer. He picked out the ones who were fit to work and spared those. There were not many.

I hid in the cellar. We were twelve people there. My elder brother and his wife and the Shapiro family. My mother was in another building. We were separated while running away. The Germans and Russians searched the cellars and bunkers and took out whoever they found. They also reached our hideout. In the house where we hid lived a fellow who worked with the local police. He had a sister who remained in his house and he asked the police to spare her life. They demanded that he show them where she was. He had no choice and showed our hideout. The Germans ordered everyone out or else they'd shoot everyone. We all came out and we were taken to the classification area. One step before the final slaughter.

I Am Saved From Death

I was taken to the place where the German officer stood. My elder brother, who was a tailor, was sent with his wife back to the ghetto I stayed there with my younger brother. We told the Germans that were the brother and sister of the man he just sent back but to no avail. He would listen to nothing. We worked but had no papers to prove it. Nearby stood a policeman with whom I went to school. He knew that we were working and convinced the German to let us go. The German believed him and we were sent back. From this place, where the classifying was done, the rest of the Jews were taken to the pits and were killed.

There were people brought to the area that tried to hide or to run away - maybe a miracle shall occur. They began to lift the floor boards in order to try to hide under the floor. The Germans saw that the number of people was too small. They found the hiding place and pulled people out by the hair. They beat them with rubber Sticks so much that I do not understand how they managed to stand up. Finally they killed everyone.

In this action more than 50% of the ghetto residents were killed. From the pits we returned to the ghetto. The situation calmed a bit but we were still very scared. Later I succeeded in seeing my mother who was in another bunker which the Germans did not as yet discover. We stayed together for a while.

The Final Extermination of the Ghetto

At the end of May, 1942 the S.S. men arrived and surrounded the ghetto. The Jews began again to hide in the bunkers, but this time the Germans knew about it in advance, found everyone and took them. At this time I was all ready out of the ghetto.

My Hideout at the Polish Gentile's Place - Borisovitch.

I had some acquaintances among the Poles. A Polish gentile, Borisovitch, helped me by employing me at his restaurant during the ghetto period. I asked him to let me work for him during the extermination. He took pity on me and agreed, and thus saved my life. On the night before the final slaughter I went to the restaurant where I worked and hid in the attic. I stayed there a few days and nights while the extermination went on inside the ghetto, and later managed, with difficulties, to move into Borisovitch's house.

During the slaughter, my mother and two brothers were murdered. Borisovitch did not fear the Germans and was not worried that I'd be found with him. He had two sisters and an old mother, who did not even know what went on in town. His sister gave me support and strength. She helped me not to lose my mind.

Borisovitch decided to save me. He hid me in a closed room and his sister would bring me food. The Germans did not especially search the Polish houses and did not imagine that the Poles could hide Jews inside the village. The Germans would enter the house, but not to search, only to find a place to rest. The greatest fear was from the neighbors.

I hid with Borisovitch during a year and three months. I lived in comfortable conditions with a humane treatment from his family. Later, some partisans by the name of Razionovtzi arrived in town. They set fire to the parts of town where the Germans resided and thus killed them. This happened in August 1943.

At this time I came out to the town and made contact with the partisans.

My Stay with the Partisans

When the partisans entered our house I told them I was a Jew and I would like to join them. They answered that they had no time to take me with them but instead they would bring me to their Headquarters and there they would decide what to do with me. I was taken to the H.Q. in a village near Dokshitz. In the H.Q. they were surprised at how a Pole managed to save a Jew and they thought I was a spy. They did not take me in since I was without a weapon and also a girl. I was left in the village of Kromivitch with a Russian peasant so that I could help her with the farm work. I was there for six months until the winter.

After a short time I heard of people from our town that were with the partisans. One of them was Zelik Tilis, who was in a different brigade out of our area.

In the village where I was, there was a second brigade by the name of Zelesniak, where Zalman Kramer fought. He helped me very much in all ways and especially to leave the house of the Russian peasant where I suffered for lack of food.

Thanks to him I joined the partisans. Not his brigade, but the brigade named after Kotozov, where Zelik Tilis also fought. This was because in the brigade of Zalman Kramer there were many antisemites who would not accept women and of course not weaponless. So I will never forget the help offered me by Zalman Kramer in these hard times. In the beginning with the partisans, I worked in the Kitchen.

After a short while we were surrounded by the Germans. Just before this took place, I came down with typhoid. I lay in the partisan hospital (a tent), near Polcek with high fever. I was sick for a month and when I finally got well, the Germans attacked from all directions. We had to escape from this area to a swamp area where we lay for a few days. The people were separated. Many were lost and many died. During the attack I was with a group of partisans. We had no choice but to break the siege by fighting the Germans. We were lucky enough to break through but only a third were left of the partisans and the rest were killed.

Until the siege I had no weapon because there were not enough for everyone. I was wounded from shrapnel that is in my body to this very day.

Freedom - 1944

After the siege we came back to our former place. We were there for some time until we heard the front nearing. A short time later we were released in July 1944.

We had nothing to go to Dokshitz for. The whole town was burnt and not one Jew was left. We stayed out of Dokshitz in a town by the name of Dolginov.

Some time later, the post office was opened in Kravitz where Borisovitch worked. He was also the manager of the post office in Dokshitz before the war. He heard that I stayed alive and together with other girlfriends, he called me back from the partisans. I started working at the post office.

I worked there until 1945 when I was taken to Moladechna. There, I worked a short time, was released and moved to Vilna.

In June 1946 I married Yosef Pren. After the wedding I quit working. My husband was a photographer and we lived in Vilna until we left for Poland in 1957. We settled in Lignitz where we lived a year and eight months.

We arrived in Israel in 1958. My husband, my two sons and I settled in Beer-Sheva.

At the memorial in Dokshitz to the victims of the German murderers.

The Jewish Resistance in Dokshitz and the Surrounding Area

(In Memorium to the Heroic Partisan Yidl Yessen)
Shabtai Ruderman/Canada

Yidl Yessen was born in 1914 in *Tumilovitsh*, in the *Dokshitz* region. He and his entire family lived in the village of *Dzedszhin* until 1942. When the German army occupied that area, the Jews from *Dzedszhin* were gathered into the *Dokshitz* ghetto.

Yidl succeeded in getting out of the ghetto before the first slaughter. He hid with peasants that he knew. It was there that he received the joyous news that his wife and mother saved themselves as well and were hiding in the *Gluboki* ghetto. He succeeded in getting in there and took his wife with him. Both of them got set up in a partisan detachment. As one who was born in the village and grew up in the region near the *Berezinaz* River, he knew the area well. The leaders of the partisans chose him as a navigator and as a liaison officer with the peasants. His deliberate, calm, cold blooded and calculated nature always aided him in carrying out his missions. A measured speaker, he always considered and listened first, thought about the issue and later spoke his opinion.

In December of 1942 *Yidl* arrived once more in the *Gluboki* ghetto. This time -- to take out youth and arms. When the *Jüdenradt* heard about his trip, they were ready to extradite him to the Germans. He was successful in escaping back to the partisans, taking with him *Leybele Rapaport* (today in Israel) and his sisters *Shifra* and *Rokhke* (the latter -- a nurse, today in America).

Yidl wanted to save his mother. He sent liaisons to the *Gluboki* ghetto several times until he succeeded, in March 1943, in seeing her. Every day she would go do manual labor with other Jews, to the *Krulevshtshine* train-junction-station, 18 kilometers from *Gluboki*. A peasant woman awaited her there and led her away into the forest.

In that period I was with *Yidl* in the forest. His sister *Itke*, his brother *Leyble*, *Mendl* (the grandson of the Jewish ritual slaughterer of *Dokshitz*) and *Sholem-Ber Freedman*.

Our group encountered a German army unit in the village of *Zashtsheshle*, in the *Haloybitsh* region, in January 1943. A bitter battle ensued. That is when *Yeshayahu Sosman* fell (born in 1910 in *Dokshitz*). Under the hail of bullet *Yidl* carried out his dead body and buried him in the village of *Rotshni*, in the *Dokshitz* region, in the sandy earth at the shore of the river.

Earlier *Yidl* had taken part in a partisan action against the German garrison in *Dokshitz* together with *Sosman*. They burned down a steam mill, which had served the Germans. *Sholem-Ber Freedman* was wounded in that action.

In February 1943, the Germans carried out a blockade against the partisans. Their guide was *Anton Trus*, a brother-in-law of the *Dokshitz* police commander, *Komulka*. Trus, from *Dokshitz*, like his brother-in-law, gave the Jews a lot of troubles and their bestiality, at times, advanced the German murders. In the *Rotshne* village, Yidl stood at an observation point in a garret; just as he noticed the Germans approaching he pointed his rifle at *Trus* and laid him out dead. *Yidl's* joy was great that he had succeeded in taking revenge on such a criminal and then -- he escaped from the Germans.

In the evening, on May the 1st, *Propelitsh* and *Krulevshtshine*. The train traffic stood still for three full days on such an important route for the Germans as the *Krulevshtshine-Molodetshne-Minsk* train route. *Yidle* also set up the destruction materials. He knew that in the village of *Zamoshe*, two kilometers from the well-armed and guarded garrison in *Krulevshtshine*, the advancing Red Army had entered and thrown weapons in a well. Additionally, the area was not far from the Germans and Yidl succeeded in getting the weapons and separating the explosive materials to use in blowing up the train tracks.

In the beginning of 1943, near the *Aszure* in the *Holubitz Pushtshe*, food and arms were air dropped, sent from Moscow. We were marched into the partisan group that carried the name of its commander, *Piyetya Tshorni* (later, it came to light that he was a Jewish boy by the name of *Peysakh Shvartz*.) Our assignment was to find out details about those stationed in the area German garrisons, transports that left to and came from the front, the numbers of divisions and names of the officers. Thanks to *Yidl* we were successful in getting a contact with the train depot supervisor in *Krulevshtshine* and with several of the men who linked the cars together. From them we received almost daily useful intelligence and information, which were very significant for us.

Thanks to that connection we were able, at the end of May 1943, to lay a mine under a platform on which there were German motorcyclists. 9 of them were killed.

What a circumstance now, after so many years, to recall all of the heroic acts of *Yidl Yessen*. I remember that in the month of March, 1944, we got an order from the other side of the front to put together a plan of the *shtetl Gluboki*, the positions of machine guns, rifles, tanks, numbers of German soldiers, etc. Thanks to our contact with a representative of the police commandant, with whom we met in the village of *Ivanovshtshizne*, as well as with the neighborhood commissar's secretary and the old engineer, *Shklenik*, we go the plan of the shtetl and the necessary intelligence. It came to be in the following way:

We needed to take the plan from a Christian near *Krulevshtshine*. It was a light night that was laden with danger for Yidl and me. Despite this we arrived safely at the designated place. We were also hungry and it was decided that we would not stay hiding there, rather go get a bite to eat in the village of *Lipove*. It later came to light that there were Germans hiding there, whose assignment it was to grab "a tongue," meaning -- a living partisan. Because of the lightness of the night we did not see them, hiding behind the little houses, when they did see us quite well and let us go undisturbed into the village. We knocked with certainty on the window of a house. All at once the nearby stable, covered with a straw roof, caught on fire from German shots and the area became bright as day. We decided to escape through the house and tore off the door -- but German soldiers awaited us there with drawn rifles. Yidl with his gun and I with my machine gun, opened fire, tore through, jumped out through the window and ran. Once again, *Yidl's* cool blooded nature caused us to be saved. He yelled to me, "Don't run to the swamp, let's go towards *Krulevshtshine*." It later turned out that the Germans were waiting all around the paths to the swamps where the partisans had their bases. We would have certainly fallen in their hands, if not for *Yidl's* cool calculations.

In the beginning of April 1944, *Yidl* got sick. I was successful, after much difficulty, to bring him the one doctor who was among the partisans -- *Lekakh*. He quickly determined that Yidl was sick with Typhus. Just then the big German siege and encircling of the partisans began, the so-called *Ushatz* Blockade. In such attacks we used to just gather ourselves in an area near a German garrison and purposefully wait out the difficult times there. But now we couldn't carry out our trick, because Yidl was sick.

The Germans brought tremendous military force from the front to that blockade and together with general Vlasov's soldiers; they made the circle around the partisans smaller, bombed them from the air and ground artillery. Many fell and were sacrificed. There was no other way out other than tearing through the blockade, notwithstanding the high price of sacrificed lives. Colonel *Rodyonov* led the breakthrough of the blockade because the partisan leader of the *Ushsatz* region left everything and escaped from the critical area by airplane.

Rodyonov gathered all of the machine guns and automatic weapons and thanks to their concentrated fire, they were able to break through the German encirclement. The colonel himself was seriously wounded and later died. That man, *Rodyonov*, who had served under *Vlasov* serving the Germans, was stationed in Krulevshtshine and sneaked over to the partisans--and as he had in *Krulevshtshine* he did in Dokshitz, kill many Germans and their accomplices. It was an important act of revenge for us Jews against the offenders.

On the 4th of May 1944, at one o'clock in the afternoon, in the village of *Rembo*, the partisan *Yidl Yessen* fell in a heroic death. Although he was weakened by illness, with gun in hand he took part in the battle against a

German division. He fell in battle like a dear soldier of the Jewish partisan-army in the terrible years of the Second World War.

May his memory be honored.

The Mass Grave of the Dokshitz Martyrs
by Efrayim Lipshitz, Of Blessed Memory

Ephriam Lifshitz

After the end of the Second World War, when I had come back from the front, my first desire was: to find *Dokshitz*, move back to my *shtetl* — perhaps some of my relatives survived, maybe some neighbors, some friends? Because even then, in the year 1945, some of us had the illusion that it was impossible and unnatural to slaughter millions of Jews in Poland, Russia, Germany, France, Belgium and other lands. Although I myself was a soldier and had seen desolated cities and *shtetls*, experienced a front of thousands of kilometers and already knew what the German murderers had done with our people —nevertheless, a spark of hope still glowed in my heart that at least some of the Jews of *Dokshitz* were able to avoid the tragic fate.

...And so, I find myself already in *Dokshitz*. The *shtetl* looks like an abandoned demolished nest. I search for the streets, alleys, nooks and corners, where but 6 years ago a full-blooded Jewish life roared and fevered — in the street, in the *beys-midrash* [house of study], in the political party meeting houses, in the organizations...

I ask a Christian if he knows if my brothers came here. He answered very calmly and indifferently that the *Dokshitz* Jews were not taken far away to other places to be killed, rather, just behind the *shtetl* to a huge dirt pit, over which the unlucky sacrifices were shot by machine guns — women, men, children, elderly, youth. Entire families were killed in this beastly manner, which only the bloodthirsty Nazis could conceive and carry out.

So, here I stand at my brothers' grave of Dokshitz martyrs. A cry is choked —but no tear shows itself in my eyes. My heart grieves — but I am not able to let out so much as a creak. I connect with the memory of the fallen, my dear and nearest who were killed as holy martyrs in God's name — and my memory wanders over into another world, the evil world of governments and people who knew about the bitter fate of the Jews and no one of them made any rulings, intervened, or demanded that the Germans stop the blood bath of us, the Jews.

Oh, *Dokshitz* martyrs — we will never forget you!

* * *

Of Blessed Memory
The Partizans

Dova Sussman-Karovitz .... .. Chaia-Esther Sussman

Left: Yehudah Rietman, Partizan (in the US)
Right: The Partisan Zelig Tielz (in Canada)

Survivors - Partizans

At the Pit

By Zvi Markman, 1970
Translation: Florence A. Ruderman, 2014

After long wandering I returned
Hoping I'd find someone alive
I trod over ashes and ruins
I thought I'd go out of my mind.

The sun dipped in guilt and in clouds
Blushed in shame and slyly peeked
Alone, unaware how, by what means
I found myself standing at the edge of the pit.

On the left -- a desecrated wrecked graveyard,
Memorial? A sole wooden cross.
The earth itself shuddered in pain --
At the one lasting witness of blood-letting evil.

My head hammers, veins throb
Legs buckle and long to escape.
A pressing weight clutches and holds,
Names surface -- face after face . . .

Mothers stand up, as little lambs-children
Just wakened from slumber
Stretch little hands out and beg, lift us up . . .
For what sins were we murdered? for whom?

Who amused himself with satanic games?
Drove some out from prayer in taless and tfiln
From wedding canopy bride and groom --
Without reason: wantonly shot.

A mesh of human beings, old and young, sons and daughters
A gruesome circle, and a manic laughter.
Intermixed sounds
Of sobs and of choking, of prayers, of song . . .

Of Chasidic melody, of lullabies' hush,
Of shofar's teruah, of the Kaddish of Nielah
Of pottery broken at marital vows,
Chants of Kol Nidre -- talesim and robes . . .

Youth wilted, unrealized longings,
And feet that never reached their goals,
Sweet dreams, tender yearnings
Of couples who promise their love everlasting . . .

Of clamor of fairs and blizzards of snow,
Disquiet and fever whirl in the air,
Chanukah candles and rattles of Purim ---
And loneness, and need, and anguish, and woe . . .

And groans of the sick and bitter laments
The murderers send out an unending curse.
Animal growls and insensate commands
The last who remain still attempt to resist.

Hands clasp aged and worn,
Eyes stare distorted and rigid
Bones, trampled, are broken
Children fall, covered over . . .

Bodies in fever, gnashing of teeth
A horrible deluge with thunder and lightning.
Burning lava erupts from volcanos,
A grueling roar of thousands of seas . . .

Flames flicker in smoke and in din,
The storm grows more bestial and wild,
A hail of bullets, blood spurts as from fountains . . .
Struck bodies fall, rolling one into another . . .

The rabbi, barely standing, adjusts the atora
Recites ere-death confession in tones of Gemorra
A ghastly choir echoes the voices of kohel
And pierces the air: Shema Yisroel!

* * * *

And then, when the abyss had swallowed up all,
The still sounding call rose up to the skies,
Calling forth brothers from border to border
Return to the land, the old land, the new . . .

Raise a memorial of splendor
That looks to the heavens with pride,
Through effort and toil build a land of renewal,
With notes now resounding: triumphant and free.

Chapter 5
The Dokshitzers in Israel and the Diaspora

The Activities of the Dokshitz Veteran Organization
By Dov Katzowitch

    Dokshitz was freed in June 1944, after the Germans retreated. The few who joined the partisans began to return slowly. Among those returning was Yosef Shapiro, Bainish Kozinitz, Yehuda Reitman, Batia Friedman, the Rozov family and others. Immediately after the freeing of the town, letters began arriving from the town Jews, the Jews who had escaped before the Nazis. Letters arrived from the faraway parts of Russia, from soldiers in the Russian army, from relatives in the United States, South Africa and South America, from Israel and other countries. One question was shouted by all these letters: Is anyone of my family alive? Did anyone manage to survive the teeth of the Nazi beast? They asked an acquaintance, a neighbor, a "good" gentile to write what happened to their families. The answer was the same everywhere: "No one is left! They are all slaughtered, murdered, exterminated!" These letters were a sort of testimony, a sort of documentation of the history of the Dokshitz Jews, for among the writers were townspeople who had left it decades ago immigrating to faraway lands, from pioneers who had "made Aliya" to Israel, from leftists who ran away to Russia, from partisans and Soviet army soldiers. However, the town was destroyed, 90% of its houses were destroyed, and the town itself had become a cemetery. It was not possible to breath in it. It was not possible to live in it - not one more day. Moreover, the gentiles of the town, wide eyed when they saw you: " So, you stayed alive?!! You were lucky!" And quickly adding, without being asked: I helped your relatives with food, shelter and everything I could... Are you thinking of staying here...?" After a "reception" like this, all you wanted was to escape your home town immediately, with giving it a second look. Many of the survivors did not want to visit it, not even for one hour. From Poland they reached the refugee camps in Germany and from there they planned to reach Israel. However, many took to the United States and their sons, today, come and visit Israel. Some of those who stayed in Russia for quite some time, arrived in Israel in 1958 - 1960, after passing through Poland.

**Some of the Members of the Committee of
the Organization of Former Residents of Dokshitz in Israel**

In 1948, on the initiative of friends Shapiro Yosef, Tzeitlin and Toibes, and with the help of members of kibbutz Ein-Shemer and Ma'anit, the Dokshitz and Parafianow Veteran Organization was formed. The first memorials were held in Petach-Tikva and it was then that the idea of a book in the memory of our martyrs was raised. With the aliya of a new wave of young people in 1958 - 60, the organization widened its activities. Now arrived in Israel, not only those who remembered the "quiet" Dokshitz, but those who were there and saw with their own eyes the destruction and annihilation of the sacred community - Dokshitz. Assemblies in the memory of the martyrs of our town took place every year. A memory board was raised to commemorate the community martyrs at Zion mountain in Jerusalem. The twenty-fifth memorial took place in 1967 in Jerusalem. A tour was taken at Yad Vashem, on mount Zion and near the wailing wall. A list of martyrs was organized and much hard work has been put in to publish this book. This is the way we keep the fire burning in our hearts. The fire we took out of our town. We meet, sometimes on happy occasions, sometimes on sad ones, but every meeting strengthens our connections and marks our path.

In 1988, a monument in memory of the martyrs of our town was erected in the Holon cemetery. Ashes of our martyrs, brought by immigrants from Dokshitz, was placed there. Moreover, in a container, in the cemetery, is a list of the martyrs. The monument can be found opposite the military section (1/9/15).

These excerpts were translated from the Dokshitz/Parafianow book in 1990.

Dov Katzovitch Secretary of the Dokshitz/Parafianow Veteran Organization in Israel.

Dokshitzers [People from *Dokshitz*] in America

by Nekhomehle Zalkind-Greber / Brooklyn, New York

I want to describe here the aid work of the *Dokshitz landsmanshaft* [society of "countrymen" or fellow citizens of a *shtetl* or town in Eastern Europe] in America (and my personal work), for our fellow countrymen before the war, and especially — after the war.

I was born and raised in *Dokshitz*. My parents, *Yisroel* and *Alte Zolkind*, were people of some means and dealt in flax and seed. Our house was on the street that led to *Parafianov* and *Gluboki*. I had three brothers: *Bentsiye-KhayimI, Eyli, Shimon* and one sister — *Elke* who was a midwife.

Later I met an Austrian young man, married him and moved to America.

The beginning of my work for the *Dokshitz* people was after receiving a letter from *Yidl Rozov* in which he wrote to me that all of my beloved and dear had been killed. He asked me to find his relatives in America. I searched for and found them and sent a package of food. I do not, until this day, know if they ever received it.

It seems that the Jews who went back to the *shtetl* after the liberation of *Dokshitz* found my letters in the post office. They began writing to me. I even received letters from *Dokshitzers* via American Jewish soldiers. Mostly they wanted me to help search for living relatives. I found many and helped them get in contact.

Later on, the ritual slaughterer of *Dokshitz*, *Yoikhonon, Yisroel Shoykhet's* son, came to me and asked me to take part in helping out a friend of his in Russia. He used to be in the *Dokshitz* party and had not gotten any help from them. I went to the president of the *Dokshitz* organization, *Shimon Vant* and asked him to call a meeting, not only of those who were already members, but via announcements in the press, all *Dokshitzers* and *Glubokiers*, to come together to participate in the aid work.

Many countrymen came, a report was generated using the knowledge we had at the time listing those who had been killed and the few who were able to survive. We gathered a sum of money, all for aid. I was elected to correspond and gather information; because I was the only one who came to America and had gotten to know the people from the *shtetl* well over the last few years.

I developed relationships with people from various *shtetls* and we gathered several hundred dollars. We also gathered some clothing and food and sent it to Poland, Russia and to the camps in Germany where many were living. We also helped them get in touch with relatives, making it possible for them to come to America. Of course, not all who came wanted our help. Once I suffered because I worked very hard and got sick, with a high temperature. But that did not stop me. Also, people didn't let me leave my work because there was nobody else who knew the *shtetl* as well as I. Many times I received letters from people who weren't from *Dokshitz*. When I asked for necessary detailed information, it came out that they were never residents of our *shtetl*.

The Zalkind Family

Our work went on like this from 1945 until 1950.

We made a big mistake when a sum of money remained and we gave it to the Joint Distribution Committee, which helped the refugees. I was personally against this, but they assured us that they are helping our fellow countrymen wherever they lived. Whether or not they did anything — I do not know.

When people turned to me from Israel about publishing a *Yizkor* [memory/memorial] Book I went to a Bar-Mitzvah celebration of one of our countrymen, were there were to be many newer immigrants who had done quite well here, but nobody wanted to give money. They knew, however, that I had helped them quite a bit so they could not say no to me. I collected 250 dollars there.

A goodhearted countryman, *Efrayim Kantorovitsh* (*Kalman Shultz's* cousin), gave 70 dollars, I gave 15 dollars and the remaining 165 dollars were collected from approximately 10 people. Obviously, this is not enough, but I could not do any more. We sent the money to *Yoysef Shapiro*.

[page 331]

Chapter 6

Our Martyrs

For these do we weep,
Along with all the holy ones of Israel,
Who lost their lives sanctifying God's name,
At the hands of the murderous Germans and their accomplices.

[Page 333]

List of Dokshitz Martyrs
(By streets)

[Note added: The list by streets is arranged as it appears in the 1990 translation when it was alphabetized and a few names were added.]

Borisover St

Aloy	Kalman-Velvel and his family	Kaplan	Beilka and 2 children
Friedman	Shmuel and family	Katz	Yosef
Friedman	Moshe-Leib, his wife and 2 children	Katz	Mota
		Katz	Mania
		Katz	Yitzchak
Gitlin	Haim	Klonski	[trans note: 1st name unknown] his wife, and his daughter Yocha
Gitlin	Yona		
Gitlin	Pese		
Gitlin	Hanna-Bracha	Kozshinitz	David, his wife and family
Gleichenhaus	Shmuel and his wife	Kremer	Eliyahu, his wife and children
Gulkovitz	Yehuda		
Gulkovitz	Zlata	Kremer	Nathan, his wife and 2 children
Harnas	Yerahmiel, his wife and 4 children	Levitan	Moshe
Harnas	Male	Ribshtein	Shlomo-Haim, with the family and 2 daughters
Harnas	Ziame		
Harnas	Leib	Rozov	Moshe, his wife and 2 children
Harnas	Sarah		
Kaganier	Eliyahu his wife and child	Rozov	Shmuel-Ber's wife and children
Kaplan	Simha		

Rozov	Rivka	Tiles	Hillel and his wife
Rozov	Altar	Tiles	Michle
Rytman	Eliyahu	Tiles	Leib
Rytman	Eda	Tiles	Moshe
Rytman	Avigdor	Tiles	Kopel
Rytman	Shlomo	Tiles	Sarah-Rachel
Rytman	Rachel	Tzeitlin	Dov and family
Rytman	Liba	Tzeitlin	Hevel and family
Rytman	Berel and 3 children	Vant	Malka
Rytman	Shalom	Vant	Shlomo
Rytman	Mirel	Vant	Rachel
Rytman	Moshe	Volfovitch	Michael his wife and 3 children
Rytman	Haim		
Shapiro	Abraham-Mendel	Yesin	Shepsel
Shapiro	Braina	Yesin	Rachel-Gitl
Shapiro	Mone	Yesin	Meir
Shapiro	Sonia	Yesin	Zev
Shapiro	Geise	Yesin	Fruma
Shapiro	Sarah-Frida	Yesin	Pese
Shapiro	Lifsha	Yesin	Shmuel, his wife and 2 children
Shapiro	Mendel and 3 sons		
Shapiro	Mendel, his wife and 2 children	Zimlin	Yitzhak
Sossman	Baruch	Zimlin	Shosha and children
Sossman	Feiga		

Dolhinover St.		Gitlin	Yerucham and his wife
Dimenstein	Aba	Gitlin	Haya-Breine
Dimenstein	Israel	Gitlin	Israel
Dimenstein	Shepsel	Hidekel	Zelke
Dimenstein	Esther	Hidekel	Riva-Elka and children
Feigelson	Eliahu	Kabatznik	Haim
Feigelson	Hasia-Ita	Kabatznik	Pese
Feigelson	Avrahml	Kabatznik	Zlata
Feigelson	Freida and 2 children	Kabatznik	Riva
Friedman	Velvet	Kabatznik	Yente
Friedman	Eshka	Kabatznik	Menashe
Friedman	Reiza	Kaplan	Yehuda-Pesach
Friedman	Sarah and child	Kaplan	Esther

Kaplan	Yankel	Levitan	Zelig
Kaplan	Hanan	Levitan	Raya
Kaplan	Hersh	Levitan	Liba
Kaplan	Rafael and wife	Levitan	Fruma
Kaplan	Mirel	Levitan	Rivka
Katz	Berke and wife	Margolin	David
Katz	Yankel	Plavnik	Sonia
Katz	Esther	Plavnik	Nachum
Kozshinitz	Zelig-Haim	Plavnik	Moshe
Kozshinitz	Eta-Rocha and children	Plavnik	Izshe
Kluft	Nachum-Yehoshua	Plavnik	Liza
Kluft	Rivka	Plavnik	Sonia
Kluft	Beile	Plavnik	Beryl
Kluft	Keile	Pliskin	Abraham-Shlomo
Kluft	Haim	Pliskin	Gitel
Kluft	Fania	Pliskin	Esther
Kluft	Alter	Pliskin	Zalman
Kluft	Yitzchak	Pliskin	Sarah
Kremer	Simcha	Pliskin	Yitzchak
Kremer	Beile and children	Pliskin	Geesha and 3 children
Kremer	Yitzchak	Rubin	Yoel
Kremer	Dvorsha and children	Rubin	Sheine
Lahotshin	Miriam	Rubin	Haya-Henia
Lahotshin	Lebe	Rubin	Fruma-Leah
Lahotshin	Gnesia	Rubin	Zalman
Lahotshin	Iser	Rubin	Ya'akov
Lahotshin	Esther	Shkolnik	Leizer and wife
Lahotshin	Zishe	Shkolnik	Sarah
Levitan	Zalman	Shklonik	Haya-Esther and husband
Levitan	Basia-Gita	Shkolnik	Menachem and wife
Levitan	Michal	Shkolnik	Mula
Levitan	Liba	Shkolnik	Zvia
Levitan	Hirshl	Slavin	Nachum-Leib and family
Levitan	Sarah	Slavin	Israel and wife
Levitan	Mendel	Srebrenik	Shaya
Levitan	Malka	Srebrenik	Musia
Levitan	Basia	Srebrenik	Yosef
Levitan	Iser	Zeidel	Ya'akov Ber and his wife
Levitan	Perel		
Levitan	Rachel		

Zeidel	Marka		

Dzshika St.		Levin	Moshe
Friedman	Zalman	Levin	Sarah
Friedman	Pese	Levin	Zalman
Galperin	Rivka	Levin	Shlomo
Galperin	Eliyahu-Natan	Levin	Bracha
Galperin	Kopel	Levin	David-Zelig
Galperin	Reizel	Levin	Shepsel
Galperin	Sarah	Segal	Haim
Kopelovitch	Musia	Segal	Dina
Lenkin	Yehoshua	Segal	Arye
Lenkin	Hoda		

Gluboker St.		Gilenson	Moshe
Akselrod	Moshe	Gilevitch	Haim
Akselrod	Dina	Gilevitch	Stira
Akselrod	Mulia	Gilevitch	Aizik
Akselrod	Sarah	Gilevitch	Berel
Akselrod	Zelig	Gilinki	Gitel and son [trans note, typo for Bilinki?]
Bilinki	Israel-Leiser and wife		
Bilinki	Yitzchak-Reuben	Glazer	Levi-Yitzchak
Bilinki	Hayka	Glazer	Moshe
Bilinki	Rivka	Glazer	Sarah
Bilinki	Yocha	Glazer	Haya
Bilinki	Leah	Glazer	Efraim
Deitz	Avraml, his wife and children	Glazer	Fruma
		Goltz	Max
Fabrikant	Leib	Goltz	Liba
Fabrikant	Hodes	Gudkin	Yitzchak
Faivishevitch	Beilke	Gudkin	Beila
Faivishevitch	Nachum and son	Gudkin	Avraham
		Kagan	Pesach
Friedman	Rachel	Kagan	Liba
Friedman	Eliahu	Kagan	Soshka
Friedman	Neche	Kagan	Aharon
Friedman	Rivka	Kagan	Golde
Galperin	Reizel	Kaminkovitch	Abraham and wife
Galperin	Kopel and child		
Gilenson	Motel	Kaminkovitch	Hava-Rocha
Gilenson	Haim-Rafael	Kaminkovitch	Yosef
Gilenson	Geesha	Kaminkovitch	Moshe

Kaminkovitch	Matale	Levit	Rachel
Kaminkovitch	Leiser	Levit	Haim- Zusie
Kaminkovitch	Gavriel	Levit	Yocha
Kaminkovitch	Liza and family	Levit	Yaakov
Kaminkovitch	Reizel	Levitan	Monis
Kaminkovitch	Haya	Levitan	Israel
Kaminkovitch	...	Levitan	Pese
Kaplan	Chiena	Levitan	Abraham
Katzovitch	Zalman-Meir	Lipkind	Bere
Katzovitch	Haya	Lipkind	Rivka
Katzovitch	Haim	Markman	Nachum
Katzovitch	Yosef	Markman	Dina
Khlabnovitch	Rashe	Markman	Hanna
Khlabnovitch	Yitzchak	Markman	Sima
Khlabnovitch	Yitzchak and daughter	Markman	Rachel
Kluft	Haya-Henya	Markman	Yitzchak
Kluft	Chashe	Markman	Kuna-Sheina
Kluft	Masha	Markman	Haya-Sarah
Kopelovitch	Moshe-Aharon	Markman	Yitzchak
Kopelovitch	Leah	Markman	Yehudit
Kopelovitch	Mendel	Markman	Nachum-Leib
Kopelovitch	Gitel	Markman	Motele
Kosovski	Yosef	Markman	Henia
Kosovski	Chiene and family	Markman	Rachel-Leah
Kozshinitz	Isha'ayahu	Markman	Abraham
Kozshinitz	Dvora	Markman	Faya
Kozshinitz	Malka	Markman	Reizel
Kozshinitz	Yonia	Markman	Haya-Sarah
Kozshinitz	Hassia	Markman	Doba
Kozshinitz	Yosef	Markman	Zusia
Kozshinitz	Pese	Perlmuter	Bera
Kozshinitz	Abraham	Pollak	Riva-Reiza
Kremer	Golde	Pollak	Leib
Kremer	Shalom	Pollak	Gita
Kremer	Berel	Pollak	Haya with husband and child
Kugel	Shmuel	Raskin	Haya-Grunia
Kugel	Sarah	Raskin	Haim-Yosef and wife
Kugel	Haim		
Kugel	Yitzchak	Raskin	Haikel (Kremer), his wife and children
Levin	Gedalyahu		
Levit	Rafael		

Raskin	Haya-Esther	Taitz	Dvora
Raskin	Shurka	Taitz	Henia
Rozov	David	Taitz	Israel-Leib
Rozov	Ester-Rachel	Taitz	Sarah
Sachartov	[trans note: 1st name unknown] and family	Taitz	Haya
		Vant	Hershel-Zelig
		Vant	Miriam
Segalovitch	Stirka	Vant	Hasia-Ita
Segalovitch	Hirshel	Vant	Zalman-Yitzchak
Segalovitch	Motel	Vant	Rachel
Segalovitch	Israel-Leizer	Vant	Hanna
Segalovitch	Etel	Vant	Zelda
Shapiro	Asher	Weinstein	Zlata
Shapiro	Mariasha	Weinstein	Ya'akov
Sheinin	R' Leib The Rav	Volfson	Mule
Sheinin	Riva	Yesin	Zundel
Sheinin	Haim-Yakutiel	Yesin	Batia
Sheinin	Shalom-Ber	Yesin	Malka
Sheinin	Boris	Yesin	Hanna
Sheinin	Dvora	Yesin	Shmuel-Yitzchak
Solovei	Yitzchak		
Solovei	Rachel	Yesin	Mache
Solovei	Chiena	Yesin	Yoche
Svidler	Mendel, his wife Sarah and four children	Yesin	Bracha-Hanna
		Yudkovski	The teacher Reuben the shochet and family
Streichstein	Leibe		
Taitz	Mordechai-Ber		

Keidershe Alley

		Friedman	Rachel
Cyrlin	Ya'akov-Ber and family	Kaplan	Moshe-Leib and family
Dameskin	Sheine-Marke	Kloiser	Mendel and wife
Dameskin	Esther	Kloiser	Shmuel-Hirsh
Dameskin	Shlomo	Kloiser	Feigel
Freidkin	Shmuel-Michael	Kloiser	Abraham
Freidkin	Israel	Kloiser	Rachel
Freidkin	Moshe & family	Kloiser	Sonia
Friedman	Moshe	Kopelovitch	Shmuel-Leib
Friedman	Chasie-Riva	Kopelovitch	Michle
Friedman	Yehuda	Kopelovitch	Berel
Friedman	Lea	Kopelovitch	Yehuda
		Kopelovitch	Zipa

Kopelovitch	Lea and children		children
Kozshinitz	Leib and wife	Perelmuter	Shimon
Kozshinitz	Esther-Malka	Perelmuter	Zelda
Kozshinitz	Dvora	Perelmuter	Zalman and wife
Kozshinitz	Abraham-Yitzchak	Perelmuter	Avramel
Levitan	Yankel-Zadok	Perelmuter	Gitel & children
Levitan	Menucha and children	Reimer	Shlomo's family
Levitan	Fruma and family	Rozov	Esther
		Rozov	Fruma
		Rozov	Nechama
Musin	David	Rozov	Sarah
Musin	Yocheved	Zacharovitch	Esther
Musin	Zusa wife &		

Polotzker St.

		Friedman	Batia
Botvinik	Faivush	Friedman	Malka
Botvinik	Rivka	Friedman	Eliahu
Botvinik	Ya'akov	Glazer	Haim-Shmuel
Botvinik	Max	Glazer	Hanna
Botvinik	Genia	Glazer	David
Botvinik	Haya	Glazer	Mirel
Budnov	Yoske	Glazer	Leah
Budnov	Sarah and family	Glazer	Raizel
Budnov	His sister and her husband	Gleichenhaus	Leib and wife
		Gleichenhaus	Nioma
Budnov	Gele	Gordon	Nechama
Dikman	Baruch	Gordon	Avrasha
Dikman	Leah	Gordon	Yonie
Dikman	Mira	Gordon	David
Dikman	Nachum	Gordon	Mina
Dikman	Sonia	Gordon	Rosa
Dlugan	Gavriel	Gordon	Mishka
Dlugan	Doba	Kopelovitch	Haim
Dovong	Hersh	Kopelovitch	Liza
Frankfurt	Hirshl	Kopelovitch	Pese
Frankfurt	Rikle	Kopelovitch	Meni
Frankfurt	Beni	Kremer	Yosef
Frankfurt	Haya	Kremer	Nechama
Friedman	Shule	Kremer	Motel
Friedman	Mendel	Kremer	Haya
		Kremer	Tzipa

Levitan	Gdaliahu, his wife and children	Sheiman	Arthur
Lipkind	Haim	Shultz	Mordechai-Velvel
Lipkind	Perel	Shultz	Marke
Markman	David	Shultz	Tzvi-Yona
Markman	Libe	Shultz	Shprinza
Markman	Reuben	Smerkovitch	Mendel, his wife and children: Tzipa, Yocha, Berl, Rivka
Markman	Tzila and son		
Markman	Mendel	Stozki	Gita and family
Markman	Doba	Tziklin	Akiva
Markman	Yitzchak	Tziklin	Tzipa
Markman	Rachel	Tziklin	Hanna
Markman	Chiene and children	Tziklin	Baruch
Markman	Rafael	Tziklin	Rachel
Markman	Dvora	Tziklin	Zalman Uri
Markman	Abraham	Tziklin	Yocheved
Markman	Esther	Tziklin	Yosef
Markman	Haya and family	Tziklin	Rachel, her husband and children
Markman	Sheina		
Price	Beril and wife		
Price	Gershon	Tzuchman	Shmuel
Raskin	Pesach	Tzuchman	Dvora
Raskin	Atshe	Tzuchman	Shalom
Raskin	Tzila	Tzuchman	Vulke
Rytman	Baruch	Tzuchman	Aharon
Rytman	Gitel	Tzuchman	Itke
Rytman	Aharon	Tzuchman	Sima
Rytman	Gershon	Tzuchman	Akiva
Rozov	Ya'akov-Hirsh and wife	Tzuchman	Reizka
		Yesin	Ya'akov
Rozov	Geesha	Yesin	Rivka and children
Rozov	Sheina		
Rozov	Henech	Yesin	Zelig, his wife and children
Rozov	Gita		
Sheiman	Sonia	Ziskind	Zelig
Sheiman	Fania	Ziskind	Shaul
Sheiman	Riva		

Shul-Hoif

Aloy	Abraham-Moshe	Kozshinitz	Vule
Aloy	Tzipa	Kozshinitz	Henia
Aloy	Itka	Kozshinitz	Moshe
Aloy	Abraham-Moshe (the shammas)	Kozshinitz	Riva
Aloy	Tzipa	Kozshinitz	Rache
Dole	Israel	Kremer	Israel
Drutz	Mendel and his wife	Kremer	Aharon
Drutz	Sonia	Levin	Shepsel
Drutz	Haya-Hinda	Markman	Simcha and wife
Feigelson	Israel-Nota	Markman	Yoske
Feigelson	Hirshl	Markman	Haim-Hirshl
Feigelson	Ya'akov	Markman	Doba
Feigelson	Gershon	Markman	David
Feiman	Esther	Markman	Yoel and wife
Feiman	Rachel-Leah and daughter	Rubin	Gershon
Feinman	Batia-Malka	Rubin	Haya-Sarah
Feinman	Sarah	Rubin	Abraham
Freiman	Zalman	Rubin	Beni
Friedman	Zelig	Rubin	Nechama
Friedman	Frada	Rubin	Leah
Friedman	Rachel-Leah	Shultz	Mendel and wife
Friedman	Batia	Shultz	Keile
Friedman	Israel	Shultz	Israel-Meir
Kaplan	Meir-Mendel and wife	Svidler	Guta
Kaplan	Shmuel-Leib and family	Svidler	Yitzchak
Kasovski	Sihlomo-Shaya	Svidler	Rachel
Kasovski	Dvora	Tiles	Rafael and wife
Katz	Tzipa (Nisan's) and 3 daughters	Ya'akov	David
Khlabnovitch	the mother	Ya'akov	Rive-Lee's
Khlabnovitch	Motele & sister	Yesin	Mendel
Kozshinitz	Zanvel	Yesin	Hayka and family
Kozshinitz	Alta & children	Zepelevitch	Mrs.
Kozshinitz	Mendel	Zepelevitch	Leizer and mother
Kozshinitz	Gita	Zepelevitch	Aharon-Leib
Kozshinitz	Zalke	Zepelevitch	Abba-David
Kozshinitz	Haim	Zepelevitch	Bracha
Kozshinitz	Sarah	Zepelevitch	Faya
		Zepelevitch	Yitzchak
		Zepelevitch	Leah
		Zepelevitch	Feigel

Zubiski	and family		Michle
the barber	Pesach, his wife and children		Muske (Chana's)
the butcher	Baruch-Shalom Zipke		Shepsel (last name unknown) his wife Etel and family
the butcher	Herzel, his wife and children		Sima (Manase's)
the tailor	Velvel and family		Yankel (Riva-Leah's)
the wagon owner	Vula and family		Zusia (Pesach's) [or Peske's]
	David (Nechama's)		

Sloboda (Suburb)		Feldman	Yechiel
		Feldman	Zlata
Alperovitch	Hirshel	Feldman	Leibe and 3 children
Alperovitch	Sasha		
Alperovitch	Shaya	Feldman	Faivish, his wife and children
Alperovitch	Doba		
		Friedman	Altar (Slave-Motl's)
Barshai	Kalman		
Barshai	Zalman	Friedman	Sarah-Leah and 2 children
Blinshtein	Reuben		
Blinshtein	Rele	Glazer	Yoshe
Blinshtein	Leizer	Glazer	Moshe
Blinsthein	Mota	Glazer	Abraham
Bloch	Shlomo	Gleichengaus	Dvonie
Bloch	Rachel-Hasia	Gleichengaus	Elke
Bloch	Zelig	Gordon	Mendel
Bloch	Chaika	Gordon	Bas-Sheva
Bloch	Hanna	Gordon	Leah
Boxer	Gershon	Gordon	Ya'akov
Boxer	Leah and children	Huberman	Hirshel (butcher)
		Huberman	Malka
Deitz	Erke	Huberman	Sheinka
Deitz	Vichne	Huberman	Shaya
Feigel	Moshe-Ya'akov	Huberman	Shalom
Feigel	Leah-Reiza	Kabatchnik	David
Feldman	Abraham	Kagan	and family
Feldman	Nathan (Kosorier)	Kantorovitch	Reuben
		Kantorovitch	Haya-Musia
Feldman	Baruch	Kantorovitch	Brayna
Feldman	Liba	Kantorovitch	Eshka

Kantorovitch	Hanna	Kugel	Nechama and husband with children
Kantorovitch	Yehoshua		
Kaplan	Eida		
Kaplan	Isar and family	Lenkin	Haim-Velvel
Kluft	Zalman-Leib	Lenkin	Pese
Kluft	Moshe	Lenkin	Yankel
Kluft	Malka	Lenkin	Shaya
Kluft	Yakutiel	Lenkin	Hanna-Liba
Kluft	Rachel	Lenkin	Haya-Brayna
Kluft	Reiszke	Lenkin	Malka
Kluft	Hanna	Lenkin	Gitel
Kluft	Greinem	Lenkin	Aharon-Ber
Kluft	Yakir, his wife and children	Levitan	Esther-Leah
		Levitan	Feiga
Kluft	Lila	Lifshitz	Mota and wife
Kopelovitch	Shmuel	Lifshitz	Etel and family
Kopelovitch	Baruch	Lifshitz	Benyamin
Kopelovitch	Liba	Lifshitz	Shifra
Kopelovitch	Menashe	Lifshitz	Zalman
Kopelovitch	Shmuel	Lifshitz	Chaim
Kopelovitch	Alte	Lifshitz	Leibe
Kopelovitch	Baruch	Lipkind	David
Kopelovitch	Menashe	Lipkind	Beylke
Kopelovitch	Zuske	Lipkind	Tuvia
Kopelovitch	Haim	Markman	Leizer-Aharon
Kopelovitch	Velvel-Leizer	Markman	Haya
Kopelovitch	Gitel	Markman	Feigel-Yehudis
Kopelovitch	Yoshe	Markman	Avraml
Kopelovitch	Shimon	Markman	Melech
Kopelovitch	Eliahu	Markman	Leib and wife
Kopelovitch	Chiene	Markman	Henia
Kopelovitch	Basia	Markman	Esther
Kopelovitch	Leah	Mindlin	Arke
Kozshinitz	Velvel	Mindlin	Zipke and husband
Kozshinitz	Alte		
Kozshinitz	David	Mindlin	Yerachmiel Mordechai-Itshe
Kozshinitz	Leah		
Kremer	Zundel	Mintz	Zelke and wife
Kremer	Henia	Mintz	Zipke and son
Kugel	Beinish	Nachman	Reuben and two daughters
Kugel	Yankel		
Kugel	Sara-Yente	Poliak	Moshe-Leib
		Poliak	Hanna

Poliak	Beril	Vorkel	Pese
Poliak	Baruch	Yanovski	Rachel and family
Poliak	Mota	Zayonitz	Shimon
Poliak	Leah	Zayonitz	Henia
Rozin	Yidel (the smith), his wife Leibe and family	Zalkind	Israel
		Zalkind	Alta
Shulgeifer	and family	Zalkind	Ben-Zion
Shultz	Eliezer	Zalkind	Elke
Shultz	Rachel	Zalkind	Shimon
Shultz	Hillel		Chavel the match maker
Slavin	Haim and family		Chone (The smith), wife Hanna and children
Slavin	Manis		
Tziklin	Abraham-Moshe		
Tziklin	Chashke		
Tziklin	Gita and husband		Haim and family
			Leizer the smith
Varfman	and family		Mote (hazan)
Varfman	Nathan		Sarah Itka and family
Varfman	Moshe		
Varfman	Reuben		Shechne the water carrier
Varfman	Ya'akov		
Varfman	Leah		Zundel
Varfman	Chana		Zusie and family
Varfman	Zishe		Erka Shimon Artzik's
Vorkel	Israel		

Ulanska Alley

Bunimovitch	Bunia	Shleifer	Yaakov
Friedman	Yitzhak-Meir	Sverdlov	Volf
Friedman	(his wife)	Sverdlov	Hana
Friedman	Slava	Sverdlov	Nota
Kremer	Leib his wife and three children Pinkhas's Gnesia and husband	Sverdlov	Yekutiel
		Sverdlov	(his wife) and children
		Svidler	Esther
		Svidler	Haya and husband
Shleifer	Yerahmiel	Svidler	Rachel and husband
Shleifer	Rachel	Svidler	Moshe

[Page 344]

List of Martyrs Given by their relatives

Varfman	Berel	Ziskind	Bashke
Varfman	Hana-Yoche	Ziskind	Zushe
Varfman	David	Ziskind	Haya-Raizel
Varfman	Gnesia	Ziskind	Rachel
Varfman	Sima	Ziskind	Sarale
Yermovski	Laizer	Ziskind	Teibele
Yermovski	Fania	Kugel	Shmuel
Yermovski	Sarah	Kugel	Sarah
Gulkovitsh	Yudik	Kugel	Chaim-Itshe
Gulkovitsh	Zlata	Kugel	Iser
Feinbloom	Shimsil	Muskat	Doba
Feinbloom	Sarah-Esther	Solovei	Arie-Lev
Feinbloom	Shprintze	Solovei	Tzipa
Feinbloom	Leah	Solovei	Mulia
Feinbloom	Sonia	Solovei	Tzipka
Teitz	Isacher	Solevei	Leah
Teitz	Feye	Nievinski	Shepsel and two daughters
Teitz	Rivka		
Teitz	Leah	Hauchman	Yakov
Horovitz	Dvora	Hauchman	Rena
Teitz	Yisrael-Lev	Hauchman	Moshe-Ishayahu
Teitz	Sarah	Hauchman	Zalman
Teitz	Haya	Markman	Mendel
Gutkin	Itsha	Markman	Beila
Gutkin	Beila	Skiben	Yitzhak
Gutkin	Avraml	Skiben	Sheine
Gutkin	Izaak	Skiben	Zev
Gutkin	Yankel	Friedman	Yisrael-Ruven
Gutkin	Chaim	Friedman	Sonia
Gutkin	Sarah	Friedman	Moshe
Huberman	Tzipa	Friedman	Shalom
Huberman	Haya-Liba		
Ziskind	Shayel		

[Page 345]

Friedman	Nachum	Kaminkovitz	Yitzhak
Friedman	Fayvish	Kaminkovitz	Hasia
Friedman	Henia	Raskind	Pesach
Friedman	Gita	Raskind	Esther
Friedman	Chaim-Yitzhak	Raskind	Tzilla
Friedman	Nachama	Vant	Shlomo
Friedman	Nachum	Vant	Rachel
Friedman	Sarah	Vant	Sonia
Friedman	Berel	Vant	Nechama
Friedman	Elke	Markman	Simcha
Friedman	Yoel	Markman	Leah
Friedman	Rachel	Markman	Yoske
Friedman	Yisrael-Eli	Markman	Chaim-Hershel
Friedman	Yasha-Leib	Markman	Musia
Levitan	Elke	Markman	Doba
Levitan	Motke	Markman	Miriam
Bielinki	Yisrael-Leizar	Markman	Batia
Bielinki	Sarah	Markman	David
Bielinki	Mendel	Piravoskin	Mordechai-Zev
Bielinki	Yankel	Piravoskin	Chana
Rosenbaum	Leiba	Piravoskin	Lipa
Rosenbaum	Dvora	Piravoskin	Vichna
Rosenbaum	Avraham-Abba	Piravoskin	Feiga
Rosenbaum	Yenta	Piravoskin	Haya
Piravoskin	Shlomo	Piravoskin	Tzvi
Piravoskin	Musia	Dvorkin	Malka
Rozov	Gita	Dvorkin	Eiga
Rozov	Mendel	Dvorkin	Avigdor
Friedman	Yitzhak-Myer	Kopelevitch	Yosef-Chaim
Friedman	Sarah	Kopelevitch	Rivka-Bluma
Friedman	Slava	Kopelevitch	Zalman-Yishiyahu
Kaplan	Nisan	Kopelevitch	Yaakov
Kaplan	Shprintze and children	Kopelevitch	Leah
Friedman	Moshe	Kopelevitch	Chana
Friedman	Chasia-Reeva	Levitan	Mendel
Friedman	Yuda	Levitan	Rivka
Friedman	Tzipa	Levitan	Zalman-Moshe
Kaminkovitz	Freida	Levitan	Chana

[Page 346]

Levitan	Aharon	Lifshitz	Chasia
Levitan	Mordechai	Lifshitz	Esther
Levitan	Roche-Freida	Lifshitz	Bella
Levitan	Leah	Markman	Ruven (son of Iser)
Deetz	Aharon	Markman	Shtshera
Deetz	Esther	Markman	David
Deetz	Verna	Kluft	Avraham-Yakov
Deetz	Miriam	Kluft	Rivka
Deetz	Avraham-Tzvi	Sosinksy	Chaim
Deetz	Sheina	Sosinsky	Motele
Deetz	Menucha	Sosinsky	Shimon
Kremer	Alter	Kluft	Nioma
Kremer	Minia	Kluft	Roza
Kremer	Chaim	Levin	Chana-Mina
Kremer	Mary	Levin	Alta
Kremer	Rivka	Levin	Anshel
Kremer	Shmuel	Kozshinitz	Haya-Sore
Kremer	Ephraim	Kozshinitz	Breina
Kremer	Aharon	Kozshinitz	Anshel
Varfman	Yakov	Meltzer	Zelig
Varfman	Zise	Meltzer	Yehudit
Varfman	Fayia	Meltzer	Baruch
Varfman	Haya-Sore	Meltzer	Moshe
Varfman	Leah	Meltzer	Yakov
Varfman	Chana	Meltzer	Arie
Varfman	Dovid-Yaakov	Meltzer	Shlomo
Varfman	Pesach-Velvel	Meltzer	Dichle
Varfman	Feivish	Meltzer	David
Varfman	Yocha	Meltzer	Gita
Varfman	Yochanan	Kozshinitz	Yenta (daughter of Moshe)
Varfman	Pese	Kozshinitz	Merke
Varfman	Micha	Kozshinitz	Chana
Munitz	Zalman-Leib	Abelson	Moshe and wife Sarah
Munitz	Alta	Abelson	Shlomo
Munitz	Tzipa	Abelson	Miriam
Munitz	Moshe-Baruch		
Munitz	Alta		
Lifshitz	Mordechai		

[Page 347]

List of Martyrs from Parafianov

Gordon	Yitzhak	Grozbin	Yosef-Yidel, his wife and children
Gordon	Tamar		
Gordon	Rachel-Leah	Grozbin	Shalom
Gordon	Freida	Grozbin	Elchanan and wife
Gordon	Gershon	Levitan	Esther
Gordon	Zev	Levitan	Shlomo
Rozov	Leiba	Levitan	Haya-Charna
Rozov	Beila	Levitan	Sarah
Rozov	Shalom	Levitan	Leah
Rozov	Haya	Grozbin	Ya'akov
Rozov	Bilka and two daughters	Grozbin	Perel
Feigelson	Avraham	Grozbin	Haya
Feigelson	Haya-Sarah	Grozbin	Leah
Feigelson	Zisila	Feldman	Michal
Feigelson	Anshel	Feldman	Sima
Getzenson	Shmuel-Chaikl	Feldman	Haya
Getzenson	Esther	Ginzburg	Etel
Getzenson	Zalman	Ginzburg	Feiga
Getzenson	Sheina	Ginzburg	Haya
Markman	Elchanon (The Shochet)	Veisblatt	Chaim-David
Markman	Malka	Veisblatt	Hana
Markman	Genya	Alperovitz	Mendel
Markman	Nachum	Alperovitz	Gita
Markman	Zlata	Alperovitz	Friedel
Meltzer	Shepsel	Alperovitz	Sheindel
Meltzer	Eshka	Alperovitz	Berta
Meltzer	Shmuel	Begin	
Meltzer	Sarah (Markman)		Ashey & daughter
Kugel	Gershon	Katz	Aharon
Kugel	Leah	Katz	Zalman
Kugel	Rachel	Katz	Minye
Kugel	Etta and son	Katz	Yossi

[Page 348]

Katz	Ezsah	Kaledetzki	Haya
Alperovitz	Lieba	Lieberman	Shmuel
Alperovitz	Avraham, his wife	Lieberman	Gershon and wife
	And daughter	Svidler	Ben-Zion, his wife
Markman	Raphael		And children
Markman	Yosef	Levin	Shabtai, his wife and children
Markman	Chana	Levin	Lipka
Markman	Berl	Levin	Briena
Markman	Chasia	Levin	Bella
Markman	Nachmia	Lieberman	Shmuel, his wife
Markman	Yechezkel		And children
Markman	Nachma-Rachel	Kooperstock	Zelig, his wife
Markman	Roza		And children
Markman	Shalom-Ber	Kooperstock	Yitzhak
Markman	Mirella	Kooperstock	Cherna
Markman	Yisrael	Kooperstock	Avraham
Markman	Mishka	Bilsky	Myer and wife
Markman	Luba	Bilsky	Rita
Markman	Beila	Varfman	David
Markman	Pesach	Varfman	Genisia
Markman	Mendel	Varfman	Sima
Markman	Rachel	Klatzkin	Arie
Markman	Zelig	Klatzkin	Pesach
Markman	Avraham	Epstein	Yidel
Markman	Yakov	Epstein	Chana
Raffelson	Hirsh	Epstein	Sonia
Raffelson	Sheina	Epstein	Zshenia
Raffelson	Haya	Epstein	Liza
Kaladetzki	Yonah	Kaplan	Yosef, his wife and children
Kaladetzki	Rachel	Kiselgof	Raizel
Kaladetzki	Sarah	Kiselgof	Myer
		Kiselgof	Sonia

Kiselgof	Haya		
Kiselgof	Rachel		
Kiselgof	Chasia	Kaminkovitz	Freida
Kiselgof	Leah	Kaminkovitz	Yitzhak
Shleifer	Chaim	Kaminkovitz	Chasia
Shleifer	Leah	Rozov	Shmuel-Aharon
Shleifer	Chunya and wife	Rozov	Liebe
Shleifer	Chana	Feigelson	Leeba

(Page 349)

Rozov	Gershon	Greenhouse	Ben-Zion
Anshelevitz	Isar	Greenhouse	Rivka
Rozov	Yisrael	Greenhouse	Uzi
Rozov	Stesha		Rachel Elka and family
Rozov	Moshe	Varfman	Dov-Ber
Rozov	Mirel	Varfman	Chana-Yicha
Rozov	Sarah	Varfman	Fania
Teitz	Zalman	Varfman	Zlata
Teitz	Raizel	Varfman	Schneur
Teitz	Tzipa	Korbman	Shifra
Teitz	Beila	Korbman	Dvora and family
Teitz	Yechka	Kaminkovitz	Laizar
Polik	Zalman-Natan	Kaminkovitz	Etle
Polik	Rachel	Kaminkovitz	Gitel
Polik	Alter	Kaminkovitz	Berel
Polik	HInda with husband	Kaminkovitz	Levka
Polik	Mordechai-Leib, his wife and children	Shferber	Yerachmiel
		Shferber	Lovka and sister
		Kremer	Alter
Gurvitz	Ben-Zion	Kremer	Mina & children
Gurvitz	Chana	Kaminkovitz	Berel
Gurvitz	Lieba	Kaminkovitz	Zina
Gurvitz	Lieka	Kaminkovitz	Zalman
Gurvita	Mishka	Kaminkovitz	Sarah
Margolin	David	Kaminkovitz	Moshe
Margolin	Itka & 2 children		

[Page 350]

List of the Anti-Nazi Fighters of Dokshitz and Parafianow Who Gave Their Lives in Battle Against the Oppressor

This section was added in 1990.

Glazer	David	May the Lord revenge his blood
Hochman	Moshe-Shaya	May the Lord revenge his blood
Katzovich	Ishe (Itzchak)	May the Lord revenge his blood
Kluft	Greinem	May the Lord revenge his blood
Kremer	Ya'akov	May the Lord revenge his blood
Lenkin	Aharon-Ber	May the Lord revenge his blood
Plavnik	Ishe	May the Lord revenge his blood
Rozov	Gershon	May the Lord revenge his blood
Rozov	Mule-Ber	May the Lord revenge his blood
Rubin	Zalman	May the Lord revenge his blood
Shultz	Hirsh-Yona	May the Lord revenge his blood

Sossman	Isha'ayahu	May the Lord revenge his blood
Tiles	Altar	May the Lord revenge his blood
Vant	Mulya	May the Lord revenge his blood
Yesin	Yidel	May the Lord revenge his blood
Yofte	Altar	May the Lord revenge his blood

Those Who Survived

Glazer	Aharon	Solevei	Zisel
Dvorkind	Berel	Poliak	Alter
Berzon	Dov	Frankfurt	Henoch
Drutz	Taybe	Friedman	Batia
Huberman	Kopel	Kozshinitz	Beinish
Hochman	Gita	Kaminkovitch	Berel
Vant	Reuvin	Kantorovitch	Hirsh
Varfman	Tuvia	Kopelovitch	Menasha
Varfman	Mordechai	Katzovitch	Dov
Ziskind	Levi-Yitzhak	Kremer	Dvora
Tiles	Zelig	Kremer	Zalman
Tiles	Alter	Kremer	Yaakov
Yesin	Breina	Kremer	Leah
Yesin	Zechal	Kremer	Tzvia
Levin	Shepsel	Rytman	Yehuda
Sossman	Doba	Shapiro	Yosef
Sossman	Haya-Esther		

People of Dokshitz Killed in Gleboki

Katzowich	Shmuel
Katzowich	Mina
Katzowich	Ita
Kosinitz	Mendel
Zalkind	Zale
Zalkind	Sarah
Zalkind	Yudashe
Zalkind	Zipa
Zalkind	Taiba

Appendix to the Dokshitz Parafianov Yizkor Book

Material Not in the Original Yizkor Book

Introduction to the Appendix

by Aaron Ginsburg
President, The Friends of Jewish Dokshitsy Foxboro, Massachusetts, USA

As the generations pass, our memory of the past recedes. As we move to the four corners of the world, we lose touch with our relatives and friends. The disruptions of the Shoah accelerated this natural process. Writing down our memories enables us to preserve them. A Yizkor book is one way to accomplish this.

A word about the Yizkor book and its translations.

When the Dokshitz-Parafianov Yizkor book was published in 1970, the Holocaust was fresh in the minds not only of those who survived, but also of the relatives who lived in the Dokshitz Diaspora. However, it was not easy to find the many people who grew up in Dokshitz. A small core group of survivors and of immigrants from the 1930s was in Israel, while others were scattered throughout the world. That core group reached out to a few souls in the Diaspora, and together, with love and tears, they wrote and gathered the material in the Yizkor book.

Most chapters of the book are in both Yiddish and Hebrew. A few parts of the book are only in Yiddish. This would imply that most of the book, if not all, was written first in Yiddish. Yiddish was the native language, the *mamaloshon*, of that generation.

In 1990 a partial English translation was published. Parts of the chapters by Zvi Markman that were in Yiddish only were not included in the translation. Two things that were added to the 1990 translation are included immediately after this introduction.

In 1995 Dokshitsy descendant Joel Alpert created a web page for Dokshitz on jewishgen.org. He also initiated the completion of the translation the Yizkor book translation. The primary donor was Ralph Ginzburg, whose parents,

Appendix to the Dokshitz Parafianov Yizkor Book
Material Not in the Original Yizkor Book

Raymond Ginzburg and Rachel Guta Lipkind were born in or near Dokshitz. The parts of the book by Zvi Markman that were omitted from the 1990 translation continued to be omitted. This translation can be found online at:

http://www.jewishgen.org/yizkor/dokshitsy/Dokshitz.html

The omissions were discovered when the Yizkor book was being prepared for printing. Many people assisted me as I had them translated from Yiddish to English, including Arie Henkin, Lisa Zimmerman, Elchanan Peres, Lyber Katz, Ira Lulinski, and Florence Ruderman.

Remembering did not stop when the Yizkor book was published. Remembering and writing those memories down has continued. The ease of communicating through the internet has enabled us to find these memories, and include several of them in the appendix.

In 2005 the Dokshitsy Disrict in Belarus wrote a letter explaining that the Jewish Cemetery had been destroyed by the government in 1965. The letter requested help "to correct a mistake that was done many years ago without disrespect to the dead. **"The Friends of Jewish Dokshitsy"** was created in response.

When I was looking for Dokshitz contacts I found a page on Yad Vashem by Sam Fogelman which began, "...I was born in Dokshits." His obituary included the names of his children. And so, I became acquainted with his daughters, Gila and **Eva Fogelman**. Eva has written "Conscience and Courage: Rescuers of Jews During the Holocaust," about righteous gentiles, such as the man that helped her father. She offered to help with the Dokshitsy Diaspora Reunion in 2010, and was the keynote speaker with, ***"Why Remember Dokshitsy?"***

In **"Despite Everything"** we read about the experiences of Michael Etkin, a child survivor. Michael learned of his mother's fate only in 1998 after sending an inquiry to the Belorussian Embassy in Israel. In 2009, after Michael died, his sons and their families visited Dokshitz, where she was killed just before the liberation. They met Nikolai Dmitrovich Chistakov, who remembered the gallows being erected for Michael's mother's execution. Rob Benjamin helped Menachem edit "Despite Everything" for the appendix.

Arie Henkin was a teenager during World War II. Like many survivors, he became obsessed with Dokshitz. When I visited him in 2014, I was overwhelmed when he opened his desk drawer which was stuffed with the many pictures from Dokshitz which he had collected. As part of the Israeli survivor community, he had known many of the writers of the Yizkor book, and he led me to their descendants. With the help of his daughter, Roni Henkin-Roytfarb, Arie shares with us details of life in Dokshitz. This is supplemented by the story of exile in Russia, and his early days in Israel. Rob Benjamin also helped edit Arie's remembrances.

In July 2017, I met **Rachel Mutterperl Goldfarb** at the United States Memorial Holocaust Museum where she is a volunteer. Rachel and her mother Dina survived the destruction of the Dokshitz ghetto in May 1942, and spent the next three years on the run. In **My Story: Three Years on the Run**, she alsp describes pre-war life, the dangers after the liberation, and adjusting to life in America.

Dan Bar-On, an Israeli psychologist, interviewed the children of Nazis. The results were published in his 1989 book, "Legacy of Silence." In 1995 my cousin Sam Gejdenson, whose father, Shmuel Gejdenson, was a survivor from Parafianov sent a copy of a chapter from Bar-On's book, **"Small Hills Covered with Trees"** to his extended family. It tells the story of German soldier who was overwhelmed by his experience witnessing the Shoah in Dokshitz and Parfianov, which affected both him and his oldest son for the rest of their lives. With Bar-On's help, Joel Alpert corresponded with the soldier's son, who invited him to visit him in Germany. When Joel visited Germany in 2005, it was too late. The son had died.

Who did the German soldier visit in the Parafianov ghetto? In "Small Hills Covered with Trees," the soldier mentions the pharmacist B and his family and the Aaron K family. The soldier's son recalled that, "My Father kept contact with the Jewish families Katz and Beltzig. Their first names Aaron Zylli and Maria stay with me."

The Soviet government created a list of World War II casualties after the liberation, which took place in Dokshitz in 1944. The secret police, the NKVD, was given the assignment. The victims that Yad Vashem lists for Parafianov come from Pages of Testimony (individual submissions), the NKVD list, and from the Yizkor book list. A victim may be listed multiple times. The NKVD listed a Bilsky family which included Marian Bilsky, his wife Chaya, and their children Rita and Nama. The Yizkor book lists them as Meier, First Name Unknown, and Margareta. Their house still stands in Parafianov, and I have visited it.

Not long ago I was contacted by Yosef Malkin. His grandmother Roza Alperovich Malkina was born in Parafianov, and moved to Moscow with her husband. She had two sisters in Parafianov, one married to a Gordon, and one to a Katz. Yosef's grandmother, Roza Malkina, submitted pages of testimony for Aaron Katz, the pharmacist in "Small Hills Covered with Trees," his wife Genya Alperovitz Katz, and their four children, Israel, Mordechai, Pinchus and Yitzhak.

Genya Alperovitz Katz (Date unknown, around 1930)

Sam Gejdenson's father Shmuel was a Holocaust survivor from Parfianov. Shmuel Markman was a member of the Markman, Ginsburg and Cirlin families. At least fifty family members died in the Shoah. When Sam

Appendix to the Dokshitz Parafianov Yizkor Book
Material Not in the Original Yizkor Book

Gejdenson was in the United States Congress, he visited Dokshitz and Parafianov and thanked the people who saved his father's life. He has shared pictures of some of some of the people who helped his father, and of those who did not survive, and also a summary of testimony from Russian trials about the atrocities in Dokshitz.

How can we remember the Jews of Dokshitz? One way is to reach into our family memories and write about and share our gleanings. Another way is to care for the remains of the Jewish community in Dokshitz and Parfianov and nearby villages and towns. **The Friends of Jewish Dokshitsy** helps to identify, mark, and care for sites in the Dokshitsy District in Belarus, conducts shtetl reunions, and organizes memorial ceremonies in the Dokshitsy District.

I would like to give a special thank you to Rob Benjamin. Rob has helped me every step of the way in the preparation of this appendix.

The Dokshitz-Parfianov Yizkor book serves a dual purpose. On the one hand, it is story of a living Jewish community. On the other hand, it is the story of the destruction of that community, and the murder of most of its residents. It is story that is about of all us, and, in our own way, we should continue to remember it and to tell it.

Aaron Ginsburg aaron.ginsburg@gmail.com

Material added in the 1990 English Translation:

Another German Failure, This Time - Payment in Dokshitz
By Dov Katzowitch, Petach-Tikva, Israel

During 1941-42 the Germans captured over two million Russian prisoners. They were treated with the familiar Nazi cruelty. The Germans did not understand that some of the prisoners suffered in their time from the Stalinist regime persecution and would cooperate with them. This could be a major reinforcement for the German army. As they did not understand this, the wave of self surrendering prisoners disappeared.

Then, in 1943 the Germans experimented: They promised a late improvement of conditions. So it happened that a few Russian prisoners agreed to serve as soldiers in Fascist-Russian units. Even before this a Russian general, Vlasov, deserted over to the German side and headed a Russian army cooperating with the Germans.

An elite unit was organized by the German security service using the Russian prisoners. As its commander was chosen Polkovnik Gil-Rodionov and its chief of staff was Malishev. They dressed in German army uniform, and only an insignia on their hats and sleeves singled them out. There were a number of German "advisors" in these companies. They operated with cruelty in Yugoslavia and Poland against the partisans.

The day came and the Germans decided to have them operate against the partisans in the Dokshitz area, mixing with the native populace and the partisan movement and reading the partisan-printed propaganda leaflets.

The Rodionov soldiers heard the truth about the German losses in the eastern front and the idea of desertion and joining the great partisan movement began to sprout in them.

Appendix to the Dokshitz Parafianov Yizkor Book
Material Not in the Original Yizkor Book

A secret contact was made between the Zelezniak Partisan Brigade and the Rodionovers in Dokshitz. Then, in order to prove the sincerity of their intentions, the Rodionovers in Dokshitz killed the Germans, attacked the Krolevshtchina railroad intersection wearing *German* uniforms, and burned a part of Dokshitz. Partisan commisars were now sent to the Rodionov companies instead of the Germans and commisar Ivan Matweiewich Timchuk was made commander of them all. Timchuk took Abraham-Yitzchak Friedman from Postovi as his aid as his loyalty was impeachable.

On Stalin's orders the Rodionov partisans were sent to the most dangerous missions in order to "wipe clean" their betrayal. Indeed they fought against the Nazis and their cooperators bravely and most were killed in the Bialorussian forests. After the release they were sent to the punishing platoons and more were killed. Few, badly wounded, survived. Thus did the Germans receive in Dokshitz another lesson in war against the Russians.

Appendix to the Dokshitz Parafianov Yizkor Book
Material Not in the Original Yizkor Book

Material added in the 1990 English Translation:

People of Dokshitz Killed in Gleboki

Katzowich	Shmuel
Katzowich	Mina
Katzowich	Ita
Kosinitz	Mendel
Zalkind	Zale
Zalkind	Sarah
Zalkind	Yudashe
Zalkind	Zipa
Zalkind	Taiba

Appendix to the Dokshitz Parafianov Yizkor Book
Material Not in the Original Yizkor Book

The Friends of Jewish Dokshitsy

By Aaron Ginsburg, President, The Friends of Jewish Dokshitsy.

The Friends of Jewish Dokshitsy, a Massachusetts (United States) non-profit corporation, was founded in 2006.

At the end of 2005 the Dokshitsy District in Belarus wrote a letter to Yuri Dorn announcing that the Jewish cemetery had been destroyed in 1965 and turned into a park, and asking for help "to correct a mistake that was done many years ago without disrespect to the dead." That letter soon made its way to Joel Alpert, who included Aaron Ginsburg in his response.

The Dokshitsy District reported that when the road next to the cemetery was being repaired, about 100 headstones from the cemetery were found. The stones were piled into the cemetery along with a few stones that were there, and the letter was written.

The Friends of Jewish Dokshitsy was created "to preserve the memory of the Jewish residents of Dokshitsy (Dokshitz in Yiddish), Parfianov, and nearby villages." Founding directors were Rochelle Ruthchild (Raichelson Family), Rob Benjamin (Raichelson, Jaffee), Richard Fein (Ginsburg, Kusinitz, Cirlin), Noah Horowitz (community member), and Aaron Ginsburg.

Our scope is wider than the Dokshitz-Parfianov Yizkor book. Begomel, 17 miles east of Dokshitz, where a Holocaust massacre took place in 1941, was in the Soviet Union between the World Wars, while Dokshitz and Parfianov were in Poland. After WWII, they became all became part of the Dokshitsy District. Jews were scattered throughout the area. Some lived in small villages such as Voznovshchina, Karalino, and Uskrimie. Others lived in larger settlements such as Krulevshchina.

The Dokshitsy District and The Friends of Jewish Dokshitsy, with the help of Franklin and Galina Swartz, worked together to restore the cemetery. This included two monuments, bricked paths, a fence, and landscaping.

Across the street from the cemetery, at the site of the Holocaust pits, a small monument was erected next to the 1965 monument. Unlike its neighbor, this one made clear that there had been a Holocaust in which Jews had been singled out AS Jews for mass murder. The 1965 monument used official language, and described the victims as "Soviet citizens."

Dokshitsy Cemetery 2008, picture by Frank Swartz

A dedication ceremony took place on Lag B'Omer, 2008 on the anniversary of the largest massacre in Dokshitsy. Attendees included Joseph and Dina Polliack (Polliack and Kapelovich), Peggy Blumenthal (Raskin), Ronald Gilman (Braverman), Marc and Tanya Izeman and their two children, (Adelson and Kusinitz), Janet Wolfe (Kapelovich), Meredith Hoffman (Chodosh, Kapalovitch, Alperov), and Aaron and Rebecca Ginsburg (Ginsburg, Cirlin, Kusinitz).

Appendix to the Dokshitz Parafianov Yizkor Book
Material Not in the Original Yizkor Book

We have also conducted several memorial ceremonies in the Dokshitsy District, In May 2015 a memorial walk in Dokshitz, included Marvin Kabakoff (Kabakoff, Portnoi, Friedman), Aaron Ginsburg, District official Valentina Randarevich and local residents. We walked from the ghetto to the site of the pits, across the street from the restored cemetery.

In September 2016, a memorial walk in Begomel included Aaron Ginsburg, 50 students and teachers from the local school, the head of the local Soviet, Nikolai Trahinin, District official Valentina Randarevich, and Vladimir Konstatinovich Gerasimonok, a childhood witness, went from the building where the victims were held to the site of the pit where they were murdered on October 2, 1941,

In May 2017, Aaron Ginsburg and school Principal Victor Korostik led a walk from the school to the site of the ghetto, and then to the site of the pit. They were accompanied by 50 students, local official Galina Azarevich and district official Valentina Randarevich. Also present was Maria Balash, who, as a child, was forced with the other non-Jewish residents to watch their neighbors being murdered. At the ceremony, the students placed stones on the monument.

Two Dokshitsy Diaspora reunions have been held to maintain interest in Jewish Dokshitsy. The first one, in Warwick, Rhode Island in 2010, was attended by about 70 people. Eva Fogelman (Fagelman) gave the keynote speech (which is in the appendix to this book), "Why Remember Dokshitsy?"

At the May 2015, Dokshitsy Diaspora reunion in Scarsdale, New York, at the home of Ira Starr (Kantrowitz, Charnas, Shulz). Eva Fogelman reprised "Why Remember Dokshitsy?"

There has been an intense effort reach to all families that have a Dokshitz connection. This includes extensive searching of the internet, writing newspaper articles, speaking engagements, a website, and a Facebook group.

Appendix to the Dokshitz Parafianov Yizkor Book
Material Not in the Original Yizkor Book

There have been several trips to Israel and to various United States locations to meet people who were born in Dokshitz or their descendants. This outreach has led to many of the items in the appendix.

Memorial Walk, 2015 Dokshitsy   Photo by Frank Swartz

There's more work to do in the Dokshitsy District. Future projects include

- Placing a monument on the site where the Jews in Begomel were killed
- Building a fence around the plot and placing a monument at the plot in Begomel where the victims remains were reburied, and
- Placing a plaque on the building in Begomel where the victims were imprisoned before being murdered.
- In Parfianov, the site of the Holocaust pit, now hidden behind a concrete wall, needs to be made accessible.

Appendix to the Dokshitz Parafianov Yizkor Book
Material Not in the Original Yizkor Book

For the latest information visit our website at jewishdokshitsy.org and our Facebook group at https://www.facebook.com/groups/jewishdokshitsy/
Our email is info@jewishdokshitsy.org

Aaron Ginsburg, President, the Friends of Jewish Dokshitsy
Foxboro, Massachusetts, USA

Why Remember Dokshitsy
Eva Fogelman, PhD
www.evafogelman.com

Fun Vanen Kumt a Yid? Where does a Jew come from? This was the standard greeting of the Jew who arrived in the New Land. To American Jews of third and fourth generation Eastern Europe, it is one big mishmash. Minsk? Pinsk? It is all the same. Most American Jews conflate Eastern Europe into one romanticized vision of the shtetl and of the Jewish city.

Nothing could be further from the truth. Each community had its own distinct culture, heritage, language, ethnography, Halakhic religious tradition – in a word, its own identity. But instead of knowing the vibrant Jewish life that was destroyed, we have ghost towns full of ghost stories.

Ghost stories are all about what happens when people and places are forgotten. Ghosts come back to haunt the living because they want to be remembered, and they want to remind the living why and how they died, and sometimes to punish the living for causing their deaths.

All Jewish towns in Eastern and Central Europe are ghost towns— they suffer from absence, they have all been forgotten. The living always have an obligation to the Jewish dead to remember how these towns became so empty of Jewish life, and, if possible, to restore some life to those towns, or, at least, to remember them.

For those of us who weren't there, *Fiddler on the Roof* was our first introduction to what the shtetl must have been like. Let me tell you a story about Joseph. Joseph is thrilled to be taking Bracha, his ninety-five-year-old mother to see the hit show, *Fiddler on the Roof*. He's excited not only because Bracha hasn't seen it before, but also because she came to America in the late 1930s from one of the many Anatevka-like Russian shtetls.

Not only does Joseph book the most expensive seats in the theatre, but he also buys Bracha some smart new clothes to wear. And on the night of the show, he even orders a stretch limo to take them there and back. He wants it to be a memorable evening and doesn't want to leave anything to chance.

On the night of the show, they arrive in style, take their seats and watch the performance. And as soon as the final curtain comes down, Joseph asks Bracha, "Well Mom, what did you think of the show? Be honest. Did it bring back any memories for you?" Bracha sits there for a while, then turns to Joseph and gives both a nod and a classic JMS (Jewish Mother Shrug). "Yes *bubbeleh*, it did," she replies, "but I really don't remember that much singing."

Broadway will not be writing our history. The historian Sam Kassow, who wrote *Who Will Write Our History: Emanuel Ringelblum, the Warsaw Ghetto, and the Oyneg Shabes Archive*, said that Ringelblum believed that Jews "needed NOT MYTH BUT HISTORY." Others argued that Jews don't need history but a covenantal memory.[1] In the Warsaw ghetto Ringelblum was on a mission to get people in the ghetto to write "from inside the event" in order for the writing of history not to be "skewed by the distorting lens of retrospective recollection and selective memory."[2] This writing of Jewish history was important to Ringelblum because he believed that the suffering of the Jewish people was a "universal story and not just a Jewish one. And evil, no matter how great, could not be placed outside of history. ...Jews were part of universal history, not outside of it. The archive not only recorded crimes; it was also part of the struggle for a better future."[3] Ringelblum was convinced that a better world will arise out of the rubble of Europe because "historical knowledge and awareness would arm the struggle for a better world."[4] Job in the Bible also stresses that we learn from our ancestors. He said:

---

[1]Kassow, S. (2007). *Who Will Write Our History: Emanuel Ringelblum, the Warsaw Ghetto, and the Oyneg Shabes Archive*. Bloomington: University of Indiana Press, 11-12.

[2]Ibid. 13.Ibid. 13.

[3]Ibid. 7-8.

[4]Ibid. 8.Ibid. 8.

Appendix to the Dokshitz Parafianov Yizkor Book
Material Not in the Original Yizkor Book

> For inquire, I pray thee, of the former generation,
> And apply thyself to that which their fathers
>   Have searched out—
> For we are but of yesterday, and know nothing,
> Because our days upon earth are a shadow—
> Shall not they teach thee, and tell thee,
> And utter words out of their heart?[5]

The generation that left Dokshitsy, and other shtetls and cities from Eastern Europe, whether at the turn of the century or before or after liberation, wanted to forget after it was decimated. There was almost a collective desire consciously or unconsciously, "purposely or passively, out of rebellion, indifference, or indolence, or as the result of some disruptive historical catastrophe" not to transmit what they knew from the past to posterity.[6]

In my own family, in 1907 my grandfather Beryl Fagelman brought his younger sister Gitta along with him on the ship to America, leaving behind his wife and two year old daughter. He worked in a lumber yard across the street from Yale University and saved enough money to bring his wife and daughter to the States. In order for his wife to recognize him at the port, he sent his picture. His father-in-law, a respected rabbi and head of a yeshiva in Dolinow forbade his daughter to come to America and resume her life with a man who lost his religious compass. My grandmother was told to either ask her husband for a divorce or have him return to Dokshitsy. In 1912 Beryl returned to Dokshitsy, leaving behind his sister who worked as a seamstress

---

[5]Margolis, M."The Holy Scriptures according to the Masoreitc Text" Jewish Publication Society of America,1917. Job 8:8-10

[6]Yerushalmi, Y. H. (1983). Zakhor: Jewish History and Jewish Memory. Seattle: University of Washington Press, 109.

in the Triangle Shirtwaist Factory and lived in an East Side boarding house where she met and married Charles Kazin that same year. In 1915 their son Alfred Kazin was born followed by Pearl Kazin Bell, both of whom became major literary critics. Alfred's daughter Kate remembers that her father was always looking for Dokshitsy on a map and could never find it. Hearing the name would make her laugh. Neither knew much about their roots. The first generation and second generation were devoted to forgetting. Gitta died before the zeitgeist of curiosity became prevalent in the third generation, which indeed wanted to connect to their roots.

In 1912, Beryl Fagelman returned to Dokshitsy, opened up a general goods store with an added bonus of a tobacco license, and had four more children. The family suffered through World War I and when Poland took over the area in 1920, my grandmother had a difficult time because she did not know Polish. Studies in school shifted from Russian to Polish. Dokshitsy did not have a high-school and the children's education was curtailed. My grandfather died in 1925, leaving behind five children. My grandmother was a meek, pious, charitable woman who had limited strength, but no business acumen. Her oldest daughter worked in the store, my grandmother worked as a seamstress, the other two girls helped her and my dad, who was twelve years old was sent to live with an aunt in Vilna, and work in her family's bakery in order to send money home. In addition, my father also studied in the Slobodka Yeshiva.

My aunts and uncle were very disillusioned with God when their father died of pneumonia at such a young age. They rejected religion, fought with their mother and joined Zionists groups, *Hachalutz* and *Shomer Hatzair*. My father in those days was more of a Yiddishist and communist. My aunt Sara was given an affidavit to go to Palestine in 1930. After five years she got emigration papers for the rest of the family except my dad who was already conscripted into the Polish army. My father was separated from his family yet again, and after the Germans invaded, and the Polish army disbanded, he escaped to live with his aunt and uncle in Ilya, **Belarus**.

My aunt Malka, who is 95 years old and sharp as can be, was part of the generation that wanted to forget. Dokshitsy for her holds very bad memories of loss, poverty, limited opportunity for education, and rebelling against her mother's religious beliefs. The only salvation was getting together with friends from *Shomer Hatzair* Friday evening and Saturday during the day.

I, who have been consumed professionally with helping others remember their past, helping people reconnect with what has been lost, finding positive ways to remember the dead and bridging the gap between present and past, find myself like the shoemaker without shoes. When I had an opportunity to ask about Dokshitsy, I was more concerned with the years of persecution. I train other professionals to ask about the life before the German invasion, and I stress that everyone had a life before the mass killings and ghettos and concentrations camps and partisans. What was the negligence on my part not to engage my father and other family members to tell me more about Dokshitsy?

Like I said earlier, one shtetl is like another. I thought I knew it from having seen *Fiddler on the Roof*. My dad left when he was twelve so it was not as important to him as his life after in Vilna, the war years and the post-liberation years. My dad had no interest in ever going back there. He said there was nothing left of the Jewish life that existed before the Holocaust. Most of the houses were burned down so I probably would not even be able to see where he lived.

The vibrant Jewish life of 3,000 Jews, which was 49% of the shtetl, was decimated. What will I see besides a ghost town? My grandfather's grave is probably not there because most of the Jewish cemetery was also destroyed.

And now, a century later there is an urgency to write an authentic history, and not let the ghosts take over. But history needs memory and the witnesses are almost all gone. So we rely on the few that are alive and scavenge through documents of those who have left a few words or images here and there. We gather at a reunion such as this to piece together the tidbits we are each accumulating to make an authentic whole.

The historian Yosef Hayim Yerushalmi says in his book *Zakhor: Jewish History & Jewish Memory*:

For if it is knowledge of the past that you seek, who is to decide a priori which fact is not potentially valuable? [What historian hasn't found an obscure detail that she needed to pursue a larger topic?] For the historian God, indeed, dwells in the details, though memory protests that the details have become gods.[7]

Jewish tradition is very much against forgetting. Yerushalmi goes so far as to say that forgetting is the "cardinal sin from which all others will flow."[8] This is emphasized in the eighth chapter in Deuteronomy:

Beware lest you *forget* the Lord your God so that you do not keep His commandments and judgments and ordinances...lest you lift up your hearts and forget the Lord your God who brought you out of Egypt, out of the house of bondage....And it shall come to pass if you indeed *forget* the Lord your God... I bear witness against you this day that you shall utterly perish. (Deut. 8:11, 14, 19).

Yerushalmi argues that peoples or groups "can only forget the present not the past. That is to say, the individuals who compromise the group can forget events that occurred within their own lifetime, they are incapable of forgetting the past that preceded them, in the sense that the individual human being forgets earlier stages in his own life history. When we say that a people

---

[7] Ibid. 115.

[8] ibid, 108.

'remembers' we are really saying that a past has been accepted as meaningful. Conversely, a people 'forgets' when the generation that now possesses the past does not convey it to the next, or when the latter rejects what it receives and does not pass it onward, which is to say the same thing. The break in transmission can occur abruptly or by a process of erosion. But the principle remains. A people can never 'forget' what it has never received in the first place."[9]

Without inquiring about the past, the mimetic tradition of Judaism, which implies, my mother carried out traditions which her mother did, and her mother mimicked what her mother did, will be lost. In reading parts in the Yizkor book of Dokshitsy certain elements of this shtetl came alive for me. The Tarbut Ivri school was of utmost importance along with the Zionist youth movement groups. While it may not be specific just to Dokshitsy, one can feel a Jewish holiday walking in the streets of Dokshitsy. The challah is braided in a ladder so that our prayers would go to heaven, Farfelekh were eaten for Rosh Hashana to symbolize the cyclical nature of the year. Fruits from Israel were used for beginning of the New Year – watermelon, dates or grapes.

We in the post-Holocaust generations are very vulnerable to falling into a trap of defining our Jewishness through a lachrymose lens – a Jewish identity based on the persecution of the Jews from one generation to another. The current effort to reconstruct our Jewish past begins at a time that witnesses a sharp break in the continuity of Jewish living and hence also an ever-growing decay of Jewish group memory. Yerushalmi suggests that history and not a sacred Jewish text is the arbiter of Judaism.[10]

By remembering the vibrant life that existed in Dokshitsy and its surrounding shtetls and cities we will be prone to identify with a life-affirming Jewish culture and tradition. By identifying with the vitality of Jewish life that

---

[9] Ibid. 108-109.
[10] Ibid. 86.

permeated in Dokshitsy, we increase the likelihood that future generations will want to embrace their heritage rather than escape it, for fear of annihilation, yet again.

Just imagine how many more Jews in the diaspora would be educated knowledgeable Jews, had they re-created more of the Tarbut Ivrit school that thrived in Dokshitsy? How many more people sitting in this room would know Hebrew, and be able to enjoy the rich text based tradition which is a Jewish trademark? And how many more people whose families were Yiddishists would be able to read Shalom Aleichem and Y.L. Peretz in the original Yiddish?

By neglecting our Dokshitsy ancestry all together, by ignoring where we came from, we also dishonor those who deserve our recognition for keeping the Jewish flame alive in the chain of a two thousand year history, and I might add, despite all odds.

And how can we even dare to want to forget those Dokshitzers in our families who were murdered by the Germans or who so valiantly resisted with so little ammunition? After the Germans invaded, they murdered a rabbi and twenty-two men. Passover, Lag BaOmer, Shavuot were never the same in this shtetl again. The Germans chose to carry out their *Aktions* on each of these holidays.

I have given you very lofty ideas of why we should remember. For the sake of history, to fill up ghosts towns with authentic history rather than myths, to learn from the past not to repeat previous evils so that the present will be a better world, not to forget the dead and what was important in their lives, and to learn about the vibrant Jewish life that had existed. All these motivations are a step removed from a more personal reason for remembering.

Many of us sitting in this room have done just fine without remembering the past. I know, this flies in the face of Judaism and common wisdom, but to be honest, wanting to remember Dokshitsy is a recent phenomenon.

- So why are we here?

- We are here because we WANT to know, not because we need to know.
- How can knowing Dokshitsy enrich our lives?
- How can it shed light on who our family was?
- How did this specific town shape our ancestors and how did it shape us, unwittingly?
- Do we pronounce certain Yiddish words a certain way?
- Do we have a custom that only a Landsmann would understand?
- Did many of us become Zionists and feel or feel that we had to choose between religion – Tradition! – and Zionism?

If we were to look into the past, we each might find that certain long-held assumptions that we got from our parents, and our parents got from their parents, all originated in this tiny shtetl, a long way from America's shores, and even though, the shtetl is long gone, we carry it within us and it's evidenced in the way we see the world. My aunts who emigrated to Israel were ardent Zionists and very secular and anti-religious. And yet, every Friday night and Saturday at lunch, a festive Shabbat meal was served and the family gathered. Growing up in a household with a religious mother this is how they reconciled the differences in the family. The vibrant Zionist movements in Dokshitsy gave my aunts and uncle a way to be Jewish when they stopped believing in God because their father was taken away from them at such a young age. My father lost his faith in God after witnessing the massacre of 1,000 Jews of Illya on Purim, 1942. He survived the war by hiding and later fighting with the partisans in Belarus. He too was able to embrace his Jewishness by joining his siblings and mother in Israel after liberation.

I am named after Leybele, my father's brother, who was killed fighting to capture Jerusalem in Israel's war of independence.

Appendix to the Dokshitz Parafianov Yizkor Book
Material Not in the Original Yizkor Book

The shtetl has been passed down from generation to generation, but probably invisibly, silently, without understanding that it was this particular town that you never knew that was still influencing you today. We are all products of our past. The past is our collective unconscious. We are not aware of it but it is there nonetheless. When we bring the past into our present, we can be more in control of choices we make.

Our past is not an illness that needs to be diagnosed. It is not a condition that requires therapy. So there goes my livelihood. But it is integral to every one of us. When you become aware that there is a whole world that existed before you and you are very much a part of it, a new consciousness and way of being in the world sets in. And finally, I think it is always important to say that as individual as each shtetl was, it ultimately saw itself as part of Klal Israel, and we cherish and celebrate what made our ancestors and us who we are, even as we embrace being a part of the bigger Jewish world.

Civilizations come and go. Of all the peoples who are mentioned in the Bible, only the Jews remain as a distinct people, more than 5,000 years later because we transmit our history to the next generation. Even a tiny shtetl such as Dokshitsy with so few people is part of that transmission. Now that we have found each other thanks to the efforts of Joel Alpert and Aaron Ginsburg, we have an opportunity to continue to create a virtual Dokshitsy. The Diaspora Museum in Tel Aviv is redoing its lost communities exhibition and we need to be present there. Yad Vashem is collecting names of Jews murdered in the Shoah and each of us needs to add to the testimonial pages of this history. Our Yizkor book needs more inserts.

History is created in the details.

And so, the next time someone asks *Fun Vanen Kumt a Yid?* we will not only be able to find it on a map, but we will enrich the person with the vibrant Jewish life that existed. And hence, there won't be room for the ghost stories to take over.

Appendix to the Dokshitz Parafianov Yizkor Book
Material Not in the Original Yizkor Book

Despite Everything, I Survived

A Holocaust Memoir by Michael Etkin

Introduction

Dear sons, our lovely daughters-in-law, and our wonderful grandchildren!

First of all, I would like to thank all of you for being here with me: My dear wife Rivka, My dear sons – Menachem, Haim, Nitzan, Amit, and Idan, their lovely wives – Mazal, Taly, Michal, and Meital.

Our wonderful grandchildren – Inbar, Shani, Eyal, Iddo, Keren, Hilla, Lior, Bar, Shay, Ben and Noam.

During the years I have been telling you, here and there, about what I had been gone through in some very difficult years in Europe until I had arrived in Israel. I told you about Krulevshchizna, about my family, about my escape from the burning Glubokie Ghetto. But always the story was told very partially, a bit here and a bit there...

In December 2002 I had reached the age of 70 and felt that it's about time to tell you the entire story: I would like you to know who was our family, from where are our origins, where was I born, why did I have to leave my house and my small Shtetl very quickly, who took care of me during these very difficult years in the forests of Belarus, etc...

A very short time after this decision, and maybe not accidentally, I dreamt an amazing dream.

In my dream, I am coming back to our wonderful house in the town of Krulevshchizna. From far away I can notice the big nice yard, the cherry trees, the birch trees, and the nice flowers which my mother Chava had planted there.

For one minute in this dream, it seemed as if I am there, where I was born, not far from the train station, where it all began. By the house I see two kids playing in the yard. These are: my twin-brother Shepsele (Shabtai) and I – Michele (Michael), or as they used to call us:

Israel-Michele and Chaim-Shepsele – the twins (di zvilling in Yiddish).

We were born to the wonderful Etkin family, grandchildren to Shaul-Rafael Etkin and Chaya-Liebe Kabakov.

The dream was very short, but I had found it to be very significant. I understood that these images, which I carry with me, and the story behind them, must be passed on to all of you – the next generations. So that you will know what happened there to our family. KNOW and NEVER FORGET!

I, Michael Etkin, feel that I represent with pride and with lots of love all of our family members, who had perished in the Holocaust. I hope to succeed in this book to reflect my entire life story to all of you, my beloved family. Hopefully, this book will not only be my life story, but become a monument, a partial reflection of a great and wonderful world that no longer exists.

Chapter 1 - My Childhood in Krulevshchizna

My story really begins with the death of my father, Menachem-Mendel Etkin from a blood infection at the age of 32, a few months before the Germans came to Krulevshchizna.

I was born in Krulevshchizna, which was built around a small train station in Belarus. It later became a central station for trains from all over Belarus. Krulevshchizna was a very small town, with a main street paved with small stones. Along the clean streets sat many wooden houses. A large river streamed by, and nearby were some nice farms with cows, sheep, horses and pigs, large wheat fields, plantations of fruit trees, and green fresh grass all over the area.

My grandfather and father had seen the great business potential in Krulevshchizna, and decided to headquarter their businesses there. A short while after this decision, they had built their big houses there. Later on, all of the rest of the Etkin family came to live in Krulevshchizna as well. All together there were 80 Jewish families living in this small town, mainly owners of some small businesses.

My father was born to Shaul-Raphael Etkin and Chaya-Liebe Kabakov in the small town of Dokshitz, in Belarus, in August 5, 1909 and died in March, 1941. He was handsome, well educated, clever, a good friend, and a wonderful father. His great sense of humor attracted people to him. Because of his great business sense, all of the Etkin family members liked to work beside him.

Menachem-Mendel Etkin

We had a large and comfortable home, many good friends and neighbors, both Jews and non-Jews.

Eva (Chava) Kaminska-Etkin and Menachem-Mendel Etkin wedding picture February, 1932

My mother, Chava (Eva) was the daughter of Michaela and Israel Kaminsky. Unlike many at that time, my parents did not have an arranged marriage. They simply met and fell in love. And they prospered. My father created multiple successful businesses which our entire extended family shared in. When my father died, he and my mother had been married only 9 years.

After my father's death, we found out mother's real strength. Despite mourning his death, she did not allow herself to cry in front of us, although I presume that she had shed many tears on her bed every night. In order to help her, she asked her sister Lea to come and live with us in our house.

Lea was already then an "old maid". Since we all knew that she would never marry, this arrangement worked for all of us. Mother had help, while Lea did not have to struggle with her loneliness.

Still, my father had been the source and symbol of the physical and cultural wealth, and everything else we had built over many years. With his death, it all started to vanish as if it had never existed.

Standing from left to right: Eva (Chava) Kaminska-Etkin, my father's uncle Hanoch (Chonke) Etkin, his wife(name unknown), Chanan Pirivoskin (husband of my father's aunt Rachel Etkin), Bomma Kabakov - a cousin, who came from Israel to visit the family in Krulevshchizna, my father's aunt Rachel Etkin, and one more unknown family relative.

Sitting: My father's grandparents: Chaya-Liebe Kabakov and Shaul-Rafael Etkin.

At the bottom, from left to right: Mike (Zelik) Hodosh - my father's cousin, my father Michael (Mishka) Etkin, his twin brother Chaim-Shepse (Shepsele) Etkin, and Greg (Hirshel) Hodosh - my father's cousin (Mike Hodosh's brother).

Eva (Chava) Kaminska-Etkin, Michael Etkin, Chaim-Shepse (Shepsele) Etkin, Menachem-Mendel Etkin at their home in Krulevshchizna, Dokshitsy District, Belarus

Appendix to the Dokshitz Parafianov Yizkor Book
Material Not in the Original Yizkor Book

Chapter 2 - The War Breaks Out

For 3 months, Chaim-Shepse and I could not come to terms with our father's death. Then on June 22, while we were still mourning, the fake peace pact between Hitler and Stalin vanished in the German invasion of Belarus. It would not take long from that day to the terrible moment in the Ghetto, when the bullets were whistling above our heads, and I had to decide whether to stay there with Aunt Lea and my Chaim-Shepse, or to let go of her hand and run out of the burning Glubokie Ghetto to the nearest forest, to the Partisans.

German infantry and tanks poured across the borders of the Soviet Union, including Belarus. That same day Minsk was bombed. But it would take another 3 months before we in Krulevshchizna and our relatives in Glubokie, Dokshitz and other towns in Belarus would feel the full impact of the invasion.

We had believed Stalin's assurances that the Soviet Union, of which Belarus was then a part, was safe from the German danger. He was wrong.

For the next few days, Chaim-Shepse and I were busy listening to the adults talk about what was coming our way. Here and there bad news started coming from different resources. Jews who had escaped from the Germans told us about massacres of Jews, and about German soldiers catching old Jews in the streets and cutting their beards. We heard of the destruction of Jewish families' houses, and the burning of synagogues and Torahs.

A few years earlier, in 1938, when we had heard about Kristallnacht, the "night of broken glass" in Germany, it had seemed both unbelievable and yet not threatening. Such things simply did not happen in our quiet, safe world. Yet now they were on their way, and panic began to spread across all of our broad family in the area. Soviet reserves were being called up, including some of our relatives

Should we leave our house, or stay?

Our family arguments began again and increased in intensity. Some said that we should sell all of our assets, as soon as possible, and move North – even to Siberia. In 1938, my 8-year old self had also taken part in these arguments, saying that we must get as far as possible from the fighting.

But many others argued that we should stay. The elderly were haunted by the horrors of the First World War, which ended 23 years earlier. Then too, they told us, it had been hard for the Jews. However, we overcame the troubles, reconstructed the businesses, and life came back into its regular course. Jews were always being killed somewhere and the Jewish people had suffered, yet survived, for many generations.

Eventually, and with awful consequences, those who wanted to stay prevailed over those who wanted to leave. None could predict the future, and none could believe that such terrible acts of genocide could happen in Europe in the middle of the 20th century.

But a few of us left. One was my aunt Rachel, my father's sister. She was a very practical woman who understood that we must get out immediately! Many others agreed with her, but, unfortunately, never followed her. As we went on with our usual daily lives and waited for developments, the 3 month "window of opportunity" to leave that opened in June was slowly closing.

My father's brothers took over managing the family businesses – the flour-mill, the carpentry, the sawmill, and the real-estate business. On the surface, life was still normal. If there was "bad water" streaming under the ground, nobody wanted to admit it. Our neighbors also continued with their daily lives. Our closest gentile neighbor, Skorochod (fast walker), kept smiling at us as usual. Echoes of the war came closer and closer, but we refused to hear them!

The Red Army retreats, the Nazis arrive at Krulevshchizna

In October, the Germans invaded our part of Belarus. The Red Army had retreated with their tanks, cannons and soldiers exhausted from almost 4 months of hard fighting and defeats. Soon, the Germans had fully conquered our entire region.

Surprisingly, THESE Germans did not harm Jews as they marched to the East. In fact, unbelievable as it seems today, they even gave chocolate to the children and cigarettes to the adults, who stood beside the roads and watched them passing by with their tanks.

I remembered very well the stories about German cruelty. I also heard their soldiers' songs, telling about how they are traveling to Moscow, in order to drink coffee in the streets of the Russian capital. I saw their tanks and cannons, and waited fearfully to see what will happen next. But most Jews felt that the worst was already behind us. Everyone waited for the Wehrmacht to pass by and then returned back to their businesses and daily routines. Even the children returned to their regular games, and I continued with my trademark naughtiness and tricks.

But I did not believe we were safe. And today, I understand how sophisticated the Nazis were then, with their lies and cunning. They had two goals: to reach Leningrad, Stalingrad and Moscow as fast as possible, and to put the Jews "asleep".

The Nazis passed by Krulevshchizna and did not return for a few weeks. Some in our family said to themselves: We were right again. There is a war, but nothing bad will happen to the Jews (I only wanted that no harm will happen to our family).

Once in a while ominous news broke our calm. Traders who moved around and beyond our region, and refugees who passed by our town told us about the horrors of the German army and the SS. Suddenly, everything seemed to be less quiet and calm. We children were told to be very careful of the German soldiers, those who just a short while ago had given us chocolates. Suddenly, we all understood that we were living on borrowed time.

When the Germans returned to our region, with different commands, some of us already understood that our lives had forever changed. The first command of the returning Germans was that every Jew leaving his house must wear a white ribbon on the sleeve of his shirt.

The evacuation of the Jews of Krulevshchizna

We never dreamt that we would ever have to leave our home, but the Nazis did not us give a chance to think. That same day, every Jew in the region got the same order: Pack a few personal items and get into the trucks for a trip to another city. This command was so sudden, so paralyzing, that we had no time for thinking, resisting or planning a rebellion, or escaping to the forests. We could only focus all our energies on trying to save as much as possible under these circumstances.

My mother and grandmother knew that we couldn't take any furniture or any large valuable items. We left them in the care of our loyal neighbors who safeguarded them until the end of the war. The women took the minimal necessary: bedding, underwear, warm winter clothes, a few pots, jewelry and some cash, which they hid on their bodies.

Worst of all that day was the uncertainty. Some of us felt deep inside that we are leaving our house forever. Others tried to keep us calm, saying that within a few weeks we would again be home as the Germans promised. But none knew where were heading, or for how long. I was among those who believed what the Germans had promised us: "As soon as we will finish handling this region – you will be able to return to your houses". Only later on, we understood the meaning of "handling the region".

The Germans started separating families: husbands from wives, children from parents. It was hard to understand the commands they were screaming. The adults, who were terrified themselves, tried to calm their even more terrified children. We did not know it then, but that day we said our final farewell to everything and everyone in Krulevshchizna. Years later I saw their faces on some old photos, which were sent to me by relatives from the USA, Argentina, and South-Africa.

It was all over fast. When the truck had arrived at our house, my mother and her sister, my aunt Lea rushed to load our belongings into it. A few German soldiers helped us getting into the truck and we drove away forever from the house, the yard, the trees, and the paved stone lane.

Glubokie

The ride in an old Russian truck was slow and uncomfortable, leaving me sick to my stomach. Luckily, it was not long, only 18 kilometers. We soon reached a familiar place, Glubokie, our mother's home town. We were given a place of our own, if it could be called that. After living for years in a spacious house, suddenly we had to get used to living in one small room for all of us! There was a small kitchen attached to this small room. The toilets were in the yard.

At first, we were shocked. We could not understand how within only a few hours, we had moved from our big house in Krulevshchizna to this small room in Glubokie, sharing a yard with many others. Later we would miss this small room, where nobody had chased us or threatened our lives. A place where we had food and water, and even a yard for the children.

The changes started coming faster. Our mother was missing from the house more frequently, and not just for to her work at the Glubokie hospital. She would leave in the morning and come back in the evening. Later, she would be gone for the whole day. And sometimes, she would leave on Sunday morning and return only for the weekend, while Aunt Lea stayed with us and took care of us.

Only later on, we understood that she was not going to the hospital, but was actually actively helping the Partisans in our region. Knowing this did not help us. We were used to mother's presence, her voice and singing, her meals, her smile and her beautiful stories. We were always asking: "Mama liubmaya, gdye ti?" (from Russian: Dear mother, where are you?)

The Glubokie ghetto survivors on the "Brother's grave"

Mother joins the Partisans to fight the Nazis

The Nazis' next move came fast. They fenced the whole area where we lived and turned it into a Ghetto. No one could get in or out without a permit. Getting caught outside could mean imprisonment or death.

Only after the war, I began putting together pieces of stories and rumors about our mother, and figured out the rest. Mother, nicknamed "Briya" (In Yiddish: Brave), could not accept the Nazi occupation and the humiliation of the Jews. With the Red Army retreating to the North, she decided to act, without any hesitation, as she always did.

She made contact with the Partisans in the forests. She had found some Jews who were working in the Germans' headquarters. They would steal German guns and ammunition and pass it to my mother and to other young Jews. My mother and the others took the stolen guns and ammunition to another contact who passed it to the Russian freedom fighters in the forests of Belarus.

It was always a one gun with a few bullets, too little to be noticed. Today I understand the personal risk she took. Anyone caught stealing a weapon was immediately executed. People were murdered for smaller crimes, and family members punished as well.

Now and then, when she returned to our small room, mother would bring news of the war between Germany and Russia. She also told us the Germans were arresting and killing Jews. "You must be very careful," she told us constantly. "We are in a hard time, and you must be very careful of the German soldiers. If you don't want anything bad to happen to you, stay near our room and our yard". She added: "If the German soldiers come here, asking where I am, tell them I am not at home, that you are also waiting for me, and you don't know where I am. Don't tell them anything!" Aunt Lea also kept an eye on us, to verify that we don't speak too much.

Mother's warning was not in vain. Every few days, German soldiers would enter our small room. They suspected her of helping the Partisans. I guess we were brave kids. Despite their frightening guns and uniforms, we kept our heads. We told them what she had instructed us to tell them. I still don't know if they believed us, but they always left us alone, without threatening or interrogating us.

Our parents' teachings proved their worth. Despite our being quite a wealthy family for years, our parents had always taught us to be satisfied with what we had. Since our early childhood, they had taught us how stand up to difficult situations. Indeed, despite everything, we were quite happy kids.

Our poor life in the Glubokie Ghetto

For the Jews who had been rounded up and sent to Glubokie, life settled into a routine that lasted from October 1941 until August 1943. The Germans vouchers for small amounts of basic food: flour, sugar, oil, bread, cheese and eggs. For fruits, vegetables or meat, you had to go through the "black market". The vouchers never provided enough. The Germans ensured that so we would always be hungry. To get some fruits and vegetables for the children, to improve their nutrition, and to break their permanent hunger, eventually some people were sneaking out of the ghetto to the surrounding villages at night.

This was a dangerous act. Whoever got caught was immediately imprisoned and not always released later. But somehow, life in Glubokie was still bearable. However inadequate, we had food. To make up for the lack of schools, now and then, a "Melamed" (a teacher) would collect a small group of kids running around in the streets, and teach them for a few hours.

From left to right: My mother – Chava (Eva) Etkin (Kaminski), the twins – Michael (myself) and Chaim-Shepse Etkin, and my aunt (mother's sister) – Lea Kaminski, 1939

My "Scar Latina" illness

In the spring of 1942, I caught scarlet fever, which was then called scarlatina. Luckily, my mother was still working as a nurse at the Glubokie central hospital. I was hospitalized until I was cured. I can't bear the thought of what would have happened to me otherwise. After a few weeks I returned home, but not to the regular routine.

By then, the Germans had begun their "Actions" with lists of all of the Jews in Glubokie. The lists included suspected Communists who were executed without their family's knowledge. One was my uncle, Dr. Yehoshua (Shiye) Geller, an excellent pediatrician married to my mother's sister, Zina. One day he disappeared and never came back. We heard that the Germans took 200 Jews into the nearest forest, and murdered them there. Now we understood that the horrors had come to us as well. The smart ones among us knew that it was now only a matter of time.

During the following weeks, we learned about many murders in the small villages near Glubokie. Some local farmers told us about Jews being murdered and thrown into mass graves. These stories made everyone in the ghetto very angry, and some Jews started looking for ways to take revenge.

The Nazis next move came very fast. Nobody could get in or out of the Ghetto, even with a permit. Whoever got caught outside of the ghetto took the risk of getting killed. From then on, we suffered more and more from lack of food and clothing, and from increasing depression and despair.

The Nazi hunts for Jews came more and more often. It was so frightening. As soon as we heard the sound of Nazi boots in the streets, we would quickly sneak to the garret where we felt safe. Then, some people wrote on the houses' walls in Yiddish: "Yidden, Nekama!" (Jews, Revenge!)

Appendix to the Dokshitz Parafianov Yizkor Book
Material Not in the Original Yizkor Book

The beginning of the rebellion

I had already told you about my mother's weapon smuggling. But she was not the only one. During our deportation to Glubokie, all of the youth-movements (Hashomer-Hatsair, HaChalutz, HaDror, and others) had secretly united to become the core of rebellion against the Germans.

Soon, groups of young organized Jewish men began ambushing German soldiers patrolling the streets of the ghetto. They would attack the soldiers at night, taking advantage of the darkness, and take their weapons to the Partisans in the forests.

At the same time, some people began escaping from the ghetto. Despite their usual thoroughness, in the Glubokie ghetto the Germans were very negligent. Instead of an electronic fence which they had installed around other Ghettos, ours was made of thin wood boards, easily be broken with one kick.

Among those who escaped was my uncle, Tana Hodosh, who was married to my Aunt Gitl (my father's sister). He escaped on the night of July 22, 1943 with his 2 young children, Zelig and Hershel, a few weeks before the Nazis burned the Ghetto down. They joined the "Shlachtonov" Brigade of Partisans, which fought against the Nazis in the huge forests of Belarus.

But many stayed, and not out of fear. As I look back 63 years, it is clear to me that if we knew what was going to happen, we would have escaped from the ghetto soon after it was fenced. But even as it began, we still did not believe that the worst could happen. The general feeling in the Ghetto was that within a few weeks the Germans would tell us we could go home to Krulevshchizna.

At 9 years old, I already understood that we must do something, and do it immediately. I repeatedly said to Aunt Lea "Let's escape. The fence is already broken in a few places. There is no problem to get out of the ghetto." But Aunt Lea had a permanent answer: "We are not going anywhere. We are staying here. Here we will live or die together."

Maybe Aunt Lea was afraid, and did not fully understand what was happening around us. As I already said, life in the ghetto was still bearable. Jews were working in the Germans' army bases, cleaning and repairing weapons, sorting the bullets, etc. Even the "Actions" were not very frequent. True, every once in a while, some Jews disappeared. True, we heard they were murdered. But since those bad things had not yet come to our doors, many still did not understand how critical our situation was.

The 3 "Actions" (Killing) in the Ghetto

The moment of truth was now very close. The first large-scale Action came on the Hebrew date of the 7th day of the month of Nissan, 1943. The Germans started searching the houses for Jews suspected of helping the Partisans. They had very accurate lists, based on information from some locals. By then, we knew that the Germans were murdering those taken out of their houses. 2000 Jews were murdered in this "Action". The Germans shot them to death in front of a mass grave in the Barok forest near Glubokie.

Although wounded, a few managed to escape by falling into the grave and hiding under the bodies. That night they escaped from the grave to the Partisans, who gave them medical treatment and aid. They were too afraid to even think of going back to the ghetto to tell us what happened. One passed by Glubokie, on his way to the forests, and told us about the horrors.

The second big "Action" took place 3 months later, on the 4th day of the Hebrew month of Tamuz, 1943. Now it was clear to us that the Germans planned to destroy the Glubokie ghetto! But they still tried to deceive us by saying that Jews who will pay them some ransom will be safe. The German authorities issued a message stating that all Jews could guarantee their safety by surrendering any gold, silver, jewelry, and diamonds in their possession. The Germans took 6 kilos of gold and jewelry, and transferred all of it to the Latvian bank in Riga. On the cargo box the Germans wrote: "FISH".

Still, briefly, life in the ghetto continued its course, even though it became very difficult and depressing. The stores were selling, children were playing in their houses, the men were working in the army bases, and the "Melameds" were teaching a Torah lesson every once in a while. The "Judenrat", headed by Lederman, contributed to this routine by organizing prayers, gatherings, theatre shows and other social activities. Jewish policemen were still patrolling in the streets of the ghetto with a white ribbon on their arm, in order to try and keep a normal manner of living.

A few still believed that we would one day go back to Krulevshchizna. This illusion finally ended on August 20th, 1943. This was the 3rd and the biggest "Action", which actually destroyed the Glubokie ghetto completely. Next, I will describe the destruction of the ghetto, and the brave Jewish uprising which began a week earlier. I will describe how I saved my life, and how I joined the Partisans in the forests of Belarus at the age of 11.

Chapter 3 – The Young Partisan

63 years after the destruction of the Glubokie ghetto, and the deaths of my beloved relatives, I can look back with pride and say "NO, we did not walk like sheep to slaughter". We fought back and killed a large number of German soldiers.

We decided to fight back when the Ghetto's leaders learned that the Germans planned to wipe us out. In a way, we were lucky. While Jews from all over Europe were being sent by trains to the death camps (which we did not yet know), the last 2 ghettos in Belarus slated for destruction were Glubokie and Meer.

The German horror was now everywhere. They had destroyed the ghettos of Dokshitz, Disna, and Bialistok. Most of the Jews there were not even put on trains. In each town, men, women, and children were concentrated in the city center, then transferred to the nearest forest in a humiliating march. After digging their own mass grave, they were shot to death. A few minutes later, the grave was covered and another great Jewish community had vanished. As had happened in the Barok forest near Glubokie, a few survived, wounded and managing to hide under the dead.

We knew that bad things were befalling Jews all over Europe, but we still could not believe the depth of German cruelty. Masters of deceit, they kept us hoping that it was only a matter of time until we were back in Krulevshchizna. We still hoped that the war would soon and that we could go back home to our nice and quiet lives. But some said "Jews, let's take revenge. Let's kill the Nazis and protect our honor".

The Glubokie Ghetto rebellion

In August 1943, the leadership of the ghetto secretly told us that the ghetto would soon be destroyed by the Nazis and that we should all be prepared to

Appendix to the Dokshitz Parafianov Yizkor Book
Material Not in the Original Yizkor Book

fight. During our 2 years in the ghetto, we had collected many weapons, ammunition, and some "cold weapons", such as light bulbs filled with acid and knives fashioned from sharpened rusty iron rods. Some of it was parachuted into the ghetto and around it by Red Army planes. At the same time, the youth movement teen-agers had received some semi-military training. It was obvious that the ghetto would not survive. It was just as obvious that we would not die without fighting and keeping our honor.

Much of what I am describing is based on data I learned from books years later, and from long conversations with friends and other Holocaust survivors from the Glubokie ghetto. At the age of 11, my twin-brother Chaim-Shepse and I saw the confusion in the ghetto, the many young men running around, and the barricades being built. But no one told us what was actually happening and what should we do. Even if Aunt Lea knew anything, she did not tell us about it. We were very frightened, and at night before going to bed, we would call our mother "Where are you, Mother? We miss you so much, and we want you to be with us."

We missed our mother's courage, her decisiveness, her determination, and her common sense. Now I understand that she could not reach us from her fighting Partisan unit in the forests of Belarus. Chaim-Shepse, myself, and Aunt Lea Kaminsky were on our own in the Glubokie ghetto.

A week before the final Nazi "Action", the rebellion broke out with grenades thrown at the German soldiers, and shooting at their tanks and army vehicles. The Germans reacted immediately. They surrounded 3 sides of the ghetto with tanks. The side of the ghetto facing the forest was left unguarded by tanks because of the German's fear of the Partisans in the forests. Later, I realized that this saved my life.

The rebellion lasted a week. Young Jewish men attacked and kidnapped German soldiers. Jewish snipers killed many German soldiers. Some Partisans who had managed to sneak into the ghetto joined the fight. The Nazis reacted very cruelly by bombarding Jewish houses, ruining and burning everything.

We felt that it was an honor to see the Germans fighting Jews, who they had considered to be weak and helpless. Aunt Lea, my twin brother, and I were hiding at home, not knowing what was happening outside. Every once in a while, I would sneak out, either to the street or to our relatives' houses, collect some information and return home.

One day, I saw German soldiers on a motorcycle chasing Motke and Yerucham Lederman, sons of the head of the ghetto's Judenrat and ran after them. The Germans killed one, but the other escaped, continuing to snipe at them until his ammunition ran out. Later on, he joined the Partisans in the forests.

The rebellion lasted a week. Finally, on August 20, 1943, the Germans decided to burn down the ghetto with a tank bombardment. The ghetto burned for 9 days, until August 28th. It was very clear to me and the others that we only had 2 choices: to be burned alive in the ghetto, or to try to escape. We decided to escape.

The Glubokie ghetto survivors

I escape and survive!

Appendix to the Dokshitz Parafianov Yizkor Book
Material Not in the Original Yizkor Book

We stayed at home until early Friday, August 20, 1943 then went out towards the ghetto's wooden fence, which was already broken in a few places. Not only we, but the entire population were preparing for the big escape. Some went to the near forest and the Partisans. Others ran towards the river.

But then we found that the Germans were waiting for us to leave our relatively safe houses for the open fields – and an ambush. For the first time, I saw death on a large scale, as the Nazis machine-gunned those escaping. I witnessed many figures falling as the bullets hit them. It was a death roulette.

This moment is frozen in my memory, as visible as if it had it happened only yesterday. Only 20 meters from the ghetto's wooden fence, Aunt Lea is standing, Chaim-Shepse and I firmly holding her hands. "We must run now!" I scream at her, knowing our time is running out. But aunt Lea, frozen from fear, stands still. "We are not going anywhere", she commands us. "We will stay here, and live or die together". "Can't you see that they are killing people?" I try to urge her, feeling suddenly more like an 18 year old than an 11 year old.. "Let's run!" "No", she insists stubbornly. "Hold my hand firmly and don't move".

At that moment, I knew I must act on my instincts, and not my aunt's instructions. Thinking no further, I cut off my hand from hers. I don't remember if she tried to stop me, or screamed after me. I did not look back. I ran through the broken wooden fence, under the tanks' cannons, towards the forest, where lay my only chance to stay alive. All who were running with me ran to survive.

It was a live-or-die raced, as simple as that. I think I survived because of an uncle's advice: "If somebody shoots at you, run in a zigzag. This way the bullets will not hit you." Running through the field, wearing a thick coat and heavy shoes in the August heat, I did as my uncle said. When I felt the coat and shoes slowing me down, I took them off and kept on running in a zigzag.

The wound. We arrive to the forest

I don't know how long I ran. I remember, like in a movie, a lot of people running, bullets whistling around me, Jews falling beside me, killed by machine-gun bullets. Since I was very athletic, I could run very fast. I knew I must not stop running until I reached the forest, which the Nazis were afraid to approach.

I did not stop running, even when I felt a sharp prick at my foot and saw the blood. I kept running. When I passed through a small stream, I saw the blood flowing from my foot. Chaim-Shepse and Aunt Lea stayed in the burning Glubokie ghetto, with another 8000 Jews. I never saw them again, and truthfully, I did not think of them while running through the big field towards the forest. Only one thought instructed me on that early Friday morning: to reach the forest trees, now only 500 meters away.

I felt myself weakening. My wound was more severe than I had thought. The bullet had crushed bones and torn flesh in my foot. But the Germans did not chase us, out of fear of the Partisans. Still, it was clear to me that I could not stay there. I was lying wounded in the field, looking for a savior, who would come and take me on his shoulders towards the near forest. My savior came very quickly. He was Motke Kraut, whom I later met in Israel, and who would become a part of our family until his death a few years ago. Without a word, he took me on his back and ran into the safety of the forest, where we knew that the Nazis would not follow. We stopped to rest and decide what to do, and which way to go in this huge forest? I did not count how many Jews made it with us to the forest, but they were not many.

Motke used his shirt to bandage my wounded foot. I don't remember how long we stayed there, waiting for something to happen. From far away we could hear the echoes of the German tanks and machine-guns, systematically destroying the Glubokie ghetto. We were lucky. Those who survived the destruction of the ghetto were murdered by the Nazis later on. Those who were wounded in the field died there.

We must survive!

After a few hours everyone relaxed, but we did not have the slightest idea where we were in the Poshcha. In Russian, a Poshcha is a huge forest, spread over tens of square kilometers, with rivers, streams, and a few small villages. While the adults sat down to think what to do next, I had moved aside, very sad and depressed, and started to cry.

For the first time during those long difficult months, I cried, allowing myself to unload the pressure on my heart, which had long been building inside me. I did not know what had happened to Chaim-Shepse and Aunt Lea, but I already knew I would not see them alive again. I did not know what had happened to other relatives and friends, who were my entire world. I kept thinking, "Why did the Germans shoot at me?" But I knew that I must be very strong from then on, no longer a child!

Most of all, I missed my mother. I knew that she was alive, somewhere in the same huge forest. I waited for her calming loving words, her soft comforting touch, her caring advice, and the feeling of safety she had always given us. My wound had started to ache, and I wondered how I would recover from this serious injury. And I began to feel guilty for leaving my brother and my aunt behind in the ghetto.

Darkness fell over the forest. The adults decided that our group would stay put, while 3 men went to the nearest village to ask for food. The 3 men pretended to be Partisans and asked, with some threats, for some food. The threats helped. They came back with vegetables, other food, and some cutlery, which they had taken from the farmers' houses. Now we could eat for the next few days. This very plain food was so delicious to me. It was a very satiating meal. Immediately after it I felt very fatigue. Luckily for us, these were hot summer days of August, so there was no problem to sleep in the open under the sky, on some improvised mattresses of forest herbs. In a way, it was better to be in the forest, without any fear from the Germans. But I was without my parents, a home, or any relatives.

The young Etkin is sent to a "Healing place"

We stayed in the forest for 2 to 3 weeks. We were safe from the Germans, because we knew that they would not approach the Partisans' bases. We even had some food to eat. But my wounded foot became infected. Motke knew that we must do something about it very quickly, or I might lose my foot.

One morning Motke said "We are going to the village. I found a shelter for you there." When we reached one of the houses in the village, Motke knocked on the door, someone opened it and we were invited inside the house. "Why did you come here? What do you want? What is the boy's name?" asked the owner of the house. "Etkin", replied Motke, "and we have escaped from the Glubokie ghetto". The man became very friendly. "If this is Menachem-Mendel's son, then – there is no problem. He can stay here with us, and he will get the best treatment."

When I look back, I think of the saying: "Send your bread over the water, and one day you will find it." I don't know whether my father gave some money to this farmer, helped him, or made a good profitable real-estate deal for him. Anyway, more than 2 years after my father's death, the villagers in our area remembered him very well. And one of them saved my life.

I can't remember the name of this farmer, his children or their family name. But I DO remember that I received good medical treatment from them, and lots of warmth. They bandaged my foot; spread a special anti-infection ointment over the wound twice a day. Later, they took me to the village shoemaker, who made a special pair of boots for me: One regular boot for my healthy foot, and one larger boot which will contain the thick bandage around my wounded foot.

This good couple made a small bed for me behind the door, hidden behind a screen. Every once in a while, I would get up and look at the chickens, the cows, and the different farm jobs. Sometimes I would help them around the farm, as much as I could with my wounded foot. I had "parents". But I could not stop missing my mother, my twin-brother, and Aunt Lea.

I stayed for about 3 months, totally disconnected from my previous world, and from Motke Kraut. I knew nothing about what was happening around me, as if the war no longer existed. I called my adoptive parents "uncle" and "aunt". Years later I wanted to return to this village near Glubokie, to thank this wonderful couple, but I could not remember its name and I could not locate it.

The Germans arrive to the village. My life is saved once again!

I rarely worried about the Germans since they came to the village infrequently. When ordered to search for Jews, they did a very cursory job and hurried back to the safety of their base. But my adoptive parents had made it very clear to me that it was forbidden for the Germans or for any of the village members to know my real identity. Furthermore, we agreed that if the Germans came to search our house, that I would lie in bed, pretending to be sick. I knew I could count on my "parents", so I did exactly as we had agreed.

One morning, German soldiers knocked on the door. I hurried to get into my bed, covered myself with the blanket, and closed the screen beside my bed. The Germans came into the house, searched it all over, and did not find anything. But before leaving, they saw my bed behind the door. "Who is this?" I heard one of them ask.

I was frightened but my fear was for nothing. My "uncle" said "This is our son. He has a high fever. The doctor said that he must stay in bed, and nobody should go near him." The soldier thought for a moment, said "Gut" (good) and left with his friends. My life was saved once again!

Here I must say something about the non-Jews in the Glubokie area, especially the farmers. Unlike the Poles and the Ukrainian killers, non-Jewish Belarussians showed us sympathy, and more. In many cases, Jews were allowed to hide in a barn or a cowshed. The farmers would give the hiding Jews some water and food, so that they could continue on their way. Most knew the Etkin family well from before the war. I do not remember even a single case of a local non-Jew informing against Jews or handing over any Jews to the Germans.

I join the Partisans

I felt good with my adoptive parents, but most of all I wanted to find my mother and my relatives, whom I was very worried about. The winter of 1943 came closer and closer. A few months after my wounded foot had healed, Motke arrived to see how I felt and to check if he could take me back to the Partisans in the forest. Motke thanked my adoptive parents, and told them that from now on the Partisans would protect them and not take any food or horses from their farm. After we all cried and said our goodbyes, Motke and I started for the forest. I did not know where were heading. I was scared.

We did not reach Motke's battalion, either because it was too far away or because Motke was worried that such a long walk would exhaust me, slow him down, and put him in danger from the Germans. So we approached the nearest Partisan battalion and soon came to a fence and a gate guarded by a Partisan. He refused to let us in, perhaps thinking we were spies. I did not know which battalion it was, or what they were doing. Motke did not give up. He told the guard in Russian "This boy escaped from the Glubokie ghetto, and was shot in the foot. He has healed and now wants to join your battalion as a trainee." The guard hesitated for a moment, and then called his commander via the radio device. The commander appeared and started to interrogate me, asking where I was from, what were my plans, and why did I want to join them.

Appendix to the Dokshitz Parafianov Yizkor Book
Material Not in the Original Yizkor Book

It was the Rokosovsky brigade, named after their commander in the Ukrainian front, I determined to stay there. I said good-bye to Motke again, and he went on his way. The battalion commander assigned me as a trainee to a Partisan named Kulke, with orders to do everything he told me to do. Luckily, the battalion had another young trainee, a 14 year old Christian boy. Despite the difference between our ages, we soon became good friends. He was an orphan, and like me, had found shelter with this battalion. We became "brothers with the same kind of problem", missing our families very much, lost children in a big war! But there was no lack of food, and we also had some clothes, although definitely not enough for a very cold Russian winter.

Me and Kulke under fire

Kulke was the ideal trainer, a very nice guy, very brave and calm. I remember once, we were riding together on a sled tied to a horse. Suddenly out of nowhere, the Germans opened fire at us. The horse panicked and the sled, full of equipment, rolled over. Kulke did not panic. He cocked his automatic rifle, which had a 50-round drum magazine, and started shooting back at the Nazis. He shouted at me "Turn over the sled and put the equipment back on it. Don't worry, I am covering you". Within minutes it was over. I fixed the sled and we got away safe and well. It was my second time under fire, but not my last.

I lived with the Partisans of the Rokosovsky brigade in the forests of Belarus for 7 months. I was without my family and friends, and always missed my dear mother, but it was good for me there. There was a fighters' spirit in this battalion, and, although just a trainee with a useless "Karabin" rifle that never shot a single bullet, I was part of it.

As a trainee, I had a few defined tasks, such as peeling potatoes, cleaning and fixing the camp, washing the Partisans' clothes, etc. We lived in bunkers dug in the ground and supported by wooden poles. Some had couches. We made mattresses from a forest grass called "Moch", and some old blankets protected us from the cold nights. In addition, local villagers gave us food, clothes and blankets.

Every morning, a few patrol groups would go out to search for nearby German army units. The others stayed to guard the camp from any unexpected enemy penetration. The women and children did all the maintenance work. Life in the forest was hard, but we managed quite well. But all the time, I could not stop thinking and worrying about my dear mother. How was she managing as a woman among HER Partisans? Did she have a toilette or a place to change her clothes? Was she cold? But I assumed she was managing, since her battalion also had other women, serving as nurses and doctors.

Our battalion strikes a German train

Sometimes we broke our routine for missions. One morning our battalion mined the railroad, in order to blow up a German train. I was lying within the Partisan lines waiting to see what would happen. The Partisans knew ahead of time when the train would pass by. They stretched a long wire, put the mines on the bridge, and waited patiently. Forward spotters reported that the train was coming. One of the Partisans lit the fuse, which burned quickly toward the mine. The mine exploded just as the train hit the bridge.

It was too late for the Germans. The locomotive and the coaches had all fallen off the bridge into a deep abyss. Some of the German soldiers who had survived the crash were crawling wounded out of the coaches. They were immediately shot by the Partisans with automatic weapons. Some managed to shoot back, but were killed immediately with overwhelming fire. In all of these raids the Partisans had the upper hand. They knew the area and hid among the trees. The Germans were in the open and exposed.

A letter from mother!

One day, I received a priceless gift: a short letter from my dear mother. I later learned that mother had heard from someone in her battalion that he had seen a red-haired child in our camp. She did not know whether was me or my twin-brother, but assumed that one of us was still alive. The letter was written on a brown paper bag. It said "My dear son, I had found out that you are in the forest not so far from me. Be a good boy. Behave well. We will meet each other soon. I love you very much – your mother."

I wanted to run immediately to find my mother in the other forest. The letter was in Yiddish, and one of the Jewish Partisans translated it for me. It was written in an unclear language on a dirty piece of paper, but still I kept it in my pockets for many months. It was the only sign I had from my beloved dear mother, a sign of love. It helped me a lot during those very difficult days in the huge cold forests of Belarus.

The letter strengthened me, and gave me a new hope. Suddenly, it seemed as if a meeting with my dear beloved mother was only a matter of time. I became very impatient, and one morning I notified Kulke: "That's it. I don't have any more patience, I am going out to the forests in order to search for my mother and live with her again. I miss her very much."

Kulke gave me his very understanding look, and asked: "Boy, this is a huge forest. Where are you going? Don't you think that you may get lost in it?" But I did not give up: "I will search for her until I will find her" I replied. "Where are you, Mother?" I asked myself. Kulke only smiled. When I started walking into the huge forest, he picked me up and locked me inside the camp. I was very angry and I tried to resist him. Now I understand that he had actually saved my life. There is no doubt that while searching for my mother, I would have lost my way in that huge forest, and maybe even gotten caught by a German patrol.

My mother's end

I did not know it then, but my mother had died about two months before the end of the war. I did not know it, and it was better this way. Many months passed until I finally understood that my mother had been killed by the Nazis, and would never come back to me. Actually, until now I did not really digest the fact that she had died.

I never stopped searching for her. Despite writing many letters to try and locate her grave, I did not receive any positive answer about it until recently. I only know that on June 3, 1944 the Nazis caught her with her Partisans' medicine troop. They took them to the center of Dokshitz, and hung all of them there. She was only 30 years old.

I do not know any more details about the death of Eva (Chava) Kaminsky-Etkin, my dear mother. But knowing her, I know she resisted her captors. She kicked them, spat on them, and did not stop fighting them until her last minute. One of the dreams, which will most probably be with me until the end of my life, is to find her grave (probably a "Brothers grave"), visit it, put flowers on it, and tell her that despite everything, we had beaten the hated Germans.

At the age of 72, I still miss her very much!

At least once a week, I listen to the nice Russian songs she used to listen to.

I really can't accept the fact that despite my longing to her – she will never be back with me.

I would like to tell you again, that my mother, Chava (Eva) Etkin, maiden name Kaminsky or Kaminska, born on January 15th, 1913, was the daughter of Michaela and Israel, part of a family of medical doctors and nurses. She was a beautiful young lady, a very talented student, and an active member in the "Hachalutz" youth-movement.

Later on, mother graduated the nursing school in Vilna, as an authorized nurse, after three years of studies. She worked with lots of dedication in the Glubokie hospital, and even found the time to take care of me, as I was a small, weak, sick child.

She was an unforgettable figure, loved by everyone: my father, her children (my twin-brother and I), her friends and the entire family. She loved all of them in return, hosting them with kindness in our warm house. The house was full of light when she was there. Our house had an atmosphere of culture, nourished by books and music. Mother never stopped singing Russian and Yiddish songs in the house and also outside in our big garden. I continue to guard her beauty and these songs in my heart.

Chapter 4 – I Search for My Mother

I had started searching for my dear mother, Chava (Eva) Etkin (Kaminsky), on July 1944 (Actually, I really wished to see her from the moment I had escaped from the ghetto). "World War 2" was still running wild in some different fronts, but for us – the Partisans in Belarus – the fighting had ended. At last we could get out of the forests.

The Nazi threat had been removed. Now we were able to travel safely in trains and trucks, without fear from any German soldier who might have sneaked into the forest and may open fire at us. I decided to search for my mother, and I truly believed that I will find her.

The fear era had ended. No more did we need to wander 15 or 20 kilometers to move our camp. We did not have to dig any more new bunkers in the ground, install the wooden couches again, fill our mattresses with forest grass, and prepare the guarding arrangements again. Now we could be relieved and let go of being on full alert 24 hours a day. It was a new positive and happy experience for us. Our lives in the forest were safe, and we had arranged them so that we would be able to fight well and survive.

The Germans defeat did not surprise us. Our patrol units reported to us about the Germans' retreat. Our patrollers (maybe I did not emphasize their importance enough) were very brave and significant fighters. During the winter time, they were dressed with white uniforms for camouflage, and in the summer time they were dressed with brownish & green clothes – like the colors of the forest, in which we were hiding.

These patrollers knew exactly when the German troops are passing by outside of the forest, and when a train full of Nazi soldiers would cross in our area – so that we could blow it with explosives. They also knew the timetable of the Germans' vehicle patrols, escorted by motorcylists in long black leather coats and helmets.

Thanks to the patrollers, many Nazi soldiers were killed or taken into captivity by the Partisans. The patrollers learned and told us that soon the hated German army would leave the territory of our beloved Belarus, then still in the Soviet Union. The Russian soldiers and the Partisans were very brave fighters, with lots of good qualities and abilities.

The German army collapses and escapes

We had other sources of information. I had already mentioned that the Soviet army had parachuted into our area some basic foods, essential supply, and weapons. Together with these supplies a few new commanders had arrived into our battalion: Romanov, Dorminyev, and Nagamayev. These commanders, which were part of the group who had established our brigade, were equipped with relatively advanced communication devices, and kept an on-going communication with the "Rokosovsky" brigade headquarters, which included three or four battalions.

The information was very consistent and fluent, and brought us great happiness in this spring of 1944. "We are winning the Nazis in every battle" declared the broadcasters. "The German army retreats little by little, and we are chasing it". "See you all in Berlin", another broadcaster said with excitement.

I was happy with them. Despite being a young adolescent, I felt that I was an equal fighter to the Russian soldiers, who had showed some very special acts of bravery. The optimism of these broadcasters had penetrated into our fighting troops, gave them additional strength and bravery to go on until the end of this period.

This information was also confirmed by the Russian newspaper "PRAVDA" (truth). It's true that this was a political, sometimes unreliable newspaper, but anyone who knew how to select the truth between the propaganda lines, could understand that now this newspaper is telling the truth. "We are winning, and soon all of us will be able to return home safely", it said. I hoped to meet my dear beloved mother, and to return to our home in Krulevshchizna. I wanted to know whether our house still existed, and were any of my family still alive?

Burnt earth

Many years later, when I speak with people and read history books, I wonder what had caused the great German army to be defeated and crushed so completely. How had what had started as a "blitzkrieg" – lightning war – which caused great destruction all over Europe and the death of many millions of people – of which six million were Jews – eventually lost its momentum?

How did the Red Army succeed to destroy the whole German war system?

In short, their mad leader had brought a disaster upon them! My conclusion, and not only mine, is that the Germans had made a few simple mistakes. Led by a madman, they did not act with pure military motives, but with egotism and insane impulses to kill, destroy, and conquer many large territories of the world. If they had only taken the time to think twice about it, they could have avoided these basic mistakes.

For example, the Germans' penetration deeply into Russia, without taking into consideration the very cold and cruel Russian winter. The Germans were not prepared for such a cold winter, which could not have been evaluated by them in June 1941. Their clothes were too thin for such a cold winter, their rifles and heavy weapons broke down very frequently due to the mud and dirt.

The deep mud had also slowed down their movements. Lots of mechanical problems had also occurred with the fast German tanks, which won many battles, but now found it very difficult to cross the deep mud, rivers and lakes. These tanks could not move any more and were eventually abandoned in the battle field. There is no doubt their mad Nazi leader had brought their end upon them, in a smashing defeat.

On the other hand, the Russian army had survived quite well, despite its inferiority. The Russian soldiers knew the territory very well, got back-up from the local population, and were tougher fighters. They could sleep on the ground, eat a small quantity of food, and survive in very difficult conditions. However, the German soldier, who might have been a good soldier, found it very difficult to adjust to the difficult physical conditions of northeastern Europe.

It's true that they had survived somehow the winter of 1942, but their forces got weaker and weaker. If they only tried to reach some conclusions, they would have understood that their soldiers could not survive another cold Russian winter. If they had only thought reasonably, they would have withdrawn their army, in order to be better prepared for the future.

However, with their stupidity – they counted too much on their large quantity of army equipment, their tanks and artillery – but they had failed in all of the fronts. They continued to go deeper and deeper with their "Blitz-Krig" thousands of kilometers into Russia, but this deep invasion became very bad for them.

If the German army generals counted on getting food supplies from the Russian villages, they were totally wrong about it. They could not count any more on any local supply of food and fuel. What was known as the "Burnt earth" policy became a horror for the Nazi army.

The Red Army commanders had planned well and followed their plan just as well. During the Russians' withdrawal, they had burnt everything. They did not leave behind any sources of food, fuel, clothes or any other resource. The Germans' long supply chains started to collapse. If we would consider the second front, which was opened in June 1944 in Normandy, we would easily understand why Hitler's army began collapsing, and withdrew very quickly towards Germany.

Now came the Red Army's great hour. Its soldiers did not only chase the withdrawing German troops. The Russian soldiers ambushed the Germans, shot them, and set off explosives on bridges and roads without any warning. I remember once, when we had reached one of the villages in our area, and found a lot of meat in the kitchen of one of the houses, we were warned not to touch it. Our commander told us that this meat might be poisoned or with hidden explosives in it.

So, where is my mother?

Our war was over, but there was only one wish in my heart: to find my dear beloved mother. The short brief letter she had sent me was still in my pocket – a sign of life from her. Indeed, I had no doubt that my mother is alive, waiting for her child in one of the villages or shtetls in our area. Throughout the war I missed her and the rest of my family. Now I decided to find them.

Now that the fear was over, it was only natural that every one of us would return to think of his family members and friends, which stayed back there. Now I was not only thinking of my mother. I hoped in the bottom of my heart, that maybe my dear twin- brother Chaim-Shepse, aunt Lea, and some of my family relatives were still alive, waiting for me.

If I was more realistic then, I could have guessed that most probably all of them had been killed by the Nazis. I saw the Glubokie ghetto being totally burnt, I heard the whistling bullets hitting the fugitives which were running in the fields towards the forest. But in August 1943 I did not want to be realistic. An 11 years old child wants to dream, to hope and to wait for the return of his beloved family members – and that's exactly what I did during those days.

Since I was always active and full of initiative, I had decided to devote my time from now on in searching after my dear mother. At the same time, the Partisans in the forests started to get organized. They packed all of their belongings, loaded them onto wagons tied to horses, and started moving towards the town of Vileke, which was also in Belarus, close to Dokshitz, Glubokie, and my childhood town, Krulevshchizna.

We did not say our farewells yet. Luckily for me, it went in stages. I did not have any relatives. Kulke and the Rokosovsky Partisans brigade were my only family. We got a command from the Red Army, saying that our Partisan

Appendix to the Dokshitz Parafianov Yizkor Book
Material Not in the Original Yizkor Book

battalion should stay in Vileike and wait for further instructions. Now I understand that the Soviet army wanted to make sure that the Germans, maybe in a last desperate attack, would not try to break through the front somewhere, taking advantage of the lack of alertness of the Red Army.

My long journey to find my mother

Our stay in Vileike was quite pleasant. Beyond our daily parades and guarding our camp, we did not do anything. During most of the day we took short trips in the area and ate food given to us by the local grateful population. They brought us fruits, vegetables, bread, fresh eggs, and even meat. I was happy that the war had ended, and that hopefully, my mother would come to me.

Since I was a young Partisan in the "Rokosovsky" brigade, I was in this camp as well, but within a very short while I became impatient. If my mother is still alive, I told myself, she must be waiting for me. I must get out of this camp and start searching for her until I found her.

But first of all, as a soldier, I needed to get my commander's permission. I approached my battalion's commander, Lieutenant Colonel Romanov, with my request. Romanov listened to me very carefully and replied: "Whether you find your mother, or not, I want you to promise me that after you complete your family duties you will come back to our base here in Vileike". I agreed without any hesitation. I felt that my mother also wanted to find her son, who had survived from the ghetto. There was no permanent transportation yet, and only a few trains were riding in this area without any schedule.

Romanov's order gave me a good feeling. I knew that I belong to a certain group in this terrible world of great cruel wars, full of blood shed. Lieutenant Colonel Romanov gave me a good feeling of belonging and care. I knew that even if I would get into any kind of trouble or problems, I could always come back to my safe secure place with the Partisans. I was very connected to them.

Now I decided to travel to Glubokie, which was about 80 kilometers away. There was no timetable for the trains. I waited at the Vileike train-station, and boarded a train, which I had believed would bring me to my dear noble mother who was waiting for me. However, I had a small problem – no money in my pockets, not one ruble. I tried to be as small as possible, so maybe the conductor would not notice me, and sat on one of the wooden benches in the train.

The train whistled and started to move. Then I was certain that I was going to meet my dear mother, whom I hadn't seen for about a year and a half, since the summer of 1943. But before that, I had to meet another person on this train: the conductor. He came closer and closer, and I carefully looked at his small scissors, which were punching the passengers train tickets. I asked myself what would happen when he reached me? I decided that no matter what, I would not get off this train, and I would tell him that I was searching for my mother. When he finally reached me, he said: "Your ticket, please".

I gave him a helpless look and decided to tell him the truth: "I don't have any money, sir, and therefore I don't have a ticket. But I must get to Glubokie, in order to find my mother". The conductor looked at me, thought for a moment, smiled and said: "O.K. boy, you can travel on this train without a ticket". He had under-estimated my age, because I was quite short. I guess he thought that I was 8 years old, although I was 11.5 with the life experience of an adult.

That was quite a relief. Such a trip to Glubokie was not an easy task anyhow in those days. Traveling alone in a train, without an adult to accompany me could have been dangerous. Gangs of criminals, who had no money, used to rob the passengers. I saw with my own eyes such a "Hooligan" (a Russian criminal), grabbing a suitcase belonging to one of the passengers. After a few minutes, he threw it out of the train to his friend, who waited there for it.

I was shocked and scared from what I had just seen. I only wanted to find my mother. It was a scary feeling, but after thinking about it logically I had reached the conclusion that nothing bad could happen to me. I didn't even have a small back pack, so nothing could have been stolen from me. Poverty was a disadvantage, but it seemed that it also had an advantage sometimes. Being a child was an advantage as well. Children and orphans usually received some help wherever they arrived. I was careful. I decided that if I would be attacked, then – I will shout for help and try to defend myself.

The disappointment

The ride took hours. The train stopped at every station, and it seemed that it did not hurry at all to my meeting with my dear mother. Finally, we had arrived to Glubokie. After asking some people where the Jews were living, I had reached the house of a Jewish family. "Your mother is Chava Etkin", he thought loudly, while my heart was beating very fast. "Yes, I think that she is alive. Go and ask the Jews in the Synagogue. I heard that some of your relatives are still alive, so maybe she is one of them."

I ran to the synagogue. I knew that very soon my journey will be over, and that within a few moments I will meet my dear mother. However, I was soon disappointed again.

"We don't know anything about Chava Etkin" they said. "But we know that your relatives, the Hodosh family, are in the town of Kurinyetz, which is not so far from here – about 2 hours by the train. You will definitely find there someone from your family." Despite being very tired, I did not wait. I ran to catch the train to Kurinyetz.

"Aren't you Chava Etkins' son"?

During my train ride to Kurinyetz, a Russian soldier whom I never saw before had approached me. Maybe he had just noticed me, and understood that I am hungry. He took out of his bag some sandwiches with meat, and gave them to me. But the real surprise was still waiting for me. "Tell me please, aren't you Chava Etkin's son?" he asked. I was totally amazed. How could he know it? How did he identify me? Maybe he knew my mother, and identified me according to a description she gave him? And maybe he confused between me and my twin-brother? Later on, I found out that indeed he knew my mother. They fought together in the Partisans. It seemed that my mother did not stop speaking about her red hair twins – an outstanding sign, which could easily be spotted. He also knew that one of the twins had succeeded to escape from the ghetto towards the forests.

I was very excited and I was shivering. "Did you know her?" I asked him with a shivering voice. "Yes boy" he answered. "Your mother was a wonderful woman, and an excellent fighter." I refused to digest that this soldier was speaking about my mother in past tense. "Where is she?" I started screaming with excitement in the middle of the train. "If you know where she is, then let's go together to search for her!" I urged him, while I was shivering from deep excitement. I wanted to find my dear beloved mother.

The soldier looked at me, and kept silent. Most probably he could not find enough courage in his heart to bring me this unfortunate message, during my searches after my mother. Later on, he said good-bye to me and went off the train, keeping the secret in his heart. I stayed there on the train. I was very sad! I wanted and needed my mother so much! I missed her so much, and felt that I could not continue without her – I would not be able to live any more without her. I missed her so much during the war, the ghetto, getting wounded, and in the forests. She was the only person left alive from our family. Or so I thought.

"Where is my mother?" I yelled at the soldier through the train's window.

He only waived good-bye to me, and went on.

A reunion with the Hodosh family

In Kurinyetz I was luckier. I located a Jew, who told me that I had some family members in the town: my uncle Tana Hodosh and his 2 sons Zelig and

Hershel. Tana was my father's brother-in-law. He was married to my father's sister – Gitl Etkin. Needless to say, Tana was very surprised to see me at his door. He probably did not think that anyone of his family had survived the tragedies of the Holocaust.

I did not know anything about Tana before our meeting. He gave me a warm welcome, listened to my exciting story, and after I told him that I am searching for my mother – he suggested that I stay at his house for a few days. "Why should you be in a hurry?" he said. "Stay with us for a while, take a good shower, eat well, and we will do your laundry. Then, you will gain some more strength in order to continue with your searching for your mother."

However, I had no patience. My mother was waiting for me somewhere (so I thought). Today I understand that I was quite desperate, and acted as a senseless child searching for his dear beloved mother. So, I said good-bye to uncle Tana, and took the next train back to Glubokie. Maybe mother got back there? But she didn't. I got sadder and sadder. I only wanted to find her! But I did not lose hope. As always, even in a very young age, I found my way out.

I refused to give up. Suddenly I remembered that mother had left some of our properties in a certain village. I decided to go there. Maybe someone there could tell me something about my mother, maybe I could use some of our properties somehow? I had no idea how many assets were there, or where they were hidden.

In the train, beside the locomotive driver

I went back to the train-station. Since I had no money for a ticket. I worked up the courage to tell the truth to the locomotive driver. "Look" I told him after climbing up to the big locomotive, "I am searching for my mother, but I don't have any money. Can I travel here beside you?" The driver smiled kindly and allowed me to stay there beside him. This way I could point at the village, to which we were approaching after a while. I had a very good memory. I remembered the village's name and the name of the family, who kept our assets.

The driver stopped the train especially for me, and I went off by a water canal. There was very heavy rain. Between me and the village houses there was a large field of a kilometer length full of water. I knew that it would be too risky for me to try and cross this muddy field – I might sink. I had to decide what to do next, and which way should I go?

I scanned the area and decided to find a shelter from the heavy rain under a bridge. Tomorrow morning, I said to myself, I will get to the village.

What should I do with our family's properties?

I slept under this bridge at night, and in the morning, I got to the village after a long walk in this muddy field. I found the house of my mother's friends, and they were very happy to see me. After they had changed my wet and dirty clothes, and gave me some food to eat – they showed me a closed room. "Here we had kept some of your family's properties, and you can take it back" she said warmly and opened the room's door, pointing at good furniture, carpets and expensive silver goods.

I looked at all of these fine goods, and did not know what to do with it. I was a 12-year-old boy, without anything, and I knew that I would not be able to carry these goods with me during my traveling. If I only knew it – I would have sold these goods, and I could have some money, which could improve my situation. But I was just a little boy, so I had left all of these fine goods to stay there.

I did not understand how these goods could be changed to money. I told my mother's friends that currently I would not take anything, because I must continue my searching for my mother, Chava (Eva) Etkin. I guess that a few years later they sold all of these goods, and took the money for themselves. They gave me some food, took me for a hair cut at the barber, and gave me some new clothes and a pair of new boots. Again, I had to decide where to go next? The most logical decision was to go back to Kurinyetz, to uncle Tana's warm house, and to ask for his advice.

I got on the train again without a ticket (with the conductor's permission), and arrived at the Hodosh' house. It seemed that uncle Tana was very angry at me. "Where are you running around so much?" he asked me with anger. "Don't you know how dangerous it is for a small Jewish boy to run alone in trains these days? Don't you know that Russian criminals can kill you for nothing? What do you think you are doing?"

I had no doubt about it. I must continue my searching for my dear beloved mother.

Uncle Tana was probably a good person, but he did not know what to do with such a knotty independent boy like me. It was clear to me that his lack of ability to control me had caused him to become very frustrated about it. Furthermore, he planned to leave Russia and migrate to America or to Israel.

Perhaps he thought that I would be a burden on him. I guess he had some personal problems as well. I know that he loved me like he loved his sons, Hershel and Zelig. Anyway, I wanted to stay with them. They were my only family now.

I escape from the orphanage

Maybe Tana thought that he was doing the best thing for me, and one day he purchased 2 train tickets for both of us to the city of Vilna, which was quite far away.

It was a very long trip. In Vilna, we arrived at a very big house, in which I was asked to stay. Only later on I understood that I arrived at a Jewish orphanage for children who lost their parents during the war. There were many children there, who needed adult supervision.

But the supervision was very poor. The Vilna orphanage turned out to be a very cold and heartless institution. The staff of workers there did not provide any warmth or love to the poor Jewish children, who stayed in it. We received a very small amount of food, and a lot of beating. The instructors were very young, uneducated, and without any experience. And they were hitting us for nothing. They wanted to take control of us in this manner. It was clear to me that I must escape from there in the first opportunity that I would have. My resourcefulness had saved me once again. I assume that if I was a different kind of child: weaker and passive, I would have stayed there, poor, miserable, and helpless. Not me! On this day I decided: I would not stay there any more.

The next day, at 05:00 in the morning, with the sunrise, I woke up. I felt weak and tired, but with a strong decision to leave this terrible place. It was not clear to me where should I go... I went out. There was no one there, except for the guard, who asked me where am I going so early in the morning? "One of the instructors asked me to buy something. I will return immediately" I replied. "Can you please let me pass the gate?"

The guard hesitated a bit, and then opened the gate. I sneaked out into Vilna's still sleeping streets. It was a smooth escape, indeed. Now I was walking around in a totally unfamiliar city, having no idea where should I go, without any money in my pockets, no food or water, sad and depressed. I had a bit of comfort knowing that I would not be back in this terrible orphanage, in which the children are starving and being beaten. It was obvious to me that I am also not going back to Tana Hodosh's house, because he might take me back to Vilna, to this terrible orphanage.

Back to the Partisans

What should I do? Where should I go? I was very confused and depressed.

Tana Hodosh's house was out of the question. My mother was not in Glubokie, not in Kurinyetz, and I had no idea where could she be. But I had to decide what to do next. I couldn't just stay in the streets of Vilna, a city with a great Jewish community in the past.

Suddenly, I remembered the Partisans and Romanov's words to me: "After you will complete your searching for your mother – I command you to return to our camp in Vileika". I was very glad. In the middle of the far and unfamiliar city of Vilna, I felt that I was not alone in this world. Once again, I got on a train without a ticket, without any money in my pocket, and within a few hours I arrived at the Partisans' headquarters in the city of Vileika.

Romanov and his friends were very happy to see me. "We knew that we can count on you" they told me warmly. "You promised to return, and you kept your word". After they showed me where would I be sleeping, I found a new friend there – a boy at my age, and we went together to the fields out of the city, to pick some strawberries.

I had not yet found my mother, but now, being in a familiar place, I felt good again, safe and secure. I knew that after I rested for a while and regained some strength, I would continue my searching for my mother. It was very difficult for me to be alone again.

Farewell to my Partisan friends

I returned to the routine life of my Partisan friends. Every once in a while, this routine was broken when some German captives arrived at our camp's "prison". They looked so miserable, hungry, thin and helpless – a total opposite of the great proud German army, who passed through Krulevshchizna three years earlier. These German soldiers looked so poor, which caused some of their Partisan guards to treat them gently. However, some other guards, who hated the Germans very much – were hitting them every once in a while, as a revenge.

After two months of routine soldiers' life, we received a command from the Red Army's headquarters in Moscow, saying that all Partisan units should stop all of their activities. All of us could return home. The Partisans' job was over. I asked myself: Where should I go? I had my plans, and I believed that I would succeed.

Our joy was mixed with sadness. Those of us whose families were alive and their houses were not hurt were very glad to return to their houses, families and work. Some others, like me, were very sad. Not only was I about to lose all of my dear close Partisan friends, who were like a family for me during a very long period of war. I had no real warm house to return to.

I was very worried about this new situation. But I had no choice. Immediately after the dismantling of my Partisan unit, I got on a train to Kurinyetz, to Uncle Tana Hodosh, hoping that he would not take me back to an orphanage, or to any other Jewish institution. I loved my uncle and his 2 sons, Zelig and Hershel, very much.

Uncle Tana understood that I was a very independent child, and so I became to be a permanent member of his family at his home. He gave me a bed, lots of food, and I even got back to school when the Hodosh family moved from Kurinyetz to Glubokie, where we got a small apartment from the local municipality. I was very glad to go back to school. I always liked to study more and more, and to broaden my horizons in many fields. My grades were very good and I was an excellent student.

It's hard to believe how the Anti-Semitism had grown in Eastern Europe with the end of the 2nd World War. Even after Hitler was only a terrible nightmare in our memories, some Polish people, Russians and Ukrainians kept on killing Jews and robbing their properties in different occasions.

Every once in a while, our Gentile classmates would bother us. But I was not afraid of them at all. I was bigger than them and I warned them: "Whoever tries to bother a Jewish child here will be sorry for it, and I will hit him."

My threats helped. Nobody bothered me anymore, and also the bothering towards the other Jewish children in my class was much less then before. In parallel with our studies, we found ourselves a source of living. Tana Hodosh took advantage of his trading talents. He bought some clothes and shoes, and we sold them together in the Glubokie market. Now, for the first time, we had some money to make a living. For a short while, we felt really good. We sold clothes, shoes and food.

Appendix to the Dokshitz Parafianov Yizkor Book

Material Not in the Original Yizkor Book

Should I stay with uncle Tana, or continue all alone to Israel? On May 8th, 1945, almost a year after the liberation of Belarus, the war had ended. Peace was back in Europe, and then in the whole world. Everyone celebrated the ending of the war with singing and dancing in the streets. Now many Jews could think about their destiny and ask themselves: Where should we go now?

Tana Hodosh wanted to go back to Poland. There, he told us, our lives would be much better. While searching for a good place to settle in, we started traveling in trains all over Poland. We were also in Austria and in Czechoslovakia. We snuck across the Austrian Alps across the border into Germany, and arrived in a huge displaced camp in Fernwald. The street names in this camp were like the names of some American states: New York, Texas, Ohio, and Minnesota. In this camp, among many other Jews, Tana hoped to find a new direction in his life for him and his family. We felt very good and free there.

During this period, I felt that on one hand I was a part of uncle Tana's family, but on the other hand, I had the feeling that the Hodosh family would go on without me, leaving me behind. Meanwhile, we continued our studies at the camp with a nice young teacher from Israel, called Aliza. She told us about the Promised Land, but when she showed it to us in films I asked myself: They want me to go there, to this dry yellow land? What would I do in this desert land?

Michael Etkin "on the tree", at the Fernwald transfer camp

That's why when my uncle suggested to me to board a ship heading to this "promised land" – I refused to do it, despite they offered me a "Certificate" (a new immigrant document). First of all, because I did not want to go there. It looked like a very depressing place. Furthermore, it was very difficult for me to leave Uncle Tana Hodosh and his family. They were the only family relatives, which were left for me, after this terrible Holocaust.

But Hodosh had already prepared himself for my farewell. Together with tens of other orphans, I boarded a train, which would take me to France.

There, in the port of Marseilles, a big wonderful passenger ship was waiting for us, the SS Champollion. This huge ship would bring me to the next stage of my life in the Jewish state of Israel.

From right to left: Mike Hodosh, Tana Hodosh, Michael Etkin, and Greg Hodosh.

Appendix to the Dokshitz Parafianov Yizkor Book
Material Not in the Original Yizkor Book

SS Champollion

Appendix to the Dokshitz Parafianov Yizkor Book
Material Not in the Original Yizkor Book

From Dokshitz to Israel

By Arie Henkin

Part One: My Father's Childhood Dokshitz Memories

By Roni Henkin-Roytfarb
Edited by Rob Benjamin

I am the daughter of Arie Henkin. He tells the rest of his story in his own words. But the story of his childhood in Dokshitz is in my words, and the images of those years are as he described them to me.

My father's grandfather, Aharon Yoel Hazan, was a Rabbi. He wrote four religious books, "Questions and Answers", "The sons of Aaron," Nechmadin Mezahav", and "Making the hearts Joyous". He lived with his wife in Tula after marriage, and died in Turkey on his way to Jerusalem.

His daughter Nina (Nehama) married my grandfather Yisrael Tzvi Henkin, who was from Disna. He and my mother lived in Kharkiv, where they had a shop selling chocolates and other sweets. They moved to Dokshitz in 1920 or 1921 after being invited by my grandmother's sister Miriam and her husband Shmuel Sheiman. My father was born in Dokshitz in 1923.

Pre-Soviet Dokshitz

Dokshitz of my father's childhood was a typical shtetl in Belorussia of the 1930s, under Polish rule. Its Jewish majority lived alongside a smaller Belorussian community and an even smaller Polish minority. The town was surrounded by Belorussian villages and some individual farms run by Polish settlers (Osadniks). These were brought into the area by the Polish government and given generous agricultural land grants. At the same time, the local peasants were crowded as the land was gradually split up among family members in inheritance.

The Henkin Family in 1929
Standing, left to right: Peska, Gnesya Dorfman (Yisrael's relative), Nina, Aharon, Seated: Yisrael Tzvi, Arie

There were also several large estates belonging to Polish squires. Particularly relevant to the Henkin family was Blonie, about a mile to the north of Dokshitz, and belonging to Wilhelmina Proshinsky. Some of the marshland separating the estate from the town was leased to our townsman Alter Chuchman, then sold to him to become 'the new extension' of Dokshitz.

This new northern extension, which the family moved into upon our arrival shortly before my father's birth, was 95 hectares. It was, divided into ten individual plots for housing and cultivation, and for a business, namely the

Sheiman-Frankfurt flour/saw mills. Most of the houses had a yard with a vegetable plot, a fruit grove, and a cowshed, in one half of which the cow lived while the other half contained hay for the winter.

Our family neither had a cowshed nor a cow. They had just a goat for a year or two, which my father had to take out to the goatherd every morning before school and bring back in the evening, over a kilometer each way, getting butted in the stomach far too often.

Some houses were divided among two families, with a kitchen in the middle (but in the case of our family the kitchen was outside). My grandparents rented the second half, for a year or two, to a new partner in the mills, a member of the Katzovich family, with his young wife and baby. A few of the Katzoviches went to Uruguay and the United States, one by one.

The Katzoviches had a peasant maid, who slept at the top of the big kitchen oven. This was where the family baked bread for the next week every Thursday and made food for Shabbos including cholent. This oven was used once a week. The bricks held the heat and it stayed warm for several days. Parallel to it was a lower oven for daily cooking.

There was no running water in the houses; all the families made do with outhouses. A communal well served each block of houses; it had a roll system with a chain to which a bucket was tied and suspended to a depth that varied with the season and rainfall status. In winter a thick layer of ice would form around the well at about the height of its opening, so my father would fear falling inside while rolling.

Once a week or once a fortnight, everyone went to the bathhouse, women on Thursday, men on Friday. As people entered the bathhouse, there was a room to put the clothing. Next was the washing room with buckets of hot water on the wall that it shared with the hot room. On the other side of the wall was the fire. After washing people went into the hot room where hot water was thrown onto the fire to make steam which made the top steps very hot.

Appendix to the Dokshitz Parafianov Yizkor Book
Material Not in the Original Yizkor Book

The steam also brought some of the dirt out, so it was back to the washing room for a final wash.

My father sat on the lowest step, while grandfather went to the top where it was unbearably hot. We could see the fire that kept things hot as we sat on the steps Almost everyone went. My grandmother preferred to bathe at home, which she did about once a month. My father had to bring the water for her bath and to empty the bath. The water went to the garden in the summer.

In the summer the cows would be led out to pasture daily. Each morning the cowherd would set out of the town center, proceeding down the main road with more cows joining, into Polotzker Street through the extension and out to the nearest farm on the marshland pasture grounds of Blonie. The Proshinsky brothers, Wilhelmina's sons, were both bachelors and both engineers – the younger was the only motorcycle owner in the vicinity, which made him an attraction as he rode past our family's house on his way to town.

The Sheimans were in-laws and next door neighbors to the north, namely at the end of Polotzker Street, with the Sheiman-Frankfurt flour mill and saw mill on their land; the neighbors on the other side were the Frankfurts, also in-laws, who rented half of the house.

My grandfather and his brother-in-law Shmuel Sheiman had a major disagreement. As a result, my father did not become a partner in his brother-in-law's mills, and they stopped talking to each other, as did their wives. This led to some unpleasant confrontations in the Schulhoyf. My grandfather went to the Staroshelever shul, and my father's Uncle went to the Mitnagdim shul. They crossed paths and exchanged heated words in front of the shul-goers. My father stood by, not understanding what they were arguing about. But my father and his cousins kept their connection. Some of the Sheimans left. The older son went to Mexico, and then he brought the younger one.

Instead of becoming a partner in the mill, my grandfather helped in the lumber industry selecting the trees to be cut down. This was far away, and he only came home twice a year, for Rosh Hashanah and Passover. When my father's brother Aharon was being treated for his injured leg in Vilna, my mother and I went with him. My sister Peska was in the gymnasium in Disna. When my grandmother collapsed, my grandfather quit his job and went to Vilna to help. When they all returned to Dokshitz, grandfather tried to go into business.

First grandfather opened a shop selling flour. Not making a living, my grandparents opened a shop at home selling cigarettes and household necessities to the laborers from the nearby mills. We created a room for the shop inside the door to the house. On Tuesdays, the market day, my grandfather and Mr. Reitman tried to buy grain at a good price from the peasants heading down Polotzker St before they reached the marketplace. Finally, he decided to go Palestine in 1935.

The distance from the house to the center, where the marketplace, the shops, the synagogues, schools and Cheyder at the Schulhoyf, the Youth Movements (Hashomer Hatzair, Dror, Beitar...), the bakery, the butcher, and everything else were located, was at least 2 kilometers. My father walked this at least twice a day. This distance may have been what put an end to the violin lessons which he took with the Friedman family, all of whom were violinists – whoever happened to be free would tutor the pupils.

Walking up south on Polotzker Street towards the center people would cross the road separating the extension from the inner shtetl and leading to Laputi, a village across the river and a mile to the northwest, with a nearby estate.

Walking past this junction into Dokshitz proper you passed the houses of blacksmith Ziklin and the Markman family and, on the other side, one of the two Orthodox churches. At the corner of the road to Laputi stood two tall, domineering crosses, one belonging to the Catholics, the other to the Orthodox Christians. Nearby was a wooden skeleton-frame of a large, half-built and deserted building, 200 meters away from the next inhabited house, that of the Reitman family.

Appendix to the Dokshitz Parafianov Yizkor Book
Material Not in the Original Yizkor Book

As a kid on his way home from the Cheyder on dark wintery nights, approaching this ominous location, my father would be absolutely terrified, despite his hand-lamp with its burning candle. Behind the black window frames there could be lurking thieves, robbers, or lunatics, maybe even ghosts out of the black block away to the right, namely the Jewish cemetery. As the years went by he remembers his fears diminished somewhat, not least because he was no longer alone. He and his friends would come home from the Hashomer Hatzair youth movement in twos or more.

The houses in Dokshitz were all made of wood except for two brick houses: the Korbman pharmacy in the market place; the Yolk house at the end of Sloboda Street, which would be transformed to serve as the governmental bakery in the Soviet era. There were also a couple of two-story buildings, one belonging to Luska Kaminkovich in the market place, with an inn downstairs and a clinic above; the other, in Borisov Street, belonged to Zeitlin, and housed the Polish police on the upper floor.

Small industries included the Gordons' brewery and a linseed factory, which employed many peasant women.

There was no public transport, no private cars, except one that was temporarily kept by Borka Yolk and a lorry temporarily kept by the Raskind brothers. The major means of transport were a horse and sledge in winter – sledges would also transport tree trunks cleaned of branches for the sawmills in winter – and horse and cart in summer. However, as the only paved streets were those of the city center and its immediate surroundings, driving around in a cart could be very tough both in spring, as the snow melted, and in heavy rain spells of the summer – the cart wheels would sink in the mud right up to the cart axle.

There were very few horse owners. These included two or three farmers and two or three balagoles or cart owners, whose horse and cart or sledge were used in a kind of shuttle service, mainly to Parafianov, some 10 km. away, to the nearest train station. This was a family business, and my father remembers that the Tiles family made a good living. It was not easy, since they had to be outside all year in all kinds of weather.

The train linked Dokshitz primarily to Vilna, some 200 km. away (YB p. 73), where the closest University Hospital was located. The links to the other towns and villages were by horse and cart or on foot.

Winter was characterized by piles of snow, occasionally reaching up to the roof. In the mornings, much tough work was needed to clear up a passage to the street or to the toilet. This was one of my father's many chores.

Children would enjoy sledging, especially down the two steep roads leading down to the river, namely Dzika and Podgorna road towards the Chuchman and Kabakov houses. Here my Uncle Aharon, my father's older brother, was injured in an unfortunate sledge accident and had his leg amputated when he was just twelve. The long hospitalization and recurring complications forced my grandfather to quit his job in Niemantzina Forest, and my father's sister to leave the gymnasium in Disna. Both, along with Gnesia Dorfman, an orphaned girl relative which our family had adopted, went to work at the Proshinsky estate on summer harvest jobs. Gnesia went to Palestine before the war.

Electricity for light was available from the Proshinsky power station at Blonie. Not everybody could afford it, however (YB p.74). Only few owned a radio, or a telephone. Even bicycles were rare, owned by the five local policemen for riding to the neighboring villages, some young clerks who took their (Jewish) girlfriends out to the country, and young villagers who would come to town on Sundays and on market days, namely Tuesdays (YB p. 84).

On market day, the villagers would arrive in their carts or on sledges, bringing in their merchandise, be it rye or linseed, eggs, chickens, perhaps a cow; at the same time they would shop for gasoline, sugar or tobacco, which they would roll into cigarettes. The women would come on foot, usually barefoot. As our family's house was right at the beginning of the street and unfenced, they would drop in to dress up a bit in the yard, putting on socks and shoes before making their appearance at the market.

Of the three Moadim – the Pilgrimage Festivals – Pesach impressed my father most. Soon after Purim the preparations for Pesach would commence (YB pp. 24-25). The Zeskind family would evacuate one half of their house which would be filled with long tables, stored as planks and stands, and brought out on this occasion. In the afternoons, after work, all the neighbors would gather in a burst of communal energy to knead, roll out, perforate, and bake the matzah dough in the large kitchen oven. Although there was a local commercial matzah factory, hardly anyone bought their matzahs there.

As a child, my father had many enjoyable activities besides the less lovable chores. He used to enjoy being taken along in a horse-drawn cart to transport and distribute manure or to spend many hours digging potatoes out of the earth, just to be given a hold of the reins for a couple of minutes or to be able to make a bonfire and bake potatoes in it at the end of the day.

An additional summer pastime would be to join up with a boy whose father had gained possession of the entire crop of an apple or pear orchard and needed to have it guarded against theft. Their fee would be worm-infested apples that had fallen off the tree pre-maturely.

Cowshed owners would bring in freshly gathered hay at the end of summer to last till the end of the winter. This hay had a wonderful smell and they loved rolling in it and sleeping on it together.

Four boys my father's age lived up the street. In summer, they would go out to Swistapoli Forest beyond the Catholic and Orthodox Christian cemeteries looking for berries, mushrooms, and even nuts that grew in a distant spot that they didn't always manage to find.

Twice at least they decided to go off during recess and look for the source of the Berezina River, famous for its historical connection to Napoleon's conquests, or rather his retreat from Russia. They never found it and barely managed to get back in time for the end of the school day, only to be duly punished.

The river was ordinarily narrow and unimpressive, barely a stream, but it could turn into a real danger in spring with the melting of the snows. The houses located between the bridge and the public bath were right on its banks. Once it overflowed and a terrible flooding resulted with many houses involved.

This river supplied water to the reservoirs in the beer factory owned by Gordon and those in the Sheiman-Frankfurt mill. A special extension was constructed there to supply water in case of a fire, which was obviously a very real threat to a saw mill. For my father and the other extension kids, however, it was a swimming pool of their own. For real swimming for all the locals there was a part of the river near Laputi, on its far side. It was a considerable walking distance away, however, with no proper path, so that only a few swimming enthusiasts got there, and only rarely. The swimming season was rather short anyway.

The public bath operated for women on Thursdays and men on Fridays. On those days water would be drawn out of the river (YB, p. 102) in a pulley system by a worker standing on the bathhouse roof, pulling down on the rope of the bucket and pouring the water into a container.

The educational system was rather rudimentary, consisting of just two elementary schools: the Polish school with seven grades and the Hebrew Tarbut school with 6 grades. The former was attended by both Jewish and gentile (Belorussian and Polish) children as well as the children of the Polish Osadniks in the vicinity. Due to transportation difficulties, the kids lived during the school week in a nearby boarding house.

The Tarbut school was of course just for the Jewish children. But of the five extension kids his age, my father was the only one to go there. All the subjects were taught in Hebrew, except for Polish language and Polish History, taught in Polish. The Tarbut was a private school with tuition, and even if there was interest not every family had the means to send their children there.

My grandfather took my father to meet the Lubavitcher Rebbe Yosef Yitzhak Schneerson when he visited Glubokie in 1934. When the Rebbe heard about the Tarbut, he said, "Not good." My father went back to the cheyder. When my grandfather left for Palestine in 1935, my mother, who was a revolutionary until she married, reenrolled my father in the Tarbut.

Those who wished to complete the seventh grade in the Polish school would make the switch at the end of Tarbut 5th grade and re-enter Polish 5th grade. This would leave the Tarbut final grade in a very reduced format. Moreover, by the end of sixth grade two of the six students in his class had emigrated to Palestine with their families. My father was also anticipating Aliya, since HIS father had already emigrated. As a result, he did not even contemplate entering a Polish school.

He continued personal Gemara lessons with a Rabbi for an hour a day. He also worked for the rest of the day with Vulya Wolfowitch, the blacksmith, who agreed to accept him as an unpaid apprentice, as was customary.

Wedding of Nahum Fabrishevitz and Belka Fabrikant, circa 1935

Standing: Nina Henkin

Sitting from left to right: Klausner, Peska Henkin, Borka Yolk, Chaike Fabrikant, Yoske Shapira, Aharon Henkin, Chaska Yolk, Nachum Fabrishevitz, bridegroom, Belka Fabrikant, bride, Leibe Fabrikant, bride's father, Hode Fabrikant, bride's mother, Chaska's mother

Children in front of table from left: Arthur Kronenberg—died (poisoned by mother Fania Sheiman, cf. Dokshitz book p. 189), Ala Kronenberg—his sister, same fate, Arie Henkin (their cousin)

Appendix to the Dokshitz Parafianov Yizkor Book

Material Not in the Original Yizkor Book

Tarbut School students – 1935

Top row, left to right: Batya Schulz Markman, Yosef Tenen (teacher), Miriam (teacher), Sarah Rozov Mirkam

Second row: Unknown boy, unknown girl, unknown boy with crown, Nacha, Arie Henkin, granddaughter of Reuvan the Shochet, Gershon Roitman;

Third row Arie Fogelman, Gita, Chana Kluft

Bottom unknown boy, Chaya Markman, unknown boy

Most of his work in summer was repairing bicycles. In winter, it was producing lighters and polishing copper containers and vessels. He had some additional income from tutoring the younger son of the local dentist, Mrs. Katzovich, since both she and her husband worked in the afternoons and an older son was away in the gymnasium.

After a year with the blacksmith my father entered the sawmills as a laborer. There were just four Jewish laborers and the rest were villagers from Laputi. It was on Sunday, the official rest day, that they were needed most for taking care of the machinery, and performing other tasks such as waxing. They were in effect the "Shabbos Goyim of Sunday".

The officials and clerks in the municipality, the province administration, and the post office, were all Poles who had arrived after the establishment of Poland at the end of World War I and the Poland-Russia war.

Most of the teachers at the public Polish school were likewise 'imported' Poles who had, however, settled in with their families, in contrast with the Tarbut teachers who, like the doctors, would be temporary and single. Noteworthy among the local Belorussian teachers was Slovik, who taught the exact sciences at the Polish school. In the Soviet era, he gave private lessons to my father and his second cousin Arthur during the summer to prepare him for skipping a grade, my father for skipping two. My father was later told that this man risked his life to hide Sonya Chuchman for a while, but the details were unclear.

The five uniformed Polish policemen, and one in civilian attire, were the true rulers. Joining their ranks was the goal of children's dreams. They represented the highest elite and ruling class. There were also some families of ranked personnel of the Border Patrols, a section of which, or possibly even a platoon, were posted locally. Their ranks were merely Corporal and Sergeant, but for the Jewish children they were the utmost peak of the social pyramid.

The local Jewish fascination with uniforms, ranks, drills, and marches was realized in the local Fire Brigade, where all these obsessions could materialize, and which was indeed all-Jewish. The children loved playing army games, organized in military formations. The commander would be a lad lucky enough to possess an old medal or some similar military object, that could be pinned on to his chest and win him the desired authority.

When it came to enlisting in the Polish army, however, it was an entirely different matter. Some of the eligible Jewish youth would starve and exhaust themselves in an effort to lose weight and escape recruitment. Such bursts of high-energy activity would sometimes benefit the community, as these youths would transfer logs from rich people's houses to poorer people's houses in a local Robin Hood fashion.

The Jewish community had two rabbis: Rabbi Sheinin for the Hassidim majority with their four synagogues, and Rabbi Golinkin for the Misnagdim who had just one synagogue. Several of the many institutions and functions in Dokshitz were likewise in twos: there were two mills; two bakeries; two feldshers, or practical physicians – a Jew named Monya Shapira, and a gentile. At this time, however, there was also an authorized imported physician, who was Jewish too. The clinic was located on the second floor of Luska Kaminkovich's house. When a physician would leave, another would be brought to replace him.

Two of the local butchers, located in the market, sold pork, but nonetheless enjoyed a lively Jewish clientele There were two mentally retarded men, both totally harmless. There were also two prostitutes: the Christian Verka who received clients at her home in an extension of Borisov Street; and Esterke who ran her business at the family home at the Schulhoyf, where she lived with her mother, sister, and younger brothers. This did not prevent my father and his friends from visiting her sister, who was a member in Hashomer Hatzair. They would usually find a Polish soldier waiting in the entrance hall for his turn to be taken to a side room.

There were several Tatar families who made a living off knitting woolen boots, all living together on the road named after them Keydersche Gäsl. My father was attracted to a beautiful girl from that tiny community and, though they shared no common friends or school or anything else, they became good friends.

The Henkins in 1938
Standing: Yisrael Tzvi, Peska, Avraham Frankfurt (Peska's husband)
Seated: Nina, Arie

Dokshitz in the Soviet Era

Everyone woke up one morning in September 1939, to a noisy roar of motor engines moving up ordinarily quiet Polotzker street. These were to be accompanied by many hundreds of Red Army units rolling on ceaselessly, and mostly on foot, towards the town center. The soldiers were surprisingly friendly to the locals who came out and stood on the roadside, waving enthusiastically. These were all Jews, since only Jews lived in the new extension at the end of Polotzker Street.

Sweating profusely in their heavy winter overcoats under the relentless sun, the soldiers refused even the water which was offered them. There seemed to be strict regulations in this issue, possibly for fear of poisoning. They did, however, generously offer the children candy. In all, there was a feeling that this was a friendly army or, in the official terminology, a 'liberating' army. This was in sharp contrast to what one may have expected having heard about looting, robbing, and raping committed by the Russian soldiers in

Appendix to the Dokshitz Parafianov Yizkor Book

Material Not in the Original Yizkor Book

previous wars. Moreover, a sense of relief reigned now, as fear of the German advance eastward diminished somewhat with the arrival of the Soviets.

When the military march was over and the initial excitement had dissolved, it turned out life had to continue in the new situation. The new reality slowly infiltrated everyone's awareness.

In the house, my father kept documents of the Hashomer Hatzair movement, passed on to him by Kalman Schultz pending his Aliyah, when he had appointed my father their trustee. Among these was a thick volume where the outgoing graduates had formulated their thoughts and opinions over the years. These were naturally pro-Zionist in orientation, hence somewhat anti-communist, as communism opposed Zionism; some also opposed Jewish movements such as the Bund or Beitar.

These youngsters with no formal education whatsoever had amazing intelligence, rhetorical ability, and grasp of world-wide problems. Little wonder that they attracted the town kids to their movement and its ideology. Indeed, when my father was 14, they were taught a course on political economy by 18-year-old Gilinson, whose words they eagerly swallowed.

Since this book obviously contained much incriminating evidence, my father and his next-door neighbor and brother-in-law, Henekh Frankfurt, set out to destroy it. They lit a fire in the stove and began tearing out the pages one by one, barely catching a glimpse of the name of the writer, of the article, and occasionally of a short segment of text before it caught fire.

Many of the writers were already in Palestine, but some, like Chaske Yolk, Berl Dvorkind, and Henekh himself, were still pending Aliyah in the town. Moreover, all still had families here. These were 'split' families who already had several members in Palestine - in our case my grandfather had emigrated in 1935, and my Aunt Peska, with her husband Avraham Frankfurt, Henekh's brother, four years later. The rest were stranded here waiting for Aliyah.

In the house they hosted the Kremer family whose house, just down the road, had burned down in a fire.

Appendix to the Dokshitz Parafianov Yizkor Book
Material Not in the Original Yizkor Book

Most of the Jewish population in the town was Zionist to a certain extent. A glance at the photographs of the organizers of Keren Kayemet (Jewish National Fund) Bazaars in the Dokshitz Yizkor Book will show the inter-class character of these Zionist activities.

Following the entrance of the Soviet army all the administrative and public institutions were closed down. Commerce was crippled, we were cut off from supplies, and money unavailable. The Polish currency was formally valid, but no one was willing to trade with it; the Soviet currency was not yet available. A few shopkeepers were forced to open their stores and sell supplies to soldiers who were in desperate need of local merchandise and not in a position to argue about its price, which was not known to the merchants anyway, in rubles.

Sometime later Shmuel Chuchman, the shoe shop owner, was accused of speculation, sentenced and exiled to Siberia or sent to prison. His family was forced out of their spacious house, right across the road from my grandparents' house. The military office, Voenkomat, was consequently housed in one half of this house, the commander and his family in the other.

The German occupation of Poland started a stream of Jewish refugees eastbound, which continued after the Soviet occupation. Among these refugees who came to live in Dokshitz was Itzik (Itzchak) Wittenberg, who was to become famous in the Vilna ghetto, when he turned himself in to the Germans to prevent them from carrying out their threat to execute a large number of inmates.

To the best of our knowledge the military representatives of the new government were three politruks – political commissars – permanently stationed in town. The first, Sluzky, was a Jew and a very good friend of my uncle Aharon. He was later moved along with his wife to the former home of the Dubnov family in Polotzker Street; the second, of Lithuanian origin, was housed in the home of the vice vicar in that same street; the third was a Russian.

Preparations got under way for elections of West Belorussian representatives to a general assembly which was to decide on the future of the area, not before expressing gratitude to the Soviet Union for liberating Dokshitz from Polish rule. These elections took place in late October 1939, when the following three candidates were elected.

The first was Leibe Rozov, a former communist who had also been appointed commander of the militia, composed almost entirely of service-eligible Jewish youth clean of any Anti-Soviet record. The second was a local villager who had been detained for a long period at the Bereza Kartuska Polish concentration camp for communist activism and had been recently released due to deteriorating health. Shortly before the Soviet era, he had come to our family's mill to grind some sacks of wheat, as all the farmers used to do. My father got acquainted with him, and they became good friends. He was later appointed regional chairman of all the local villages (gmina). The third was a woman.

As expected, all the representatives supported unification with Eastern Belorussia, and all Dokshitzers subsequently became nationals of the Soviet Union.

My father knew little about life downtown, as he continued to work in the saw-mill next to the family house in the new extension, on the outskirts of the town. He was paid in flour, which is what the customers paid with at the mill. When he later took private mathematics lessons with Joseph Kaminkovitch, he paid with the same flour.

The mill continued to operate as before, except that an executive committee was elected, which included my seventeen-year-old father. The actual management was left for the time being in the hands of Hirshl Frankfurt, Henekh's father. A former owner, he was liked and respected by the workers. However, life was not easy under communism for individuals associated, rightly or wrongly, with either Zionism or capitalism, as both were considered negative, unreliable elements in the present atmosphere, and aroused suspicion.

Thus, after a while Hirshl chose to move to Neeman, where one of his sons, Benny, was employed in his profession as a chemical engineer. The youngest son, Henekh, also moved there and was enlisted in the army; and Avraham was already in Palestine with my father's sister Peska. Only their daughter Chaika remained in Dokshitz, married to Shalom Chuchman.

Several other families moved out of Dokshitz for similar reasons. Those included Chaske Yolk and her mother and husband, Yakov Kazinitz, who moved to Vileyka; my father's cousin, Rivka Sheiman-Shleyfer and her husband and daughter also moved out.

However, these fears did not materialize. No measures were taken against Zionists – none were exiled to Siberia. This was, of course, unfortunate, since expulsion could have saved thousands of lives.

Despite the financial hardships, for the young generation this period was a true revolution. Previously, there had been no horizons nor prospects for the future, other than the hope of emigrating to Palestine with its closed borders; suddenly all the barriers were removed to education, public positions, professional training, etc. One of the major events was the opening of an evening school.

Till now there had been seven Polish classes and six Hebrew classes. Upon graduating from the Hebrew system, one could continue to Polish 5th to 7th grades, but that too would soon be over. Only few could afford gymnasium studies in Vilna, Glubokie or Disna. My father's sister Peska and Chaska Yolk did go on to study in Disna; and from my father's age group only Bebe Katzovich did so – he was later to become the chairman of the Association of Former Residents of Dokshitz in Israel.

Almost all the youth, certainly the Jewish youth, seized this opportunity to return to school. My father enrolled in grade five of the evening school. When that was over, the school principal approached my Uncle Aharon with the

Appendix to the Dokshitz Parafianov Yizkor Book
Material Not in the Original Yizkor Book

suggestion that my father should take private lessons in mathematics (and Communist Party History!) during the summer. This would be in order to cover the syllabus of Grades six and seven.

There was a teacher in the Polish school and then in the Russian school named Slovik. Uncle Aharon arranged with him to give lessons to my father and to his second cousin, Arthur, so they could jump a grade. Arthur, the one whose mother poisoned him and his sister (Yizkor Book pages 22, 128, 160). Arthur and his sister were a year or two younger than my father. His mother was my father's first cousin and they lived next door.

My father and Arthur were able to enter grade eight, which the Soviets were compelled to open for the sons of some Eastern functionaries. These included the second Party Secretary, Voronov, whose family was Jewish. He was housed in the Wolfovich villa on Borisov Street, after the Polish forest director who had rented it had been moved out. The regional council (Ispolkom) chairman, Wilensky, also Jewish, was housed in the Levitan house on Dolhinov Street. The third secretary, Levin, also Jewish, was lodged on Polotzker Street in the house belonging to the Gordons, who were moved to their brothers' house out in the back yard.

As the number of their children did not justify opening a class, both locals and some Polish gymnasium students would be encouraged to apply for the entrance exams. School in the Soviet era was, incidentally, the only place and time when Jewish and Polish youth interacted as equals.

The extended school absorbed many teachers from Russia, all unmarried except the principal who had a family. They were housed along with the locals in parts of houses.

As there was a serious shortage of imported supplies, there were almost no books for purchase. Everyone had to make do with one copy for the whole class. The only store in town would occasionally have the most basic supply. The Soviets had their own exclusive store where supply was relatively abundant, but this too was limited per family.

In the evenings, there were still get-togethers in Hashomer Hatzair, where landscape photographs of Palestine and the commandments of the Boy Scouts were promptly replaced by posters of Stalin, Lenin and the Motherland; also, the songs taught there were now in Russian, and included 'Katyusha', Prashchenye, Kakhovka... Everyone picked up the language fairly quickly, as it was rather close to the local peasants' Belorussian, which everyone knew. In fact, my father was told that in early childhood he actually spoke Russian, as the family came from Russia, where both my Aunt Peska and Uncle Aharon were born.

In fact, the official language of the new Belorussian Republic, Belorussian, was close enough to both Russian and Polish to be confusing. At school the only lesson conducted in Belorussian was Belorussian itself, the rest being in Russian. But my father's 8th grade graduation certificate, received June 20, 1941 with distinction in studies and behavior, was written in Belorussian and adorned with photographs of Lenin and Stalin.

In general, throughout this period the Soviets were friendly towards the locals. My father especially remembered the daughter of the second secretary, Sonya Voronov, a classmate and good friend. Almost every day after school he would go to her house and would be invited in, even if her parents were home.

His companion on these visits was his cousin Arthur. Arthur's mother, Fanya, was my grandmother's niece. She and her husband, Dr. Kronenberg, lived at Tshekhanov, near Warsaw, where Arthur and Ala were born. When their father died, the children would spend their holidays at their grandparents'; and when the pre-war tension rose, Fanya moved with them to Dokshitz. She worked at organizing, distributing, and instructing about defense equipment against air attacks. When the Russians entered, she got a job in the health system. This lasted through to the German occupation, when, tragically, she put an end to her own life along with that of her children (YB pp. 189, 228, 255).

Appendix to the Dokshitz Parafianov Yizkor Book
Material Not in the Original Yizkor Book

Activities that were initiated in the town and surrounding villages included folk dancing and choirs. The nearest village, Laputi, sent a troupe of dancers to perform in the Eastern region. One summer day a massive happening took place in the Swistapoli forest clearing, where all the guest and local dance troupes performed.

A spacious Dom Kultury (house of culture) was erected at the end of Borisov Street — formerly the large house of an estate owner, it had been taken apart and brought into town to serve as a center for entertainment and cultural activities.

It was impossible to get accepted into the Communist Party, even for local ex-Party members, so no one tried. To enroll in the Komsomol youth movement, special recommendations were needed from Party and Komsomol members, but this was problematic, since these were all newly arrived, and did not know the candidates. Consequently, the enrollment process was conducted at a public gathering where the audience was invited to speak up and refer to the candidate and his suitability.

For example, during the discussion concerning my father's older brother, my Uncle Aharon, a youth stood up and recounted a conversation that had taken place at Vant's, the barber. Aharon, who then held the prestigious post of director of the consumers' department (Potreb Soyuz), had declared that he would willingly quit his post to join his father and sister in Palestine. This, by the way, did not prevent his acceptance.

Sadly, Aharon did not survive the war. Fortunately, my father and his mother did, as did his father and sister who were already in Palestine. As the last of the Dokshitzers in the family, my father said he considered it a privilege to be able to write some memories of this humble but unforgettable shtetl and dedicate them to the memory of all the Dokshitzers who remained there.

Siberian Exile, Aliyah and the War of Independence

By Arie Henkin,
as told to Aaron Ginsburg
Edited by Rob Benjamin

It's a long story.

In the middle of the night the NKVD in plain clothes came to our home told my mother and I, "You are being moved to the far areas of Russia." It was June 20, 1941.

We understood that my brother Aharon had been arrested and that because of that we were being sent into exile. Aharon worked for the government managing supplies (food and other things) for both the locals, and the separate shop that was for Russian officials only. He got this job because he became a close friend of one of the Russian politruks, Slutsky, who was Jewish. When he got the job, he took a room in the center of town and didn't live with us. Because he had lost a leg, it would have been difficult for him to walk to work from home.

Aharon Henkin and Slutsky (Russian Politruk)

Appendix to the Dokshitz Parafianov Yizkor Book

Material Not in the Original Yizkor Book

We never found out what happened to him. We only assumed they had killed him, likely without a trial. When the war started so suddenly with the Germans, they didn't have the means to transfer the prisoners into Russia. As a result, they probably just killed all of the prisoners. This was particularly likely in the case of Aharon whose leg had been amputated, and who would have been less mobile than others.

We were put on a train in Parafyanova while more people were arrested. Two days later, on June 22, 1941 the train left for Siberia. It was the same day that the Germans invaded Russia. We were allowed to take 50 kilograms. We took mostly clothes and a few small items

When we got to Siberia, we stayed in a town called Barnaul, which is in the Altai area. Three groups of Jews ended up in Barnaul, the 20-30 young volunteers from Poland, a large group of Lithuanians, and a large number of Russian Jews as well. Since it was the Lithuanians who kept the prayers, we met them for the holidays. Not because I was interested in praying but because I was interested to meet more Jews.

After WWII started in Europe, in September 1939, half of Poland was occupied by the Germans, and half by the Russians. Now many Jews from the German area escaped to the Russian area. Since there was not enough work for all the youngsters, the Russians suggested that they go into Russia to work. This was the source of the Jewish volunteers in Barnaul. They were considered Soviet Citizens.

A few weeks after the war between Germany and Russia started, there was an agreement between Russia and the Polish government in exile, which was in London. The Sikorski–Mayski Agreement restored Polish citizenship and released all the Polish citizens, many of whom were Jews, who had been arrested. The released and the volunteer workers could now work wherever they wanted, if they could find a job.

And then there were the Russian Jews. Because when the Germans started the war with Russia, the Russian Government transferred a lot of factory workers from the areas that are going to be occupied by the Germans to Siberia. Now, they didn't deliberately move only the Jews - they moved all the people who were workers in factories. But It just happened that many of the managers in those areas were Jews. Originally, there were only a few Jews in Barnaul. One was an old watchmaker who was still repairing watches. Another was a young lady who managed the youth clinic. And another was the manager of the hospital. So, two doctors and a watch maker.

The local people didn't know what Jews were. They didn't know we were Jewish. Because in Communist Russia you were not allowed to say "Zhyd". You know the word "Zhyd?" "Zhyd" means Jew in Polish and Russian. Since this was generally used in a bad way, the Soviets prohibited people from using the word "Zhyd." It was an offense that could send you to jail if you called somebody "Zhyd."

When we came there, I started to work in digging for buildings. After a very short time, they sent me by lorry to a factory of doors and windows, just to pick up the finished doors and windows, to load on the lorry. But since I used to work on these same machines as a youngster in Dokshitz at my uncle's lumber factory, after I finished the Tarbut school and was waiting to join my father in Palestine, I recognized the machines. I came up to the manager and said I knew how to operate them. He was happy to have a grown-up worker. The workers were only women and older teenagers because all the men were mobilized for the war. I started to work in the furniture factory and became, how to say, the engineer of the factory.

But then, I learned somehow that they were going to teach drivers. Now in Russia, if you're promoted to a higher post then all the doors are open. If your new post is higher, more important, then you're free to move. Otherwise I would not have been allowed to leave the place I worked.

I went to a driving course, two or three months. They were teaching how to drive two kinds of lorries and one private car. We had to know each detail, and to know how to repair. It was comprehensive but took a lot of time. Only after

I completed the course, we went out for a few lessons of practical driving, and before you knew it you were a driver.

I became a driver. And after less than a year of driving I learned that they were going to open a technical school for technicians (who would work in construction) who had completed the eighth class at school. I had with me the certificate of the eighth class with distinction. If you didn't have eight classes, you studied for four years. But If you did have eight classes, in less than two years you became a technician. This was another opportunity to advance in the Soviet work place.

The technical school had been evacuated from Leningrad. There was no building available, so classes were held in the High School in the evenings. During the day, I finished my high school education. I studied for high school on my own and only went there for exams.

The manager of the technical school, which only had 8 students, warned my mother that if I went to the high school he would release me to the army. I went to high school unofficially and got a certificate with distinction in the Russian language, adorned with the usual pictures of Lenin and Stalin, that I had completed the 9th and 10th grades.

The Russians realized that most the youngsters were killed in the war. They lost millions and that there would be nobody to rebuild Russia after all the losses. So, they came up to youngsters and exempted them from service. Moreover, I was Polish, which meant I was free from going to the army. I became a student.

All this time, I was with my mother. She didn't have to work. because of age. She was getting 400 grams of bread. I was getting 800 grams. There was a little more food available to buy, but not much.

We came to Russia with some clothing and some things that we could sell. Because we had also all the clothing of my brother who was arrested, since we didn't know that we shall not see him again. And we could sell it on the black market. So, my mother sold some of the things we had. At least to buy some more bread and food and so on, also on the black market.

In the meantime, we got in contact with my father who was in Palestine since 1935. We knew that he worked in Shemen. Shemen is a big olive oil factory in Israel. It was one of the few factories that existed. It also produced soap and toothpaste, and other products connected with oil.

We wrote to Shemen without knowing where in Shemen he was. But he got it, which meant that we were in contact again. And he started to send parcels, mainly products of Shemen. Some pieces of soap and other products of Shemen - in Russia, it was like gold. We did not have to ask; he knew what was needed in Russia. He kept on sending parcels. This is how we managed to survive.

My sister Peska, the one in the photos, who married Avram Frankfurt – she was already in Palestine too.

World War II in Europe ended in May 1945. In exile, I was lucky. I got something of an education, and I avoided serving in the army.

Then came the day that we were allowed to return to Poland. But the part of Poland where I came from wasn't Poland any more. After the Germans retreated, the Russians had made it part of Belarusian SSR. I was a Polish citizen but my home was no longer Poland.

I got to Poland anyway, but to a formerly German part; we were allocated houses of Germans. The Germans took their possessions, but the houses were furnished. We were waiting to go to Palestine, where my father and my sister were. We went to the British embassy in Warsaw and got certificates to go to Palestine. But it took half a year to arrange it.

We didn't work. A Jewish organization called, that I later learned was the Joint, looked after the Jews who came from Russia into Poland. We were allowed to leave for Palestine because the Poles were happy to get rid of us, the Jews.

Finally, we came to Palestine in December 1946. One of the first things I did was to visit everybody we knew, and we knew people all over the country. My mother was with my father and wasn't interested in going to meet people, so I went alone. I didn't have to work because my father had saved money during the years he was in Shemen. He lived in a small room in the factory, which they gave him, so he didn't have to pay rent and had little need to spend money. This meant I was free to go around.

Nobody drove in those days. There were few cars. In those days, people would stop and give you a lift. Or you could take the bus. The people who came in the '30s, most of them were in kibbutzim. So I could go from one kibbutz to another - Hatzor, Beit Zera, Ayelet Ha-Shachar, and so on - there was always somebody from Dokshitz.

As I was going around visiting friends, my mother registered me into the Technion, the technical university in Haifa. She had the papers that I finished my education in Russia so she talked to a friend of hers who offered to register me to the Technion. She did this without me knowing it, while I was still going around.

In '47 school started. But then the war started too, the Independence War. I was drafted along with all my Technion classmates and mobilized for a year and a half.

First I got basic training. REALLY basic. For one week only, we trained with stones instead of grenades, with broomsticks instead of rifles. We were not allowed to shoot because British might hear us and confiscate the weapons. Even though the war had already started, they were still in the country. They confiscated any guns and ammunition we had, so we had to hide everything. That was all the training you got in order to get into the army.

Then I went back to school, to the Technion – we were, after all, still students. In about two months they mobilized us again. We went to help defend Safed. Safed was surrounded by Arabs. We had to break-in to the town. After a month, we went back to the Technion.

In another two months, there was a general mobilization. One of our duties was bus duty. Between Haifa and Zichron there were three Arab villages. Two soldiers out of uniform were on each bus. If the bus was attacked, they got their rifles and grenades and fought back. After things calmed down, the rifles and grenades were hidden again under the floor in the case the British came by.

Then we had to fight for Haifa. This was the real thing. Haifa is on a mountain, Jews lived on top, mixed population in the middle, and Arabs below that. Here and there was some shooting. But we decided to take control of the whole city. This took about two days. I and two other boys in a house in the mixed area. The Arabs went down to the harbor and by road or boat and fled to Akko and nearby villages. A British military vehicle saw that we were shooting and sent a bomb through the window. Luckily, we were unharmed.

Next from Haifa to Nahariya, which was surrounded by Arab villages, on the boat "Hanna Senesh." We took control of the area. After Nahariya, we went to Akko. We were bused to Ein Hamifratz, a kibbutz south of Akko and with other units went to Akko on foot. The main place we had to fight for was a two-story concrete police station. We surrounded that place. We had a special kind of bomb. We sent it into the fortress. After some fighting they surrendered.

By this time Israel had declared its independence. All the units in the area assembled to swear loyalty to the State and the Army.

Then we went to Rosh. All the units in Rosh Pina were scattered among the olive groves. The nearby Jordan River was the border with Syria, which was on the East bank. A little bit East of that, Syrian Army units held the high ground.

The plan was to cross the river at night by boat, surprise the Syrians and capture the post they were holding. I was going be among the first wave of troops. We were going to pull the boats across the river with ropes. The story I heard was that the ropes we had were too short. The official story is that we ran out of time to move in all our units and their equipment. With dawn approaching, we quickly withdrew to our side of the Jordan. We were pinned down and tried to dig some trenches, but it was hard rock, and we could only dig down about 20 centimeters. For the whole day, we were under fire from the Syrians above. About ten of our people were killed. Only after dark could we retreat to safety.

The next night, we were sent by bus to an unknown destination. After a few hours, the plans were canceled and we came to back to the olive groves.

The night after that, July 15th, 1948 my unit climbed up to a deserted khan (fort) on a hilltop named Yarda to "rest." We were the third unit that was sent to "rest" at Yarda. Instead, we found ourselves face to face with the enemy. At dawn, they attacked from all sides with massive artillery and infantry. Five tanks fired at our positions from about 200 meters.

The front line was forced to retreat after many casualties, and my group became the front line. We were a newly formed unit from remnants of units that had lost too many men to continue, and did not know each other.

We were in two parallel rows of about 10 soldiers each. The khan anchored one end of our line. The Syrians attacked us head on. A few of them outflanked us by going around the deserted khan and occupying a ditch behind the building parallel to our line. On my own initiative, I went into the khan and through a window opening threw two grenades and shot some bullets from my Sten into the ditch below. I ran back to our position, picked up two more grenades from my friend Isaac, and ran back up. I threw them from the fort and also fired my gun, just to make sure. Peeping through a little slit in the wall, I saw that the enemy had evacuated the position.

On my way out of the khan, I was hit by a bullet in the shoulder, just 2 centimeters from my throat. A paramedic bandaged me up. Some 15 minutes later we were ordered to retreat. Eight men in our unit were dead.

On my way down, I found a friend lying unable to move. His clothes had somehow got tangled. I untangled him and we went on, crawling all the way among thistles and rocks till we were reunited with the main group and I was hospitalized.

I was recommended by my commanders for an award, probably the Gibor Yisrael award for bravery, the only award in those days. But Prime Minister Ben-Gurion decided that since there were 12 tribes of ancient Israel, that only 12 heroes would be recognized. So, all I have are the memories, two short letters from my commanders – and a scar.

I asked to be released from the army to take care of my parents. I have a letter written by my commander saying I was a good soldier, who by the way was recommended for an award for bravery under fire, and should not be released. The senior commander used exactly the same words to deny my request.

Batia Cohen Henkin, Roni Henkin-Roytfarb, Arie Henkin in 2014

Appendix to the Dokshitz Parafianov Yizkor Book
Material Not in the Original Yizkor Book

My Story: Three Years on the Run

by Rachel Mutterperl Goldfarb

edited by Rob Benjamin, Janet Zucker, and Aaron Ginsburg

Life before the War

I want to tell my story as a memorial to my family and about 2,500 fellow Jews of Dokshitz who were executed by the Nazi regime, for no other reason than being born Jewish. My own experiences have taught me that hatred, especially when born of prejudice and amplified by jealousy or greed, may cause a person's own neighbors to treat a him in a vile and inhumane way.

Chevel Dov (Beryl) Mutterperl

Rachel, Dina, and Shlomo Mutterperl. Picture recovered by a neighbor after they fled the Dokshitz ghetto.

I was born Rachel Mutterperl on December 2, 1930, in Dokshitz. For a small town, it had pretty good-sized Jewish community of about twenty-five hundred people. My parents, Chevel Dov Mutterperl and Dina Mindel Mutterperl, were both born in Dokshitz. I had a brother, Shlomo, three years younger than I.

My father was called Beryl. His father's name was Shlomo, for whom my brother was named. My father had one brother and two sisters. The brother lived locally on Polotzker St. One sister immigrated to the United States, and lived in Washington, DC.

Top row: L-R Bere's sister, Edya Dameskin, Rae's cousin, daughter of her father's sister. Man in top row, Bera (Rivka's husband), Bottom Row, Rachel Mutterperl, Rivka (Bere's wife Rae's cousin)

My mother's parents were Aaron Mindel, who was born in Dunilovichi, and Hinda Baila Friedman, who was born in Dokshitz. They referred to grandfather as Moses. He was tall, had a grey beard, and wore a frock. He was a mitnagid. He was an orphan. A shidduch was made with my grandmother when they

Appendix to the Dokshitz Parafianov Yizkor Book
Material Not in the Original Yizkor Book

were kids. They grew up in the same house, and as children used to argue. When they got older and they were told they would be getting married, they argued with their parents, initially refusing. Eventually, they raised six children together, and during my own childhood, they appeared happy together.

Before the war life was pretty good. Both my parents had businesses. My mother had a yard goods store. My father was involved in several businesses. He supplied meat to the Polish garrison at the nearby Russian border. He also exported flax, which was used to make rope, flax oil, and flax seeds. The seeds would be used in producing oil. He also exported meat, pigs and apples.

I especially remember the apples. He used to rent orchards and would sometimes take me along when he went to oversee them. Once Father took me when he viewed an orchard which was right on the Russian border. In the evening, as we were sitting outside, we could hear the Russians on the other side playing their accordions and harmonicas and dancing.

Both of my parents traveled because of their businesses. My mother took me on one of her trips to Vilna, where at some of the stores I was given presents.

With my family being in business, we had a pretty good relationship with the White Russians, the Belarusians. Some of our household help, such the laundresses and my brother's governess, were gentiles. I remember visiting some of their acquaintances in the surrounding villages. There were some good times, horseback riding and playing with their children.

My brother and I had tutors. I started my education rather early, and according to my mother, I could read by the time I was three. Believe it or not, I enrolled in the Tarbut school at the age of three. It was fortunate for me because I got a little more education than I would have gotten otherwise.

The Jewish holidays were really important in our community. In our family, Shabbat started Friday afternoon. Preparations were ready. The table was laid. The candlesticks were on the table and the challahs were placed near the candlesticks. There was always Friday night dinner. On Shabbat, no cooking was done and families gathered.

The Jewish community was always organized. The Gemilut Chesed Society, a community organization set up to perform acts of loving kindness, functioned like a bank. If someone was in dire need, he could get help.

My father was active in the Jewish community. He was also very helpful to some of his gentile friends. Whenever they were in need of money to help them through hard times, he would buy from them, and I guess he must have advanced them money. It stood us well in our escaping from the ghetto. It probably also cost my brother his life.

My father was a Zionist. I was taught Hebrew at an early age. I spoke fluent Hebrew and remembered enough of it that after liberation, when I met up with the Jewish Brigade after we crossed the border into Italy, I had no difficulty communicating. I think he always contributed to the Jewish community and to Israel. I remember the little tzedakah box and the discussions about Zionism in the house. Some cousins had gone on Hachshara, preparing to go to the land of Israel, Eretz Yisrael, getting mostly agricultural training and living in kibbutz-like communities. I remember the pioneer movement Hechalutz, the patriotic songs, and learning about some of the heroes.

There were also Jewish Socialists. I had a cousin who had gone to Russia during the revolutionary period. We never heard from him. All I did was see pictures of him. I never actually knew him, but that was my father's sister's son.

I don't recall being aware of anti-Semitism as a young child. If there was some, I guess either I was sheltered from it or, just as any other child, was involved in my own things. If I ventured out into the non-Jewish community, it was normally to my parents' acquaintances. With my parents having businesses, and especially my mother having what was probably the largest yard goods store in the area, there were always non-Jewish people coming and going from the store, which was in front of the house. The store and house were connected.

I had a close relationship with some of the maids that worked in our house, and with one maid in particular who was Catholic. Sometimes she took me to church with, even though her my parents had forbidden this. However, she wanted to go to church. In order to fulfill her own duties of taking care of us, she brought us with her to church, as did some of the other girls that worked for us. When you go to church as a child and you observe, you learn how to do what everybody else does. It came naturally to kneel and to cross myself, a ritual I learned in church that probably saved my life.

My father died in 1937, after a trip to the border with Germany. He came back broken hearted. He said that he had heard human cries from cattle cars and that he couldn't figure out what was happening. According to my mother's reports, he seemed to be ailing after that, and died in 1937. Mother continued with the business and became the mainstay of the family.

The Russian occupation begins

Once the Germans declared war on Poland, we knew that the Germans would be coming. Poland was divided and we were occupied by the Russian forces. We knew the Germans would come, but we did not know how quickly it would happen.

When the Russians came in, all of a sudden, we were identified as bourgeois. The store was closed. In order to hide her stock from the Soviets, my mother quickly distributed a lot of her fabric to her nearby customers. She told them to use what they needed for themselves, and save the rest for her so my mother would have something to trade for food and necessities. With some of the fabric, clothing was made. First my cousins wore them, and then they were passed down to me. She also left some of her better clothing, such as fur and sheepskin coats, with gentile friends.

The Russians also confiscated personal property. One of my parents had brought back an alarm clock from one of their business trips. That was a novelty at that time, and the Russians were crazy about them. They called them "chasy," which means clocks, watches. I remember that one strapped an alarm clock onto his arm with my mother's silk stocking.

From her buying trips to Warsaw, my mother also brought back silk lingerie and nightgowns, which looked like dresses. (They didn't have nylon back then, it was all silk.) The Russians confiscated them, and Russian women paraded wearing them in the streets, as if they were gowns.

Since we were called bourgeois, meaning rich Jews or rich people, we expected to be deported to Siberia. We were packed with bundles by one of the doors, waiting for the knock on the door. That's what they did with rich people, resettling them. Perhaps because my mother was a widow, we weren't deported. If only we had been one of the families that was deported to Siberia!

The Russians closed the Tarbut school and we went to a Russian school. The Russian school started out right away with indoctrination. Children were encouraged to join the Pioneer movement, and in so doing become part of the Communist system. The symbols were a red scarf and a badge with a hammer and sickle on it. I had a difficult time becoming a member because of my mother's status. The only way to become a member was to excel in school, which I did, and then I got my red scarf. My mother thought becoming a Pioneer was a good idea because maybe we wouldn't be deported.

It was during the Russian occupation, in about 1940, that my father's mother, Sarah Chana Mutterperl, died.

Stories filtered down about how the Jews in Germany were being taken out of their homes. Jews from Poland ran away, fearing the Germans. Some of them returned to German-occupied Poland because the conditions under the Russians were so bad.

There was an awareness of oppression under the Germans, but I don't think anybody thought about being just shot to death, being eliminated or wiped off the face of the earth. As a child, of course, I didn't think about it, but I don't think the general community was prepared for holocaust.

**Sarah Chana Mutterperl,
my father's mother.**

Under the Germans in Dokshitz

The first sense of brutality after the Germans arrived was when the Russian prisoners of war were driven through the town. They were treated with great cruelty. They were in terrible condition, without shoes, without proper clothing, hungry, looking dilapidated and drawn. They went begging for food and water.

The Jewish people have always been taught to help. People ran home to get water and something to drink with. If somebody attempted to give them...or, unable to hand it to them, throw them, anything, any food and whether caught it or not, the Germans beat and even shot several of the prisoners. I don't recall them turning on the ones that were trying to give them the food. The Germans turned against the ones that went for the food, and I think this is why it left such a lasting impression on me; if a man is hungry and reaches for something, he gets beaten and in some cases shot.

Everybody became aware of the fact that the Jews were not treated well. There were beatings. Then Jews had to wear an arm band, a white arm band with a yellow star on it. I wanted to wear a white blouse so when I wore the arm band it would not show too much.

Shortly thereafter it was required that we have a yellow star sewn onto all our clothing, inner clothing and outer clothing, on the left side in the front and the right side in the back. That was so you could be identified when both coming or going. A Jew was not allowed to venture out without the yellow star. If you were caught, you would get beaten. I think there were even a few instances where Jewish people were shot.

Wearing the star, for the first time I felt I was being singled out and pointed to. I went from living in a family that was quite comfortably situated financially and feeling part of the upper crust to becoming part the lower crust. All of a sudden wearing the Jewish star made me a less of an important person than I was before.

I remember being spit at. Part of the prescribed new behavior was that a Jew had to accommodate the non-Jewish person. I remember having to get off the sidewalk when a non-Jew approached. Poland being as far northeast as it was, winter started in about October and lasted until Easter time, which meant that there was snow and when the snow melted a little bit because of traffic going through, it was mud. So, you had to step off into mud. That was degrading. If a Jew had to wear the yellow star, he was set aside...he was set apart from the community. He was pointed to.

I recall quite early when some of our valuables were taken. The Germans formed an organization made of Jews and appointed one of them as a leader to be the intermediary between the German command and the Jewish community. I remember having to give up some valuables to help with the war effort.

The Germans supposedly let the Jews govern themselves, however, the appointed committee had to supply the Germans with what they wanted. They extracted money, valuables, and all types of metal. A lot of the cooking utensils were brass or copper. They wanted those. And this committee was supposed to collect it and deliver it.

That was 1941, and the ghetto did not get established for several months. If a person reported that a Jewish household had valuables, he might be rewarded with a portion of whatever wealth would be seized. So, there were lots of informers. Anybody saving a Jew, collaborating with a Jew, stood to lose his life or his health because a good-sized beating can leave one maimed, or worse.

The Germans kept the Jews in line mostly by promising that nothing would happen to them as long as they cooperated. If however, a Jew were caught defying German orders, there would be retaliation.

I recall a few men who escaped to the forest, and became the first partisans. When that became known, the first thing the Germans did was gather some people in the open area where the synagogue courtyards were and shoot them or take them away to be shot. They may have shot several in the ghetto itself but most of the time they would take more people and then let them some return to tell how the other ones died.

The synagogues ceased to exist as they did before.

Our house was in the ghetto, which was created in the fall. The ghetto was around the synagogue courtyards because that was where the concentration of Jews lived. The street was the border of the ghetto. The houses on our side of the street all had enclosed courtyards facing the street.

Our house was situated in such a way it was a gated area fronting the street. The main streets were the best location and our house had a gate between the two businesses, my father's and my mother's. The house was in the back and so was the warehouse. My family had built a double wall in the warehouse. The space was two and a half to three feet wide. Access was through an attic. That space was used to store for documents and things for the house.

In the ghetto, we tried to observe Shabbat normally. If the Nazis took you out to work, you had to go. Some were taken to work either cleaning or doing laundry, whatever the Germans needed done. Some were shoemakers or tailors. They fared a little better because they were needed.

I remember a Passover seder in 1942. A table was set up and everybody sat on wall-to-wall beds. That was probably the last seder in the ghetto. We celebrated with the people that lived in the house. Some were family, some not. Probably for the first time in my life, I observed the baking of the matzoh. It was done at night in hiding. Baking was set up in one of the houses and everything was blacked out.

The destruction of the Dokshitz ghetto

Slowly but surely the Germans started to weed out some of the people from the ghetto. Those that were able to work were taken to work details. Since it was a garrison town with a military barracks, the Nazi's occupied the barracks and took Jewish details there to work. They needed laundresses, they needed cleaning of the stalls, tending to their horses, preparing their food. And, of course, someone to shine their boots. They had an obsession about shiny boots. If anybody did not adhere to orders, they never came back. Some of them were beaten and some of them were just shot.

If the Germans counted 50 people for a work detail and somebody escaped and 49 came back, the penalty they extracted from the people in the ghetto was ten for one. The victims were shot in front of the rest of the population of the ghetto. Some people volunteered, older people. They figured their life is at an end anyway, nothing is going to help them survive.

They took away the less able and the smallest and shot them. It was a process that the Germans used to eliminate people and to make the ghetto smaller, easier to control.

Appendix to the Dokshitz Parafianov Yizkor Book
Material Not in the Original Yizkor Book

There was awareness of what was happening, but there was no place to go. A few people did manage to get out. The severe reprisals probably kept others from leaving even if they were able to. The first ones to suffer in the reprisal would be the escaped person's family. It's very difficult for a person to save his life knowing that his family is going to pay for it.

The Germans and their accomplices gathered Jews and shot them. They eliminated everybody with bullets. Sometimes live people were suffocated by the bodies on top of them. A few people that I know managed to crawl out from under the dead bodies at night and get away.

I remember stories that people were made to dig their own graves. In front of the cemetery, there was a big pit...I guess a sand pit. From what I heard that is where the majority of the people were shot. I remember hearing that some of the Jews had to throw dirt or sand or whatever over the bodies. Those people had been at the edge of that pit and had come back. There were small groups that were killed and then there were what they called reducing the numbers, I guess.

Normally the strongest ones were the ones that survived because the Germans could use them. The Germans needed some people to do their chores and kept alive the most able. Every time that the people in the ghetto became aware that they were going to take some of the people away, whoever could, hid. If they were not found, they could survive.

We survived because we were in hiding when the ghetto was liquidated. This started about May 5, 1942, and lasted until around Shavuot. My entire family survived until that point. The ghetto was surrounded. Word had it that something was going to happen, but nobody ever knew what it was to be.

Whenever something like this happened, the women and children were the ones that were put into hiding and the men, the big protectors were left out. There was just so much space to hide.

After reviewing my mother's documents, I realize that my grandfather, her father, who was with us in the ghetto, had arranged a way for us to get into the hiding place and also some supplies so, when they were shrinking the ghetto, we could hide until things got quiet again.

My family and quite a number of other people hid there, whoever could fit in. When the Germans started to knock on the door, it was who could make it, and at a certain point, the door was closed and that was it.

Hiding were me, my mother, brother, grandmother (my mother's mother) and some other people. My grandfather did not make it into the hiding place. Just how many other people, I don't know because it seemed like whenever somebody went out to investigate, they didn't return.

We could hear quite a bit of what was going on. We couldn't see. There was lots of shooting going on and then it became quiet. We did not have any more bread or water.

Everybody came to loot, especially to our house. It wasn't just the Germans that were against us. The gentiles in the community were against us too. I'm not going to say all of them. I wouldn't be alive today if it were all of them, but a great number were.

Our part of the country was very poor. Looting appealed to a lot of the people, being able to take over somebody else's wealth. Even though by the time we came into the ghetto a lot of it was stripped, there were still some things left. In Dokshitz people didn't even have shoes. My husband still kids me about how I come from a small town where you walk barefoot. You only put on your shoes when you came to the market place.

We stayed in the hiding place for eight to ten days, until it became totally quiet. We could hear the gentiles talking. I think my mother overheard somebody saying, "Everybody's gone from here and it's time to occupy the house, to take the house." Then it would be very difficult to get out.

The decision was made to try to get out. My grandfather also had prepared another hiding place, excavating it under a wooden floor. We thought if it was quiet, then it was all finished. We tried to get out from of attic and into the house.

Appendix to the Dokshitz Parafianov Yizkor Book
Material Not in the Original Yizkor Book

My grandmother was caught coming down from the attic. I remember hearing my grandmother during the encounter. I was by myself. That I remember very clearly. Whether it was by Germans or whether by gentiles, I don't know. She was pulled away, and she was beaten. They asked her, "Where are the rest?" My grandmother said, "Everybody is gone, I'm the only one that was hiding in the attic."

My mother, my brother, and I were the first ones out, I think, and we hid under the floor. Also, three children, from what I remember, got in with us. I remember my mother trying to reach for my grandmother and trying to protect us at the same time. My mother very quickly covered the boards from the floor and held onto them.

On the run

When night fell, my mother took us to escape. We ran out from the second hiding place, crawling over bodies. Our first attempt to cross the Berezina River failed; it wasn't safe enough.

We used to bathe in the Berezina River, which was one of the boundaries of the ghetto. She knew where the water was shallow. She took my brother on her shoulders and me by the hand. The other children were on their own. We crossed the river.

After crawling over bodies and hiding in the shadows we encountered two men with rifles. Mother had some valuables. I have a picture of one of the valuables because my grandmother had sent a picture of this particular watch on a heavy golden chain to her daughter in the United States, my aunt. Mother said, "Look, I can make you rich. Put your hands out and I'll give you whatever I have." She asked them to put their rifles on their shoulders. Mother wound the watch around the fingers of one of the guards, saying, "This way it won't fall off. Put it away quickly because the Nazis will take it away from you!" Greed helped us. Before they hid their trophies, and had their rifles ready, we ran.

We hid in a bath house. People usually bathed in a bath house before the weekend. This was the middle of the week, so we could hide there during the day and at night we ventured again out to hide.

All three of us were together until my mother left me in the bath house and took my brother to place him into hiding. I guess she figured she'll place him and place me someplace safe and then she'll fend for herself. Unfortunately, it didn't work out that way.

It was known that we were someplace around. I don't know if they recognized my mother. They could easily figure out where we were going to, who our friends were, and which village we would go to.

Mother went to a family that was very friendly with us, actually very good friends. We used to go to their house at Christmas time and help decorate the Christmas tree. The man agreed to hide my brother. He told her that my brother was okay because he had a son the same age, or close enough in age, and that he could pass him off as his own. However, we had to go.

This man had a sister who was a friend of my mother's. We went to her house. She gave us some clothing and she gave us something to eat and drink. No sooner did we get settled when a little boy was sent from the other house to tell them that the Nazis had gotten my brother because the man's mother-in-law got mad at him and she told the Nazis that he was hiding a Jewish child. He tried to deny it and they beat him so badly that he remained a cripple. We saw him after we were liberated by the Russians. His sister told us very quickly, "Here is some bread, please go."

The wheat grows pretty high in our part of the country and I remember hiding in the wheat field. I remember gentiles passing, farmers passing and talking about what was happening in town, the fact that all the Jews were being killed. They really did a clean-up job.

At night, we managed to get over to my brother's governess's house. She used to take us to church with her so I was a little familiar with the procedures in church. She offered to go to the town to see what happened to

Appendix to the Dokshitz Parafianov Yizkor Book
Material Not in the Original Yizkor Book

my brother. "If he's alive," she said, "I'll try to get him, and raise him like my own. I have no children and would like to have him." She came back and told us that he was shot. My mother recorded date as May 8, 1942. She was afraid to hide us because everybody knew the connection and she had just come from town inquiring about my brother.

Then we went to another gentile family. Again, my mother chose very, very carefully as to where to go, who she would think would be the least belligerent. We went to a widow's farm because my father had helped to save the woman's property after her husband passed away. She was French. Her late husband was Polish. She had two sons and a daughter. My mother felt that that was a good place to go.

When we arrived, she wasn't home. Her daughter, who must have been about a couple of years older than I, was home. The daughter knew us very well too, and she hid us.

Most of the houses had an oven in the center of the house. Everybody had to bake bread. It was used as an oven and to keep warm. It was built out of bricks and it had shelf. A lot of the farmers would sleep there in the wintertime because the oven would be heated up. She put us there. Normally there was some sort of a curtain that was drawn across it, so that's where she put us and that's where we stayed until the mother came back.

As in many villages, the big pastime was to get together and to talk. We were up there and this woman crawled up and sat down right in front of the curtain and talked to the people that were sitting on benches. They were discussing what had happened in the town. She knew we were there because when she came home her daughter had informed her that we had come and where she hid us.

We probably stayed there a couple of nights, until things quieted down. The woman was afraid to hide us because she hired some people from the village to help run the farm.

We saw her after the war. My mother corresponded with her briefly and sent her some money. She had talked about going back to her people. At one point, she wrote my mother to stop sending letters. After a while the letters came back unopened and we never heard from her again

My mother told her Glebokie would be the next stop for us. She got in touch with some people, and was told, "Yes, it's safe." She dressed my mother in her clothing, me in her daughter's clothing, and sent her son as if going to the market. He took us in a wagon and let us off in the marketplace in the city of Glebokie.

If it had been discovered that she was hiding us, our lives and hers would have been ended. She was a righteous person. She was a good person. I thank God that there are some people who did not side with the Germans and who had a conscience and who had love of humanity and wanted to help people.

My mother chose very carefully. She figured if anybody had any kind of a debt to pay, and, of course, if they were good people, they were likely to help us. This particular woman had nothing to gain by turning us in, but she had a lot to lose. I remember her telling my mother, "Your husband came to my aid when I thought that life was over for me. I'll do anything I can do to help you out."

The Glubokie ghetto

We waited until evening when people were coming back from work and joined the Jews returning to the ghetto from their assignments of labor. We had no papers. If you didn't have any papers in the ghetto, you couldn't work. If you couldn't work, you didn't go out on work details.

If you didn't have papers, you could be seized on the spot if the ghetto was being shrunk.

Mother was very inventive in ways to try to save us. One of her many acquaintances in Glubokie was involved with the committee that that was the ghetto's go-between with the Nazis. He had lost a daughter in one of those supposed transfers to other ghettos. Her name was also Rachel. She was

Appendix to the Dokshitz Parafianov Yizkor Book
Material Not in the Original Yizkor Book

taken because she had left her documents at home. Her father gave me the documents. The documents made me old enough to go out on work details.

I didn't have any skills, so I worked in a spinning mill that was outside the ghetto. If a thread broke, I had to quickly grab the ends and tie them together so the spinning machines could keep going.

Mother stayed in the ghetto. To survive, you had to be productive. The German Army wasn't prepared for the climate, so they needed lots of gloves, socks, scarves and hats. Mother couldn't knit for the life of her. I learned how to knit scarves and socks because my mother couldn't produce enough. I hated to knit gloves. Those fingers...they were complicated. In the ghetto I learned to knit and read at the same time.

The Glebokie ghetto went through the same process as the Dokshitz ghetto. It was constantly being consolidated. People were taken away. The ghetto became smaller and smaller. All the signs were that the Glubokie ghetto would be liquidated too.

Mother had a lot of acquaintances among the non-Jewish population. Some of them would have probably hid us, but they were afraid of their neighbors. The Nazis had offered five kilos of sugar for exposing a Jew. Sugar was a very sought-after commodity. Those that would have done something good-their hands were tied. However, one farm woman was very helpful. Mother would go out into the marketplace, she would dress in the clothing that she got from this woman, and she would go out into the market and try to barter something for food.

Mother met a gentile friend of my father at the market. She told him that she wanted to escape. He told her where the partisans were, and she asked him if she could obtain a gun. He had hidden some of our valuables and mother told him whatever it costs, get me a gun. He came back two weeks later to the marketplace, Mother was watching for him, and she got the gun. He put it in a basket with some eggs on top because the Nazis were very cleanliness conscious. Pull out an egg and if it breaks, it gets on their hands. She smuggled the gun with us in a basket when we left the ghetto.

One time when they were shrinking the ghetto-they called it a resettlement-my mother followed the advice of a man named Yosef Pren. He was a portrait photographer, an excellent photographer. The Germans made full use of his talents. They set him up in a house outside of the ghetto as a photographer. I think he mostly took photos of the Germans to send back home. He had to return to the ghetto every night. They told him that particular night that he should get out of the ghetto and stay in the house. He told mother that I should come with him.

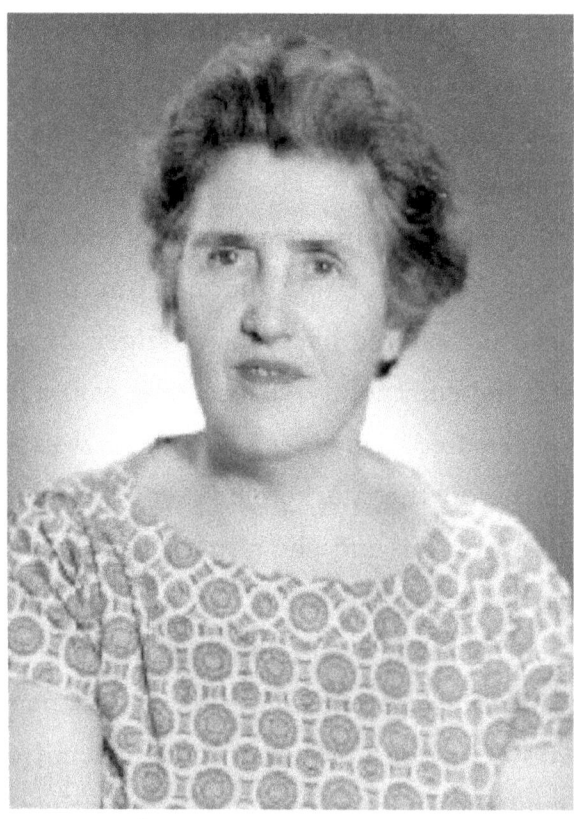

Dina Mutterperl
Photograph by Yosef Pren

Appendix to the Dokshitz Parafianov Yizkor Book 371
Material Not in the Original Yizkor Book

We started out with him, following him a short distance out of the ghetto. Some Jewish women started to say, "Hmm, she thinks she's going to get away with it, they won't recognize her." Mother made me go with him, follow him, and she stayed in the ghetto. I had to follow at a distance, and he hid me. We went up to the attic of the house and watched what was going on.

We saw the Jews being gathered into an open field. We watched them being separated, a group here, a group there. Their papers were examined and some taken away and some returned back to the houses. The ones that were taken away were shot. The next day after the massacre, we returned to the ghetto. Fortunately, my mother survived and I found her.

Yosef Pren survived. After the war, while in Poland, he married a distant cousin of his, Basha Friedman. She was from Dokshitz, and was also distant cousin of my mother. During the Russian occupation, she was a telephone operator in Dokshitz. She tells her story on page 301 of the Yizkor book. For more than a year, a Pole named Borisovitch hid her in his house in Dokshitz. She then joined the partisans. When the Jews were not so kindly asked to leave Poland, they immigrated to Israel, where he made his living as a portrait photographer. When we visited Israel in 1978, he took a picture of my mother, which I still have.

He was able to communicate with the outside much easier and he helped communicate so that we could escape. We knew where the partisans were at that point and took the chance.

My mother was determined to get out of the ghetto and join with the partisans. She figured she has to have not just the gun, she has to have something else with her in order to be accepted. Who would want a woman and a child?

The leader of the Glubokie ghetto was not really defiant but he understood what was happening to others. We used to meet at the leader's house. He had a daughter my age and he very much wanted his children to survive. The leader's sons also wanted to get away. His brother-in-law was a physician. My mother felt that if she brought someone like the physician with her who could contribute, she would be more welcome to join the partisans.

The physician and a couple of others decided that they were going to make a break for it. Unfortunately, others got wind of it. Had it just been our small group, we might have made it. They made a tunnel under the barbed wire fence so that they could crawl out into an area that was close to the woods and make a run for it. The people who realized what was going on went ahead of us and drew attention to themselves. They crawled out and we heard the shots. We were in the last wave to get out and we realized we couldn't make it.

The leader was summoned to a meeting with the Germans, and to bring his family along. They were arrested and taken out of the ghetto. The leader and his wife were shot. His sons defied the Germans. They and their sister escaped. The older son was shot and died of his wounds. The younger son and the daughter hid in the ghetto for a short time. They were afraid to be in contact with any of the Jews. Some people had hard feelings against their father, because he had been the liaison to the Germans. In his position, I guess there were times when he knew about things and it was a matter of saving the majority. And the Jews were so worried about their own well-being, their own survival, that they were ready to turn them in to the Germans.

The son escaped and became a hero in the partisans. I believe he and his sister both survived.

There were several things that kept people from escaping. One was the family unit. It wasn't everybody for himself; maybe more people could have survived if they had left their families. If you tried to escape with a family and with children, it becomes much more difficult. The men did not want to leave their wives and children. Some of them did. Some of them figured they'll get out and maybe they'll bring their families. Some of them did bring their families. But how do you put yourself in the position of perhaps being the cause of somebody else's death, and then live with yourself?

Appendix to the Dokshitz Parafianov Yizkor Book
Material Not in the Original Yizkor Book

We were surrounded by people who were not looking to help us but to hinder us. There was no place to go. The partisans did not get well organized until the fall of '43. There were little groups here and there. My mother was very much in touch with the first partisans...there were a few of the young men who escaped to the forest. The way they accumulated weapons was by staking out some roads and finding a lone German soldier passing by who they could kill and take his weapons. That was the only way to take the weapons from a soldier.

It was kill or be killed. They accumulated a few weapons. Some of the Russian prisoners of war had also escaped. When people are treated like this, it doesn't matter. The line between life and death becomes very, very narrow, and it's a matter of..."Well, do I get killed and end my suffering or do I escape and have a chance to live," and then it's much easier to escape.

But when you're the cause of the rest of your family's deaths, it's very difficult.

There was no place to run. You lived amongst the population that was ready and willing to hand you over to the Germans again. It was only under the threat of fear that those people provided the food to the partisans. Once the partisans were able to get some weapons and once they had made contact with the Russians behind the lines, then it became much easier. When the front was organized, the Russians sent leadership, ammunitions and some supplies. Other than that, whatever supplies, whatever fighting supplies there were, were only very primitive or what was taken from the Germans.

I remember quite a number of people who wanted to escape from of the ghetto. Some of them were successful.

But there was really no place to go. You were in a situation that you're damned if you do and you're damned if you don't. You don't want to die. You know you're going to die. Hope is what keeps us all living. The hope was that maybe the Russians are going to regroup and liberate us before the Germans have a chance to kill us. And as long as the Germans could elicit some sort...some sort of labor or some sort of valuables from the community, we were still of some use.

With the Partisans

In 1943, we escaped from the Glubokie ghetto in broad daylight. On market day, Mother dressed me and herself as if going we were going to work. We left with the work details and we kept on walking outside the ghetto. Then we skipped off to the side, having prearranged to meet with a gentile woman who was to lead us out of town. She met us and brought us some clothing. We quickly changed into peasant clothing. It wasn't much different from what we were wearing, but nonetheless helped to hide our identity. We even hitched a ride with the Germans on a truck. They were going down the road. They stopped. We were walking with this woman. They asked if we wanted to ride, where we were going…

She took us to a village eventually and from that village…Mother already had contacts, and from this village we went on.

We reached the partisans. It was a small group of about 20. They were a forward group. Their mission was to undermine German progress to the Russian front. The leader of the group was an escaped Russian prisoner.

The Russian Army laid down their weapons and became prisoners of war. They didn't want to fight. Some of them, mainly the leadership, had military training. The foot soldiers were just handed a gun and told, "Shoot out there and go fight the enemy."

They were hungry, they were tattered. When they were mistreated by the Germans they were looking to escape and they would break free. They ran toward the forest. Some of them were shot and some of them escaped. And that's how the partisans got formed in the forest.

The partisans said to my mother, in so many words, "So what good are you to us? Well, you have a gun, that's fine. Can you shoot it?" She said, "You'll teach me. However, I'm an excellent cook." There were a few Jewish men there and they eased the way for us.

Appendix to the Dokshitz Parafianov Yizkor Book
Material Not in the Original Yizkor Book

Mother became a cook. She knew very little about cooking other than observing. But she was very inventive, again. I did whatever I was told to do. Sometimes I peeled potatoes until I couldn't feel my fingers. I used to count the ammunition and package it up for distribution to the partisans. I could take apart a rifle and probably could clean it faster than a soldier. My little fingers managed to get into places where big fingers couldn't get in. It was a matter of what was your worth to the partisans. Everybody had to have a certain worth.

There weren't that many Jews among the partisans. They knew we were Jewish. There was quite a bit of anti-Semitism in the partisans. There weren't many Jewish women.

As much as surviving mattered, the only thing available was pork and I would not eat pork and neither would my mother. My mother cooked it for the partisans but we never ate it. We'd sooner eat just a potato. When she made soup, she served our portions before adding in pork for the rest of the group.

Our partisan group was at the edge of the forest. We were not with the main group. Our job was to disrupt communications, communications meaning train deliveries. We would go out and loosen the bolts to some of the railroad tracks so a train could not go on, thus disrupting the delivery to the to the front lines, and sometimes managing to blow up a couple of carloads of ammunition. It had to be done in a manner that would not be too suspicious, that could be accepted as an accident, in order to avoid retaliation.

We lived in villages. Sometimes in a house, a dirt house, and sometimes just under the stars. The Germans were occupied at the front lines; they were not living in every house, nor in every village. They were afraid of those deep forests. The forests were so thick, but also very muddy. That area is known as the Polotski Bloty. the marshes. You could sink into those marshes and never come out. They could not go in with a vehicle.

The Germans prided themselves on their cleanliness. If they got dirt on their boots, they didn't like it. They were not very apt to venture into the forests and marshes. Every so often they would venture in to discourage the partisans from going to close to the railroad stations, and the railroad tracks. When they attacked, we would run into the forests and live under the stars. When they pulled back, we returned to the villages. I don't know if the villagers received the partisans with open arms, however they had to go along with the tide.

The partisans told the villagers that if they ran to the Germans, they could not return to their homes and their families, and warned them about how the Germans treat would them. By then the Germans were the feeling the heat.

The villagers were afraid of the Nazis because the Nazis started to take away their farm goods, their animals and ship them to the front. The villages were at the edge of the forest because you can't farm in the forest, especially when there were marshes. The villagers didn't want their animals destroyed. They used to put their animals in the forest. The partisans guarded them. The partisans didn't take much from them, but they did take supplies to eat. The villagers started to share with the partisans because that was the only way to keep what they had.

Once my mother and I got separated in the forest. I didn't know where I was, nobody was there. All I could hear was the Germans calling and shooting. They knew people were around. They were calling out, "Give yourself up and you will survive," and spraying bullets over the area. It's better to get shot than be lost in the forest. I went out to a clearing and watched the bullets hit the dirt in front of me. They make a little puff when they hit the dirt. Then I heard my mother calling me. It didn't take me a split second to turn away and run. I remember it very clearly.

I never thought about giving myself up. Sooner be shot than give myself up. I was willing to walk into a bullet. At that point, there were no Jews alive that we knew of in any of the surrounding towns. Knowing that I'm Jewish and knowing what awaited me, it was easier to take a bullet at random than to have somebody point a gun between your eyes.

Appendix to the Dokshitz Parafianov Yizkor Book
Material Not in the Original Yizkor Book

By the time we came into the partisans, they had a command structure. The commanders came from Russia. We were with a special group so there was just one commander over this small group of people, but there was a chain of command over the brigade, and there were several brigades. The one that we were with was called Medvedev.

When partisans went out on assignments to do their either demolition or sabotage, many of them were captured. I remember when a Jewish woman was captured. She was returned in a potato sack in pieces. The Germans were trying to teach is that if you tried to do that to us, we'll show you what we can to do you. It never stopped anybody going out again.

I got sick with typhus in late 1943. The partisans had set up a makeshift hospital deeper in the forest where it was safer. The Nazis did not venture there. Mother got me into a wagon and took me to that hospital. There were no doctors in the hospital. There were a few people who knew how to extract bullets and how to sew up wounds. Rachel Rappaport from Glebokie ran the hospital. She had just gotten her credentials as a midwife. She could thread a needle and sew into flesh, and acted as a surgeon. She had relatives in Dokshitz and we knew her very well. When I arrived, she shaved my head. My temperature was 106. She got me through. By then it was 1944, and the front lines had shifted. Rachel married Michael Friedman, who was a partisan. They settled in New York. Michael eventually became a shammas in a synagogue.

When we were with the partisans, they attacked Dokshitz. They were probably attacking the German Army post to make it easier for the upcoming Russian offensive. Mother didn't want the Germans to use our house. She asked the partisans to torch it, and they did. A lot of other buildings burned in the resulting fire.

Closer to liberation in early 1944, the Germans tried to rid the forests of the partisans. They were already in retreat. In order to be able to fight the war, they had to get rid of this monkey on their back that was inflicting all kinds of disruptions. In addition to the Germans there was a Ukrainian military unit that had turned themselves over to the Germans. They fought on the German side and did dirty work for the Germans, including blockading the partisans.

They surrounded every exit from the forest. They pushed the partisans deeper into the forest and managed to capture quite a number of us. We were captured together with some partisans and some of the villagers because the villagers ran too. They were afraid to stay, and also some of the partisans made them go with them because blending into the population provided protection. This happened while my mother was with me in the hospital, so we were not with our group. We were on our own.

The villagers were just as scared as we were. Mother was hiding and some of the villagers did not know her. She had changed tremendously. She was a pretty stout woman, and she looked like a skeleton. Her features hadn't changed. She was afraid that someone would realize she was Jewish or that someone would recognize her. She wore a kerchief like an old Russian woman that hid her hair and most of her face. All you could see was her eyes and her nose and her lips. She spoke only Polish, so they referred to her as a szlachta, an upper-class Pole. They hated that because they were Belarusians. I would go out and try to procure food. My head was shaved after the typhus, and I wore boys clothing because that's all that was available. At one point, I had a pair of German boots that I stuffed with rags because they were too big.

We were brought back to the forest near our home town, Dokshitz. To the Germans we were just a couple of more villagers. I looked very much like a boy. Our captors, a brigade of Croatians led by Germans, started to separate the women from the men. The Germans had this phobia not to keep men and women together, even boys and their mothers, and they were going to separate me from my mother. That was my biggest fear. "Junge, madchen, madchen, junge [boy, girl, girl, boy]," they said. They started to argue whether I was girl or a boy. I said I was a madchen, a girl, and since my mother identified herself as my mother, they presumed that she was a gentile who was harboring a Jewish child.

Appendix to the Dokshitz Parafianov Yizkor Book
Material Not in the Original Yizkor Book

They knew I was Jewish because I said the word madchen. It's very similar to the same word in Yiddish. I understood the German conversation. Most of the gentiles did not catch on to German.

I started to cry, "Mommy." My mother was brought and we were put on the scaffolding. They were going to hang me for being Jewish. If she wanted to survive my mother had to tell them that I'm Jewish. My mother said, "Hang me first so I don't see my child being hanged. I worked for the Germans, I worked for the Nazis as a laundress and my daughter, being young, managed to learn some words." All of a sudden, I became a darling.

We were housed in some barns with no food. When the children went out to try to scrounge up some food, I went too. One of the priests gave the children food, including me. Everybody knelt and thanked him and did the normal observances, and I knew how do to them properly too.

Then they let us go. The villagers were returned to the villages because the partisans had dispersed and were not in the area. We went with them. However, even in the villages, Mother had to hide. It was in the spring of 1944.

We survived by living with the villagers, but the Germans were very close by. Mother tried to stay out of the way. I was the one that had to organize some food and I was the one that went out and brought news. Supposedly she was sick and couldn't move.

One woman told my mother, "Dorka, somebody recognized you. You better get out of here." My mother's name is Dina, but in Russian it was Dorka. So Mother took me by the hand again and we fled. How long can you hide amongst a population of non-Jews, especially my mother, who was known throughout the area? There were some people that were sympathetic too. They told us where there were some partisans beginning to organize again.

We rejoined the partisans. We joined up with a group and that group joined up with another group. By the latter part of the occupation, when the Russians were advancing, we partisans had communication with the Russian armies. We knew that the Russians were coming. We knew which direction they were coming from, so we headed in that direction to join up with them. We had a very long march to try to get out of the way of the armies. Eventually, we met the Russian Army, and were liberated.

Liberation

When the liberation came, I remember vaguely, very vaguely, sleeping in a house and not worrying about anything. It was still very unsettled. To give you an example, no sooner did the war end when we had to again be very wary because some of the population, when they realized there were some Jews that remained alive, tried to eliminate us. We were despised, we were not wanted.

My mother went back to Dokshitz to see who else might have survived. She also went to look for some buried valuables. One of the neighbors gave my mother a picture of me with my mother and brother that she had found in the trash. She took my mother into her house to show her that she had taken care of everything my mother had left with her. She also returned my mother's coats. Later, when we went to Lublin, my mother was able to sell these so we had something to live on.

She said that people had dug around our house looking for buried money or valuables, but hadn't found anything. My mother was able to find the things she had buried, which helped us to survive. She said, "You are welcome to stay the night, but there are people here that are still killing Jews. I don't know if you would survive the night, or if I would survive if I help you" So Mother took the picture, took some bread, and fled again.

She joined me back in Glebokie. We lived there for a short time and then moved to Krulevshchina. We were with the Katz family. Marsha Mirman Katz's brother sponsored their immigration to the United States after the war, and tried but failed to do the same for my mother and I. Mr. and Mrs. Katz had a son. Mother and Mrs. Katz earned some money by baking rolls and selling them to the Russian soldiers going to the front lines

My mother wanted to get out of the Russian area. The Russians asked partisans to enlist in the work force. Mother and Mr. and Mrs. Katz enlisted and rebuilt water towers for the railroad. We lived on a work train, sharing part of a boxcar with the Katz family. The railroad stations were pretty much destroyed, and the only movement of troops was by railroad. Restoring the stations and the railroads was urgent in order to move the army towards the front lines.

We were heading toward Central Poland. We knew that the Americans were pushing from the other side, and realized that the Russians and the Americans would eventually meet. Our objective was to get as close to that area as possible and to go over to the American side.

It didn't happen that easily. First, we headed towards the Baltic Sea. Mother thought going straight toward Germany was the best way to get to Italy. However, when we came to Prussia, conditions were terrible. The Germans had mined anything and everything that they could. They mined the chandeliers. They mined the equipment in the houses. They mined themselves so when the Russians went to remove the bodies, they were killed. It was very dangerous.

My mother ran into a Red Army general. He was a doctor, accompanying wounded soldiers back to Russia. After a short conversation, he hinted that he was Jewish and he said if you think that the Germans were bad, wait and see what anti-Semitism and hardships awaited us if we remained in Poland. He advised her to head south. He heard there were some Jews in Lublin in Southern Poland. He arranged for the box car we lived in with the Katz family to be hooked onto a train heading in that direction.

While we were going through Poland, two Jewish boys jumped into our box car. They were fleeing for their lives. They eventually made it to Italy.

Now we headed south. When we came to Lublin, the war was still going on. My mother got the Red Cross to provide a document that said I was born in Lublin. My mother was trying to make sure I did not get sent to Russia.

Our intention was to reach land of Israel. That was the only haven. When we got to Lublin, there were already a few Jews from Palestine, probably Polish born, who came to organize the Jews and prepare them for the trek to the land of Israel. From there we went to Czechoslovakia and then to Hungary. The purpose of the journey was to get into areas that weren't Russian-occupied.

In Czechoslovakia, we heard that the war was coming to an end. We stayed in Hungary for a while, where Poles were not very much liked and Jews were definitely not liked.

When we crossed the border between Hungary and Austria we met British troops who sent us back to the Russian side. We already had guides that were sent by the Zionists. We had to cross the Alps. We went through some of the passes in the Alps. When we crossed into Italy we found out that the war had ended.

We were cold. We were hungry. We were frozen, not just cold, and I saw a blue and white flag with the Jewish star. I was sure I was hallucinating. It was the Jewish Brigade. We were well received, "Where are you from?" I came from a little town nobody heard of. And of all the people to meet, I met my governess's brother.

I couldn't get over it. I ran for my mother. Mother met him. Mother remembered when he had left for the land of Israel. He had a little tiny soldier's bible. He gave it to me, so that I would not forget my studies. I had not spoken Hebrew since about 1941. To be able to communicate, to be able to speak, to be able to get my feelings across and to understand what was being said, was probably the most joyous time that I know of. I think it was more joyous than coming to the United States. I still have that bible.

We stayed with the brigade for about three days. We were put in trucks. A boat was waiting some place in Italy. Our truck broke down. There were quite a number of Jews that were collected near Bologna in Italy and needless to say when a truck breaks down, you don't go any further. We missed that boat. We missed three boats. We even missed the Exodus. It was pretty clear that it was difficult to get into Palestine.

My mother had pushed very hard to survive and to not just to survive by herself but also to save me. It's an obsession to try to stay alive. She managed to find gentile acquaintances who owed her favors. One family that had a lot of our possessions took a big risk to smuggle food to us into the Glebokie ghetto. They even smuggled a gun in to my mother and they helped smuggle us out, and that was taking an even greater risk.

Mother was a child during the First World War. She helped with the family. She went into business early in life. Not only did she run a business but she also helped a sister get into business in a neighboring town. Mother was a woman who ventured out into the world. She used to go to Lodz and Warsaw to buy yard goods. Vilna was the main place. She wasn't somebody that came from the hinterlands and just stayed in the hinterlands. She had a very good head on her shoulders.

Throughout the war and the hiding and the freezing and the starving, my mother remained strong and was able to go forward. After the war my mother fell apart. We're all strong during bad times, but we fall apart during good ones, and I think that's the time when it finally hit her. I've survived, but...

Mother was very sickly after that. I would say more dead than alive. She developed asthma which was diagnosed psychosomatic asthma in the United States. The slightest excitement would bring on an attack, and unless I got her a shot of adrenalin, God knows what would happen. When we were supposed to leave to meet the Exodus she had a very bad attack of asthma She was taken to the hospital. I thought the world had come at an end because we were not going to get out of there. We were not going to get to Eretz Yisrael.

I think she came to the realization that the struggle to survive had ended. But she was missing everybody. She felt that she was a big business woman who could do most anything, but the thing that mattered to her the most, saving her family, she wasn't able to do.

Until the day of her death, she kept on talking about what she should have done and what she could have done, but of course if she could have done it she would have done it.

To America

Mother had heard that you could put in an ad into the Forward, and she remembered writing to my uncle and aunt in the United States. My aunt was my father's sister, Shirley Mutterperl Gotkin, who lived in Washington, DC. She was married to William Gotkin, who was also from Dokshitz. They were childhood sweethearts. He promised he would marry her. She was 14 when my uncle went to the United States.

My Uncle had a grocery store. When he felt he could afford to get married, my father sent his sister to Cuba. My uncle went to Cuba and married her, and they returned to the United States. My uncle had Gotkin relatives in Wisconsin in the lake area, in Sheboygan. One of his cousins married a Rosen. They had a fishing and tackle shop.

My Uncle had Freedman and Kotz relatives in Washington. Sam and Katie and their son Stanley Freedman were not related to my mother's Freedman relatives. My mother described our Friedmans as the klezmer Friedmans.

Somebody saw our name in the paper and alerted my uncle, William Gotkin. He wrote to the Forward, who forwarded his letter to us. We made contact and he was willing to help. He wrote, telling us not to try to go anywhere, that he would try to get us over. He made out papers but the Polish quota was full, so we couldn't come. My Uncle had to post a bond of $5000, and had to promise to provide us with shelter, food, clothing, medical care, and provide for my education.

The displaced persons who were waiting to go the United States were sent to a camp in Bari, Italy. They were letting just a trickle in. My mother realized we were not going to get in under the Polish quota. The American Consul had no problem going along with my mother's claim that she was Russian-born. The Russian quota was not full because for years very few people had immigrated from Russia to the United States. On November 17, 1947, we arrived in the United States under the Russian quota.

My mother never really adapted here. She was never any longer what she was. She had to struggle to earn a livelihood. Since coming to this country, I'll tell you I've worked...I don't remember ever not working.

My Uncle put me in a private school right away. I caught up. I went to summer school. Some of the children of my mother's friends coached me. After completing Junior High, we moved to New York. Mother thought that she was going to be able to get a job there and manage better. The language was not as much of a problem. Washington isn't a city where somebody without money and without a profession can easily survive. She did not want to be dependent on my uncle and aunt. We didn't find it that easy in New York.

I worked while I went to Brooklyn's Samuel Tilden J. High School, which I completed in 2 1/2 years. Hebrew was offered. I needed a language requirement and that was an easy language requirement. I could get a lot of credits by just taking one semester and taking the regent's examination.

My counselor was Mrs. Rief, a German woman. She was very apprehensive when she found out I was assigned to her. I learned years later from her obituary that she was Jewish.

Ms. Rief felt that she had to set things straight. She helped me a great deal in judging people on their merits. She helped me get through and adjust to school. She interceded with teachers to get me extra help. Someone gave me elocution lessons after school. She taught me how to deal with some of the prejudices in school, and made me aware that I have something to pass on too.

Thanks to Mrs. Rief, I became very much aware of the importance of passing on Jewish knowledge. She got me to substitute in Hebrew class. If the teacher couldn't make it, there were very few Hebrew substitutes, and I guess I was a better substitute than anybody they could get to babysit. I remember her saying to me, "Well you know it and you can impart more than somebody else." It became a matter of imparting.

I hated New York. When I graduated high school, I wanted to go to college. The only way I could go to college was with my uncle's help. I returned to Washington and managed to get a very good job and go to school at night. I liked the environment in Washington much more than the New York environment. Mother came back with me. But she could never get a decent job in Washington, so it was a matter of just surviving.

What I've experienced in America means quite a bit to me: going to school, freedom, being able to walk the streets, being able to hold my head up high, being an equal even though I wasn't an equal. I was still living a nightmare, but nonetheless I had all the opportunity and could take advantage of those opportunities. I was an equal in being able to pursue the goals that I had set for myself.

I became less observant than I was before the war. I think integrating into society meant an awful lot. Going out on a date and having to go to a kosher restaurant and not being able to go out on a Saturday night up until a certain time, not being able to get a job that I needed so badly other than working on Saturday.

My first experience was when I went with a friend of mine from school to look for a summer job. Every job I went for I had to work on Saturday. I had to ride on Saturday to get to my job. I think it's little by little those feelings break down. You do one thing and then you allow yourself to do the next thing. There's no such thing as being slightly strict.

wedding, Rachel Mutterperl; l-r William & Chashka (Mutterperl) Gotkin, Rachel Mutterperl Goldfarb, Dina Mutterperl, Henie Gotkin (mother of William).

Adjusting to America wasn't too difficult for me. When I came to my uncle's house, I became the fourth daughter. I was probably a little bit resented by the others but my uncle was a very smart and good-natured man. It was very important for young ladies on their sixteenth birthday to get their first fur coat. Well, low and behold, his daughter was made to wait to get her first fur coat until I came here and we got identical ones. I can understand now why my cousin resented me a little bit.

In 1952 I married my husband, Harvey Goldfarb. My husband's mother was one of six. Her siblings were in the United States or Canada. My husband's family had a visa, but they did not get out in time. My husband, a survivor, remembered the address of an uncle in Canada. He contacted one of the relatives in the United States, who tracked him down at a d.p. camp, and arranged for him to come to Washington in May, 1946 on the visa that he had. We met when I first got to Washington. A lot of the survivors socialized together. We reconnected after I graduated. He's older than I am. When I was 17 and 18, I was a child compared to him, but when I was twenty it was a different story.

Today, I guess my life is the same as in any American family. My children went to college. They've got nice professions. They are devoted children. We try to let them live their own lives. Sometimes they think we probably put more requirements on them than they would like, but nonetheless we have a good relationship with them.

Sources:
1. United States Holocaust Memorial Museum Oral History, RG Number: RG-50.030*0082 Date: 1991 September 05 (interview of Rachel (Mutterperl) Goldfarb).
2. First Person Series, Conversation with a Holocaust survivor (Rachel (Mutterperl) Goldfarb [2013 season], United States Holocaust Memorial Museum.
3. Interviews, Rachel (Mutterperl) Goldfarb by Aaron Ginsburg, 2017.
4. Email messages, Rachel (Mutterperl) Goldfarb and Aaron Ginsburg, 2017.

Legacy of Silence
Encounters with Children of the Third Reich

By Dr. Dan Bar-On
Permission granted by Tammy Bar-On

Chapter 9, pages 200-217

Small Hills Covered with Trees

Rudolf answers my ad in the local newspaper: "Children whose parents witnessed or took part in the persecution or extermination of Jews andlor Gypsies and who are willing to participate in a research project by an Israeli psychologist at the local university, please . . ." He calls and says he will speak only to the Israeli interviewer. We set up a time for the interview, and I agree to meet him at the bus station.

Compared to the interviewees I seek out, about whose parents, and their role during the war, I have detailed information, the ad respondents are a mystery to me until they tell their stories. I usually reach the meeting place a few minutes ahead of time in order to see the person arriving—how he approaches-the station, what he looks like, if he seems troubled or at ease, if his expression changes when he recognizes me. But Rudolf is already waiting, glancing impatiently at his watch (although I am not late). He is tall and looks like a manager in some local firm. A strong handshake. I can sense his excitement. He starts talking immediately, but I steer him into small talk because I want to reach my office, where the tape recorder is set up. When we finally reach my room and I invite him to sit down, he pulls a yellowed sheaf of papers from his briefcase.

R: I was born April 4, 1930, in Wuppertal, the son of an unemployed textile worker. My father was out of work at the time. Before he lost his job, he was employed as a master craftsman in a textile plant. But there was a great deal of unemployment in the area, and he was laid off too.

B: Are you the only son?

R: I was the only son until 1940, when my brother was born. He's still alive. He was born on January 14, 1941, in Wuppertal. I spent those very early years more or less pleasantly until my dad found work again. He found a job later, I'm not sure exactly when. We were living in quite a primitive little house. Although he was out of a job, my father built himself a small house in a garden. He was very enterprising, but the thing about him—right up until he died he was a very pious and believing Christian. And that has accompanied me through my entire life—Christianity, being a Christian. At home we would pray— have a Bible hour and sing together. There were also others who'd come over to our place in order to read the word of God together.

I experienced National Socialism right from the start. OK, not from the very beginning, the years before 1930, but after Hitler came to power in 1933 it began to be a reality for me. For me it was something I was born into, I couldn't question it. It was something quite normal. When I'd see the soldiers marching outside, the Hitler Youth marching past, for me that was something: I wanted to march too. My mother would say to me, "Just wait, see what happens, you don't know . . ." "Mama, I'd like to be in the Hitler Youth too!" "Just wait and see first." Well, I joined the Hitler Youth in 1940. The war had already begun. I advanced through the ranks very quickly, went to a leadership school, and became a squad leader (Jungenscharfuhrer). Later I became a platoon leader with a group of thirty boys under my command. That's one side of it. I experienced all that directly and with a feeling of joy.

Now I finally had what I'd been longing for. Now I was a leader, I was able to command, although I was still just a child.

There is something very theatrical in his way of talking. I wonder if this is his usual manner or if it is due to his excitement in recalling and relating the events of the past.

B: How old were you then?

R: I was only eleven when I went to the course where young leaders were trained. I was twelve when I became a squad leader and thirteen or fourteen when I made platoon commander. In any event, something very peculiar happened at that time . . . well, not peculiar, but something that had a powerful formative influence on me. My father had found work again even before that, but he wasn't happy. He tried to find a position that was more challenging. So he went to work with the railroad. It was called the Reichsbahn then. He laid track at first, then he was a station conductor, and later on he worked with the signal box. He always felt attracted to the track gang, the guys who laid track, but he was also preaching sermons as a member of a Protestant congregation of the Free Church, a congregation that was independent but still Protestant. So he was a preacher. The railroad was his job and being a preacher his love. And his family—his children—were his pride and joy, his great love. He did a lot of Sunday school lessons with small children, taught them about the Bible. Actually he lived just for the family, for his congregation.

Naturally he had to work, and he had this enormous garden. My father was a very believing and religious person, as I said and he was filled with a great deal of love. I felt protected in his love. Whatever my father said was right. Then the day came when my father was approached by the Nazi Party, by the National Socialist German Workers' Party. He was already a member of the NSV, the National Socialist Welfare Association. He collected money for the Party and distributed ration cards—those cards were quite common at that time. So he was already active in the NSV and was asked to join the Party. I can recall that this had been discussed once at home. I had listened and thought about it. I myself was in the Hitler Youth and my view was "Dad, you have to join the Party!" First he resisted. Then he thought that maybe it would be a good idea after all if he joined up: maybe he could advance more quickly, make headway in his profession and—just maybe—be in a position to shield his congregation. At that time, they didn't want such Christian congregations—I think it was a passing phase for National Socialism at the time. After the war they would have done away with the church congregations anyhow. I oscillated back and forth between the Hitler Youth and the congregation. I was undecided and psychologically unfulfilled. I loved the Hitler Youth more and more. Religion became more and more unimportant to me. I felt invigorated and full of life. They knew how to do that. The Hitler Youth leaders were good at animating young people, motivating and preparing them psychologically for tasks they would carry out later on. It went without question in my eyes that what the Fuhrer said and did, that was the truth. He was almost more of a god for me than the real God . . .

B: Could you give an example of how the leaders did that?

R: We used to have evening get-togethers when all the boys would sit in a large room. The room had black wallpaper, completely black. The benches were dark red. Up front there was a picture on the wall, not of the Fuhrer but of a famous Germanic king, along with two lamps that shed a dim light on the picture. It was quite dark in the room. Then we were told stories about the ancient Germans, our Germanic forefathers. The Aryan race, which has the sole right to lead. We would sing songs in a minor key. It penetrated very deeply into our souls. We felt this very deeply. We believed everything, and we were very proud to be members of this Germanic race and leaders to boot. Young leaders, tribal leaders within this race, this new Germanic race. Young people who were now setting out to rule the world—they really wanted to rule the world. So for us what was predominant was what engaged our feelings. That wasn't the only thing though, not just such evening gatherings. Marching

Appendix to the Dokshitz Parafianov Yizkor Book
Material Not in the Original Yizkor Book

out on the street, marching like soldiers ... we youngsters already felt like grown-up soldiers. The music that accompanied us, played by the Hitler Youth, with flags and drums through the streets—everyone had to salute our flags, and we were proud to be full members! The fact that we were children was used to prepare us for what was to come. I say for what was to come, but what was that going to be? We were as yet unable to grasp what "later on" might be. We didn't know what was really involved. Who had told us? No one spoke about it.

[Sighs] But now I have to return to the subject of my father. My father was inducted as a railroad man and sent to Russia, to Poland. To be more precise, my father was sent to Parafianovo. [Placenames appear in their Russian form; these are small villages in Belorussia, between Vilna and Smolensk.] That's between Vilna and Smolensk. He worked as—what they called during the war an adjunct work-squad leader. He had a section of track to take care of. It was between Parafianovo and Smolensk, maybe three hundred to five hundred kilometers. I can't give you a definite figure. It was his job to maintain this section of track, which was frequently attacked by partisans. They blew up the tracks so the trains would be derailed. But the most important thing, the thing that had such a formative influence on him—which is why I'm here—and on me, was an experience he told me about after he returned. He came back earlier than expected. There was a Jewish ghetto in Parafianovo. A lot of Jews had been brought together and concentrated there in one area, where they were allowed to live. These Jews also worked for the German railroad. A large number were used to help maintain the tracks. For example, there was—I just can't forget their names—there was Aaron Katz, Maria, and the cook for the men my father worked with. This cook was Jewish. I can't recall her name. I think Dolla was her first name, or people called her that. My father could go into the ghetto and speak with the Jews there.

Since he was a convinced and religious Christian, he also spoke with them about the Talmud and the Scriptures, our Holy Bible. And they saw that they both believed in a common God, except that, for the Jews, Jesus is a kind of strange chapter inserted in between. In any event, they understood that they were equal. And basically, we Germans are also a tribe of Israelites. If you assume that certain tribes developed up north and that the Germanic tribes, the so-called Germanic tribes, are a conglomerate of many peoples, they are also a tribe of Israelites. Not that this is important, it's something secondary. [Very agitated] Well, the day arrived when the ghetto was surrounded by the SS. They asked my father, "How many do you need?" And he told them, "I need all of them." "No, I need a few heads," the officer said, "they're all to be shot." So now you have this Christian, with a soft and childlike heart. He stands there and can do nothing! What should he say, "Shoot me too"? He had children and a wife of his own . . . What was he to do? [Almost shouting at me] He didn't have such great courage. He couldn't resist. He was unable to save his Jews—after all, they were his brothers, he had lived with them. First, a woman was shot. She had given birth the day before. She was tossed down into the grave. [Crying] Whether they also shot the baby, he doesn't know, he didn't know that. Then he ran away and cried bitterly. And a young SS soldier ran after him and said, "I can't go on either! I've killed so many, I just can't go on!"

In any case, he was criticized after that. I could read you a letter written by my father to make things clearer, a letter he wrote right after the end of the war. He became very ill and was released from service too, following this experience. He wrote the letter only after the war because he was afraid to put anything at all down in writing during the war, during the National Socialist period. Let me show you. It's an old letter, and here is also the confirmation that my father was in the east and had been given an early release.

His hands shaking, Rudolf hands me the two documents he has brought with him. He is sweating. I can see that the documents are old and have been carefully kept in a nylon bag. I can also see that they are written in an old-fashioned hand and that on one, the words Our Guilt appear at the top. I offer

Rudolf a glass of water and suggest that he read the documents to me himself, since I would have difficulty with his father's handwriting. He starts with the one that carries the swastika, aformal certif~cate of the Nazi railroad authority. Then he reads hisfather's letter, dated May 16, 1945.

Our Guilt

Finally now, after many weeks of a serious illness that almost robbed me of my senses, I find myself able to com~nit to writing those things that (so soon) made me ill and have so completely shattered my nerves. I intend to narrate events one after the other in the course of writing and to present a reason for having chosen the above title.

Until 1941 I had been active for many years as the director of a Sunday school for children. Our parish served in external and internal missionary activities in China. It was my favorite task to be involved in service to children. Since I generally had a great many friends (through my work with the children), the Party believed it had found the right man for its National Socialist Welfare Program (NS-Volkswohlfahrt, NSV) activities. At the same time I was working for the National Railways (Reichsbahn) and had a very low income. On the basis of my work as block chairman of the NSV and as an employee of the Reichsbahn, I became a member of the National Socialist German Workers' Party onJune 1, 1941.

I was also promised that I could retain my faith, but shortly after I became a member of the Party, I was forbidden to hold Sunday school classes. That was the first blow. I had to keep silent and put aside my favorite activity.

I was transferred to the town of Parafianovo in Poland to work as head of an auxiliary work squad on February 9, 1942. Among others, there were also some 247 Jews—men, women, and children—living in the town. The Jews were put to work at all kinds of jobs but generally lived in a closed ghetto. We Germans (four men) were assigned a Jewish cook by the name of Dolla, a sweet young girl with red hair, who was very, very clean. My fellow soldiers did not treat her with much respect, since she was, after all, Jewish. But she soon noticed that there was someone there who treated her with love, and we became friends, though no one was supposed to notice. I became sick one week, a bad cold, and Dolla called the Jewish pharmacist Belzik, who procured excellent medicines for me. My fellow soldiers began to taunt me about this friendship with a Jew, and even started to criticize and complain. When I regained my health, I visited the ghetto for the first time. Visiting the ghetto was forbidden and a punishable offense. Due to my illness, I was allowed to go to the pharmacy that was located in the ghetto.

So I visited the pharmacist in the ghetto for the first time, and I was pleased to meet several wonderful human beings: the Jewish women Maria (Mr. Belzik's daughter), Rita (a teacher), and Lilli (a piano teacher), as well as the Aaron K. family. These people proceeded to tell me all their cares and worries. I was confronted with one tale of woe after another. These Jews, whether young or old, were each given a ration of three hundred grams of bread week after week, this and nothing else, month after month. The great misery among these poor people now became evident to me. I then tried in every possible way to help them, and since I knew that they were God's own people, I began to beseech him and to help where I could.

I was very happy when we were joined by a new fellow soldier who shared my view, Mr. S. from Munich, who faithfully pitched in, helping these poor people wherever help was needed. We had to go about it very cautiously and could only pay visits to people late in the evening, though each time, the Jews were overjoyed when we came. I noticed, however, that their troubles were growing from day to day, because everywhere there was talk about Jews being shot. Their questions became ever more pressing and urgent: What will become of us? I tried then to explain to them that the living Lord would not abandon them, and at home, in my room, I myself engaged in a fervent struggle with God and asked him for help. Yes, in my distress I said, "Lord, I will serve you faithfully forever, but please let these people live." As a result of

Appendix to the Dokshitz Parafianov Yizkor Book
Material Not in the Original Yizkor Book

this terrible distress and misery, our relationship became very, very close. It went so far that we even knelt down together to ask our Father for strength in all these matters. One evening, when I was visiting them again and we were all sitting together, I quietly sang the song "Guten Abend, gut' Nacht" [Brahms's Lullaby], accompanied on the guitar. When we came to the words "Tomorrow, God willing, you'll be awakened once again . . . ," Rita broke out in sobs and said, "I feel so strange." The rest of what she said was lost in sobbing. That was the last night of her young life.

Rudolf is crying and searches desperately for his handkerchief while continuing to read.

Early the next morning, we suddenly heard that the ghetto was surrounded by the SS. The Jews were herded together and forced out of the ghetto into an open area. There they had to take off their shoes, coats, and jackets, and they began to weep loudly. A boy of about fourteen tried to run away but was shot immediately. In response, a Jewish man became extremely angry and began to rebuke the SS; however, he was brutally beaten on the spot, so that he had to be transported in a vehicle. The men of the village were forced to dig a large hole, and everyone—children and women, young and old—had to lie down face to the ground. Among these miserable creatures there was a woman who only the day before had given birth to a child. That woman was the first who had to stand up and go to her grave (and the grave of all). I saw how this woman tottered and reeled, clutching her almost naked infant and crying bitterly, asking for her life. She was pushed brutally into the hole and then shot.

Rudolf is unable to go on reading and sobs heavily. I am stunned, distressed, and wait until he regains enough control over his tears to continue.

I went as fast as I could to my room, heard shots again and again, and collapsed at the foot of my bed. Now I lost everything. I had followed the Lord faithfully for twenty-eight years, and now this horrible thing occurred. I had believed right to the last hour that the Lord would preserve these people as a result of my prayer, but then I cursed God and all men.

Rudolf stops again, bursting into tears.

I wanted total oblivion (ich wollte von nichts mehr wissen) Apparently abandoned by God and all of humankind, I carried out my duties in total apathy and hardly knew in subsequent days what was happening.

My fellow soldiers—except for S.—called me a coward and a "lover of Jews." Jews were being shot everywhere, in Glubokoe, Dokshitsy, Vileika, Budslav, and Krulevshchyzna. I had one small consolation when I came to Dokshitsy ten or twelve days later and met the captain. His first question was, "Where is Maria?" (Maria was the pharmacist's daughter in Parafianovo, liked everywhere as a result of her universally respected love for human beings.) I said, "Maria is dead." The captain began to cry. He grabbed my hand and said, "It's a rotten shame!" (Schweinerei). I didn't see him again after that, but I knew that his heart was also bleeding with grief. Eighteen hundred Jews had been shot in this village. There was great commotion and shouting. I ran over to see what was happening, and to my horror I saw Jews emerging from subterranean caves, some eighty to a hundred people, a terrible picture of misery and suffering. They were crying for water, emaciated, their faces white as chalk. Hardly able to utter a sentence, they dropped to their knees and begged for their lives. Without receiving anything, they were pushed and herded into a barn. I watched as a girl about the age of ten, who had hidden herself in a hay shed and was now almost completely emaciated, was carried past me. This poor girl looked more like a pile of bones than a human being, and this bundle of misery and agony, it too was carried into the barn. As long as I live, come what may, I will never forget this horrible sight. I can't help myself. It was just too horrible and made me sick for the rest of my life. I just can't comprehend how human beings can be such beasts. These images haunted me day and night.

After a few weeks I was sent to a field hospital in Vileika because of hypertension. But then I collapsed completely, since I was not allowed to tell anyone of my suffering. And this suffering became even more intense when I realized that I was a member of such a band of murderers and criminals, a band that would not have spared my life if I had objected. So I got sicker and sicker and was sent to Vilna. There, for the first time, I had fainting spells and mental disturbances. They didn't know the cause, and they asked me all kinds of questions, but I didn't tell them a thing, since I couldn't trust anyone, including the doctors. After that I was released and sent home to Germany accompanied by a soldier. Back home my condition got worse, to the point that I could hardly walk without someone to accompany me, since I was suffering from the enormous weight of the events I had experienced. After some time, I was reproached by the local section of the Party for not having ~as they saw it) a National Socialist outlook on things. My general outlook was more religious in orientation than anything else. When I subsequently wanted to talk about my experiences, I had to be so careful and cautious (pretending as if I thought this and not that) that I became very sick and Dr. D. considered it advisable for me to be placed in an institution. I was afraid they were going to get rid of me there. Shortly after this, I had to enter City Hospital for observation. It was there that I revealed all my suffering to Dr. L. and explained everything to him. Dr. L. did not belong to the Party. He understood me completely and advised me to try to forget things—something that was, and is, impossible.

On April 14, 1945, I was suddenly approached by a man in the street, who came up to me and said, "We know who you are. You've been undermining the work of the Party now for some time. You're a dirty saboteur and that's going to cost you your life!" I didn't know what was happening. What had I done? I took a few steps and must have collapsed on the spot. Witnesses say I was going on about "common murderers, brown bandits, and shootings of Jews." People thought I was insane. I remained in this condition for several days. I had, in any case, been sick and unable to work since December 17, 1944, but now I was completely finished. Dr. G. and Dr. S. were at my bedside. When I regained my senses a bit, I asked myself, "What have I done!"

I had confided in several families and told them about this crime in Russia. Whether they remained silent I don't know. In addition, I had also not given away the presence of a man who had been living away from his unit for a year and a half, about whom I was often questioned. I covered for him whenever I could. I couldn't allow him—someone who quite early on had seen through all the lies—to fall into the hands of that pack, who wanted to build a so-called "workers' paradise" on the blood and bones of the dead.

I can't understand that there are those who wish to kill me because of this, since anyone who has a fairly just view of things must admit that if we had won the war, then there couldn't be a just God in heaven, one who could give his blessing to such bloody deeds.

On May 3 or 4 when he visited me I told Dr. S. about everything, particularly about Russia. And I can say that he cried bitterly and was ashamed of his . . . [document illegible]. When I asked him, "Can God . . ." [document illegible], he replied resolutely and with determination: "Never!"

I doubted God in Parafianovo, but ask him today for forgiveness. He was not on the side of those who perpetrated such injustices, and he expiated those bloody deeds.

R: So that is the end of the letter. That was the experience. And let me tell you that this man suffered right up until the end, until he died, and if you want to know when that was, I can tell you. He's been dead now some eight years. He wasn't able . . . and was given early retirement. He was a bit absentminded. But you must understand: the thing that shaped and molded me, what influenced me, was that I was unable to comprehend what my father was talking about. I had been so fanatic about this idea of National Socialism . . . But when he returned from Poland and told me these things—I was able to understand various things by this time—I was unable to go on believing in it. A cause I was ready to sacrifice my life for—these people had done such a thing? First I accused him of being a deserter! I did not believe his story, I could not believe it. [Agitated] So then I was bothered by doubts. What should I do? I was a leader in the Hitler Youth, but what should I do? I lived in a constant state of inner tension. I didn't know what I should do. Though I must say that in the course of time, that feeling disappeared, it dissipated. My father spoke less and less about it, he withdrew more and more into himself. More and more, the only person he spoke to was my mother. He turned away from me, because I was unwilling to take off that uniform. He turned away from me, and I could see that he was extremely ill, seriously so, because of it. Yet I couldn't follow in his direction. But then there was an experience that actually opened up once again the wound he caused in me by what he'd said.

B: What was that?

R: Well, it was in '43 or '44 I think. They showed the movie Jud Suss. It was a film against the Jews, but I didn't recognize it as an inflammatory film. For me it was a simple fact: that's how Jews are. The film portrayed them as the dregs of humanity. So there was this contradiction in my mind. There was "Jud Suss," this carefully polished character in this horror film—that's the expression you could use today— which destroyed young people spiritually and prepared them to . . . something they could never vindicate: to pass judgment on a people I had never experienced directly or seen. [Gets up and walks around restlessly] OK, I had seen some Jews with yellow stars. For me they were just people wearing a yellow star—the Poles had a P and the Ukrainians a U—for me these were second-class people. And I used to hear remarks, during those years you could hear again and again shouts of "Jew! " "Lousy Jew! " "Criminals! " "Vultures! " "Bloodsuckers! " Or "TheJews are responsible for the war!" The Jews were guilty of everything. There was nothing the Jews weren't responsible for. Then this film Jud Suss was made.

Appendix to the Dokshitz Parafianov Yizkor Book
Material Not in the Original Yizkor Book

I forgot one thing: Kristallnacht in 1938. I hadn't been a witness to that. I didn't see what happened, I only heard about it. I heard them talking about a shoe store, a Jewish shoe store—I think it was called Rosenthal's—and that it had been smashed and shoes were lying all over the street. They carried out a child wrapped in a lamp shade. Everything was gone, the Jews were gone. But those events occurred on the periphery of things as far as I was concerned. At that time, for me the Jew was someone so small and inconsequential . . . They weren't an independent people, didn't have an independent state. Jews were nothing, just nothing.

Once my father came to me and said, "Rudolf, Rudolf, listen." He noticed that we were drifting farther and farther apart. I was also aware that we were growing more and more distant. Then he said, "Rudolf, we have to sit down and have a serious talk." That was during the war, but at times he had very clear, sane moments (lichte Momente). "We've talked so often about the Bible. You've read the Bible yourself, and I've read both the Old and New Testaments. You know that the Jewish people are in fact a people in their own right, God's chosen people. It is so and will remain that way. You can't, we can't deny that. No matter how many Christians curse them, the Jews are the chosen people. The Jew is the hand on the clock of history: whatever happens to him, from that you can read the course of history and time. Just remember one thing: if you lift a finger against the Jews, you can cut off that finger because you are going to lose it! Never attack a Jew. Be careful, cautious, and have respect for the Jews." Then he told me a few more things from Jewish history, from the Old Testament. After that I was filled with a sense of fear. He said to me, "Do you believe in Jesus?" I said, "Yes, Dad, I do believe in Jesus Christ." "But you know who he was, don't you?" and I said, "Yes, he was a Jew, right?" "OK, so do you believe in Jews now?" and I said, "Yes, Dad, I do. I'm sorry." And then I started to cry. I cried a lot. I was so sorry that I had been so blinded by this idea, that I had been led astray, led astray again and again. But even what my father said to me—said to me in tears, and I noticed that he was sick—even what he said to me I didn't believe, so profound was the influence of the National Socialists, of their propaganda.

A long pause. Rudolf sits down and wipes his forehead with a handkerchief.

And then I was apprenticed in 1944, I got an apprenticeship in the railroad, the Reichsbahn. I wanted to be a locomotive engineer and in '44, I was sent as an apprentice to a plant where locomotives were repaired. This plant had its own fire brigade, since such plants were often attacked and bombed during the war. Now because I was the only one who had been in a leadership position in the youth movement—I was the only Hitler Youth leader among the sixty apprenticed trainees—I was given the job of getting them to assemble in formation in the early morning; I had leadership status once again. I also had to join the fire brigade at the same time and went out with this brigade a few times after heavy air raids.

I was involved during the last big raid—it was the end of '44 or the beginning of '45, I can't remember. There was a raid and we were called out to see what we could save. The buildings were on fire. And then I saw something. As a young man, I was a runner, a messenger— we didn't have any radio equipment. I had to supervise the inspection of hoses, make sure the hoses were laid properly and weren't leaking. And I noticed that under a hose lying on top of some debris, there was something dark red, shining there underneath. I said, "Mr. B."— he was the chief at that time—"Mr. B., there's something over there!" He had the debris cleared away and I could see a woman lying there. She had run downstairs and out the front door, and a bomb had exploded right in front of her. Shrapnel and a lot of debris went flying, and this woman was killed. They lifted her out, and then I felt sick: her lower body was ripped open, and everything inside came tumbling out. Now I had seen a great many dead people those months but this was the worst thing I'd witnessed. I started to feel sick, and Mr. B. said to me, "OK, go on home."

Well, that was the end of my activity in the fire brigade. That was shortly before the end of the war. What I did after that was . . . But I was no longer filled with such conviction. Now I understood what my father had told me at the end: you can't justify and accept it.

During the last half hour, Rudoy has been very agitated, and I actually start to worry. But he wants to go on, as if a hidden volcano has finally erupted.

R: Though I must admit that I felt split and divided. After the Americans marched in, people said, "Now the Hitler Youth is finished." I felt a certain sadness, not because of the fact that the Hitler Youth was done for, but because I was no longer able to meet all my friends. That camaraderie was something I missed.

Those were actually the main experiences. I wanted to tell you that, well, that a family can be destroyed during a war by these things. My father passed away, but before he died, he lived in a kind of twilight, a constant twilight, psychological and mental. He would only work with clay. He used to have this clay brought in and . . . Now I want to mention something that once again concerns those two religions, where you can see the schizophrenia . . . He had a board, and on this board he fashioned and shaped mountains and small hills covered with trees. Down below, at the foot, he made a creche with Jesus lying there inside, and there was a path that led up to a synagogue above. So he wanted to make this connection (in his unconscious) between Christianity and the Jews. He was unable to cope with the notion that a Christian had been able to do such things against a Jew. In his state of mental twilight, he wanted to restore this connection. And he died with that. He didn't die as a Christian or as a Jew: he was something in between.

In front of me I see the son of an exceptional father, the only person I've heard of who lost his mind because he could not go on living a normal life after he witnessed the massacre of Jews. I hug Rudolf and thank him for talking with me. As we walk out, he says that he has never told anyone about it before, but when he saw the ad in the newspaper, he knew the time had come to bring his father's letter out into the open, to tell his father's story—which is now his own.

We arrange to meet again a few days later. Rudolf arrives with two heavy folders in which he has carefully collected the songs from his days in the Hitler Youth. He looks more relaxed, ready to go on.

R: I had certain other experiences in the Hitler Youth that were especially memorable and important for me—for example, when I was promoted. Those were moments when my soul was lifted up again. They'd make a campfire in the evening, although it was prohibited on account of the air raids, but they would let us know: OK, no enemy aircraft in sight. Promotions were usually announced on Hitler's birthday, April 20, and on November 9 [November 9 marked the anniversary of the failed 1923 Munich Putsch; it was a sacred day on the National Socialist calendar]..... It was all done in a very military atmosphere, with torches and songs . . . [Singing] "Holy Fatherland in danger, your sons gather in around you . . ." And this was sung in a minor key, which makes you feel a bit melancholy, and it would rouse our spirits. Then they would announce the promotion: Comrade so-and-so is now promoted to the rank of squad leader, effective as of such-and-such a date. They would pin on the special ribbon, and you'd go home through the streets swelling with pride. You already felt like a young representative of National Socialism.

Later on—I have to say, not at that time but later on—I had this thought: What would have happened if my generation had been sent to carry out these murderous acts? OK, people were killed during air raids, but we never killed, we didn't get that far, thank God. But just imagine, what if this generation, which had been psychologically trained and geared up for it, what if this generation had been let loose on mankind? Then what occurred with the Jews, why it would pale in comparison—it would have been nothing. So that's what I have to tell you: we would have been worse. We could have done it without any doubts whatsoever. [Agitated] We were trained to hate from a very early age.

B: Did you have any friends at school who were Jewish, or were there any Jews in your school?

R: No, no, none. Wait a second, there was one: she was half-Jewish. I started school in 1936, and there was a girl—we didn't know this at first—who was half-Jewish. She told me after the war that they had— I was no longer at that school then—that the other children had stripped her naked in the street, because they heard she was halfJewish. Even young children had been indoctrinated to the point where they could pull the clothes off a classmate and shout, "Jew! Jew! Jew!" She told me this after the war. She still lives here. She's married to an Englishman. She said she wouldn't want to marry a German.

And there was something here in town, not very long ago, at the zoo. I don't know whether you heard about it. There's a large hall at the zoo where meetings are held, and it was hired out by the police. The police had a celebration there, and a police officer, who was functioning as a kind of master of ceremonies, said, "What do you answer to'Sieg'?" And a few young men shouted, "'Heil'! " That was the salute the Nazis used to use. The policeman really didn't mean any harm by it, I know that. They had all been drinking a little . . . But this Jewish woman was there and she filed a complaint against the policeman. He was temporarily suspended from service, and then there was some sort of punishment. I don't know exactly how it turned out. Anyhow, it was in the paper. She was a classmate of mine. Her brother and father—or her brother and mother, one of them died before that - were murdered in the camps. Aside from that, I had no otherJewish classmates. There weren't any left. It is astonishing, but I didn't actually have any direct experience of Jews being sent to concentration camps. I didn't know about it. I only knew that Jews had to wear a yellow star—I knew that later on—a yellow star. They were marked and singled out so that you could recognize them as Jews. Though I must emphasize again and again, it was also true for the Poles, the Ukrainians . . . it wasn't anything . . .

B: After your father told you his story, did you ever discuss it with friends?

R: I wasn't able to discuss it with my friends. That would have endangered my father.

B: What happened between you and your friends after your father came back?

R: Actually, there was no break, no rupture between me and my friends. I think you have to view it in this way: the overriding, all embracing concept was the Hitler Youth. National Socialism was a phenomenon that accompanied this organization. Only in a subconscious way was all this hammered into us: National Socialism and Adolf Hitler. Basically, in terms of our behavior, we remained young children, only that, via our subconscious, they attempted to prepare us for the later phase. After all, we were still immature, still under the age of eighteen. You couldn't get rid of our childlike character. That was something that remained.

Maybe I should tell you about one more experience. I told you that I was a trainee with the Reichsbahn, and that I was a youth leader there. I wasn't all that good as a student, and I wasn't the best among the apprentices, but I was the leader. So we young guys—you can see from this just how young we still were—we got up on a hill during recess and started throwing stones, as boys sometimes like to do, a kind of game. There were two sides, two groups, and we were throwing stones at each other. The winner was supposed to get a bottle of soda water or something. So I heaved a heavy stone and hit a boy right in the stomach. He got really angry, and he shouted, "You goddamn Nazi pig!" And that was during the war! I ran over to him and said, "What did you say?" "You goddamn Nazi pig!" Whammo, I gave him a left and right to the nose, and he dropped to the ground. Then I told him, "Just you wait. I won't forget this." I told this kid, "You watch out!" Now what comes is like the seed that has been sown in a child and begins sprouting unconsciously . . . [Stands up and walks around the room waving his arms] I threw a stone at him and hurt him, he felt pain and shouted at me' "You Nazi pig!" His father had been in a concentration camp as a Communist, and he always stressed the fact that he wasn't a Nazi. He said this spontaneously, even though the Nazis were in power. And I told him, "Just you wait, I won't forget this!" Now that tiny seed began to sprout. It was still very small. But if it had grown, I probably would have turned out to be one of those who could have killed someone for saying such a thing . . .

[Sits down again, trying to calm himself] I recall that when I was a leader in the Hitler Youth, I . . . in Germany we have people who, as you would say in slang, are "brown noses," people who want to make trouble. Well, I loved to go around dressed in my uniform. I even went to school in uniform, to work—I was very proud. And at that time Russian civilian laborers weren't allowed to drink any alcohol. Then an incident occurred that I have to tell you about. There was this Russian civilian laborer. I was out with a lot of boys, and this drunken Russian laborer came along. I asked him, "Where are you coming from?" Me, just a child. And he stammered something in his drunken stupor. I said, "Do you want to have a fight?" He said, "Yeah." So I slugged him. He smashed his face into the big window of a grocery store. There was a pointed grille covering it, and his whole face was cut and scratched. No one did anything to me, though. After all, they couldn't hit me. If anyone had done such a thing to me while I was wearing that uniform, he'd have ended up in a concentration camp. Terrible, right? Anyhow, my father found out about this incident and he gave me the worst spanking I ever had. He really walloped me! It was the right punishment. But, as I said before, the small seed had started to germinate, to grow and sprout: "I won't forget that, you'll see!" "You Russian, listen, you're not worth a damn thing! I can do something to you, even though I'm much smaller, and you can't defend yourself, you can't do anything!"

Appendix to the Dokshitz Parafianov Yizkor Book
Material Not in the Original Yizkor Book

Rudolf is in a kind of trance. He is staring at the ceiling, trying to bring out the memories that have plagued his conscience all these years. I listen carefully, wishing I had a camera tofilm this interview. The stories continue to pour forth, however disjointedly, one after another.

R: Then there was this Frenchman ... My uncle lived between Brandenburg and Berlin, and he had a fruit farm—he made a living growing strawberries, apples, and tomatoes—and a Russian, a Pole, a Serb, a Frenchman . . . these were the people who had to work for him. Early in the morning there was the "funeral procession." That's what we called it. There was this old German soldier who could hardly stand on his legs, and he led the French POWs off to the various fruit farms. And when they would pass a farm where one of them worked, he'd leave the group and go on in. They walked very slowly, took a lot of time, this German soldier and that French POW. Once I spoke with the Frenchman, whose German was rather good. I was actually quite surprised that I didn't react differently. We were sitting together between the rows of strawberries, and he told me something about his attitude toward the German people and National Socialism. I let him talk and didn't react at all, although I was very bothered by what that Frenchman was saying. He said, "Pay attention to your own history, the history of Germany. Don't always go on carping about the Jews, the French (because the French had been our archenemies). Just take a long, sober look at your own history, without rose-colored glasses. Take your history as it really is, what really happened, and then form an opinion. How much hatred do you Germans have in yourselves? How far do you expect to go with it? How many more do you plan to exterminate in the name of this hatred?"

So, as you can see, that idea stayed with me, what he said, though I myself was deeply indoctrinated. OK, if you place all these little piles of impressions one next to the other, you can understand my reaction—the way I experienced it later on, the way I reacted to myself. I almost felt like Judas in the Bible, that disciple who committed suicide. Yes, well, more than that I ... I have such a modest heart, wouldn't harm a fly . . . But they had swelled up my heart. They were able to deform a person's heart.

Then the war ended. If it hadn't ended, I don't know, I'm not sure I would have forgotten all that. I mean, it's especially easy to manipulate children at that age, and where you can get at the children, that's where—at least this is what I think—that's the history of the people. If you can drill the notion into their heads: you are from a tribe, a race that is especially valuable. And then you tell them something about the Germanic tribes, their loyalty, their battles, how Germanic women let themselves be hitched up to carts to fight against the Romans. You, you're a child of this race, a people that dealt the Romans a destructive blow in the year 9 A.D., all that sort of thing. Then there were the songs. I'm especially affected by songs. When they would sing those songs glorifying the deeds of the Germanic tribes, such as [singing] "The sons of the people ride on silvery stallions, born from a divine multitude, warrior of the Nordic people, they ride in silence to the far fields of the northern lights, on secret paths they greet elves at the shore of the pounding sea." Or "Holy Fatherland, your sons crowd in around you." How does it go on? "What we swear is written in the stars, he who directs the stars will hear our voice . . . before the foreigner robs you of your crown, O Germany, we would prefer to fall side by side." Or "The flag is dearer than death." Death was nothing. The flag, the people—they were everything. You are nothing, your people everything. Yes, that's how children were brought up, that's how you can manipulate a child . . .

He is singing, talking, and crying, shifting back and forth between one memory and another.

We meet again a year later. Rudolf is willing to be interviewed on videotape: he will do it for me, for the research, for humanity. When he reads his father's letter during the filming at the studio, he cries again, and this time too, he does not seem able to find his handkerchief.

We walk out together when the taping session is over, and I thank him for coming. He tells me that his own children did not want him to come. They do not want to have anything to do with this chapter of the family's past. Their motto is "past is past." They want a life of their own. Outside the studio, we shake hands warmly, and Rudolf walks slowly away into the darkness. I suddenly realize how lonely he must be, carrying his father's letter: *"Our Guilt."*

Postscript

After reading this poignant chapter in Dr. Bar-On's book about the town from which my paternal grandparents had emigrated, I wrote to Dr. Bar-On, asking for the address and name of "Rudolph" (not his real name), so I could contact him.

I wrote a letter to "Rudolph" explaining my interest in this whole affair. He answered me in German, which a dear friend translated for me. In his letter, he was warm and welcoming and even invited me to visit him in his home.

Unfortunately, it took me several years to find my way to Germany at which time I attended the inaugural of the "Memorial to the Murdered Jews of Europe" in Berlin in May 2005. I wrote to Dr. Bar-On, because I had misplaced "Rudolph's" address, so I could finally meet him. Dr. Bar-On's response was that "Rudolph" had just passed away due to cancer a couple of months before. We have since learned that Professor Bar-On died on September 4, 2008.

Joel Alpert, Coordinator of the Yizkor-Books-in-Print Project
September 11, 2015

Appendix to the Dokshitz Parafianov Yizkor Book
Material Not in the Original Yizkor Book

Testimony from Trials by the Russian Government of the Nazi Murderers and their Belorussian Accomplices

Mass shooting of innocent old people, women, children, burning them alive and enslaving Soviet citizens in Germany was conducted under the order of German authorities by officers, soldiers of the Nazi troops, c.q.:

1. Ebeling, Deputy Gobietscommisor
2. Kaz, Comandant of "Ghetto"
3. Benz, Head of Parfianovo station of Belostok Rail Roads
4. Claus, Captain, Oriscommandant of the town of Dokshitsky;
5. Ungerman, Administrative officer, etc.
6. Gartman, Administrative officer, etc.

These people committed atrocities unseen in the history of mankind

Below are excerpts from eye witnesses' evidences:

1. Kramer, Shaya Kusclevich, born 1909, resident of the town of Parfianovo
2. Levitan, Gendel Aronovich, born 1925, resident of the town of Parfianovo testified:

On May 30, 1942 Nazi gendarmery has come from the city of Glubokoe to Parfianovo railway station. Early in the morning led by deputy Gebietcommisar Ebeling, gendarmery herded the Jews living in Parfianovo into "Ghetto". Men, old men, women and little children were put all together in the building of the club-house, remodeled for accommodating POW. After that, instructed by Gebietcommissar Ebeling and commandant Benz, Nazi gendarmes started to take people out in small groups of five. Every one was stripped naked and beaten up by rubber clubs and butts. When I (Levitan) was taken outside, I saw puddles of blood and was also beaten up by a rubber club until I lost consciousness. Continuing the atrocities in the club-house, all

Appendix to the Dokshitz Parafianov Yizkor Book
Material Not in the Original Yizkor Book

Jews were drawn up, including old people and children, and were led to the shooting site, on the territory of Parfianovo station. On the site where mass shooting was supposed to take place, a hole had already been dug out. Gendarmery forced people to come up to the hole and machine gun shooting began. People started to scatter around the place. After herding people up again, Nazi beat several old people, women and children with rubber clubs and pushed them in to the hole alive. Seeing such atrocities with my own eyes, I rushed for safety. When the machine gun opened fire, I pretended to be shot dead and fell into the ditch and stayed there up until night fell. I could see all the atrocities on that day. A lot of old people, women and children were shot. In July 1942, Nazi gendarmes caught 2 Jews. Their names were:

1. Levitan, Shlyoma
2. Gilbert, Rubin

They were beaten up with rubber clubs, stripped to the underwear and hanged on the telegraph poles along the road from Parfianovo to the village of Veren'ki.

Most active in shootings were Ebeling, Benz, Giko, Foreman of the Parfianovo station, as well as many others, whose names I don't know.

3. Kuchko Zahariy Yakovlevich, born 1880, resident of the village of Osovo of the Yankovsky region testified:

In January 1943 instructed by Nazi commandant gendarmes and soldiers came to the village of Osovo, burnt down houses, arrested villagers. They also burnt alive the Kovels family: Peter, Elena Mikhailovna and Semyon, their son born 1936. All in all, five people were burnt in that house. After that, there were mass shootings. Twelve villagers were shot with rifles and Tommy guns. I saw the bodies. Another eye-witness of shootings was Vasily Aldorovich Parliyanovich, resident of the village of Osovo. He saw the Zan'ko's family shooting. They were beaten by butts, Nazis wanted to take Maxim Zanko to the city of Dokshitsy and shoot him there but he refused to go anywhere and was shot outside of his house in the village of Osovo. Maxim's mother popped out of the house crying " You shot my son, shoot me". The entire Zanko's family was shot right on the street.

4. Andrievsky Viktor Mikhailovich, born 1894, resident of the villageof Maslovichi of the Porplischensky region.

5. Voitehovich Bellya Gippolitovna, resident of the village of Telshi of Porplishcensky region. Two eye witnesses testified:

Living two hundred meters away from the Dokshitsy-Glubokoe road, we saw with our own eyes in July 1943 the Nazi herding Russian POW's along that road. Every POW, who could not march further, as they were all exhausted, was shot. So over three days of July Nazi shot 11 POW. We don't know their names, as there were no ID's with the bodies.

5. Anoshkovich Vasily Ivanovich, born 1880, resident of the village of Vorgany of the Brabuchensky region testified:

In May 1942 Nazi detachment came to our village and herded for hard labor in Germany the following citizens:

1. Vargan Semyon Antonovich

2. Vargan Elena Semyonova

3. Zhilyonok Yakim Ivanovich

4. Apanashkevich Ivan Ivanovich

5. Apanashkevich Nikolai Konstantinovich

6. Vargan Igantiy Ivanovich

7. Kahanovich Ivan A lexandrovich

8. Voitehoivh Pavlina Andreevna

9. Shitel Alexander Konstantinovich

10. Vargan Konstantine Nikolaevich

11. Kahanovich Maria Ivanovna

12. Malinovskaya Emilia Stanisslavovna, etc.

SS Detachment encircled our village, herded villagers to the central place in our village, selected above citizens and forced them to go for hard (slave) labor in Germany.

7. Stadolink Polikarp Ivanovich, born 1891, resident of the village of Makarevichi of the Grabuchensky district, testified:

Nazi detachment came to our village on February 15, 1944 and shot my wife on the street (Stadolnik Maria Emundovna) next to the barn and shot my son (Stadolnik Boleslav Polikarovich), born 1927 who was in bed ill. Also, in our village were shot:

1. Dolchenok Petr Ivanovich;
2. Gritsevich Iosif Marianovich;
3. Skurat Stefanida;
4. Polyanina alexander Vasilievich.

All villagers were herded onto the central square and the above people were shot before the eyes of all people. I also was there and saw the shooting. The Nazis did not allow us to bury them. Our villagers could bury them only 10 days after the shooting, when the Nazi moved out of our village.

8. Sivko Ivan Frolovich, born 1898, resident in the village of Gnezdilovo of Gnezdilovsky district testified:

In October 1943, a group of Nazi of approximately 85 people came to the village of Gnezdilovo and put it on fire. The Nazi burnt many people alive in their own houses.:

1. Kolyago Vasily Stepanovich
2. Kolyago Anton Ivanovich both tried to escaoe through the window but were shot. The Nazi also burnt a little girl Kovel Elena, born 1943.

In addition, Nazi shot three imprisoned soldiers of the Red Army at a distance of approximately one kilometer from th e village of Gnezdilovo was caught by Nazi and was shot on the cemetery of the village of Yuzhnoc Gvazdilovo.

9. Kurilyonok Anna Petrovna, born 1922, resident of the village of Ryzhovka of Porplischensky district:

10. Pashkevich Adelya Ignatievna, born 1916 resident in the village of Degtiary of Porplischensky

11. Stepanets Semyon Mikhailovich, born 1916, resident in the village of Sloboda of Porplischensky district.

All the threee testified: we live not far from the road to the village of Sitsy, next to the forest. We saw Soviet men, women, and children being herded, as well as Italian POW's, walking along the road from Parfianovo to Dyatki. The column was stopped and turned left, i.e. to the road to the village of Sitsy. Soon after that we could hear gun (machine-gun) fire. Soviet citizens and Italian POW's were shot. Same shooting recurred more than once over two days. IN the first day after the the arrival of the Red Army in our district. I went to the forest and saw 5 big holes camoflauged with green turf and green tree branches. On one of the trees under the bark I found a note, which read in Russian "We were executed by Nazi butcher: Russians-600 person, Italians-200 persons. Take vengeance Nazi butchers for our blood, for women and children shot by Nazi."

12. Ozenblovsky Andrei Ivanovich, born 1909 resident of the city of Dokshitsy testified:

In March 1942 under the instruction of Glubokoe Gebietcommissar, there were started arrests of Jews living on the territory of the city of Dokshitsy. The Jews were herded in "Ghetto" and mass shootings of women with babies, old and young people began. I saw it with my own eyes. Jews in groups of 100-150 people were led to the hole, which was dug next to the Jewish cemetery in the city of Dokshitsy, they were forced to undress and the shot. Babies and little children were not shot, rather they were stabbed with bayonets or thrown alive down into the hole. One could hear moans of the wounded and cries of children. Over three weeks of mass shootings the Nazi killed about three thousand Jews. On the same day, the Nazis executed almost 100 active Soviet workers.

Appendix to the Dokshitz Parafianov Yizkor Book
Material Not in the Original Yizkor Book

In addition to mass shootings, Nazi shot daily 1-2 unknown people in the vicinity of Dokshitsy brewery. Rumors go that there are about three hundred people were shot. Also, Nazi herded many residents of Dokshitsy to Germany for slave labor.

13. Podberesskin Mikhail Filippovich, born 1880, resident of the village of Rechnye of the Nesterovsky District, testified:

In February 1943, I saw the following residents of out village killed:

1. Anikovich E.T.
2. Pet'ko E.I.
3. Shul'gat S.T.
4. Gnyran M.S.
5. Podberesskiy S.F.
6. Podberessky V.T.
7. Vasilevich M.A. and some others.

In total 23 residents of the village of Rechnye were killed, 10 of them were burnt

1. Kazachyonok T.D. with his family
2. Kazachyonok wife
3. Kazachyonok 7-year-old daughter
4. Kazachyonok daughter, born 1942
5. Kazachyonok daughter, born 1943

Material supplied by Sam Gejdenson (7/14/99)

418   Appendix to the Dokshitz Parafianov Yizkor Book
Material Not in the Original Yizkor Book

Photographs of Martyrs of Dokshitz

Photographs and identification provided by Juljia and Shlomo Gejdenson

Zalman Gejdenson, brother to Shlomo - Murdered in 1943 at age 20, two days before the end of the war. He had hidden in woods.

Appendix to the Dokshitz Parafianov Yizkor Book
Material Not in the Original Yizkor Book

First from the left: Zalman Gejdenson. Murdered in 1943, age 20 by German Nazi bandits. All of his other friends pictured here were murdered in 1942.

Youfa Palinska helped the Gejdenson brothers for 12 months. Youfa Palinska with her daughters Helena, Ludka, Michalive, Fadzia.

Maria Stankieicz (91 years old). Helped the Gejdenson brothers for 12 months. Maria is with her daughter Broma Korcyn. They live in Dokszyc (Dokshitz).

Esther Gejdenson - murdered in May 1942 with her husband Rabbi Samuel Gejdenson and their daughter Sonia Gejdenson in Parafianov, near Dokshitz.

They were the parents of Shlomo Gejdenson.

Sonia Gejdenson in the middle and her friends were murdered by the German Nazis and their helpers in 1942. She was 22 years old. She was the sister of Shlomo Gejdenson.

Appendix to the Dokshitz Parafianov Yizkor Book
Material Not in the Original Yizkor Book

Sonia Gejdenson was killed in 1942 at age 22 by the German Nazis.

Shlomo Gejdenson's Grandfather

INDEX of the Translation Only

A

Abel, 129
Abelson, 134, 239
Aharon, 6
Akselrod, 228
Alchziov, 157
Aloy, 225, 233
Alperovitch, 234
Alperovitz, 240, 241
As, 148
Avrom-Moyshe the sexton, 81

B

Baden Powell, 66
Bar-Massada, 51
Barshai, 234
Bassuk, 183
Ben-Moshe, 44
Berkeh, 37
Berzon, 246
Bialik, 8
Bielinki, 238
Bigun, 148
Bilinki, 228
Bilsky, 241
Biyelinki, 56
Bland, 183
Blank, 189
Blinshtein, 234
Bloch, 101, 102, 103, 104, 159, 161, 192, 234
Blokh, 105, 109, 110, 152
Borisovitch, 208, 209
Borochov, 46
Botvinik, 152, 231
Boxer, 234
Brener, 202
Brodsky, 42
Brown, 183
Budnov, 231
Bunimovitch, 236
Butwinik, 163, 164, 165, 166, 168, 206

C

Chuchman, 58
Cyrlin, 230
Czar Nicholas, 114

D

Dameskin, 230
Deetz, 239
Deitz, 228, 234
Dergatchow, 170, 171
Dikman, 231
Dimenovsky, 159
Dimenstein, 226
Disha, 9, 11
Dlugan, 231
Dobeh-Musyeh, 37
Dole, 233
Doroschenko, 181
Dovong, 231
Drutz, 233, 246
Dubin, 176
Dvorkin, 238
Dvorkind, 246

E

Epstein, 241
Erke the blacksmith, 8

F

Fabrikant, 228
Faibush, 8
Feigel, 230, 233, 234, 235
Feigelson, 226, 233, 240, 242
Feiman, 233
Feinbloom, 237
Feinman, 233
Feldman, 234, 240
Feygin, 152
Finkelman, 182
Finster, 168
Fishkeh the barber, 81
Fogelman, 97
Foss, 140
Frankfort, 122
Frankfurt, 121, 231, 246
Freedman, 159, 211, 212
Freidman, 166
Freiman, 56, 161, 163, 233
Friedman, 56, 117, 161, 169, 173, 174, 175, 177, 181, 182, 196, 205, 220, 225, 226, 228, 230, 231, 233, 234, 236, 237, 238, 246

G

Galperin, 228
Gejdenson, 141
Getzenson, 240
Gheler, 185
Ghitleson, 185
Gilenson, 55, 56, 84, 228
Gilevitch, 228
Gilinki, 228
Ginsburg, 21, 111
Ginzburg, 240
Gitlin, 166, 225, 226
Glazer, 164, 169, 173, 175, 182, 228, 231, 234, 244, 246
Gleichenhaus, 225, 231
Gleichenhous, 160, 167
Glekhengoz, 71
Gleykhenhoz, 82
Glinkin, 15
Golkowitz, 167
Golts, 56
Goltz, 84, 228
Gordon, 51, 56, 60, 81, 126, 153, 174, 231, 234, 240
Grabsky, 42
Greenhouse, 243
Grinboym, 84
Gronam, 159
Grozbin, 240
Gulkovitsh, 120, 237
Gulkovitz, 225
Gurewitch, 176
Gurvitz, 243
Gurwitch, 166
Gutkin, 237

H

Halbanowitz, 132
Harnas, 225
Hartman, 159, 160, 164, 165
Hauchman, 237
Havel, 189
Hidekel, 226
Hochman, 244, 246
Holtz, 167
Horovitz, 237
Huberman, 234, 237, 246

I

Isakson, 182
Itshe, a son of the bath-keeper, 62

J

Juttkovsky, 167

K

Kabakov, 58, 60
Kabatznik, 226
Kagan, 155, 228, 234
Kaganier, 225
Kaladetzki, 241
Kaledetzki, 241
Kaliosov, 171
Kamaiko, 177
Kamankovitz, 46
Kamankowitz, 132
Kamenkovitz, 133
Kaminkovitch, 179, 228, 229, 246
Kaminkovitz, 48, 238, 242, 243
Kanareyke, 41
Kantorovitch, 234, 235, 246
Kantorovitsh, 62, 224
Kantrovitch, 169
Kapelovitsh, 74
Kaplan, 54, 86, 162, 201, 225, 226, 227, 229, 230, 233, 235, 238, 241
Karovitz, 216
Kasovski, 233
Kastrol, 148
Katsovitsh, 119, 120, 121
Katz, 225, 227, 233, 240, 241
Katzenelson, 183
Katzovich, 244
Katzovitch, 161, 184, 221, 229, 246
Katzovitsh, 113
Katzowich, 173, 247
Katzowitch, 220
Kazinitch, 163
Khasiye, 74, 75, 76
Khaya-Tsishe, 63
Khlabnovitch, 229, 233
Khoydesh, 82
Khyeneh-Soreh-Tzipeh, 37
King Zigmond, 5
Kiselgof, 241, 242
Kishka, 3, 5
Klatzkin, 241
Kleiner, 133
Kleynboym, 84
Kloft, 159
Kloner, 132
Klonski, 225
Kluft, 227, 229, 235, 239, 244
Komankowitz, 132
Komolka, 159, 162, 165, 203
Komulka, 127, 151, 160, 165, 166, 167, 212
Kooperstock, 241
Kopelevitch, 238
Kopelewitz, 64
Kopelovich, 169
Kopelovitch, 124, 173, 228, 229, 230, 231, 235, 246

Kopelowitz, 124, 125
Kopilovitch, 182
Koplovitch, 167
Korbman, 243
Kosovski, 229
Kosovsky, 156
Kosowsky, 156
Koton, 182
Kovalsky, 159
Kozinitch, 182
Kozinitz, 157, 220
Kozshinitz, 225, 227, 229, 231, 233, 235, 239, 246
Kozshiniyetz, 56
Kramer, 159, 179, 208, 209
Kremer, 154, 225, 227, 229, 231, 233, 235, 236, 239, 243, 244, 246
Kugel, 56, 84, 229, 235, 237, 240
Kuggel, 125, 128
Kuladitzki, 144
Kurokin, 77
Kuzinitz, 128

L

Lahotshin, 227
Lederman, 174, 175, 182, 186, 189
Ledermans, 174
Lenkin, 136, 228, 235, 244
Levin, 164, 228, 229, 233, 239, 241, 246
Levit, 229
Levitan, 52, 87, 96, 133, 139, 141, 142, 147, 148, 152, 159, 225, 227, 229, 231, 232, 235, 238, 239, 240
Libeh-Frumeh, 62
Lieberman, 241
Lifshitz, 125, 156, 214, 235, 239
Lipkind, 163, 165, 229, 232, 235
Lipshitz, 155, 214
Litvin, 159
Lochovski, 195
Lukhovski, 116
Lulinski, 21, 111

M

Madeyski, 82
Malishevski, 5
Malka, 11
Malnikov, 157
Margolin, 183, 227, 243
Markman, 21, 26, 69, 71, 72, 83, 97, 101, 103, 110, 111, 112, 132, 135, 140, 143, 144, 151, 159, 163, 165, 167, 217, 229, 232, 233, 235, 237, 238, 239, 240, 241
Markov, 171, 198
Marks, 46
Marx, 8, 81
Meltzer, 239, 240
Melzer, 128

Mendalei, 8
Mendl, 74, 80
Mikulsky, 35
Milchman, 182
Mindlin, 235
Mintz, 235
Mirkens, 158
Mirska, 183
Molinovsky, 116
Moniya the barber-surgeon, 74
Monya the barber-surgeon, 40
Mopassant, 8
Mordkhe, 77
Motles, 77
Moyshe the bookbinder, 84
Munitz, 239
Mushin, 151
Musin, 136, 159, 231

N

Nachman, 235
Nicholas the Second, 36
Nielevitsky, 112
Nievinski, 237

O

Ostrogski, 5

P

Patzvitch, 181, 182
Perelmuter, 231
Peretz, 8
Perlmuter, 229
Pintzi, 89
Piravoskin, 238
Plavnik, 120, 121, 166, 169, 227, 244
Pliskin, 152, 227
Poliak, 125, 235, 236, 246
Polik, 175, 176, 178, 243
Pollack, 111, 137
Pollak, 229
Polotnikov, 91
Pren, 204, 209
Presman, 53, 54
Price, 232
Pristorova, 42
Proshinski, 59, 60

R

Rabbi Eliezer, 106
Rabbi Sheinin, 162
Rabbi Velvl, 71
Radoschkovitch, 169

Rafalson, 144
Raffelson, 241
Rapaport, 211
Raskin, 229, 230, 232
Raskind, 159, 238
Reb Alter the sexton, 113
Reb Berke Yoshe, 77
Reb Berkey Yoshe, 74
Reb Dovid Zisheh, 37
Reb Leyb, 113
Reb Lipeh, 37
Reb Mendl, 76
Reb Mendl the shoykhet, 76
Reb Sholem, 37
Reb Tzvi-Hersh, 38
Reb Tzvi-Hirsh, 36
Reb Velvl, 77
Reb Yakov- Yosheh, 37
Reb Yoel, 56
Reb Yoyel, 74, 75, 76
Rebe Yoyel, 74
Reimer, 231
Reitman, 166, 220
Ribshtein, 225
Rietman, 216
Ritman, 152
Roderman, 174
Rodyonov, 213
Rolan, 8
Rosenbaum, 238
Rothschild, 42
Rozin, 236
Rozov, 74, 75, 87, 94, 132, 220, 222, 225, 226, 230, 231, 232, 238, 240, 242, 243, 244
Rubashkin, 186
Rubin, 227, 233, 244
Ruderman, 211, 217
Rytman, 226, 232, 246

S

Sachartov, 230
Sagalchik, 170, 171, 172, 174, 176, 177, 179
Scheinman, 135, 205
Schultz, 137, 162
Segal, 228
Segalovitch, 230
Shainen, 205
Shapira, 123, 179
Shapiro, 128, 134, 149, 207, 220, 221, 224, 226, 230, 246
Sheiman, 232
Shcinin, 230
Shferber, 243
Shimon-Arye, 63
Shklenik, 212
Shkolnik, 227
Shleifer, 167, 236, 242
Sholem the bagel-baker, 62
Shosyeh-Khayeh, 37
Shoykhet, 222
Shtshaglov, 175
Shtshegolov, 176
Shultz, 7, 224, 232, 233, 236, 244
Shvartz, 212
Sigaltchik, 181, 199
Simchelevitch, 172
Skiben, 237
Skibin, 111, 112
Slavin, 227, 236
Smerkovitch, 232
Sokolov, 171
Solevei, 237, 246
Solovei, 230, 237
Solovey, 54, 87, 91, 132
Solovey-Zamiri, 124
Solovitchik, 181, 182
Sosinksy, 239
Sosinsky, 239
Sosman, 211
Sossman, 125, 127, 128, 161, 226, 245, 246
Spitchonk, 159
Srebrenik, 227
Stcheglow, 197
Stishe, 37
Stozki, 232
Strathoff, 159
Streichstein, 230
Strothoff, 167
Susman, 176
Sussman, 126, 216
Sverdlov, 236
Svidler, 230, 233, 236, 241
Swiedler, 169
Sztokfisz, 2

T

Taitz, 230
Tamarkin, 91
Taragonski, 195
Taragonsky, 159
Taytz, 84
Teitz, 237, 243
Tielz, 216
Tiles, 154, 226, 233, 245, 246
Tilis, 208, 209
Timchuk, 172
Timtchuk, 196
Toibes, 221
Tolstoy, 8
Tomarkin, 53, 54, 76, 77
Tonik, 176
Trus, 212
Tschuchman, 132

Tschuhman, 57
Tshorni, 212
Tsiklin, 134, 154
Tzaduk, 84, 85
Tzeitlin, 221, 226
Tzicklin, 159
Tziklin, 232, 236
Tzoduk, 79
Tzuchman, 232

U

Ulshvitz, 5
Ungerman, 159, 165

V

Vant, 222, 226, 230, 238, 245, 246
Varfman, 116, 152, 236, 237, 239, 241, 243, 246
Veisblatt, 240
Velble, 156
Velvl, 39
Vinboim, 128
Vlasov, 213
Volfovitch, 226
Volfson, 230
Vorkel, 236

W

Wallwel, 11
Wand, 157
Want, 160
Warfman, 156, 163, 164, 195
Weinstein, 230
Weinstien, 174
Winitch, 159
Witwitzki, 189
Witwizky, 165

Y

Ya'akov, 233
Yanovski, 236
Yashka, 169, 174
Yassin, 127, 128, 174
Yehuda-Peysakh, 114
Yenteh- Dvosheh, 37
Yermovski, 237
Yesin, 226, 230, 232, 233, 245, 246
Yessen, 211, 212, 213
Yifat, 94
Yishayes, 78
Yitzchak, 182, 225, 227, 228, 229, 230, 231, 232, 233
Yochleman, 182
Yochniewitch, 159
Yoel, 39
Yofeh, 134
Yofte, 245
Yoshe, 77
Yudkovski, 230

Z

Zacharovitch, 15, 231
Zalke, 114, 233
Zalkind, 156, 222, 223, 236, 247
Zalman, 196
Zamir, 46, 87, 92
Zamiri, 46, 87, 125
Zayonitz, 236
Zecharovitch, 12
Zeevlotzki, 181
Zeidel, 227, 228
Zeitlin, 138
Zelmanovitz, 50
Zepelevitch, 233
Zeplovitch, 174
Zimlin, 226
Ziskind, 135, 136, 175, 232, 237, 246
Zolkind, 222
Zoska, 170

Appendix to the Dokshitz Parafianov Yizkor Book
Material Not in the Original Yizkor Book

INDEX of APPENDIX

A

Adelson, 258
Aleichem, 269
Alperov, 258
Alpert, 249, 251, 257, 271, 411
Andrievsky, 414
Anikovich, 417
Anoshkovich, 414
Apanashkevich, 414
Azarevich, 259

B

Balash, 259
Bar-On, 251, 389, 411
Bell, 265
Beltzig, 252
Belzik, 396
Ben-Gurion, 352
Benjamin, 251, 253, 257, 322, 344, 353
Benz, 412, 413
Bilsky, 252
Blumenthal, 258
Borisovitch, 371
Braverman, 258

C

Charnas, 259
Chistakov, 250
Chodosh, 258
Chuchman, 323, 328, 334, 338, 340
Cirlin, 252, 257, 258
Claus, 412

D

Dameskin, 354
Dolchenok, 415
Dolla, 393, 395, 396
Dorfman, 323, 328
Dorminyev, 305
Dorn, 257
Dubnov, 338
Dvorkind, 337

E

Ebeling, 412, 413
Esterke, 335
Etkin, 250, 272, 273, 274, 275, 276, 277, 285, 296, 298, 302, 304, 311, 312, 314, 319, 320

F

Fabrikant, 332
Fabrishevitz, 332
Fagelman, 259, 264, 265
Fogelman, 250, 259, 262, 333
Frankfurt, 324, 325, 330, 336, 337, 339, 348
Freedman, 384
Friedman, 255, 259, 326, 354, 371, 377, 384

G

Gartman, 412
Gejdenson, 251, 252, 253, 417, 418, 419, 420, 421, 422
Geller, 286
Gerasimonok, 259
Gilbert, 413
Gilinson, 337
Gilman, 258
Gil-Rodionov, 254
Ginsburg, 249, 252, 253, 257, 258, 259, 261, 271, 344, 353, 388
Ginzburg, 249, 250
Gippolitovna, 414
Gnyran, 417
Goldfarb, 251, 353, 387, 388
Golinkin, 335
Gordon, 252, 330
Gotkin, 384
Gritsevich, 415

H

Hazan, 322
Henkin, 250, 251, 322, 323, 332, 333, 336, 344, 352
Hodosh, 276, 287, 311, 312, 315, 316, 318, 319, 320
Hoffman, 258
Horowitz, 257

I

Ivanovich, 414, 415
Izeman, 258

J

Jaffee, 257

K

Kabakoff, 259
Kabakov, 273, 274, 276, 328
Kahanovich, 414
Kaminkovich, 327, 335
Kaminska, 302
Kaminski, 285
Kaminsky, 275, 291, 302, 304
Kantrowitz, 259
Kapalovitch, 258
Kapelovich, 258
Kassow, 263
Katz, 250, 252, 380, 381, 393
Katz's, 380
Katzovich, 324, 333, 340
Katzowich, 256
Katzowitch, 254
Kaz, 412
Kazachyonok, 417
Kazin, 264, 265
Kazinitz, 340
Kluft, 333
Kolyago, 415
Korbman, 327
Korcyn, 420
Korostik, 259
Kosinitz, 256
Kotz, 384
Kovel, 413, 415
Kramer, 412
Kraut, 294, 297
Kremer, 337
Kronenberg, 332, 342
Kuchko, 413
Kulke, 299, 301, 308
Kurilyonok, 415
Kusinitz, 257, 258

L

Lederman, 289, 292
Levin, 341
Levitan, 341, 412, 413
Lilli, 396
Lipkind, 250

Lulinski, 250

M

Malinovskaya, 414
Malishev, 254
Malkin, 252
Malkina, 252
Maria, 252, 259, 393, 396, 398, 414, 415
Markman, 249, 250, 252, 326, 333
Mikhailovich, 414
Mindel, 354
Mirkam, 333
Mutterperl, 251, 353, 354, 358, 370, 384, 388

N

Nagamayev, 305

O

Ozenblovsky, 416

P

Palinska, 419
Parliyanovich, 413
Pashkevich, 416
Peres, 250
Peretz, 269
Pet'ko, 417
Pirivoskin, 276
Podberesskin, 417
Podberesskiy, 417
Podberessky, 417
Polliack, 258
Polyanina, 415
Portnoi, 259
Pren, 370, 371
Proshinsky, 323, 325, 328

R

Raichelson, 257
Randarevich, 259
Rappaport, 377
Raskin, 258
Raskind, 327
Reitman, 326
Reuvan the Shochet, 333
Rief, 385
Ringelblum, 263
Rita, 396
Roitman, 333

Rokosovsky, 299, 305, 308, 309
Romanov, 305, 309, 316, 317
Rosenthal, 402
Roytfarb, 251, 322, 352
Rozov, 333, 339
Ruderman, 250
Ruthchild, 257

S

Schneerson, 331
Schultz, 337
Shapira, 332, 335
Sheiman, 322, 324, 325, 330, 332, 340
Sheinin, 335
Shitel, 414
Shleyfer, 340
Shul'gat, 417
Shulz, 259
Sivko, 415
Skorochod, 279
Skurat, 415
Slovik, 334
Slutsky, 344
Sluzky, 338
Stadolink, 415
Stadolnik, 415
Stankieicz, 420
Starr, 259
Stepanets, 416
Swartz, 257, 258, 260

T

Tenen, 333
Timchuk, 255
Trahinin, 259

U

Ungerman, 412

V

Vargan, 414
Vasilevich, 417
Vasily, 413, 414
Verka, 335
Vlasov, 254
Voitehoivh, 414
Voitehovich, 414
Voronov, 341, 342

W

Wilensky, 341
Wittenberg, 338
Wolfe, 258
Wolfovich, 341
Wolfowitch, 331

Y

Yakovlevich, 413
Yerushalmi, 267, 268
Yolk, 327, 332, 337, 340

Z

Zalkind, 256
Zan'ko, 413
Zanko, 413, 414
Zeitlin, 327
Zeskind, 329
Zhilyonok, 414
Ziklin, 326
Zimmerman, 250
Zucker, 353

www.ingramcontent.com/pod-product-compliance
Lightning Source LLC
Chambersburg PA
CBHW082006150426
42814CB00005BA/240